I0819136

PAUL AND JUDAISM

AN ANTHROPOLOGICAL APPROACH

Second Edition

TIMO LAATO

CONCORDIA PUBLISHING HOUSE · SAINT LOUIS

For Anne,
with love.
Proverbs 31:29

Erstlich soltu wissen, das die heilige Schrift ein solch Buch ist,
das aller ander Bücher zur narrheit macht.

Firstly, you should know that the Holy Scriptures constitute a book
which turns the wisdom of all other books into foolishness.
Martin Luther

Published by Concordia Publishing House
3558 S. Jefferson Ave., St. Louis, MO 63118-3968
1-800-325-3040 • cph.org

Unless otherwise indicated, quotations in this volume are translated from the German edition.

The quotation above from Luther is from *D. Martin Luthers Werke: Kritische Gesamtausgabe*, vol. 50 (Weimar: H. Böhlau, 1914), 659; *Luther's Works: American Edition*, vol. 34 (Philadelphia: Muhlenberg, 1960), 285.

Manufactured in the United States of America

Library of Congress Cataloging-in-Publication Data

Names: Laato, Timo, 1963– author
Title: Paul and Judaism : an anthropological approach / Tim Laato.
Other titles: Paulus und das Judentum. English
Description: Second edition. | Saint Louis, MO : Concordia Publishing House, [2026] | Translation of: Paulus und das Judentum. | Text in English. Translation from German.
Identifiers: LCCN 2026007646 (print) | LCCN 2026007647 (ebook) | ISBN 9780758682017 paperback | ISBN 9780758682246 ebook
Subjects: LCSH: Paul, the Apostle, Saint—Relations with Jews | Bible. Epistles of Paul—Theology | Bible. Epistles of Paul—Social scientific criticism | Jews in the New Testament
Classification: LCC BS2655.J4 L2313 2026 (print) | LCC BS2655.J4 (ebook)
LC record available at https://lccn.loc.gov/2026007646
LC ebook record available at https://lccn.loc.gov/2026007647

---

1 2 3 4 5 6 7 8 9 10 35 34 33 32 31 30 29 28 27 26

CONTENTS

Paul and Judaism: An Anthropological Approach

PREFACE TO THE SECOND ENGLISH EDITION

THE FIRST EDITION of *Paul and Judaism: An Anthropological Approach* has been out of stock for a long time. It was written as a doctoral thesis in German and published in 1991 by Åbo Academy Press. Fairly soon thereafter it was translated into English and then published in 1995 in the series South Florida Studies in the History of Judaism. Since its publication, it has been a recognized contribution to the ongoing discussion about the New Perspective on Paul that was triggered by E. P. Sanders's well-known masterpiece and standard work *Paul and Palestinian Judaism: A Comparison of Patterns of Religion*. Without doubt, his book set the ball rolling in the current direction.

Hence, I am pleased to publish the second edition of *Paul and Judaism: An Anthropological Approach*. In comparison with the first edition, I have made minor changes throughout and polished the English. I have added here and there and expanded my argumentation. Additionally, I have strengthened and intensified my line of reasoning. Chapter 7, "Paul's Mindset: From Solution to Plight?" is new, as is the epilogue on the new quest for Paul.

Once again, I thank Bror Erickson for correcting my English. He has been of invaluable aid for me, as always. The original German text of the first edition was translated into English by T. McElwain.

It was Bror Erickson and Professor John Pless who contacted Concordia Publishing House and recommended the second edition of this book for publication. Dr. Jacob Corzine, vice president of publishing at Concordia Publishing House, soon picked up the reins and brought the whole process to a swift conclusion, together with Jonathan D. Schultz, president and CEO of Concordia Publishing House. Laura Lane as an editor for the professional book team has done a marvelous job. Especially Joshua H. Cook and Dawn Mirly Weinstock have upheld a high level of competence and know-how in preparing my manuscript for print. I would like to applaud their great skill and express my deep gratitude to you all.

Further, I appreciate very much that I have regained the rights of my book from the University of South Florida. In addition, I have made use of the following articles of mine in the second edition of my book:

"Paul's Anthropological Considerations: Two Problems." In *The Paradoxes of Paul*, 343–59. Vol. 2 of *Justification and Variegated Nomism*. Edited by D. A. Carson, P. T. O'Brien, and M. A. Seifrid. WUNT 2/181. Mohr-Siebeck, 2004.

"'God's Righteousness'—Once Again." In *The Nordic Paul: Finnish Approaches to Pauline Theology*, 40–73. Edited by L. Aejmelaeus and A. Mustakallio. Library of New Testament Studies 374. ESCO 374. T&T Clark, 2008.

"*Simul Iustus et Peccator* through the Lenses of Paul." *JETS* 61, no. 4 (2018): 735–66.

Some parts or passages of these articles are inserted in this book with permission.

Last, I am fully aware of the fact that our books are nothing in comparison with God's own Word. They are even less than nothing if his holy name is not glorified in everything we do. Therefore, I do hope that this book will confirm the biblical and confessional Lutheran teaching in all respects.

For we cannot do anything against the truth,
but only for the truth. (2 Cor. 13:8)

Timo Laato

PREFACE TO THE GERMAN EDITION

IN THE FIRST place, I have God to thank that my doctoral thesis should ever have been completed at all. He has brought me through weakness, illness, and hindrances in the most marvelous way. Only in retrospect do I recognize the full extent of his providence, which often rose above my own reason. Whenever I found myself "stuck" in my work, the Almighty again and again showed the way out of my troubles. Human words do not suffice to express my deep gratitude.

Next, I would like to thank my dear wife, Anne. She has kept faithful in good days and especially in bad times. My work is figuratively speaking written with her sweat. All these years until now, I have with confidence given over to her the upbringing of our three very lively children, Taisto, Marjareetta, and Tapani.

Moreover, I express my deep gratitude to my "Doktorvater," Prof. J. Thurén. He has truly been unstinting in engaging his student in long and intensive discussions. His constructive criticism has fundamentally improved my argumentation. The close and gentle contact between us stood the test of my going in my own way.

During the preparation of my research, I worked with many other professors as well. Professor of Old Testament theology and Judaism, K.-J. Illman, gave me many important pieces of advice. He introduced me to the project "Church and Judaism" under the leadership of Prof. H. Räisänen. This provided opportunity for discussion with New Testament scholars in Helsinki. Räisänen has especially maintained my interest in the present theme with his thought-provoking theses and compelled me to rethink some points in my exegesis. I dare to hope that my work will likewise inspire him to think differently.

From the winter semester of 1989–90 to the autumn of 1991, I enjoyed the privilege of studying under Professors H. Hübner and G. Strecker in Göttingen. Both made it possible through their efforts to prolong my grant. In addition, the former served in the role of opponent in my defense committee and is responsible for honing the style of my original German edition.

I would also like to thank student of theology M. Quaschning, theology candidate J. Reller, and theology student K. Bergmann, whom I excessively loaded with various language problems in my original German edition. Theology candidate K. Merten and Mrs. D. Henschke kindly perused the whole work and gave my German a final polish.

The idea for the design and cover comes from Mrs. R. Kujala. Mrs. T. Ahlbäck carried the idea out.

Nothing would come of academic research without money. Finally, I will thank the following funds and organizations which supported me with financial help:

Deutscher Akademischer Austauschdienst e.V.

Emil Aaltonen Foundation

Hedvig Sophia Palmbergs Testamentsfond

Kirkon Tutkimuskeskus

Martin-Luther-Bund

Stiftelsens för Abo Akademi Forskningsinstitut

Suomen Akatemia

Suomen kulttuurirahaston Varsinais-Suomen rahasto

Svenska Litteratursällskapet i Finnland

The city of Turku

Åbo Akademi Press assumed the cost of production.

Not to be forgotten are the engagement of my parents. They have supported my studies without reservation and even financially—although grieved by the obstinacy of their youngest son. To have grown up in a harmonious family has left a tender and permanent impression upon me. I am only ashamed not always to have taken the well-meaning advice of my parents more seriously.

Timo Laato

WHY THIS SECOND EDITION OF *PAUL AND JUDAISM: AN ANTHROPOLOGICAL APPROACH*?[1]

PAULINE RESEARCH CONTINUES to triumph. The debate broadens and deepens, yet it also becomes more difficult and complicated. The present debate was launched in 1977 with the publication of E. P. Sanders's extensive work *Paul and Palestinian Judaism: A Comparison of Patterns of Religion*. Later, there has been talk of a whole new perspective: the New Perspective on Paul.[2] This concept comprises a large number of scholars who do not always agree on interpretations. Yet they do have something in common, otherwise it would not make any sense to speak of a new wave of research. The Christological argument can at least be mentioned as one common denominator: Paul did not discard the Jewish religion based on its assumed legalistic soteriology—that it was built on merit and led to vainglory. His main reason was simply (and slightly simplified) that it was not *Christ*ianity; in other words, it denied Christ as Savior, Messiah.[3] This argument is also accompanied by a strong emphasis on salvation that is meant for everyone, heathen as well as Jew. As an apostle to the Gentiles, Paul had to regard God's plan of salvation as broader than before. He could no longer

1 Here, I follow some preliminary remarks in my article "'God's Righteousness'—Once again," in *The Nordic Paul: Finnish Approaches to Pauline Theology*, ed. L. Aejmelaeus and A. Mustakallio, ESCO 374 (T&T Clark, 2008), 40–41. The quotations from other sources are taken from the originals.

2 To read more closely about the research history, see S. Westerholm, "'The New Perspective' at Twenty-Five," in *The Paradoxes of Paul*, vol. 2 of *Justification and Variegated Nomism*, ed. D. A. Carson, P. T. O'Brien, and M. A. Seifrid, WUNT 2/181 (Mohr Siebeck, 2004), 1–38. See also chapter 2 below. For the concept of "the New Perspective on Paul," see chapter 2.3. below.

3 E. P. Sanders, *Paul and Palestinian Judaism: A Comparison of Patterns of Religion* (Fortress Press, 1977), 501. His short and provocative thesis was: "In short, *this is what Paul finds wrong in Judaism: it is not Christianity*" (552).

stay inside the narrow boundaries of Mosaic Law. Particularism had to give way to universalism. The old covenant had been replaced by the new.[4]

The debate has since advanced. The Christological argument has been accompanied and, in a way, explained by anthropological analysis: Paul's view on man's ability to obey the Law became much more pessimistic after he experienced conversion on the road to Damascus. He no longer believed in the ability of free will to break the power of sin. No man can help himself. The synergism of Judaism (cooperation of God and man within the prerequisites of the Sinaic covenant) must be rejected as worthless. It leads man to trust in the "flesh" and to boast of self-righteousness (Galatians; Rom. 3:27; 4:2–5; 9:30–10:3; Phil. 3:3–9). Man is totally corrupt and therefore fully unable to save himself or even contribute to his salvation. His only hope lies in the boundless mercy of God, which is received on account of Christ through faith alone. In this we hear a reformation heartbeat—naturally!—although at some point it was thought or claimed to be silenced, and the most enthusiastic hastened to toll the death knell in order to precipitate the burial.

The anthropological analysis that completes the Christological argument has been elaborated especially by T. Laato in his doctoral thesis, originally published in German: *Paulus und das Judentum: Anthropologische Erwägungen* (Åbo, 1991). It was translated into English and published under the title *Paul and Judaism: An Anthropological Approach* (trans. T. McElwain, South Florida Studies in the History of Judaism 115 [Scholars Press, 1995]). Although at this point it is too early to draw any final conclusions, it seems that the anthropological analysis has entered the present debate on the relationship between Paul and Judaism to stay. It cannot be ignored—except in tendentious research.

There is still disagreement on many details, but the importance and centrality of the main subject is the most significant and essential point. To support this claim, some brief scientific surveys of the present state of the debate are presented here. D. A. Hagner concludes:

> The result is that Paul abandoned the synergism of Jewish soteriology for the monergism of total dependence upon the grace of God in Christ. Laato concludes, rightly in my opinion, that Paul thus repudiates the Jewish understanding of righteousness and the Jewish soteriology. We may compare these conclusions to those of Stephen Westerholm [. . .].[5]

---

4 Especially E. P. Sanders: *Paul, the Law and the Jewish People* (Fortress Press, 1983). After him many others.

5 D. A. Hagner, "Paul and Judaism: The Jewish Matrix of Early Christianity: Issues in the Current Debate," *Bulletin for Biblical Research* 3 (1993): 122.

Furthermore, S. Westerholm performs a broad survey of Jewish literature. He basically corroborates the findings of Laato and concludes finally:

> The anthropologies of Paul and Judaism cannot, then, be considered in isolation from their respective "soteriologies": different plights demand different solutions, and (as Sanders has reminded us) different solutions demand different plights. Broadly speaking, our survey of the literature supports the notion that Paul's anthropology, in corresponding to his "soteriology," is a good deal more "negative" than the anthropology typical among his contemporary Jews.[6]

In another context, Westerholm writes:

> But (the post-Damascus) Paul believes that human beings, at enmity with God and in slavery to sin, have neither the ability nor the inclination to submit to God's law. (Laato, among others, has reminded us that the pessimism of Paul's "anthropology" is not typically Jewish, and that it inevitably leads to a distinctive soteriological emphasis.) It follows (as those who stress the "apocalyptic" aspects of Paul's thought are wont to remind us) that, for Paul, a new divine act of creation is needed before people can be "put right" with God.[7]

M. Seifrid agrees fully:

> The very issue that Sanders's paradigm isolates within Paul's post-Damascus thought and thus removes from consideration, namely, the nature of the human plight, turns out to be the pivotal juncture at which Paul engages his contemporaries.[8]

Earlier, he wrote accordingly:

> In anticipation of our following discussion, we may say that Paul's surprising statements concerning the law make sense given his view of the fallen state and moral inability of the human beings (Laato 1995).[9]

Also, C. A. Gieschen asserts:

> Timo Laato, a Finnish Lutheran scholar, has challenged Sanders's position on the role of the works of the Law in maintaining one's righteous status with his 1991 dissertation that was later translated and published as *Paul and Judaism: An Anthropological Approach*. Laato argues that a key difference between first-century Judaism and Christianity was the anthropological presuppositions of their respective soteriologies or, to put it simply, their respective

---

6 See S. Westerholm, "Paul's Anthropological 'Pessimism' in Its Jewish Context," in *Divine and Human Agency in Paul and His Cultural Environment*, ed. J. M. G. Barclay and S. J. Gathercole, Library of New Testament Studies 335 (T&T Clark, 2006), 71–98.

7 Westerholm, "The 'New Perspective,'" 37.

8 M. Seifrid, "Unrighteous by Faith: Apostolic Proclamation in Romans 1:18–3:20," *Justification and Variegated Nomism*, vol. 2: *The Paradoxes of Paul*, ed. D. A. Carson, P. T. O'Brien, and M. A. Seifrid, WUNT 2/181 (Mohr Siebeck, 2004), 144.

9 M. Seifrid, *Christ, Our Righteousness: Paul's Theology of Justification*, New Studies in Biblical Theology 9 (InterVarsity Press, 2000), 95.

> understandings of man's nature after the fall and the role that fallen nature is able to play in salvation.[10]

P. T. O'Brien affirms:

> [. . .] there are significant anthropological differences between Judaism and Paul. [. . .] Sanders' contention, however, has been challenged: the anthropological presuppositions of Judaism clearly differ from those of the apostle.[11]

Similarly, T. George states:

> In one of the most incisive criticisms of the new perspective published thus far, Timo Laato, building on the work of H. Odeberg, has compared the anthropological presuppositions of covenantal nomism, as sketched by Sanders, and Paul's own soteriology. He has shown [. . .].[12]

H. Blocher concludes:

> Exegetical studies in the present volume have shown that Paul did elaborate the doctrine of human guilt, helplessness and condemnation as the foundation of his gospel.[13]

On the other hand, T. R. Schreiner generally states:

> E. Sanders (1977) rightly criticizes the caricature of Jewish legalism that has infiltrated biblical scholarship. But he goes too far to the other extreme. Laato (1991) contends rightly that Paul repudiates a synergism that was present in Jewish theology [. . .].[14]

Furthermore, in another context Schreiner concludes:

> Laato (1991) argues that the central difference between Paul and Palestinian Judaism lay in their estimate of anthropological ability. I believe he is largely correct here.[15]

---

10 C. A. Gieschen, "Paul and the Law: Was Luther Right?" in *The Law in Holy Scripture: Essays from the Concordia Theological Seminary Symposium on Exegetical Theology*, ed. C. A. Gieschen (Concordia Publishing House, 2004), 132. He has the following subheading II D: "The Contrasting Anthropologies of First-Century Judaism and Paul."

11 P. T. O'Brien, "Was Paul a Covenantal Nomist?" in *The Paradoxes of Paul*, vol. 2 of *Justification and Variegated Nomism*, ed. D. A. Carson, P. T. O'Brien, and M. A. Seifrid, WUNT 2/181 (Mohr Siebeck, 2004), 270. In his article, he often refers to Laato.

12 T. George, "Modernizing Luther, Domesticating Paul: Another Perspective," in *The Paradoxes of Paul*, vol. 2 of *Justification and Variegated Nomism*, ed. D. A. Carson, P. T. O'Brien, and M. A. Seifrid, WUNT 2/181 (Mohr Siebeck, 2004), 453.

13 H. Blocher, "Justification of the Ungodly (*Sola Fide*): Theological Reflections," in *The Paradoxes of Paul*, vol. 2 of *Justification and Variegated Nomism*, ed. D. A. Carson, P. T. O'Brien, and M. A. Seifrid, WUNT 2/181 (Mohr Siebeck, 2004), 484. Among others, he refers to Laato.

14 T. R. Schreiner, *Romans*, BECNT 6 (Baker, 1998), 174.

15 Ibid., 154 n. 14 *et passim*.

J. R. Harrison summarizes the present state of research as follows:

> T. Laato (*Paul and Palestinian Judaism: An Anthropological Approach* [Atlanta 1995]) is a sound example of the approach required. He charts from the intertestamental and rabbinic literature how Judaism embraced an optimistic anthropology in its concentration on human free will (*ibid.*, 65–75). The synergistic approach of Judaism, Laato argues, stands in contrast to Paul who, because of his pessimistic anthropology of human depravity (*ibid.*, 75–146), emphasized salvation by grace alone (*ibid.*, 147–168).[16]

Apparently, the first person to give a positive statement like the previous ones was L. Aejmelaeus in his German review of Laato's dissertation:

> Laato's dissertation is a clearly written and sharp apology for the apostle to the Gentiles, who has received a bad reputation in recent decades because of his polemic against Jewish "works-righteousness." In this book a model is constructed with which a person can make sense of the Pauline logic and argumentation in his opposition with the Jews without thereby simultaneously becoming antisemitic himself.[17]

Finally, P. M. Sprinkle concludes the ongoing debate quite well as follows:

> In other words, Judaism believed that people were capable of contributing something to their salvation, while Paul believed that people could contribute nothing to their salvation. Covenantal nomism itself, the critics say, assumes a rather positive view of the human condition, while Paul clearly had a pessimistic view. While some scholars pointed this out early on, a full-scale treatment of the anthropology was lacking until Timo Laato published his dissertation, *Paul and Palestinian Judaism: An Anthropological Approach.* Laato argued that Paul's pessimistic view of the human condition calls for a more radical emphasis on divine agency in salvation. [. . .] Many opponents of Sanders and the New Perspective have taken Laato's conclusion at face value. They have assumed that Laato's study ended the discussion, hammering the proverbial nail in the coffin.[18]

All the previous surveys adequately show the present state of the research. Hence, it is necessary to take the anthropological analysis into account when

16 J. R. Harrison, *Paul's Language of Grace in Its Graeco-Roman Context*, WUNT 2/172 (Mohr Siebeck, 2003), 101 n. 18.

17 L. Aejmelaeus, review of *Paulus und das Judentum: Anthropologische Erwägungen*, by Timo Laato, *SJS* 13 (1992): 170: "Laatos Dissertation ist eine klargeschriebene und scharfe Apologie für den Heidenapostel, der in den letzten Jahrzehnten wegen seiner Polemik der jüdischen 'Werkgerechtigkeit' gegenüber einen schlechten Ruf bekommen hat. In diesem Buch wird ein Modell konstruiert, womit man die paulinische Logik und Argumentation in seiner Auseinandersetzung mit dem Judentum verständlich machen kann, ohne daneben gleichzeitig selbst antijudaistisch werden [. . .]."

18 P. M. Sprinkle, *Paul and Judaism Revisited: A Study of Divine and Human Agency in Salvation* (InterVarsity Press, 2013), 126. He himself deals with anthropological presuppositions especially in the Dead Sea Scrolls. In the end, his conclusions do not differ much from the *opinio communis* in New Testament scholarship. See below 4.1.1.

contemplating and drawing the outlines of a New Perspective on Pauline theology. A mere Christological argument is not enough. One can rightly ask—with reference to the present academic debate—whether the Christological argument is understood in-depth or even correctly without anthropological analysis. Hence, we need to heed again the arguments in *Paul and Judaism: An Anthropological Approach.* It represents a significant contribution to the ongoing academic debate.

PAUL AND JUDAISM

AN ANTHROPOLOGICAL APPROACH

1. INTRODUCTION

IT SEEMS THAT Christian churches must again and again analyze and appraise their relationship to Judaism as the "parent religion" of Christianity. Because today Christian churches consist mostly of "Gentiles,"[1] a dialogue between both parties requires a better understanding of the criticism Paul, the apostle to the Gentiles, brings forward against Judaism. New Testament scholars must therefore search for a satisfactory answer to the question *why* Paul (or the later Christian Church) never succeeded in preventing or settling the conflict with Judaism. Only then can the Christian-Jewish dialogue move on and start to think in terms of removing the theological controversies between church and synagogue.

Until the 1970s, exegetes and other theologians almost without exception considered the whole question closed. They took for granted that the Jews (at least those in New Testament times) depended on their good works and tried to earn their own salvation. Only after his conversion could Paul protest and break the prevailing conception. He concluded that no one gains salvation on account of his own merits, but that each one receives it as a gift by faith in Christ. From then on, the matter was straightened out. The controversy between Paul and Judaism over the different prerequisites for salvation (human works versus divine grace) resulted in the parting of the ways.[2]

The publication of E. P. Sanders's work *Paul and Palestinian Judaism* in 1977 paved the way for a radical turning point in the history of research.[3] He argued that salvation in Palestinian Judaism was not based on human merits or good works. The pertinent writings from about 200 BC to AD 200 show that salvation takes place by divine grace within the covenant. The observance of the Law explicitly serves as a means of staying in the covenant. An exception proves the rule. In 4 Ezra, salvation depends on perfect sinlessness. All sinners are condemned. Their falling back on the covenant is indeed to no avail.[4] Just as in Judaism in general, Paul teaches the salvation of humankind out of divine grace,

1 The concept of "Gentile" naturally refers here to "non-Jew."

2 See below 2.1.

3 See below 2.3.

4 Sanders 1977, 419–23.

namely, through faith in Christ. Notwithstanding, he still considers the fulfilling of the Law as necessary for staying "in Christ."[5] Accordingly, he renounced the Jewish soteriology since they had refused Christ, but not because they allegedly rejected divine grace.[6]

In succeeding years, Sanders's monograph has been widely received and accepted with approval, particularly in the English-speaking world. To say the least, he has without exaggeration completely and perfectly overturned the views of Old and New Testament scholars about Judaism. At the same time, he has once again brought to the fore the old question about the rupture of Paul with Judaism.[7] The old answers are no longer necessarily compelling; the academic discussion strives forward and seeks new answers.

The main task of this study is to compare Pauline and Jewish religion, proceeding from the research position of Sanders already mentioned. It is obviously impossible to carry out a comparison of a plethora of details within the framework of a single volume. My interest applies above all to the relationship between divine grace and human works. As the present-day state of research at least in the English-speaking world has directly developed from the breakthrough of Sanders's theses, a critical examination of his overview of research history and an analytical discussion of the methodological basis of his outcomes provide a fundamental point of departure. As a result, the reader obtains a more comprehensive and complete understanding of the problems still to be resolved. Far and away the most stirring and thrilling cause of dispute arises from Sanders's thought-provoking proposal that Paul and the Jews did not, strictly speaking, disagree on the relationship between divine grace and human works.[8] But what then was their bone of contention exactly? Why did they ultimately have their fervent confrontation? Sanders seems unable to answer such questions in a satisfactory manner. This is fundamentally because of deficiencies in his methodological procedure as he fails to take sufficiently into account the anthropological approach to each religion.[9] So his method has to be modified and amplified in order to attain a more persuasive clarification of the break between Paul and Judaism. The present work will serve that urgent purpose.

In consideration of my task, it would be important to know precisely which sort of Judaism Paul criticizes in each case. Unfortunately, he does not always tell his readers more about his adversaries. The question often remains quite obscure. Indeed, Paul criticizes Judaism in a more general way (cf. in particular Romans 2–3, 9–11) without specifying what kind of Judaism it is all about

5 Op. cit., 543–49.
6 Op. cit., 549–52.
7 See below 2.3.
8 Sanders 1977, 549–52.
9 See below 3.3.

on every occasion.[10] Albeit he obviously turns against Wisdom of Solomon in Romans 2[11] and mentions his own Pharisaic past as a warning example in Phil. 3:4–9,[12] his reproach finally applies to Judaism as a whole. Consequently, the complexity of the exegetical analysis expands and increases. The following two main alternatives open up: either Paul has been unable to make any explicit difference between heterogenous groups in Judaism, or he has been able to take the manifold Judaism as a sufficiently homogenous phenomenon to the exclusion of any further differentiation. In the former case, the issue concerns from which Judaism Paul precisely broke off in various contexts. In the latter case, the issue concerns why Paul broke off from the whole body of Judaism in a variety of limited contexts.

In the progress of the survey, I avail myself, as it were, of a zoom technique. History of research (chapter 2) gives an overview of the problem area. From the wide picture, it will become apparent how several different scholars rate in each case the relationship between divine grace and human works in Judaism. Also, it will appear whether they ultimately regard Paul's break with Judaism as a deliberate resolution or a precipitate solution. The focus here lies on the problems so far presented. The outlook of Paul still remains in the background since the very general nature of the overview permits no identification of noteworthy distinctions in the details of perceptions among diverse scholars. They all agree (or sufficiently so) that divine grace as opposed to human works displays a central issue for him.

A section enlargement follows the general overview. Now attention lies on the methodology of Sanders ("a comparison of patterns of religion"), since at present his results stand in the limelight of exegetical research. The critical analysis of his definition and application of method (chapter 3) shows some very serious cracks in the foundation of his conclusions. It will turn out here that he ignores the question of human ability, although he does suppose a specific response to it. This deficiency has led to distinct distortions in the big picture. To all appearances, Sanders's juxtaposition of Palestinian Judaism and Paulinism truly falls short. His portrayal of them needs more "exposure" or clarification.

Hence, a further section enlargement engages interest. This time the focus moves to the anthropological presuppositions of the Jewish and Pauline patterns of religion (chapter 4) since they are mainly missing in Sanders's angle of view. He has not zoomed in to reveal them. The completion of his fuzzy and blurry presentation adjusts lenses especially on Paul because some focal details in Pauline anthropology have been partly or totally overlooked in New Testament

10 See below 6.7.

11 See below 4.2.1.3.

12 See below 6.6.

scholarship. In regards to Jewish anthropology, mainly a summary of research results will catch the eye.

On close reflection, mere details remain patchy unless integrated within a big picture. Consequently, the many implications and the overall significance of anthropology for the Jewish and Pauline patterns of religion zoom into focus (chapter 5). This kind of clarification ensures the right exposure and facilitates the true comparison.

The comparison between the Jewish and Pauline patterns of religion places the break of Paul with Judaism in a new light. Next, his vehement disputes over the requirements for salvation come into view (chapter 6). Some sharp snapshots should be mediated from the heat of combat.

In the end, the decision must be made in which order all the images are presented. Sanders suggests that Paul thinks "backward," in other words, from solution (Christ is the Savior) to plight (the whole humanity is in need of Christ on account of their corruption) and not vice versa. Hence, he maintains that the first photos are shown last, and the last photos are shown first. It remains to be seen if he does justice to the object of the picture folder, namely, if soteriology comes before anthropology or anthropology before soteriology in Pauline theology (chapter 7). In the final chapter, I join the sketched images together and hope that the collection is representative (chapter 8).

As if all this were not enough, in this second edition I offer as an epilogue a new photo session that provides an optimal viewing angle. There, the images are adjusted to correspond to the vivid portrait of the apostle Paul, providing a detailed cross-sectional view of the vibrant features of his person. In my high-resolution wallpaper, he is seen as never before, though remaining the same faithful apostle of our Lord Jesus Christ.

2. AN OVERVIEW OF RESEARCH

2.1. The Weberian Position

In his critical overview of research, Sanders initially makes the comment that, until the nineteenth century, Christian theologians in general stressed the similarities between Judaism and Christianity.[1] They tried, for instance, to illuminate the Christological dogmas of the church by referring to the Jewish speculations about Logos and Memra.[2] Toward the end of the nineteenth century, however, everything changed. Christian theologians began to perceive Judaism more and more as an antithesis to Christianity.[3] Sanders does not analyze the shift in perspective further. It seems that the change came with the great impact exerted on thought during the preceding century by G. W. F. Hegel, who introduced and elaborated his highly sophisticated scheme of thesis, antithesis, and synthesis as a pattern to explain the historical development. By the middle of the nineteenth century, F. Chr. Baur had reconstructed the growth and expansion of Christianity by means of Hegelian philosophy: the Jewish particularism of the early church in Jerusalem (thesis) was opposed by the liberating universalism of Paul (antithesis), and they later merge into Catholicism (synthesis).[4] F. Weber was the first to consistently outline Judaism as an absolute antithesis to Christianity in his work originally entitled *System der altsynagogalen palästinischen Theologie aus Targum, Midrasch und Talmud* (1880). However, after his death it was revived by F. Delitzsch and G. Schnedermann and published under the title of *Jüdische Theologie auf Grund des Talmud und verwandter Schriften* (1897).[5]

1 Sanders 1977, 33. He supports himself from Moore 1921, 197–221.

2 Ibid. See also Moore 1921, 233.

3 Ibid. See also Moore 1921, 233–41.

4 On the dependence of Baur on Hegel's philosophy, see Goppelt 1980, 28.

5 Sanders 1977, 33. See also Moore 1921, 228–37. Cf. further Schechter 1961, 23; Sjöberg 1939, 154–55.

Weber conjures up a very gloomy picture of rabbinic soteriology. To begin with, he deals with the story of the fall in Genesis 3.[6] It brought or initiated an alienation between humanity and their Creator.[7] Therefore, they have to return to him, owing penance and obedience as the "means of salvation."[8] Only then and in that way could they attain achievements by which they might earn the grace and benevolence of God.[9]

The establishment of the covenant at Sinai led to the canceling of the consequences that Adam's fall had imposed on humanity. At that moment, the lost glory of Paradise was restored to the people of Israel.[10] However, their bliss and happiness did not last long. Their worship of the golden calf marked their own fall into sin.[11] From then on, they are obliged to win back the original status lost by their forefather in his rebellion against God. It happens through penance, obedience to the Law, and expiation.[12]

In addition, there are other means of earning righteousness, particularly "good works," which entail alms and deeds of charity (for example, to feed the poor, clothe the naked, and visit the sick).[13] Further, the different merits of the forefathers make up for the many deficiencies of the descendants.[14]

The Jews will be judged on the basis of their works. Their coming judgment strictly depends on the preponderance of their evil or good deeds. In this world no one knows whether he has fulfilled the commandments in sufficient measure. Therefore, all must live in fear and trembling.[15]

Various means of penance (offerings, repentance, the Day of Atonement, sufferings, vicarious sufferings, death, and good works)[16] efface sin and restore the sinner to the covenant. Still, they do not guarantee him certain and final salvation.[17]

Sanders rates Weber's sketchy description of Jewish (or rabbinic) soteriology as typical of the New Testament exegetics. The cast-iron criteria of *System der altsynagogalen palästinischen Theologie* became predominant in wide academic

6 Weber 1897, 259. He delves into the rabbinic reflections on the fall more broadly (see op. cit., 218–25).

7 Ibid.

8 Op. cit., 259.

9 Op. cit., 259–62.

10 Op. cit., 271.

11 Op. cit., 274.

12 Op. cit., 276–77.

13 Weber 1897, 284. The rabbis distinguish between works of the Law and "good works" (those which go beyond the duty imposed by the Torah). See further Billerbeck 1926, 160–61; 1928, 559–60; Heiligenthal 1983, 280.

14 Weber 1897, 292–97.

15 Op. cit., 279–84.

16 Op. cit., 313–34.

17 Op. cit., 334–36.

circles.[18] Apart from the theory of the two falls (the fall of Adam in Paradise and the fall of Israel at Sinai), they in general gained broad acceptance and support. Sanders recognizes a direct line from Weber to Bultmann. Mediating members in the line are W. Bousset and H. Gressmann.[19]

Sanders resurrects the old reproach that Bousset has entitled his book on apocalyptic Judaism *Die Religion des Judentums im neutestamentlichen Zeitalter* (1903, 1966 [4th ed.]).[20] As is well-known, the apocalyptic tendencies and perspectives constituted only one movement in the Jewish religion of that time. Other trends made themselves felt simultaneously.[21]

The undoubtedly in itself accurate criticism brought forward against Bousset indicates no understanding of the historical circumstances under which he was writing his book. Before his monograph *Kyrios Christos* (first edition 1913), leading scholars of history of religion did not yet primarily analyze Hellenism, but rather Judaism, in order to track down the essentials influencing nascent Christianity.[22] They regarded the Apocrypha and Pseudepigrapha as the most relevant and significant Jewish sources. Moreover, they assumed that those writings reflected the Jewish "folk piety" (*Volksfrömmigkeit*) which the Christian movement in part absorbed. As expected, the rabbinic material drew less attention or no notice at all. It was supposed to depict the Jewish "learned piety" (*Gelehrtenfrömmigkeit*) which had only very little to do with the Christian movement.[23] The undervaluation of the rabbinic material was also defended on the basis of methodological difficulties. No one knows for sure which specific traditions stem from the time of the New Testament or before.[24]

It is therefore not surprising that Bousset speaks of *the* Jewish religion in the New Testament era even if he largely concentrates on his limited source material, particularly on the Apocrypha and Pseudepigrapha.[25] We can expect nothing else from a specialist in history of religion at the turn of the twentieth

18 Sanders 1977, 38–39, 42, 44, 47. Many critics follow him, as Beker 1978, 108; Best 1982, 66–67; Brooke 1979, 248; Caird 1978, 538–39; Dahl 1978, 154; Hagner 1979, 25; McNamara 1979, 68–69; Mußner 1986, 42; Neusner 1980, 59–60; Saldarini 1979, 299. Cf. Heiligenthal 1985, 546–47; C. Wolff 1986, 421–25. Gundry (1985, 4 n. 9) ascribes to Sanders the view that "Weber's theory of Israel's falling from grace through worship of the golden calf is necessary to the affirmation of legalism in Judaism." In reality, Sanders does not postulate anything like that. On the contrary, he emphasizes that New Testament exegetes generally share Weber's sketchy description of rabbinic Judaism with the exception of the theory of two falls into sin (1977, 38).

19 Sanders 1977, 39, 44, 47. Cf. Limbeck 1971, 13–15, 36.

20 Sanders 1977, 34 and n. 11.

21 Particularly Neusner 1984, 91–141, 195–203.

22 K. Müller 1983, 69.

23 Hoheisel 1978, 25–26; Moore 1921, 243–44; K. Müller 1983, 69–70.

24 Ibid.

25 Bousset 1966, 6–47.

century. But nowadays, it seems no longer plausible to summarize the Judaism of New Testament times without taking into account a much broader basis of the Jewish literature.[26]

On the one hand, Sanders sturdily suggests that Bousset took over his presentation of Judaism from Weber.[27] On the other hand, Sanders strongly suspects that Bousset read his own interpretation of the Apocrypha and Pseudepigrapha into the rabbinic texts.[28] The two explanations contradict each other. They cannot be in force at the same time. It seems that neither one strikes home.

It is unlikely Bousset read his own interpretation of the Apocrypha and Pseudepigrapha into the rabbinic texts. He himself underscores that rabbinism does not conclusively amount to late Hellenistic Judaism.[29] The Jewish religion fundamentally changed in character with the fall of the political state and the parting of ways with Christianity. Consequently, whoever attempts to reconstruct late Hellenistic Judaism on the basis of the rabbinic texts is building on sand.[30] Besides, Weber's analysis of rabbinic literature, for obvious reasons, does not have much effect on Bousset, who examined late Hellenistic Judaism mainly by means of the Apocrypha and Pseudepigrapha.[31] Afterward, various rabbinic quotations were added in the third edition (1926) by H. Gressmann.[32] He also corrected the title of the book, which from then on has been called *Die Religion des Judentums im späthellenistischen Zeitalter*. Through his crucial contribution, the influence of Weber on Bousset's results increased substantially.

The edition revised by Gressmann corroborates Weber's theses. Rightly, Sanders perceives that the doctrine of God's distance and inaccessibility arises

26 Hoheisel 1978, 32–33. Cf. K. Müller 1983, 69–101. See already Moore 1921, 244–46; Perles 1903, 6–19, 21–24.

27 Sanders 1977, 39, 42.

28 Op. cit., 34 n. 11. Sanders writes: "He [Moore] was entirely correct [. . .] in objecting to defining Jewish piety on the basis of such sources as IV Ezra (also post-70!) and reading that piety into Rabbinic literature, as did Bousset and Köberle, among others." For sure, Moore (1921, 241–48) takes a stance against Bousset's position but does not give to understand that Bousset delineates rabbinism through his own interpretation of the Apocrypha and Pseudepigrapha.

29 The concept "late Hellenistic Judaism" is obsolete. It is used here only to quote Bousset himself.

30 Bousset 1966, 41.

31 Bousset 1966, 6–39. He (op. cit., 50) evaluates Weber's book as follows: "Ein nur mit Vorsicht zu benutzendes Hilfsmittel zur Kenntnis der zeitgenössischen pharisäischen Theologie ist F. WEBERs Werk [. . .]. Hier ist die spätere rabbinische Theologie geschildert und nirgends ein Versuch gemacht, das Ältere vom Jüngeren abzuscheiden, vielmehr alles auf eine Fläche aufgetragen." On the whole, Bousset seems to criticize Weber mostly for his handling of the sources but not so much for his analysis and interpretation of the rabbinic texts.

32 See Lohse 1966, v–vi; Sanders 1977, 56.

as the dominating theory.[33] It is further unheard of that the merits of the forefathers are not transferable to others because Judaism disposes of no sacraments that can mediate the excess merits of the forefathers to their posterity.[34]

Besides Bousset, Sanders lays the responsibility for the deep-rooted pervasion of Weber's theses in New Testament scholarship mainly on two authors. First of all, P. Billerbeck prepared the most ground for and paved the most direct route to broad consensus.[35] His popular multivolume *Kommentar zum Neuen Testament aus Talmud und Midrasch* (1922–28, more reprints) has become a well-known standard work. Appealing to the authority of H. Strack, the original author deals with the soteriological system of the ancient synagogue in a short supplement.[36] There, Billerbeck states, in agreement with Weber, that Judaism is "a religion full of self-redemption" ("eine Religion völliger Selbsterlösung"). It leaves no room for a Savior who would die for the sins of the world.[37]

R. Bultmann too continues along the same line as Weber, Bousset, and Billerbeck.[38] He depicts Jewish soteriology before the destruction of the second (or third) temple in particular in his book *Das Urchristentum im Rahmen der antiken Religionen* (1949; 1954 [2nd ed.] = 1963 [3rd ed.]; 1976 [4th ed.]). Startlingly, there is no limiting of relevant sources here, but, for example, the Apocrypha, Pseudepigrapha, and rabbinic sayings are quoted alternately one after the other.[39]

Right from the start, Bultmann recognizes that a very strong consciousness of election, the covenant, and the history of salvation permeates the Jewish thought and informs all of it.[40] Nonetheless, he maintains that Judaism badly falls short. Israelites made the error of binding themselves to their holy history. They broke off contact with the present and refused to take responsibility for the time being. God is no longer in a real sense the God of history. One does

33 Sanders 1977, 39, 212–14. See Bousset 1966, especially 373–84. His notion of God's distance and inaccessibility in Judaism is found already in Weber (1897, 148). Among others, Hoheisel (1978, 30–31) and Moore (1921, 242, 247–48) criticize Bousset precisely for the same reasons.

34 Bousset 1966, 197–99. Lüdemann (1987, 349–50) points out that Bousset in his later publications outlines a little more positive picture of Judaism.

35 Sanders 1977, 43.

36 Billerbeck 1928, 3–13.

37 Op. cit., 6.

38 Sanders 1977, 39, 44, 47 (cf. also 8 n. 6). *Pace* Thielman 1989, 7. Thielman maintains: "There were, of course, notable exceptions to the anti-Semitic tone of works like Windisch's, and Rudolf Bultmann is undoubtedly the most important." But later he adds a short remark: "When speaking of Judaism generally or of Jesus' relationship to Judaism, Bultmann could talk of 'Jewish legalism' in a manner with which Moore had no sympathy." See op. cit., 8 n. 42.

39 Cf. op. cit., 43–44.

40 Bultmann 1954, 62.

not experience him directly here and now, but only thrust into the past by his revelation.[41]

On the whole, in the course of time the ritual aspects of the Torah gained more and more supremacy and dominance. The number of commandments increased to the extent that scarcely anyone could know them, let alone practice them.[42] In consequence, the Law induces no "radical" obedience determining all fields of life. Some area of daily challenges to which it does not apply is always found. In those specific conditions, an opportunity opens up for the Jews to behave for their own benefit as they try to accomplish extra good works and in so doing atone for their offenses.[43]

The juridical understanding of obedience resulted in the idea that on the Last Day all deeds would be weighed against each other. The outcome depends on whether the good works outweigh the evil or the evil works the good.[44] On the one hand, it promotes uncertainty of salvation. But on the other hand, it provokes complacent self-righteousness.[45]

From Sanders's perspective, the adherents of the Weberian position do not doubt in the least that Paul's criticism of Jewish soteriology indeed shows itself justified. The Jews promote the worst kind of legalism. They indeed try to earn salvation through their works.[46] Their illusion collapses through the apostolic proclamation of the Gospel.[47]

In the main, Christian scholars were the first who adhered to the Weberian position.[48] They made the general assumption that postexilic Judaism had degenerated into a legalistic religion.[49] No doubt, they also took for granted that the degenerate Judaism remained far behind Paulinism or Christianity in general.[50] Their reasoning inevitably carries the consequence that the Judaism in New Testament times serves as an example of complete contrast to Christianity. From then on, their overall conception became predominant in the following generations of scholars.

Further, Sanders objects that Christian theologians since Weber have on purpose set Judaism in an unfavorable light in order to show and prove the

41 Op. cit., 62.
42 Op. cit., 64, 68–69.
43 Op. cit., 72.
44 Op. cit., 74.
45 Op. cit., 74–75.
46 The eternal fate of the Gentiles goes unaddressed here. The rabbis themselves discuss that issue only sporadically and quite often very differently. See, e.g., Hruby 1968, 232–45; Sanders 1977, 206–12.
47 Sanders 1977, 33–59.
48 Hoheisel 1978, 40; Sanders 1977, 55.
49 See Hoheisel 1978, 59.
50 Ibid.

superiority of Christianity.[51] In demonstration of his thesis, he does not provide any concrete evidence. Here, two short historical examples will suffice.

Bousset at least in part contrasts Judaism and Christianity with each other in his attempt to underline the supposed central dogma of Christianity.[52] Already in 1900, A. v. Harnack had identified the "simple teaching" of Jesus as the essence of the New Testament message. It roughly means something similar to God is a loving Father and all people are his children.[53] Bousset takes his view from here and moves on. He equates the kernel of Judaism with the notion of God's distance and inaccessibility. Then he concludes that a shift in thinking broke forth with Jesus (or Paul or Christianity generally), who was indeed the very first to dare reject false conventional theology.[54]

Bultmann too maintains the necessity of his own hermeneutical concept against the black background of Judaism. It is no coincidence that he rates extremely negatively the Jewish interest in God's salvific action during the history of salvation.[55] As is well-known, he himself suggests that those concrete events in the past, at least for the "real" and demythologized Christianity, matter very little or not at all. It seems that he indeed promotes his hermeneutics at the expense or to the detriment of another kind of theology. He criticizes the Jewish preference for the past in order to convince his Christian readers of his specific presupposition that Christ, who is present in the apostolic kerygma here and now, who then through the proclamation bestows a new self-understanding and who only by dint of preaching changes human existential conditions, constitutes the fundamental of Christianity.[56]

Although Weber's theses on rabbinism (or Judaism in general) have almost been canonized in New Testament scholarship, they hardly ever achieved full-scale acceptance in the academic world. There were all the time corrective modes of thinking. Unhappily, dissenting opinions did not always gain the recognition they would have deserved. In what follows, the focus will rest on the criticism against the Weberian position. The discourse with Sanders must stay in the background, since he nowhere thoroughly accounts for introducing the arguments of his predecessors in-depth.[57]

51 Sanders 1977, 33–59.
52 Cf. already Perles 1903, 84–85.
53 Harnack 1900, particularly 40–45.
54 Bousset 1966, 377–78.
55 Bultmann 1954, 62. See above.
56 Bultmann 1988, 52–63.
57 Sanders 1977, 1–12, 33–59.

2.2. The Anti-Weberian Position

2.2.1. The Development Up to E. P. Sanders

Perhaps unsurprisingly, Jewish scholars were the first to contradict the Weberian position.[58] Among the most prominent and proficient of them was without doubt S. Schechter. His work *Aspects of Rabbinic Theology* already appeared in 1909 (further editions). He mentions with biting irony that the (mainstream) exegesis of the Pauline epistles leaves room for an astonishing alternative:

> Either the theology of the Rabbis must be wrong, its conception of God debasing, its leading motives materialistic and coarse, and its teachers lacking in enthusiasm and spirituality, or the Apostle to the Gentiles is quite unintelligible.[59]

Schechter does not conceal his ultimate antipathy for Weber's *System der altsynagogalen palästinischen Theologie*. He considers it to be a prime example of a fundamentally faulty understanding of rabbinic theology. It is full of fatal mistakes. Yet it has become "the chief source of information for the great majority of the writers." Weber simply turns rabbinic theology upside down. He penetrates first the material principle (legalism) and second the formal principle (written and oral tradition) of nomism. Much later, he proceeds and examines the Jewish notion of God. In doing so, he gives the impression that God truly has nothing to do with the Torah or that he has more or less forsaken his own people or that "he is himself a feeble reflex of the law."[60]

In his survey, Schechter sketches an altogether different description of rabbinism. To start with, the rabbis do not consider God distant from the world. They teach that he continues to care for his creation.[61] The relationship between God and Israel is particularly intimate and near. They show their mutual love for each other in a covenant.[62] Most of the rabbis regard Israel's election as a decisive manifestation of divine benevolence and compassion. They do not take it as an achievement to be earned through human merits.[63]

The Jews do not observe the Law in hope of reward from God. Instead, they serve him for his sake. They know perfectly well that a good work must be carried out with pure motives. Notwithstanding, God "does reward goodness and does punish wickedness."[64]

58 Hoheisel 1978, 31.
59 Schechter 1961, 18.
60 Op. cit., 23–24.
61 Op. cit., 21–45.
62 Op. cit., 46–56.
63 Op. cit., 57–62.
64 Op. cit., 162–63.

In no case does a Jew experience the Law as some sort of heavy burden. Rather, he enjoys observing the commandments. He rejoices in them.[65] The fulfillment of the Torah strengthens the mutual ties of love between God and his people.[66]

Salvation does not exactly depend on the number of commandments that will be observed. Whoever is able to "accomplish at least *one* law in a perfect manner," he "possesses the virtue of saving."[67] Surely the doctrine of the merits of the forefathers "plays an important part in Jewish theology." Nevertheless, its significance "is reduced to very small proportions" in rabbinic soteriology.[68] Different means of expiation (suffering and death, offerings, and Day of Atonement) mediate divine grace and take away guilt.[69] Without repentance, they all are self-evidently ineffective.[70]

Schechter especially undertakes to correct the Weberian caricature of rabbinism. Hence, he does not directly discuss the question of Paul's break with Judaism, in other words, why Paul then so strenuously reproached and rejected Judaism. What ultimately lies behind their severe conflict?[71] Without a clear answer, Schechter at any rate seems to suggest that the "apostle to the Gentiles" does not fully do justice to the Jewish side.[72]

A few years later, another Jewish scholar, C. G. Montefiore, set the academic discussion a step forward in his work *Judaism and St. Paul: Two Essays* (1914). He examined particularly the exacerbated or aggravated relationship between Paulinism and Judaism, a theme that Schechter, as already shown, had ignored in his survey. In fact, several years earlier, Montefiore had raised the issue in his article "Rabbinic Judaism and the Epistles of St. Paul" (1901). There he brought up the solutions developed in his book.[73]

65 Op. cit., 148–69.

66 Op. cit., 167: "The Law is thus a means of strengthening the mutual relations of love between God and his people. The fulfilment of the Law was, in the eyes of the Rabbis, a witnessing on the part of the Jews to God's relationship to the world." Later, Sanders (1977, 420–23 *et passim*) defends a similar position. See below.

67 Op. cit., 164–65.

68 Op. cit., 170.

69 Op. cit., 293–312.

70 Op. cit., 293–94.

71 *Pace* Sanders 1977, 6: "Schechter, of course, took the second view [that the apostle to the Gentiles is wholly incomprehensible]. Paul's critique of Judaism was not to the point: therefore Paul could not be understood." In effect, Schechter in no place takes a clear stand on the conflict between Paul and Judaism.

72 Cf. op. cit., 18.

73 Sanders does not take the article into account. See his register of literature (1977). Stein (1977) does not refer to the article either, despite his explicit intention in his monograph to penetrate Montefiore's publications.

Montefiore attempts to outline rabbinism from the beginning of the fourth century to the end of the fifth century AD.[74] In his Jewish sources, he does not find a single indication that the Jews should earn forgiveness for their sins. Instead, he concludes that they put their strong trust in the grace of God, who has established the covenant and expiatory means on their behalf. Hence, everyone who resorts to the atonement of the sacrificial offerings with repentance receives divine mercy for his transgressions.[75] For certain, Montefiore leaves it to others to decide how Palestinian Judaism may have appeared in the first century AD. He assumes, nonetheless, that salvation according to the common contemporary conviction did not depend on human merits.[76] It was rather Hellenistic Judaism in the first century that far more insisted on the legalistic principle of earning eternal life. In consequence, it would be exclusively Hellenistic Judaism that Paul accused of self-righteousness and boasting in one's own efforts.[77]

On this specific condition, Montefiore only modifies the traditional theory that Judaism as a whole degenerated after the exile (cf. J. Wellhausen).[78] He maintains that the degeneration affected merely Hellenistic Judaism. As a result, Palestinian Judaism would have remained free of deformation.

H.-J. Schoeps, also a Jewish scholar, represents a similar conception. In an article (originally appearing in 1942) published in his collected monograph *Aus frühchristlicher Zeit: Religionsgeschichtliche Untersuchungen* (1950), he deals with the haggadic material on the election of Israel.[79] It is solidly based on the evidence for sovereign divine initiative. On the whole, the rabbis stand firm in the Old Testament position (Deut. 7:7–8 as an example). They maintain that Israel has not gained her special status among the peoples of the world because of her merits. It harkens back to God's amazing grace. He made that decision in his benevolence.[80] For sure, works of the Law are important, but they have their place solely within the covenant, not outside it.[81]

In his later monograph *Paulus: Die Theologie des Apostels im Lichte der jüdischen Religionsgeschichte* (1959), Schoeps asserts that Hellenistic Judaism represented another kind of Judaism. It had in a very disastrous manner distorted the Old Testament heritage. First, the distortion touches the content of the Torah. Hellenistic Judaism reduces the Torah, including the haggada as well as the halakah, to the bare legal (or legalistic) document (*nomos*). Second, the distortion touches the close relationship between the Torah and the covenant.

74 Montefiore 1914, 15.
75 Op. cit., 17.
76 Op. cit., 87–91.
77 Op. cit., 92–112, 126–29.
78 For the significance of Wellhausen, see, e.g., Limbeck 1971, 11–12, 35.
79 Schoeps 1950, 184–200.
80 Schoeps 1950, 196–97.
81 Op. cit., 198–99.

Hellenistic Judaism isolates the Torah from its genuine context, that is, from the covenant.[82] Paul has committed the same fatal faults. He has misunderstood Palestinian Judaism since he came from Hellenistic Judaism.[83] Here, Schoeps apparently goes a step further than Montefiore, who—departing from his German colleague—strongly insists that Paul did not even know Palestinian Judaism (to say nothing of misunderstanding it).[84]

At any rate, in agreement with Montefiore, Schoeps presumes that Paul criticizes Hellenistic Judaism for self-righteousness and boasting in one's own efforts but does not pass judgment on rabbinic Judaism. The two main movements differ from each other both in a geographical and theological sense.[85]

On close reflection, Schoeps contradicts himself as he maintains that "as a result of the post-biblical lack of clear doctrinal standards, even in the Palestinian schools there is *hardly a clear presentation* of the relationship between the Torah and Berith [covenant], that, namely, what Paul calls the νόμος or ὅλος ὁ νόμος actually represents an instrument of the Berith, a statute and organ of the covenant" (italics mine).[86] Strictly, he supposes and suggests that both Palestinian and Hellenistic Judaism have in a fatal manner falsified the Old Testament heritage since they have isolated the Torah from its correct context, that is, from the covenant. Where now is the previous contrast between Palestinian and Hellenistic Judaism? And if Palestinian Judaism had also degenerated, was that not grounds enough for Paul to criticize it for egoistic and legalistic soteriology? And had he utterly misunderstood Palestinian Judaism? Oddly, one seeks clear-cut answers from Schoeps in vain. In his later writings, he seems to waver in his opinion.

The first Christian scholar to protest against the Weberian position was G. F. Moore.[87] Already in 1921 he published an essay with the title "Christian Writers on Judaism." It gives a short overview of what Christian authors at different times have written about the Jewish religion. Moore critically analyzes

82 Schoeps 1959, 224–30, especially 225.

83 Ibid.

84 Montefiore 1914, 92–112. *Pace* Räisänen 1980, 65: "Nevertheless, both Montefiore and Schoeps assume that Paul's picture of Judaism *as known to him* is in itself accurate. But the form of Judaism Paul knew was an inferior one. According to these scholars, Paul was ignorant of the nature and quality of Palestinian Judaism and based his critique on the allegedly deteriorated piety of Diaspora Judaism." See further Räisänen 1983, 181. The quotation does not do Schoeps justice.

85 Schoeps 1959, 21, 216–27.

86 Op. cit., 225: "infolge der nachbiblischen Insuffizienz hinsichtlich von Lehrnormierungen auch in den Lehrhäusern Palästinas *kaum klare Vorstellungen* über das Verhältnis Thora-Berith bestanden haben, daß nämlich das, was Paulus νόμος bzw. ὅλος ὁ νόμος nennt, tatsächlich Instrument der Berith, Satzung und Organ des Bundes darstellt" (italics mine).

87 Hoheisel 1978, 37.

the majority of the pertinent works from the beginning of the Common Era to the beginning of the twentieth century. His focus rests on the newer literature, among others the studies of Weber and Bousset.[88]

In agreement with Schechter, Moore categorically and drastically discards the conception that the rabbis would in the main consider God as distant from the world. He thinks that neither Weber nor Bousset, who have maintained such positions,[89] offer convincing arguments. Both read their own thoughts into the source material. Weber mainly induces the rabbinic utterances on the "mediating hypostasis" (for instance, Metatron, Memra, Shekinah). On the basis of them, he instantly draws his conclusion that God holds himself distant from the world. Moore calls into question Weber's argumentation. He exposes the absurdity of it.[90] On the other hand, Bousset mostly induces the apocalyptical visions of *caelum supremum*. On account of them, he immediately draws the same conclusion that God holds himself distant from the world. Moore calls into question Bousset's argumentation as well. He equally exposes the absurdity of it.[91] Through their descriptions of the heavenly temple, the apocalyptic writings rather emphasize God's holiness and majesty (cf. Isaiah 6) but not, for example, that God exists and remains somewhere far away "in heaven."[92] If Bousset had taken heed of rabbinic theology,[93] he would have achieved absolutely different results.[94]

In his outstanding trilogy *Judaism in the First Centuries of the Christian Era: The Age of the Tannaim* (originally published in 1927–30, further reprints), Moore deals with rabbinism in-depth. On the basis of the Tannaitic material, he indeed sketches an entirely different picture of the Jewish religion than does Bousset on the basis of the apocalyptic literature. They are more like mirror images of each other.

Moore delineates the following main lines in rabbinic theology:

> The rabbis believe in an accessible and nearby God.[95] In his benevolence and compassion, he has established a covenant with the Israelites. He swore thereby always to look after and watch over them.[96] The covenant originates in his

88 Moore 1921, 228–37, 241–48.

89 See above 2.1.

90 Moore 1921, 233–34. He does not explain what the Jewish concepts of "intermediaries" mean, if not that God holds himself distant from the world. In his later work, Moore (1948–50, 1:419) explains that the rabbis speak of "intermediaries" in order to avoid anthropomorphism.

91 Moore 1921, 247–48.

92 Ibid.

93 Moore speaks of rabbinism as "normative" Judaism (op. cit., 244–45). Rightfully, his usage has been criticized. See, e.g., Sanders 1977, 34 n. 11.

94 Moore 1921, 242–48.

95 Moore 1948–50, 1:359–85, 423.

96 Op. cit., 1:219–34, 398.

divine initiative, not on the basis of human merits.[97] Since God chose Israel, all Israelites, excluding the unrepentant sinners, take part in the future kingdom.[98] Yet good works do not become superfluous. They still count. God desires an obedient people. Exactly for that reason, his people desire to obey his will as it is documented in the Torah.[99] The rabbis do not satisfy themselves with an external fulfilment of the Law. They demand that the Law be fulfilled for the highest motives (such as love of God and awe of his holiness).[100] In practice, everyone knows that he at least occasionally goes astray. In order to win salvation, he need not live up to all the commandments with absolute perfection.[101] Instead, he should atone for happenstance transgression through repentance and expiation (day of atonement, offerings, sufferings, death).[102] God certainly shows his mercy on the repentant.[103] His favor toward his own people increases even more through the merits of the forefathers benefiting more readily the collective than the individual.[104]

Only in passing does Moore deal with the anti-Jewish polemics of the Pauline letters, especially the epistles to the Romans and Galatians. He sets up a far-reaching theory later accepted by Sanders.[105] He assumes and suggests a kind of "reverse order" of the apostolic thinking: Paul has started with his categorical statement that there is no other salvation but faith in Christ. As an inevitable consequence from his prior premise, he then concludes that the Judaism that rejects his Gospel falls short.[106]

Some New Testament scholars seem to postulate that "traditional Lutheranism" necessarily sympathizes with the Weberian position.[107] Their prejudice, however, results from the fact that they did not satisfactorily become familiar with Lutheran works.[108] In Sweden, H. Odeberg has energetically confronted every kind of misreading of rabbinic theology. The Swedish original of his important work *Fariseism och kristendom* appeared in 1943 (1980 [4th ed.]), the English edition, *Pharisaism and Christianity*, first in 1964.

97 Op. cit., 1:398, 2:95.
98 Op. cit., 2:94–95.
99 Op. cit., 2:89–111.
100 Op. cit., 2:95–100.
101 Op. cit., 1:495, 2:94.
102 On means of expiation, see op. cit., 1:497–506. On repentance, see op. cit., 1:507–34.
103 Op. cit., 1:535–45.
104 Op. cit., 1:543.
105 See below.
106 Moore 1948–50, 3:151.
107 Especially Sanders 1977, 53, 55, 57, 100, 176, 228, 296, 436, 492 n. 57 *et passim*. Besides, see also F. Watson 1986, on nearly every page!
108 Cf. Beker 1978, 110; Dahl 1978, 154, 157 n. 1.

For Odeberg, rabbinism represents Pharisaism.[109] He practically equates the two, which currently appears somewhat audacious.[110] Besides, he portrays Christianity for its part using the Johannine and Pauline materials in particular.[111] For obvious reasons, there is here no significance or relevance in delineating the controversy between Johannine "Christianity" and "Pharisaic" Judaism. In the following, the emphasis solely rests on the controversy between Pauline "Christianity" and "Pharisaic" Judaism.

In his *Pharisaism and Christianity*, Odeberg regularly follows the argumentation in another book that is hidden behind the enigmatic abbreviation "LJI." He does not decipher what the two roman characters and one roman numeral stand for, but it is the book *Die Lehren des Judentums nach den Quellen. Erster Teil*[112] (published already in 1920 by Verband der Deutschen Juden).[113] The first volume explicitly focuses on *Die Grundlagen der jüdischen Ethik*, while the second and the third volume deal with various different issues. The preface to the second edition from 1999 regards the entire series as "the essence of Judaism in three volumes" ("die Essenz des Judentums in drei Bänden") or "a publishing masterpiece" ("ein verlegerisches Meisterwerk") or "this legacy of German-Jewish thought" ("dieses Vermächtnis deutsch-jüdischen Denkens"). It rapidly reached the rank of a standard work. It also became a bestseller.[114] The preface concludes:

> The "Lehren des Judentems nach den Quellen," however, present an outstanding intellectual achievement: they denote the climax of Jewish learning in twentieth-century Germany.[115]

To begin with, Odeberg, in broad agreement with the ethical teachings in LJI, depreciates many misinterpretations of rabbinism (for example, the conception that the rabbinic ethic is casuistic,[116] that it completely concentrates on

109 Cf. Odeberg 1980, 9–40 *et passim*. He again and again cites rabbinic sayings as Pharisaic utterances.

110 See, e.g., Sanders 1977, 60–62.

111 Odeberg 1980, 41ff.

112 See Laato 2007, 171–73 (in reference to J. Svartvik).

113 The organization was founded in 1904. Its ultimate goal or ambitious intention was "die Gleichstellung der jüdischen Religionsgemeinschaft mit den beiden christlichen Kirchen." See Laato 2007, 171.

114 Ibid.

115 Ibid.: "Die 'Lehren des Judentums nach den Quellen' jedoch stellen eine herausragende geistige Leistung dar: sie bezeichnen den Kulminationspunkt jüdischer Gelehrsamkeit im Deutschland des 20. Jahrhunderts." Already in the first edition of the book series, it interestingly reads as follows: "Möge sie [this book in three volumes] dazu beitragen, Vorurteile zu beseitigen und in weiten Kreisen eine gerechte Würdigung des Judentums herbeizuführen."

116 Odeberg 1980, 13–24.

external deeds without any concern for internal disposition,[117] that it rests on the egoistic purpose of earning rewards and escaping punishments,[118] that it depends on and reckons with the merits of each person).[119] Next, he moves on and in full agreement with LJI maintains that the exact contrast between rabbinism and Paulinism culminates in the question of the freedom of the human will.[120] The rabbis underscore that man has free will. Hence, they suppose that with his own strength he can do what God demands.[121] Instead, Paul underscores that the whole of mankind lacks free will (in spiritual matters). Hence, he maintains that they cannot in their own power do what God demands.[122]

In his overall understanding of rabbinism, Odeberg has in large part adhered to the theological overview of LJI. He has not gone rogue or set out on his own.[123] Yet in his juxtaposition of rabbinism and Paulinism, he offers an important contribution to the constant discussion in soteriological issues. He postulates that the anthropological difference makes the real big difference. This is what results in the parting of the ways. The rabbinic soteriology in part is based on human achievements since man can and must cooperate with God. In contrast, the Pauline soteriology is not in the least based on human achievements since man cannot and should not cooperate with God in order to gain salvation. He needs to be reborn, so to speak. The transformation in terms of "new birth" naturally takes place without his merits.[124] Furthermore, Odeberg finally seeks to demonstrate that in his critique of Jewish self-righteousness and

117 Op. cit., 25–26.

118 Op. cit., 27–30.

119 Op. cit., 31–34.

120 Op. cit., 41–82.

121 Op. cit., 49–52, 66–68.

122 Op. cit., 52–55, 73–74.

123 For the similarities of argumentation in Odeberg's *Fariseism och kristendom* and LJI, see Laato 2007, 171–72. This in part new and heavy evidence enables Svartvik (2007, 179–80) to accuse Odeberg of plagiarism. His accusation rather seems like some kind of overreaction. It hardly does full justice to the neutrality of historical research and the objective consideration of relevant data. It is instead more to the point to point out that Odeberg closely follows the argumentation in LJI. He allows the prominent Jewish scholars to define their Jewish religion through their well-known standard book on the Jewish set of beliefs. In so doing, at least he does not succumb to any vile deformation of rabbinism. True, Odeberg does not reveal to his readers what LJI stands for. He does not tell them that he quotes from it and repeats its main thoughts. But those who know what is going on understand that he always gives the floor to the Jewish experts who wrote their bestseller in Germany in German and whose work was even published in Germany by a German-Jewish organization. Notwithstanding, Odeberg also strongly criticizes Pharisaism from his own Christian convictions and warns Christianity of the perilous Pharisaic "leaven" (cf. below). After the Second World War, he modified and mitigated his text in the new editions of *Fariseism och kristendom*.

124 Odeberg 1980, 73–74, 93–100.

self-praise, Paul does not overshoot the mark. His criticism concerns the optimistic anthropology and its ensuing soteriological consequences in Judaism.[125]

Lastly, it might be of interest that in his (Swedish) review of Odeberg's *Fariseism och kristendom*, the Jewish scholar Schoeps, who himself thinks and argues differently (see above), still commends the book and applauds the great expertise of the author. His critical remarks revolve around the political opinions prevalent in Germany in the early 1940s.[126]

To all appearances, most of the adherents of the anti-Weberian position originate from the Anglo-Saxon world (Schechter, Montefiore, Moore).[127] It is also notable that Odeberg's work was translated into English. In the German-speaking world, Schoeps stands out as the one who deviates from the common mainstream representation of Judaism.

Taken as a whole, the examination of the anti-Weberian position reveals far more variance and heterogeneity than in the case of the Weberian approach. Certainly, a broad consensus exists that the common or mainstream conception of rabbinism or Judaism as a legalistic religion of the worst kind turns into a complete failure and fiasco. Still, Schechter, Montefiore, Schoeps, Moore, and Odeberg do not reach agreement on the reasons why Paul breaks with his Pharisaic past. What lies behind his morbid critique of the Jewish soteriology? Schechter suspends his judgment altogether. Montefiore assumes that Paul criticizes only the degenerated form of Hellenistic Judaism. Schoeps concurs and

125 Op. cit., 52–60, 64–65.

126 Schoeps 1944. Despite his high respect for the academic expertise in *Fariseism och kristendom*, Schoeps criticizes Odeberg's political views which seem to reflect some kind of pro-German or even pro-Nazi commitment. Later, Svartvik (see 2006, especially 118–245) tries to turn Odeberg's *Fariseism och kristendom* into a vile pro-Nazi propaganda. However, he ignores that LJI represents the best Jewish knowledge at that time. How could Odeberg, who in his *Fariseism och kristendom* follows LJI (see above) with slavish precision, suddenly promote only disinformation and indoctrination? Moreover, Svartvik does not even mention Schoeps's review of *Fariseism och kristendom*, in which he, as a Jew, acclaims the academic value and worth of the book. See especially my contribution to the ongoing discussion (Laato 2007, 169–74). Odeberg disassociated himself from anti-Semitism in his installation lecture when he was appointed to a professorship in Lund. At that time, he was even accused of Judaistic exegesis. Now, the pendulum points in the opposite direction! During the Second World War, Odeberg invited rabbis or other Jewish persons to join his Erevna (an academic discussion and research group). He had cultivated good relationships with them. Apparently, he was never a hard-boiled Nazi, even if his political views were more or less naive (Laato 2007). In his reply to me, Svartvik (2007) repeats his prior accusations and adds some new ones. Yet he still overlooks the main problem: it does not seem plausible or reasonable to suggest that Odeberg in his *Fariseism och kristendom* depicts a pro-Nazi "falsarium," if in his argumentation he follows a Jewish standard work and gains recognition from his Jewish colleagues. Here, Svartvik obviously owes his readers a good answer. It does not make any sense to continue the discussion with him before that. For a well-balanced presentation of the discussion, see Kreß 2022, 167–68.

127 See also Sanders 1977, 55.

adds that Paul has also misunderstood Palestinian Judaism. Moore underscores that Paul rejects Judaism because of his exclusive Christology. Yet Odeberg underlines that Paul rejects Judaism because of his pessimistic anthropology instead. The divergence of views is ostensibly why the anti-Weberian position did not have any decisive influence or direct bearing on New Testament exegesis. In contrast, the Weberian position has not divided into opposing camps. Consequently, it more easily dominates the academic discussion.[128] Only E. P. Sanders has caused a shift in thinking and a turning point in research.[129] Hence it seems justifiable to introduce his innovative and seminal contribution in a separate section.

2.2.2. E. P. Sanders

In his impressive and epoch-making work *Paul and Palestinian Judaism* (1977), E. P. Sanders fervently confronts and opposes the Weberian line of reasoning. Weber and the "Weberians" misconstrue rabbinism already by means of their prejudiced presumption that the rabbis provide a kind of systematic theology.[130] Bousset concentrates on the Apocrypha and the Pseudepigrapha. He does not pay sufficient attention to the rabbinic sources even when trying to describe the religion of Judaism.[131] Billerbeck cites many Jewish writings and rabbinic sayings without reference to their context. In doing so, he distorts their apparent or plain meaning.[132] Bultmann depends mostly on secondary literature but has not particularly studied rabbinic literature himself.[133] He avails himself of the anti-Weberian works of Schechter and Moore in order to corroborate the Weberian interpretation of rabbinism.[134] Sanders further criticizes Protestant scholars for projecting the Lutheran-Catholic dispute onto the time of the New Testament, whereby Judaism takes the role of Catholicism and Christianity the part of Lutheranism.[135]

In his own study of rabbinism, Sanders avails himself of the Tannaitic literature alone.[136] Hence, his criticism of Weber, Bousset (and Gressmann), Billerbeck, and Bultmann lacks a certain degree of force where their source materials exceed the Tannaitic literature.[137] He does not prove or demonstrate

128 See above 2.1.

129 See below 2.3.

130 Sanders 1977, 69.

131 Op. cit., 34. Sanders depends on Moore (1921, 243).

132 Sanders 1977, 42.

133 Op. cit., 43.

134 Op. cit., 44.

135 Op. cit., 57.

136 Op. cit., 59–60.

137 See Weber 1897, Einleitung § 2; Billerbeck 1922, vii–viii; Bousset 1966, 6–47; and Bultmann 1954, 232–39.

that, for example, the Amoraic sayings represent a different sort of soteriology that is at odds with the Weberian position (or the adherents of the Weberian picture of rabbinism).[138]

Sanders attaches weight to the covenant as the indisputable foundation of rabbinic theology.[139] However, he does not in the Tannaitic literature find any unequivocal answer to why God established a covenant with Israel. There are differing explanations. They occur simultaneously and are in force at the same time. They lay emphasis either on the sovereignty of God or on the merits of Israel. Both alternatives are equally true. Neither the one nor the other amounts to a doctrinal system.[140] According to the former, God chose Israel out of pure love. According to the latter, God did not choose Israel arbitrarily or at his pleasure.[141]

The covenant is based on a mutual relationship between both parties. Since God has chosen Israel as his own people, Israel will act as his own people in order to please him.[142] Correct conduct will take the Torah as norm.[143] The rabbis nowhere complain that the detailed instructions of the halakah might become a heavy burden or cause a lot of resentment. Instead, they consider and experience it as a great privilege and pleasure to possess the right knowledge of the divine will.[144]

The rabbis maintain that the Law must be fulfilled with the right intention. They push for acceptable motives. As a consequence, they encourage obedience to the commandments out of love for God or simply because the commandments are good in and of themselves.[145] As a result, the Torah, for example, should not be kept out of fear of punishment or in hope of reward. Yet disobedience causes punishment or obedience receives reward.[146]

The weight of sins against merits does not constitute rabbinic soteriology. The idea of "heavenly bookkeeping" does not indicate that God counts the evil and the good deeds with meticulous precision in order to decide the place of everyone in the future world on the basis of whether their good works are in the majority. No, his last judgment will not amount to his day of reckoning in this

138 E. Sjöberg, for example, points out that the rabbis of the Amoraic era, unlike those of the Tannaitic epoch, give more weight to the merits, especially in the question of זכות אבות (Sjöberg 1939, 51–52), the eternal destiny of the Gentiles (op. cit., 83 n. 2, 86) or conversion (op. cit., 163–64, 166).

139 Sanders 1977, 84–107.

140 Op. cit., 87–101.

141 Op. cit., 98–101.

142 Op. cit., 107.

143 Op. cit., 106–7.

144 Op. cit., 110–11.

145 Op. cit., 120.

146 Op. cit., 117–25.

definitive sense.[147] Rather, the rabbis follow up a parenetic aim in their warning that someone will be condemned according to a single sin or that he will be saved according to a single merit or that the eternal verdict will fall in accordance with the preponderance of sins or merits.[148] All those various sayings in their own specific way urge a Jew to be obedient to the Law as though his next act were decisive over his everlasting destiny. They do not announce in any dogmatic sense that he inherits the coming kingdom only if his good deeds outweigh the evil ones.[149]

All Israelites (including the עמי הארץ) will enter the world to come and enjoy life after death unless they deny God or throw off the yoke of the covenant.[150] An exception confirms the rule: the Sadducees will not enter the world to come because they do not put their faith and trust in the resurrection. They are acted upon according to the principle of "measure for measure." Nevertheless, they were still regarded as Israelites and full members in the covenant.[151]

The basic thought of God's benevolence and compassion stands firm in rabbinism. It involves the recognition that he forgives every kind of sin. He assures his grace to the repentant. In contrast, the unrepentant are lost.[152] In the event that a Jew transgresses the Law, he must with repentance diligently seek the remedy through expiatory means (temple cult, Day of Atonement, suffering, death). His guilt will be wiped out. No one needs to live in unknowing suspense. God keeps what he has once promised to Israel. He will certainly have mercy on them.[153]

The rabbis regularly discuss the question of cause and effect. They ponder which merit or merits (זכות)[154] have brought about happiness and success in the course of history. As a rule, the Jews earn for themselves concrete and material things but not—note well—for example, their future place in the world to come.[155] In fact, the Tannaitic literature provides no evidence for the illusion that a person might pass through the day of judgment because of the merits of the forefathers.[156]

147 Op. cit., 125–47, especially 146.

148 Op. cit., 141, 146.

149 Ibid.

150 Op. cit., 147–50, 152–57.

151 Op. cit., 150–52.

152 Op. cit., 157.

153 Op. cit., 157–80.

154 Sanders (1977, 183–84, 187–88) notes that the concept "merit" does not exactly correspond to the Hebrew זכות.

155 Op. cit., 189: "Now we must note that these rewards for merit are almost without exception quite concrete historical rewards and are not soteriological."

156 Op. cit., 197.

Hence, salvation depends on a personal relationship with God. The rabbis by no means regard him as distant or remote, nor do they consider him as inaccessible. He has not left Israel to cope on its own, nor has he forsaken the Israelites. They live in intimacy with him.[157] They feel close to him particularly as they meditate on and practice the Torah,[158] or as they pray to him.[159]

On various occasions, Sanders repeats his central conclusion that the Jew does not fulfill the Law in order to enter the covenant but rather to remain in it, in other words, that he does not earn his salvation through his works.[160] Among the different Palestinian Jewish writings from about 200 BC to AD 200, only 4 Ezra stands out as an exception. The author suggests that each and every person must work very hard and reach moral perfection to finally gain eternal life. The other Palestinian Jewish texts (the Tannaitic literature, the Dead Sea Scrolls, Sirach, 1 Enoch, Jubilees, the Psalms of Solomon) do not share the same soteriological view, neither do certain Hellenistic Jewish sources (Philo, Joseph and Aseneth).[161] Therefore, it seems plausible to think that salvation in Judaism generally and particularly during New Testament times depends on God's grace.[162]

Last but not least, the urgent question arises why then Paul broke off from Judaism, assuming that it did maintain a proper balance between divine grace and human works, in other words, provided that it did not turn into a religion of self-righteousness and self-praise. He must have had some reasoning for his rejection. Evidently, Sanders tenders Moore's solution, although he does not directly express himself on it. Both put their emphasis upon the exclusive Christology of Paul. He must break with Jewish soteriology on account of his conviction that no one nor other can save but Christ.[163]

157 Op. cit., 212–17. See further p. 222: "It thus appears that at the very heart of the Rabbis' supposed legalism is the feeling of intimate contact with God."

158 Op. cit., 217–23.

159 Op. cit., 223–33.

160 Op. cit., 84–101, 104–7, 147–50, 233–38, 419–23.

161 For Palestinian Judaism, see Sanders 1977, 419–26 (cf. already 1976, 15–22, 39–44). For Hellenistic Judaism, see Sanders 1976, 22–44.

162 Sanders 1977, 426–28.

163 Op. cit., 442–47, 474–75, 549–52. For sure, Sanders in short mentions Moore's solution (op. cit., 6). However, Sanders does not concede that he directly or precisely follows it. He simply takes it over and makes it his own. In the second section of his book ("Paul"), Sanders does not depend upon Moore in even one instance (cf. op. cit., Index of Names, s.v. Moore). For Moore's Christological solution, see above 2.2.1.

2.3. The State of Research

The ongoing exegetical debate applies in the first rank to Sanders's prominent work *Paul and Palestinian Judaism*. His thoughts and theses immediately excited worldwide attention.[164] Not surprisingly, in 1978 he received the National Religious Book Award for his research.[165] By 1985, *Paul and Palestinian Judaism* already appeared in unabridged German translation and by 1986 in Italian.[166] An undetermined and unknown number of academic articles and monographs relate to the problems or questions that it has brought up for discussion.[167] The debate now begun shows no sign of ending. More and more biblical scholars and experts on Judaism are joining it. Nowadays, the so-called New Perspective on Paul has been inspired by Sanders and his imposing work *Paul and Palestinian Judaism*. In recent years, it has become a hot topic and a talking point that goes back to him.[168]

Sanders's influence on the current state of research comes into view through the response his conclusions have initiated from the very beginning. The reviews as a rule rank his *Paul and Palestinian Judaism* as a masterpiece, even when obviously not lacking in critical remarks.[169] The following survey of

---

164 In his foreword to the fortieth anniversary edition of *Paul and Palestinian Judaism*, Chancey (2017, xi) rightly writes: "Rarely in biblical scholarship has a book made such an immediate and lasting impact as did *Paul and Palestinian Judaism: A Comparison of Patterns of Religion*." See below notices of several reviews.

165 According to Hagner 1979, 25.

166 *Paulus und das palästinische Judentum: Ein Vergleich zweier Religionsstrukturen* and *Paolo e il giudaismo palestinese: Studio comparativo su modelli di religione*.

167 Cf. Laato 2019. See also below, especially chapters 3 and 6.

168 Chancey 2017. Similarly, Laato 2019. In reference to Chancey (2017, xvi–xxiv), Sanders (2017, xxviii) will disentangle his *Paul and Palestinian Judaism* "from the confusing conglomeration of view called 'the new perspective on Paul.'" Nonetheless, his monumental work has at least inspired the later development or movement. Besides, different scholars do have something in common. At least they represent "a rich chorus of voices that perpetually remind the larger guild of biblical studies that the days of unchallenged negative generalizations about Judaism are over" (Chancey 2017, xxiii). In addition, the Christological argument is often a common denominator as well: Paul did not discard the Jewish religion since it was allegedly based on legalistic soteriology but rather for the reason that it amounts to a denial of Christ as Messiah. In Sanders's well-known words, "*this is what Paul finds wrong with Judaism, it is not Christianity*" (1977, 552). Further, the Christological argument is generally accompanied by a strong emphasis on salvation for all, Gentiles as well as Jews. The apostolic proclamation could no longer stay inside the narrow boundaries of the Mosaic Law. Particularism has to give way to universalism. See Laato 2008, 40–41. Notwithstanding, the concept of "the New Perspective on Paul" comprises a large number of scholars who stand for a wide spectrum of deviating interpretations (op. cit., 40).

169 Chancey 2017. The criticism of Sanders will be examined particularly in the following chapter.

some of them (in a very abbreviated form for practical reasons) may serve as a short résumé.

J. Neusner,[170] an American Jewish scholar in rabbinism, designates Sanders's monumental work as one of the most ambitious contributions in Pauline research during the last twenty-five years.[171] It offers an effective apology for rabbinism and a heavy-laden criticism of incompetent or malevolent estimations of Judaism.[172]

S. Sandmel, a Jewish New Testament scholar, writes that his praise of Sanders's masterpiece is "virtually unstinted."[173] He holds it "to be one of the very great works of New Testament scholarship of our time." In addition, he really admires "the thoroughness" of the author's scholarship, "the clarity of his thought," and "the sensitivity of his understanding."[174]

M. McNamara considers Sanders's work as the most important publication in the field for a whole generation. The far-reaching outcomes of his *Paul and Palestinian Judaism* will certainly guide the direction of research for years to come.[175]

B. R. Gaventa holds it essential that New Testament scholars get to know and try to understand the relationship between Paul and the different forms of first-century Judaism. Sanders's work, especially his criticism of earlier methods in the comparison of religions,[176] marks a step forward in the right direction, leading academic research to more effective exegetical analysis and application of biblical studies.[177]

H. Hübner notes that Sanders's *Paul and Palestinian Judaism* ranks among the most ambitious and influential publications on Paul. No doubt, it is destined to become a standard work. It certainly represents the beginning of the way ahead and a step forward.[178] However, the high quality of Sanders's important study is mainly due to the first part, in which he characterizes the pattern of religion of Palestinian Judaism, and not so much to the second part, in which he sketches the theology of Paul.[179]

---

170 Neusner's review in *History of Religions* 18 (1978): 177–91, was revised with a short addition and published for a second time in vol. 2 of *Approaches to Ancient Judaism*, ed. W. S. Green, 43–63 (1980). The pagination referenced here follows his later publication.

171 Op. cit., 59.

172 Op. cit., 60.

173 Sandmel 1978, 159.

174 Op. cit, 160.

175 McNamara 1979, 71.

176 For Sanders's argumentation, see below 3.1.

177 Gaventa 1980, 42.

178 Hübner 1980, 448.

179 Ibid.

Other reviews contain similar words of appreciation and approval.[180] But there is no need for more of the same. The preceding examples will suffice. They demonstrate that Sanders has truly done groundbreaking work and paved the way for new perspectives. Reviewers do not exaggerate in saying that his masterpiece *Paul and Palestinian Judaism* should be on the bookshelf of every exegete. It will be impossible to ignore his theses in the future.[181] Indeed, he "did what apparently no New Testament scholar had done before."[182] In 2017, his *Paul and Palestinian Judaism* was once again reprinted as a fortieth anniversary edition.[183] Actually, all current new interpretations of Pauline theology (see, e.g., N. T. Wright, J. D. G. Dunn, and J. M. G. Barclay) are still based on this grandiose book of Sanders.[184] Similarly, the editors of *Perspectives on Paul: Five Views* (2020), S. McKnight and B. J. Oropeza, confirm in their preface: "In many ways, the decisive impetus for each of the perspectives here was the 1977 book by E. P. Sanders, *Paul and Palestinian Judaism*."[185]

In consideration of the current state of research, some obvious outcomes arise from the main lines of the historical survey and the overview of the prominent proponents of the Weberian and anti-Weberian views (see above). At least, the following three conclusions stand firm:

(1) The Weberian interpretation of rabbinism resp. Judaism in general no longer receives any tangible support.[186] Instead, Sanders's depiction of Palestinian Judaism finds approval in wide circles.[187] The best example is H. Räisänen's

180 Beker 1978, 110; Best 1982, 65, 71, 74; Caird 1978, 543; Dahl 1978, 153, 157; Drury 1978, 236; Hagner 1979, 25, 27; Heiligenthal 1985, 546–47; Horbury 1979, 118; Jacques 1979, 898; King 1980, 141, 144; Klauck 1986a, 77–79; Malina 1978, 190–91; Mußner 1986, 42; Nickelsburg 1979, 173, 175; Oberforcher 1987, 213–14; Saldarini 1979, 299, 303; Sandmel 1978, 158, 160; Schelkle 1986, 64–65; Uotila 1986, 512–13; Vicent 1986, 428; Westerholm 1979, 131, 133; C. Wolff 1986, 421, 424–25. However, Bietenhard's review is the exception that proves the rule. He considers Sanders's work to be wrong from the ground up (1986, 279: "als ganzes im Grundsatz für verfehlt")!

181 First, Chancey 2017, xiv: "In retrospect, the extent to which scholars immediately recognized the paradigm-shifting significance of *Paul and Palestinian Judaism* is remarkable. [. . .] The book was quickly hailed as a stunning masterpiece." See also Caird 1978, 543; Drury 1978, 236; Hagner 1979, 27; Horbury 1979, 118; King 1980, 141, 144; Malina 1978, 190–91; McNamara 1979, 71; Murphy-O'Connor 1978, 126; Nickelsburg 1979, 175; Saldarini 1979, 299; Westerholm 1979, 131, 133.

182 Chancey 2017, xi.

183 Chancey 2017; Sanders 2017.

184 Laato 2019.

185 McKnight and Oropeza 2020, ix.

186 See especially Chancey 2017, xxv: "Most scholars recognize that the simplistic charges of Jewish legalism that once filled the pages of New Testament scholarship were based on ill-founded and often unidentified assumptions." Beker 1978, 108; Best 1982, 71, 74; Brooke 1979, 248; Caird 1978, 539; Dahl 1978, 154, 157 n. 1; Hagner 1979, 25; King 1980, 42; Neusner 1980, 60; Saldarini 1979, 299; Sandmel 1978, 158–59; Thielman 1989, 25.

187 See the following reviews: Beker 1978, 108–11; Best 1982, 65–74; Brooke 1979, 247–50; Caird 1978, 538–43; Cooper 1982, 123–39; Dahl 1978, 153–57; Drury 1978, 235–36;

monograph *Paul and the Law* (1983). Axiomatically, he underlines already in the preface that Sanders "cogently and with great expertise" argues "for a view of Palestinian Judaism rather different from that still prevalent in much New Testament scholarship."[188] What's more, Räisänen goes so far as to introduce Sanders's "illuminating" work "like a gift from heaven" for his own quest.[189] No doubt, it is correct if a scholar in advance informs his readers and from the start gives them an account of whether or not he agrees with a certain perspective or a specific reading of the texts. That might be indeed commendable. However, here a person might pause to reflect on the fact that Räisänen nowhere makes himself clear about what kind of gift from "heaven" he received, in other words, to what extent Sanders's characterization of Palestinian Judaism holds true or not.[190] Räisänen simply presumes that Sanders is right. Then he demonstrates what consequences follow from such a presumption.

(2) The clear-cut differentiation between Palestinian and Hellenistic Judaism in New Testament times offered by Montfiore and Schoeps no longer finds approval. The distinction they made does not match the reality. Rather, it seems exceedingly artificial. By all accounts, there has never been a trenchant borderline between Palestinian and Hellenistic Judaism. In the first place, Hellenistic influences invaded Palestine very early.[191] In the second place, the Jews of the Diaspora never broke their close contacts or relations with their countrymen in Palestine.[192] In addition, Sanders postulates that the main soteriological principles in Palestinian and Hellenistic Judaism coincide with each other,[193] which further calls the conclusions of Montefiore and Schoeps into question.[194]

(3) Odeberg's approach has not been rejected, but neither has it been accepted. In the long run, many of his arguments have sunk into oblivion. In reality, they were never integrated into research.[195] At last, it is high time to

---

Gaventa 1980, 37–44; Hagner 1979, 25–27; Horbury 1979, 116–18; Jacques 1979, 898–99; King 1980, 141–44; Malina 1978, 190–91; Murphy-O'Connor 1978, 122–26; McNamara 1979, 67–73; Neusner 1980, 43–63; Nickelsburg 1979, 171–75; Saldarini 1979, 299–303; Sandmel 1978, 158–60; Westerholm 1979, 131–33. See also Chancey 2017.

188 Räisänen 1983, preface.

189 Ibid.

190 Cf. op. cit., 166. Räisänen repeats here his praise from the preface. Without substantiation, he asserts that "with the publication of the pertinent studies" especially by Sanders "the discussion has been carried a long step forward."

191 Especially, Hengel 1969, 105–7, 191–95, 453–563. See further Davies 1980, 5–6; Hoheisel 1978, 32 n. 189; Räisänen 1983, 181 n. 99; Sanders 1976, 11–12; Stein 1977, 32–33; Thielman 1989, 12.

192 Hengel 1969, 105–7, 191–95. See further Davies 1980, 6–7.

193 Sanders 1976, 39–44.

194 Räisänen 1983, 181–82.

195 With the exception of reviews, I know of no academic publication dealing with Odeberg's views more in-depth.

examine Odeberg's overall view in the framework of an academic study. The central question concerns his notion that Paul broke off from Jewish soteriology because of his pessimistic anthropology.[196]

It remains to be hoped that Sanders has ultimately brought the final end to all ill-founded or trumped-up presentations of rabbinism and Judaism.[197] He has with good reasons demonstrated that the Weberian position is approaching caricature. In much New Testament scholarship, it is often a matter of sheer ignorance and lack of right knowledge rather than of outright malice. But now the shift in focus has taken place. The turning point in research history is already here.

Sanders correctly emphasizes that the rabbis (or the Jews in general) have not forgotten the benevolence and compassion of God, who shows his constant love for them in the gracious context of the covenant[198] or through means of expiation.[199] Hence, they did not believe in a remote God, who lives somewhere far away in isolation from Israel or the world in general and reveals himself as inaccessible. Instead, he makes himself known as the Creator and Benefactor of all his creatures.[200] Furthermore, Sanders rightly puts an end to the deep-rooted consensus that weighing good deeds against bad ones constitutes rabbinic soteriology. The Jews did not commonly reckon their works in the hope of gaining salvation according to the majority of their merits. They (as little as anyone else) did not perform such a calculation. In the case of sins, they should first of all repent and put their trust in divine leniency. An attempt to outweigh some transgressions with works of compensation does not bring about salvation.[201]

Yet a further examination of Sanders's position is still needed. Ultimately, the most urgent question concerns his analysis of the relationship between divine grace (covenant) and human works (obedience to the Law).[202] Does Paul

196 See above.

197 See, e.g., Beker 1978, 108; 1980, 340; Best 1982, 71; Brooke 1979, 248; Caird 1978, 539; Dahl 1978, 154; Hafemann 1981, 148; Hagner 1979, 25; Heiligenthal 1985, 546–47; King 1980, 42; Neusner 1980, 60; Saldarini 1979, 299; Sandmel 1978, 158–59; Vicent 1986, 428; C. Wolff 1986, 421, 424–25. Cf. further Patte 1983, 96–104.

198 Sanders 1977, 84–107, 180–82, 236–37. See also Hoheisel 1978, 137–40; Hruby 1969, 30–56; Neusner 1980, 47–48; Schechter 1961, 57–58; Segal 1985, 53–62; 1987, 147–65; Sjöberg 1939, 26–27.

199 Sanders 1977, 157–82, 235–36. Similarly Hoheisel 1978, 167–72; Moore 1948–50, 1:498, 520–35; Schechter 1961, 293–312.

200 Sanders 1977, 212–33. Already Perles 1903, 129–30. See further Hoheisel 1978, 140–43; Hruby 1965, 230–37; 1967, 44–48; Limbeck 1971, 190–95; 1972, 44–48; Moore 1948–50, 1:368–69, 398, 423; Schechter 1961, 21–46.

201 Sanders 1977, 125–47. See further Gundry 1985, 7; Segal 1985, 55; 1987, 150–51. Snodgrass (1986, 78) formulates his position a little more warily: "There is an emphasis on weighing good deeds against bad in some writings and on the keeping of ledger books in others, and this cannot be dismissed as easily as Sanders would like."

202 See Gundry 1985, 7.

really not find any room for critique of the Jewish soteriology with the exception of his exclusive Christology? In other words, does he simply think that the salvation-historical progress has pushed past his former Pharisaic religiosity? Especially because of Odeberg's tentative argumentation, it is worth a careful examination whether anthropological reasons also play an important role in that radical confrontation.[203]

203 For the later development of the ongoing academic discussion, see Laato 2019 (cf. also Laato 2008, 40–44).

3. E. P. SANDERS'S METHOD

A Comparison of Patterns of Religion

3.1. Definition

Sanders shows his dislike for the traditional methods of comparing religions. He considers comparison of essences and comparison of individual motifs unsuitable in the context of comparing Paul and Palestinian Judaism with each other.[1]

The method of comparison of essences comprises fatal defects. In the comparison of two religions, their inner essence, their supposed core, should be summarized in a phrase or line (faith versus works or liberty versus Law, a spiritual religion versus a materialistic and commercial religion).[2] Yet a short proposition or a simple concept can never do an entire religion justice.[3] Further, the question of "essence of religion" has often in practice been used by Christian scholars to prove and demonstrate the superiority of Paul or Jesus or Christianity in general over Judaism.[4]

The method of comparison of individual motifs also falls short, although the thought that a religion may be portrayed as the sum of its parts is not in and of itself inadequate. In the first place, the elements of one religion are often compared with the elements of another in order to identify their origin. Simply, the two religions are not accurately treated in the same way. For instance, one starts with Pauline motifs and looks for their origin in Judaism, but he does not handle Jewish motifs for their own sake. As a consequence, no true comparison follows. In the second place, the context and the significance of the motifs are commonly overlooked in one (or sometimes both) of the religions. The same

1 Sanders 1977, 12.
2 Op. cit., 12–13.
3 Op. cit., 13.
4 Ibid.

motifs might occur in different religions and yet have differing significance in their respective contexts. Their distinctive settings in the theological scheme should be taken at face value.[5]

In contrast, Sanders prefers a method that makes a holistic comparison of the religions possible.[6] For his purpose, he creates a "comparison of patterns of religion."[7]

By the phrase "pattern of religion" Sanders does not denote an entire historical religion, all of Christianity, Judaism, Islam, Buddhism, and the like, but rather "only a given, more or less homogenous entity," for example, Paulinism.[8] Further, a pattern of religion does not include every theological doctrine or religious idea within a religion. The term "pattern" points toward the question of how one goes through the religion from the "logical"[9] starting point to the "logical" conclusion. Excluded from the "pattern" proper are such speculative questions that relate to the how of creation, the time of the end, and the nature of the afterlife. However, those questions and their answers could still affect the pattern of a religion.[10]

The phrase "pattern of religion," positively defined, delineates how a religion in general functions. Main questions are *How a person gets in* and *How a person stays in* or *How does a religion admit and retain new members.* Daily activities and rites, such as prayers or washings, have no decisive relevance per se except only within the overall context of the pattern of religion.[11] In short, it is worth noticing on what principles they are based and what happens if they are not observed and the like.[12]

On the whole, Sanders approaches the questions of traditional systematic theology pertaining to soteriology. Nevertheless, he disregards it as inadequate. He rather speaks of pattern of religion. It has some certain advantages over the concept of soteriology. First of all, the former covers a much more wide-ranging area than the latter.[13] The pattern of religion includes the beginning point of the religious life and its goal and end, as well as the steps in between.

5 Ibid.

6 Op. cit., 16.

7 Op. cit., 16–18.

8 Op. cit., 16.

9 Sanders does not explicitly define what he means by the term "logical." He seems to suggest that each religion contains different, coherent stages. One achieves the goal of a specific religion when he goes through those stages in order. Cf. below.

10 Sanders 1977, 16–17.

11 Op. cit., 17: "This [sc. the notion of how a religion functions] may involve daily activities, such as prayers, washing and the like, but we are interested not so much in the details of these activities as in their role and significance in the 'pattern' [. . .]."

12 Ibid.

13 Sanders assumes the knowledge of what soteriology stands for in general. For the content of the concept, see below 3.3.1.

Second, the concept of soteriology has many connotations which are not always "entirely appropriate." For example, it may involve a preoccupation with otherworldliness or imply that all are in need of salvation since they have lost it on the basis of original sin. However, most forms of Judaism have no interest in the transcendental reality or the idea of inborn depravity. That is why those connotations would cause fatal misinterpretations. Hence, it makes sense to speak about the patterns of religion instead of soteriological categories.[14]

A pattern of religion has to do with the thought or the understanding that lies behind religious behavior, not just the externals of religious behavior. For example, from cultic practice one may infer that the ritual of a religion has a certain function in the religious life of the adherents. Their awareness or perception of the significance of the ritual is worth noticing. However, they themselves have not necessarily articulated a systematic theology or created a theological system wherein the ritual takes a logical position. Even so, the ritual stands in close relationship with other elements in the religion. Therefore, the pattern of religion turns out as a coherent whole.[15]

On the whole, a pattern of religion consists of separate motifs. Still, the focus lies more on the setting or place of different motifs within the proper framework of each religion. The emphasis does not directly fall on a comparison of a motif in some part of Judaism with a similar motif in Paul. Rather, once "the various entire patterns clearly emerge, the comparison can take place, and not before."[16]

In the comparison between Paul and Palestinian Judaism,[17] two principal dilemmas arise. First, one must compare the writings of one individual with the large bodies of Palestinian Jewish literature despite the risk of upsetting research equilibrium. In this case, there seems to be no other choice. The nature of Palestinian Jewish literature renders it almost impossible to isolate the thoughts and views of "individuals comparable to Paul."[18] Second, the New Testament does not represent only one pattern of religion. It obviously encompasses several differing models and paradigms. An ample analysis of them and a rough grouping of their diversities would create confusion and hinder meaningful conclusions.[19]

---

14 Op. cit., 17–18.

15 Op. cit., 18.

16 Ibid.

17 Sanders puts it into his own words: "Comparing an individual on the one hand with the large bodies of Palestinian Jewish literature on the other [. . .]" (op. cit., 19).

18 Ibid.

19 Op. cit., 19–20.

3.2. Application

Sanders applies his new method, "comparison of patterns of religion," to Palestinian Judaism (Tannaitic literature, the Dead Sea Scrolls, Sirach, 1 Enoch, Jubilees, the Psalms of Solomon, 4 Ezra) and Paulinism (the so-called authentic or genuine epistles).[20] Consistent with his own definition, he discusses aspects that reveal how one gets into each respective religion and how he stays there. He does not deal with some issues that do not directly belong to the pattern of religion but still have influence on it.[21]

In short, Sanders calls the Palestinian Jewish pattern of religion "covenantal nomism." He delineates the overall structure of it in the following main points:

> (1) God has chosen Israel and (2) given the Law. The Mosaic Law implies both (3) God's promise to maintain the covenant and (4) the requirement of obedience. (5) God rewards obedience and punishes disobedience. (6) The Law provides for means of atonement, and (7) the atonement reestablishes the broken covenantal relationship. (8) All those who through obedience, atonement, and God's grace remain in the covenant will be saved.[22]

At large, the overall Jewish pattern of religion includes that one gets in (enters) the covenant through acceptance of the Law and stays (remains) in the covenant through fulfillment of the Law.[23] Significantly, both the election (see above, point 1) and ultimately the salvation of Israel (see above, point 8) depend on divine grace, not on human achievement.[24] Obedience does not earn God's mercy as such. Rather, it effects remaining in the covenant.[25]

Not every single Palestinian Jewish document contains every one of the structural elements in covenantal nomism. Yet even the apparently missing elements are provided. For example, the requirement of obedience in 1 Enoch implies that God has given the Law (see above, point 2), although the author does not explicitly mention the giving of the Law.[26]

For sure, not all the Palestinian Jewish documents conform to an absolute uniform system. For example, the Qumran definition of the covenant and the commandments differs from the rabbinic. But there is still agreement on the primacy of the covenant and the need or necessity to obey the Law. Therefore, despite apparent differences, the same pattern of religion prevails in Qumran and in rabbinism.[27]

---

20 Sanders 1977, 33–428, 431–556.
21 See above 3.1.
22 Sanders 1977, 422.
23 Op. cit., 419–22.
24 Op. cit., 422.
25 Op. cit., 420.
26 Op. cit., 423.
27 Ibid.

In a strict sense, only 4 Ezra falls out from covenantal nomism insofar as the author requires perfect fulfillment of the Law (8:33, 37). His extreme and radical demand for upright conduct corroborates the idea of earning salvation.[28] Nonetheless, the close correlation between the covenant and the succeeding obedience remains unchanged also in 4 Ezra. It reiterates, in agreement with the rest of Palestinian Judaism, that Jews stay in the covenant through their obedience. They act in this faith.[29]

In contrast with Palestinian Judaism, Paul indeed presents a pronounced soteriology. Hence, the concept of "soteriology" seems suitable or adequate in establishing his pattern of religion. But insofar as it belongs very close together in the systematic theology with other specific loci, such as Christology, eschatology, or anthropology, the concept of "pattern of religion" takes precedence here also.[30]

To begin with, Sanders works out the center and "beginning point" of Pauline theology.[31] Following especially A. Schweitzer, he gives the participatory categories preeminence over the juristic terminology, in other words, the message of a new existence "in Christ" over the declaration of justification in faith.[32] The participatory categories best and most evidently express what Paul intends. For sure, he accepts the general Christian understanding of Christ expiating the sins of the world through his death on the cross. Strictly speaking, he means something else and totally different by the Gospel, namely, that Christ brings with him a new dominion. The world as such is subjected to the demonic dominion of sin. Through faith alone one is released from the dominion of sin. At the same time, he then crosses over into the dominion of Christ.[33]

After his preference for the use of the participatory language, Sanders sets up two central convictions or assertions in Pauline thinking:

1. Jesus Christ is Lord. He will soon return and deliver all who believe in him.
2. Paul has the task of preaching the Gospel. God has called him to be the apostle to the Gentiles.

28 Op. cit., 421–22.

29 Op. cit., 420.

30 Op. cit., 433.

31 Op. cit., 434–41.

32 Sanders gives the following arguments for his view: The juristic categories are not uniform (op. cit., 491–95). The discussion of repentance, forgiveness, and guilt is lacking (op. cit., 503). The doctrine of justification substantiates further no other doctrine, such as ethics (op. cit., 439, 441). By and large, Paul apparently prefers the participatory categories instead of the juristic ones (op. cit., 502–3). Therefore, the former are encountered in the context of exhortations and sacraments (op. cit., 503). Besides, fornication and idolatry are damned as sins in 1 Cor. 6:12–20 and 10:6–14 since they create a relationship that is incompatible to union with Christ (ibid.). Moreover, juristic language is sometimes pressed into the service of participatory categories, but never the reverse (ibid.).

33 Op. cit., 463–68.

Both conceptions belong together and form the sum of Pauline theology.[34]

Next, Sanders undertakes to overthrow the standard interpretation that Paul would have started from the problem (man is sinful and in need of a Savior) and then afterward reached the sole solution (Christ is the Savior). It happened the other way around: Paul rather started from the sole solution (Christ is the Savior) and then afterward found the problem (man is sinful and in need of a Savior).[35] Salvation means liberation from the power of sin and incorporation into the body of Christ (see above).[36] Therefore, from his original Pharisaic standpoint, Paul could not have come to the conclusion that all humankind is under the power of sin. He must have deduced his ultra-pessimistic idea from his Christological soteriology: insofar as Christ has the dominion over those who believe in him, it follows out of rational necessity that sin has dominion over those who do not believe in him.[37] As an argument for the sovereign power of sin, Paul later depends on the incontestable fact that all men sin. In that manner, he tries to prove his claim.[38]

Sanders calls the Pauline pattern of religion "participatory eschatology." He delineates the overall structure of it in the following main points:

> (1) God sent Christ to save all, the Jews and Gentiles alike. (2) One "participates in salvation" by becoming one person with Christ, dying and rising with him. (3) However, the transformation will not be completed until the Lord returns. (4) Meanwhile, one who believes has been released from the power of sin, and he is free to live his life in Christ and do what is good. (5) Since Christ died to save all, they all must have been under the dominion of sin, "in the flesh" as opposed to being "in the Spirit."[39]

In short, the Pauline pattern of religion entails that one gets into Christ by faith and stays in him through bringing forth "the fruit of the Spirit."[40]

No doubt, Paul suspends covenantal nomism.[41] Notwithstanding, his pattern of religion still resembles to a great extent that of Palestinian Judaism.[42] According to them both, one is saved by the grace of God and remains in the state of salvation through keeping the commandments of God.[43] Ultimately, Paul disallows Judaism only on account of his Christological conviction. Since he proclaims that Christ is the sole reason for the coming rescue on the Last

34 Op. cit., 441–42.
35 Op. cit., 442–47, 474–75.
36 Op. cit., 442.
37 Op. cit., 443, 499.
38 Op. cit., 499.
39 Op. cit., 549.
40 Op. cit., 444–47, 451–53, 515–18.
41 Op. cit., 511–15.
42 Op. cit., 543.
43 Ibid.

Day, Judaism that refuses Christ has already failed and fallen into the abyss of eternal misery.[44]

3.3. Toward a Judgment of the Method

3.3.1. Critique of Definition

Without going further into the problematics, the reviewers have on the whole accepted Sanders's criticism of both methods, the comparison of essences and the comparison of individual motifs.[45] For certain, he shows persuasively why a comparison of essences of two or more religions is hardly adequate: a religion in its entirety cannot be summarized in a single phrase or line or concept that supposedly outlines the core of the respective religion.[46] Yet his argumentation against the comparison of individual motifs fails to carry conviction.

Sanders finds, as already shown, the following weaknesses in the comparison of individual motifs:

1. It is customary to compare the elements of one religion with the elements of another to identify their origin.
2. Either the context of the motifs or their significance in the religion is usually overlooked.[47]

Neither of the two objections stands up for critical analysis:

(1) Reasonably, it is always only the elements of one religion that can be compared with the respective elements of another. Comparing individual motifs, one in no case proceeds otherwise.

When a scholar of religion compares the elements of one religion with the elements of another to identify origin,[48] he combines two entirely different questions, namely, the factual comparison of motifs and the genetic clarification of their origin. The latter does not necessarily belong together with the former. It goes well to compare motifs from distinctive religions with one another and not end in clarifying their origin.

Comparison of motifs and genetic clarification are both in themselves legitimate tasks.[49] There exists no reason from this to criticize the comparison

44 Op. cit., 549–52.

45 Beker 1978, 108; Gaventa 1980, 42; Hafemann 1981, 146; Neusner 1980, 48–49, 59.

46 Sanders 1977, 13.

47 Ibid.

48 Sanders (op. cit., 13) writes: "[. . .] it is usually the motifs of *one* of the religions which are compared with elements in the second religion in order to identify their origin."

49 See Brooke 1979, 248: "Moreover, because of his denial of the value of comparison through motifs, [. . .] Sanders fails sufficiently to consider the scholarship that has so greatly advanced the understanding of the tradition-history of much early Jewish

of individual motifs. A comparison of motifs shows similarities and dissimilarities in usage of a motif in two (or more) religions, while a genetic clarification searches for the origin of a motif. Admitting that scholars of religion have customarily carried out either or both the comparison of motifs and the genetic clarification totally incorrectly or half seriously or one-sidedly, Sanders would have been able to tackle the task better.

(2) Besides, admitting that scholars of religion have commonly overlooked the context and the significance of motifs, Sanders would have been able to take into consideration in more depth and detail those disadvantaged aspects. In order to avoid the misuse of a method, one must not forego the method itself. As they say: *Abusus non tollit usum*.[50]

For very good reasons, the comparison of individual motifs hence shows itself as an adequate method in the comparison of religions.

Although Sanders does not succeed in establishing an opposite standpoint, it does not necessarily follow that his own method, the comparison of patterns of religion, proves superfluous. The same texts should or could be examined with distinct aims and by diverse methods as long as objectivity is not lost. What, then, does Sanders wish to compare, and what method does he use for his purpose?

On close reflection, the comparison of patterns of religion is merely a variant of the comparison of individual motifs. Sanders determines which motifs make up such a whole that enables a comparison between the chosen religions. He explicitly concentrates on the motifs which elucidate the "soteriological pattern"[51] of a religion. Other motifs are disregarded. It is worth noticing that the context and significance of motifs should be taken into consideration not only in the comparison of patterns of religion but also in the comparison of individual motifs.

In practice, it has always been necessary and compulsory in the comparison of religions to limit the infinite number of different motifs and accordingly focus on central and relevant motifs case by case. Sanders wishes to set up a common

literature [. . .]." Cf. further Sanders 1973, 458: "Genealogical questions should be pursued by *Motivsgeschichte* [*pro Motivgeschichte*]."

50 Sanders takes G. W. Buchanan and D. Flusser as examples that scholars of religion in their comparison of motifs often overlook the significance and the context of a motif (1977, 13–16). Later, and without further ado, he affirms to have shown that the procedure of Buchanan and Flusser exemplifies the weaknesses of the method (op. cit., 14–15). Here, Sanders ignores the fact that both falsely use the method. Cf. already Sanders 1973, 455: "The characteristic weakness of this *approach* [that is, the comparison of individual motifs] [. . .] is that a conclusion about some of the parts *may* lead too quickly to a conclusion about the whole" (italics mine).

51 Sanders himself characterizes "pattern of religion" as "the soteriological pattern" but prefers the former, being more general (see already 1973, 457). Cf. also Gundry 1985, 2–3.

rule that shows the special character and pertinent uniformity of religions with the intention of comparing those "wholes" with one another. He maintains that the comparison of patterns of religion delivers effective results in this respect.

In addition, Sanders concentrates on the place of motifs in a pattern of religion, while in the comparison of individual motifs one rather examines the motifs themselves.[52] As two (or more) religions are compared, it scarcely makes sense or serves any rational purpose to study and analyze every single religious motif even down to the finest detail. Otherwise one runs the risk of not seeing the forest for the trees, namely, that the uniformity of the respective religions may not come into sight for all the individual motifs. In his innovative methodological approach, Sanders leads the way and shows how he goes into the essential. He leaves aside less important specifics.

Hence, the comparison of individual motifs and the comparison of patterns of religion differ more quantitatively than qualitatively.[53] Sanders proceeds with a comparison of individual motifs insofar as he delves into certain motifs, however not as such, but rather with respect to their place within a pattern of religion. His methodological disposition in *Paul and Palestinian Judaism* provides a great model for ongoing comparison of religions.

Despite his quite comprehensive methodological discussion, Sanders defines his task negligently, which has brought about much perplexity for his readers. Many reviewers raise the objection that in his introduction he indeed promises to compare the religions in their entirety, but he does not keep his promise in the essay itself. There, he only answers questions of how one gets in and how one stays in Judaism and Paulinism respectively.[54]

Without doubt, the former objection touches a sensitive point in Sanders's argumentation. To begin with, he searches for a method that makes it possible to compare religions in their entirety. The comparison of patterns of religion

52 Sanders 1977, 18.

53 Cf. Brooke 1979, 248. He writes: "Since it is Palestinian Jewish literature that the author [Sanders] compares with that of Paul, the admission and standing of members within a particular religion must primarily be understood as literary themes, and this is not so very different from the study of motifs which Sanders seeks to discredit." Similarly, Gaventa 1980, 42: "Instead, what is actually produced here is perilously close to an examination of particular motifs (covenant, law, soteriology) or even to a reduction of each system to an essence (covenantal nomism, participationist eschatology)." In accordance with Gaventa, N. A. Dahl (1978, 157) and A. J. Saldarini (1979, 300) point out that the concepts "pattern" and "essence" do not differ greatly one from the other (cf. also Lüdemann 1983, 48 n. 64). Still, the comparison of patterns of religion does differ clearly from the comparison of essences of religion; the former rather concerns itself with the comparison of individual motifs. See above.

54 See Best 1982, 72; Brooke 1979, 248–49; Cooper 1982, 124 n. 7; Dahl 1978, 155–57; Gaventa 1980, 39–41; Gundry 1985, 2; Hafemann 1981, 147–48; Meeks 1980, 27; McNamara 1979, 72; Neusner 1980, 48–50, 55, 59; Saldarini 1979, 300.

should serve that purpose excellently.[55] Still, Sanders in the following passage defines the concept of pattern of religion differently and suggests that it no longer includes a historical religion in its entirety.[56] Later, he adds an explanation and admits that he will take into account mainly the systematic theological issues concerning soteriology.[57] The smooth alteration from "a religion in its entirety" to "a soteriological pattern of religion" hardly seems wholly justified. It remains unclear what Sanders really aims to do: Does he wish to compare religions in their entirety or only patterns of religion? Or does he actually mean that he compares religions in their entirety through their patterns of religion? The scales might tip to the latter alternative. Apparently, Sanders maintains that certain distinctive elements in the religion form a holistic entity. Therefore, he reduces a religion in its entirety to its pattern of religion.[58]

For certain, there is no debate that Sanders does not compare religions in their entirety through their (soteriological) patterns of religion.[59] His methodological discussion does not utterly coincide with what he in fact desires to compare and what he then also brings into comparison.

Further, Sanders's negligent definition of the task has drawn other objections as well. Several critical remarks against his methodological discourse develop from his unclear disposition of purpose. Evidence for the limitations and shortcomings of his procedure will follow below.[60]

Sanders becomes equally confusing as he formulates the two central questions of pattern of religion. He does not precisely disclose *where* a person gets in and *where* he stays in. Fortunately, the reader possesses more implicit information on the problem. As Sanders explicitly tells, he principally discusses

---

55 Sanders (1977, 12, 16) does not explain why the comparison of soteriological patterns of religion should make possible the comparison of religions in their entirety. Cf. my criticism below.

56 See especially op. cit., 16: "What is clearly desirable, then, is to compare an entire religion, parts and all, with an entire religion, parts and all; to use the analogy of a building, to compare two buildings, not leaving out of account their individual bricks. [. . .]. By 'pattern of religion' I do not mean an entire historical religion [. . .]." Tellingly, the chapter rubric reads: "The *holistic* comparison of patterns of religion" (italics mine). Cf. also Best 1982, 66: "Instead, Sanders insists, we must compare the entire 'pattern of religion' in first-century Judaism with the entire 'pattern of religion' found in Paul. In fact, however, Sanders gives this terminology a specific meaning [. . .]."

57 Sanders 1977, 17.

58 Cf. Brooke 1979, 248: "[. . .] he [Sanders] takes it for granted that religions are reducible to such functional patterns."

59 Cooper 1982, 124 n. 7: "It is not a complete description of Palestinian Judaism as a religion, but an investigation pursued with one topic under consideration, namely soteriology—or, as Sanders prefers to call it, the question of 'how getting in and staying in are understood' (p. 17). Much more remains to be done by way of systemic description."

60 See below.

soteriological issues.[61] Logically, he should then answer the questions of how someone enters the range of salvation and how someone stays there. Sanders further turns his method on the Jewish and Pauline texts in order to answer the question of how one gets in the covenant (for the Jewish religion) and "Christ" (for the Pauline religion) and how one stays there.[62] In that case, he obviously does not, for instance, put emphasis on sociological aspects.[63]

In the first place, N. A. Dahl, J. Neusner, and A. J. Saldarini maintain that the concept of pattern of religion takes up such questions that are central for Paul and Christianity but secondary for the rabbis or Palestinian Judaism as a whole.[64] They contend that Sanders forces Pauline categories onto his Jewish sources through the thematic sieve of grace and works. He does not attempt to understand the most relevant literature from the Pseudepigrapha to the Tannaitic texts with its own conceptuality.[65]

Sanders has defended himself against this criticism. In his rejoinder, he asserts that the contrast between grace and works (an explicitly Christian perspective) directed or dominated the previous discussion of the relations of Paulinism and Judaism. In order to analyze and assess the state of research in the early 1970s, Sanders had to start from the prevailing use of language. However, he did not assume to continue the "traditional" contrast between Judaism and Paulinism in the sense of a religion of works against a religion of grace. Indeed, he considers a comparison of that kind as absolutely inadequate.[66] Instead, he has created a new method, the comparison of patterns of religion, that more accurately deals with a "relatively neutral question." For sure, the questions of getting in and staying in are encountered in certain texts more often than in others. But they are as such neither especially Christian nor particularly Pauline.[67]

Further, Sanders underlines that in his *Paul and Palestinian Judaism* he made a significant effort to find out why some distinctive and significant Jewish motifs (for example, repentance and forgiveness) do not have any great impact on Pauline thinking. For all of this, he does not in his analysis force the Jewish

61 Sanders 1977, 17.

62 Op. cit., especially 419–23, 543–56.

63 Against Deidun 1986, 43: "[. . .] Sanders compared the religion of Paul with Judaism in the light of their respective answers to the soteriological questions, how one 'gets in' and how one 'stays in' the *community* of those who are to be saved" (italics mine).

64 Dahl 1978, 157; Neusner 1980, 50–51, 56; Saldarini 1979, 300. Consistent with them, Best 1982, 72; Gaventa 1980, 40; King 1980, 142–43; Uotila 1986, 513. Cf. Caird 1978, 539; Sandmel 1978, 159.

65 Ibid. Brooke 1979, 248, writes a little rashly: "The limitations of the pattern of religion derived by the author from *Rabbinic* literature [. . .]" (italics mine).

66 Sanders 1980, 68.

67 Ibid. See further Sanders 1985, xii.

sources through Pauline categories but rather demonstrates that Paul proves himself unresponsive to the chief motifs of the Jewish religion.[68]

In the course of the intense debate, neither Sanders nor his critics have sufficiently taken into consideration that the concept of pattern of religion especially aims at the question of how one gets from the logical starting point to the logical end point of a religion.[69] A methodological procedure of that kind indicates an absolutely neutral issue. Every religion has some "place of departure" that leads through different "stages" to a distant "goal" ahead. Besides, it does not seem very plausible that only Paul and Christian theologians consider the relationship between grace and works. For certain, in Judaism (as well as in other religions) at least a certain interest rests upon the constant interaction between the human and divine commitment in the process of salvation (or any ultimate destination or outcome).[70] The New Testament hardly stands out as the first document relating to the soteriological matters. As is well-known, Paul and Christian theologians in general put an emphasis on the contrast between grace and works. Sanders would have probably forced the Jewish material into a Pauline framework if he had read the contrast between grace and works into rabbinic texts or pseudepigrapha.[71] But if he aims to uncover the human and divine role within covenantal nomism, he certainly does not analyze his Jewish sources from a Christian perspective.

Besides, the adherents of a certain religion cannot proceed and move on from its logical starting point to its logical end point without first getting into that religion and then staying there. Sanders therefore rightly explains his main intention with his two principal questions. He wants to know how a person gets into the religion and how a person stays there. He promotes neither Christianity nor Paulinism.[72] The two questions become central since they adjust the rather

68 Sanders 1980, 68–69. For more on this, see below 5.3.

69 Sanders 1977, 16–17. See above 3.1.

70 Cf. Sanders 1980, 68: "Discussing grace and law, I should add, is not entirely foreign to either Jewish material or Pauline [. . .]."

71 Sanders (1977, 297) explicitly and strongly denies that Palestinian Judaism would set grace and works against each other: "The heightening of both the perception of God's grace and the requirement of obedience is instructive for understanding Judaism generally, for it indicates that 'grace' and 'works' were not considered as opposed to each other in any way. I believe that it is safe to say that the notion that God's grace is any way contradictory to human endeavour is totally foreign to Palestinian Judaism." Cf. the following quotation: "One might have expected the Rabbis to develop a clear doctrine of prevenient grace, but grace and merit did not seem to them to be in contradiction to each other" (op. cit., 100).

72 Nicely, Gundry 1985, 3: "In Sanders' defense, however, he does not conceive of soteriology narrowly. It covers all the essential points of religion, i.e., all the requirements for getting in and staying in. Whatever their number, these essentials include both beliefs and practices." Correctly, Murphy-O'Connor 1978, 122: "Cette [Sanders's] manière d'aborder la question est incontestablement juste, car les deux religions se proposent de

general question of how to go from the logical starting point to the logical end point of a religion.[73] The same methodology functions just as well in Islam or Hinduism (or any other religion): How does a Muslim get into Islam and stay there? How does a Hindu get into Hinduism and stay there? No one has brought forth an argument that prevents the application of the "pattern of religion" to another religious context. In short, Sanders has indeed developed an objective method. He has not based it on any intra-Christian premises.

Certainly not all of the holy writings within a religion need to address to the same degree the question of how a person gets in a religion and stays there. Neither need they encompass every element of a pattern of religion. However, a religion in its entirety shows how it functions and how to get in and stay there.[74] As a result, the comparison of patterns of religion proves highly relevant for the comparison of religions in general.

B. R. Gaventa unlocks another somber methodological problem in the comparison of patterns of religion. She emphasizes that it seems to her completely impossible to compare the whole of Palestinian Judaism with the whole of Paul, since we have no wholes to compare. On the one hand, the Palestinian Jewish literature is so complicated that no one has so far been able to describe its pattern of religion. On the other hand, the Pauline epistles are likewise so fragmentary that hardly anyone has ever been able to put together anything like "the whole Paul." Perchance in the near future we shall even find new Pauline letters that will overturn some of the premises now predominating. Nowhere (not once in his most organized letter to the Romans) does Paul give a firm systematic exposition of his manifold theology, but rather a mixture of his reactions to specific occasional situations.[75]

On the whole, one cannot help but think that Gaventa is tilting at windmills. In the final analysis, she hardly takes into account what it is all about. True, she strongly argues against the attempt to compare religions in their entirety. Yet she makes no criticism against the comparison of soteriological patterns of religion. Insofar as Sanders in effect does not compare whole religions, but rather only soteriological patterns of religion,[76] he certainly takes upon himself no absurd task. The extensive Palestinian Jewish literature is hardly so complicated and each of the Pauline epistles so fragmentary that one could not figure out how a person gets in and stays in the covenant or in Christ. Later, it will become palpable that Sanders's concept of "pattern of religion" does not contain all of

faire quelque chose, c'est-à-dire de sauver leurs membres." Cf. Best 1982, 74; Dunn 1983, 99–100; Lüdemann 1983, 47 n. 54.

73 Sanders 1977, 17.

74 See above.

75 Gaventa 1980, 39–40.

76 See above.

the elements in the systematic concept of "soteriology."[77] As far as I know, no one has tried to pretend that we cannot delineate the main contours of Jewish and Pauline soteriology. The alleged lack of sources or the supposed obscurity of their content produce no real problems for Sanders, seeing that he aims to sketch just the soteriological patterns of Palestinian Judaism and Paulinism.

Besides, in the comparison of patterns of religion, the main soteriological tenets of a religion are brought for close examination and further analysis. In all likelihood, a new Pauline epistle would therefore not initiate a radical change and shift in the understanding of the principal thoughts in the currently existing Pauline epistles. Sanders is perfectly correct in confining himself to the material handed down. He has indeed every reason to avoid speculation about ancient texts to be discovered in the future.[78]

In short, Gaventa's objections do not bear up. Instead of writing on the comparison of soteriological patterns of religion, she in general criticizes the comparison of religions as wholes. In her defense and on her behalf, it must be said that Sanders himself has caused the confusion through his neglectful formulation of his task. The reviewer finds herself in a very difficult position if she cannot take the words of an author or a scholar at face value. No wonder that enormous misunderstandings follow.

Like Gaventa, Sanders does not succeed in pinning down an exact definition of the concept of pattern of religion. He maintains abruptly and promptly that the pattern of religion consists of more than soteriology in the common sense.[79] The bewildered reader asks in what aspect does the pattern of religion consist of more than soteriology. For sure, Sanders hastens to add that the pattern of religion includes the beginning point of the religious life and its goal and end, as well as the steps in between.[80] Yet he does not explain what soteriology in the current meaning involves. The reader cannot therefore follow the argumentation. The reader searches in vain for reasons why the pattern of religion really consists of more than soteriology in the common sense.

It turns out that, strictly speaking, Sanders does not stick to his own thesis. Immediately, he hastens to remark that the concept of soteriology brings with it several "inappropriate" implications, especially the concentration on the transcendental and the doctrine of original sin, while the concept of pattern of religion remains free of such conditions.[81] Hence, it fails to carry conviction to

77 See below.

78 Cf. Gundry 1985, 3 n. 6: "Gaventa adds the objection that there are no wholes to compare, since we have only a few, occasional letters of Paul and since our knowledge of rabbinic Judaism in Paul's day is sketchy. But this objection only expresses the limits of historical research. Surely Sanders means 'whole' so far as data are available."

79 Sanders 1977, 17.

80 Ibid.

81 Op. cit., 17–18.

maintain categorically that the pattern of religion consists of more than soteriology. Rather, it shows that the opposite is true: the concentration on the transcendental and the doctrine of original sin belong to soteriology but not to pattern of religion.

Besides, Sanders later mentions that Pauline soteriology is attached to Christology, eschatology, and anthropology, while he limits himself exclusively to the Pauline pattern of religion.[82] Once again, it turns out that a pattern of religion does not contain all the elements of soteriology—to say nothing of the fact that also hamartiology (inclusive the dogma of predestination), pneumatology, ecclesiology, as well as the doctrine of sacraments, belong to Pauline soteriology. Without doubt, the pattern of religion does not cover all of the connotative aspects in soteriology.[83]

Knowing that concentration on the transcendental and the doctrine of original sin are missing in Palestinian Judaism in general does not lead to a hasty conclusion that those implications in the concept of "soteriology" show themselves inappropriate for the comparison of Palestinian Judaism and Paulinism. It is not only about presence but also absence of the connotative aspects in soteriology: "To be or not to be." Thus it is worth knowing that concentration on the transcendental and the doctrine of original sin are missing in Palestinian Judaism in general. If one compares, for example, the anthropological presuppositions in Paulinism and Palestinian Judaism, the juxtaposition initiates and necessitates a truly in-depth analysis of why Paul, unlike the Jews, did reckon with the doctrine of original sin or the absolute corruption of humankind or the like. The more general question of sin entails the more particular question of original sin. As a consequence, the academic focus lies on human incapacity or capacity as a whole. In effect, Sanders himself proceeds along the same lines in his exegesis. He examines in detail the issue of repentance (a further implication in soteriology), although he suggests that it does not have much influence on Pauline theology in contrast to Jewish covenantal nomism.[84]

To sum up, balance in the comparison of patterns of religion does not fall short through the many implications of soteriology. Sanders does not succeed in establishing his position that pattern of religion excels soteriology. Neither of his arguments hold up, because

1. a pattern of religion consists of nothing more than soteriology in systematics.
2. soteriology includes no "inappropriate" connotations.

82 Op. cit., 433.

83 Cf. Saldarini 1979, 299: "Thus defined, a pattern of religion covers part of the area called soteriology in systematic theology."

84 Sanders 1977, 546 (see further his Index of Subjects, s.v. "Repentance").

In comparison with soteriology, pattern of religion still has two advantages:

1. Since all kinds of implications cling to soteriology, they might result in numerous detours or many side roads in the implementation of the academic study and survey. Quite the reverse, the concept of pattern of religion offers a more precise point of departure and a more accurate process of research. In consequence, irrelevant or unrelated details may be set aside.
2. The concept of pattern of religion is compatible in those cases where a full-scale soteriology is missing, as, for example, in the case of Sirach, where belief in eternal bliss and damnation seems to vanish.[85] In such contexts, the language of soteriology would eventually lead astray, because it could easily call forth associations with a life after death. If instead one speaks of pattern of religion, the risk of unintentional misunderstandings disappears.

Later, Sanders returns to the implications of soteriology and puts his main emphasis on the connotations associated with the doctrine of original sin. He points out that various speculations about the origin of disobedience[86] (as well as notions about the nature of the future world) lie outside the pattern of rabbinism. It is therefore unnecessary to discuss them. Nevertheless, Sanders perceives that the rabbis lack a doctrine of original sin or the absolute corruption of humankind in the Christian sense.[87] He observes their theological reflections that humanity has an inborn propensity to rebellion and disobedience, but no one is born as a sinner and in constant need of redemption.[88]

It seems once again that Sanders comes too quickly to his conclusion. Rightly, the problem of the origin of disobedience may well lie outside the pattern of religion. Yet it should not for that reason be ignored as irrelevant. Sanders himself admits that factors not strictly belonging within the pattern of religion can still have some bearing on it.[89] It is by no means impossible that the question of human ability may have an impact on the pattern of religion. Sanders does not justify his conclusion to the contrary. He only says so.

In reality, Sanders's definition of pattern of religion postulates or stipulates the question of human ability. He explicitly deals with concurrent themes

85 Sanders (1977, 333–34) speaks of soteriology in Sirach but uses the concept explicitly "in a very limited sense" (op. cit., 333).

86 Sanders (op. cit., 114) here uses a pleonastic expression. He speaks of a "sinful disobedience."

87 Ibid.: "Yet it is important to note that the Rabbis did not have a doctrine of original sin or of the essential sinfulness of each man in the Christian sense."

88 Ibid.

89 Op. cit., 16–17.

such as soteriological issues[90] or the relationship between grace and works.[91] He cannot complete his study without reference to anthropological concepts and conceptions. Necessarily, the critical question arises concerning what a person within the scope of a particular religion is able to do on behalf of his salvation. On the other hand, Sanders examines how a religion functions in the view of its adherents.[92] Once a religion functions, there must be at least one or more adherents who can live, and do in fact live, in accordance with the pattern of that religion. Sanders mostly counts or enumerates, describes or illustrates the different steps in the (Jewish resp. Pauline) pattern of religion. Oddly enough, he avoids the relevant and significant inquiry of where people get the power to move from step to step and finally reach the goal of the religion. It thus remains open how a religion in the strict and direct sense of the word functions or who ultimately gets in and stays in. Obviously, Sanders's discourses urgently need a lot of completion here. He stopped his thinking halfway through.[93]

In conclusion, the outcomes of the survey so far fall into two groups listed below, the first are points of agreement, and the second are points of disagreement between me and Sanders:

I 1. The comparison of patterns of religion does not arise from a distinctively Christian or Pauline point of departure. It is an objective method.

2. The source materials will suffice to delineate the patterns of Judaism and Paulinism. The academic survey can be accomplished on the basis of them.

II 1. Sanders does not formulate an entirely new method. Rather, he develops the comparison of individual motifs to the comparison of patterns of religion as he examines certain relevant religious motifs especially with regard to their place in the pattern of religion.

2. Sanders claims to compare religions in their entirety but in fact compares only their soteriological patterns of religion.

3. Sanders defines and describes how a person gets in the sphere of salvation and stays there, even though he does not explicitly state it.

90 Op. cit., 17.

91 Sanders 1980, 68–69.

92 Sanders 1977, 17.

93 Cf. Sanders 2009, 49–52, and how slightly he deals with the question of anthropology (or human ability). He reduces it to a short and shallow discussion about the relationship between grace and works. (His contribution was reprinted in 2016, 77–80.) Moreover, Sanders draws some important conclusions that evidently presume the question of human ability. See below 3.3.2.

4. Sanders dispenses with the concept of soteriology because it does not include all of the elements in the concept of pattern of religion and further provokes many inappropriate implications. In effect, the concept of pattern of religion does not include all of the aspects in the concept of soteriology. Besides, soteriology does not provoke any inadequate implications.
5. Sanders disregards the question of human ability, although he assumes an answer to it by his very definition of pattern of religion.

3.3.2. Critique of Application

Several reviewers have missed wider source materials in Sanders. He refers neither to targumim,[94] 2 Baruch and the apocalyptic literature in general (except for 1 Enoch and 4 Ezra),[95] *Pseudo-Philo*,[96] Josephus,[97] mystical and ascetic texts of Jewish origin,[98] the anti-Jewish polemics from the Gospels[99] or the Acts of the Apostles,[100] ancient historians of Judaism,[101] nor to archaeological discoveries in the Middle East.[102] He fails to take into account social relations in ancient Palestine[103] or the pertinent distinction between abstract theology and concrete religion, that is, the recurrently observable difference between the theory and practice of the adherents.[104]

In my opinion, Sanders definitely refers to sufficient material. He studies Tannaitic literature, the Dead Sea Scrolls, Sirach, 1 Enoch, Jubilees, the Psalms of Solomon, and 4 Ezra.[105] His sources well and widely characterize Palestinian Judaism during the time from 200 BC to AD 200.[106] The gravest weakness may be that the apocalyptic literature does not receive the attention it deserves. This criticism, however, takes on more importance if one shows that the apocalyptic literature in general rejects covenantal nomism.[107] Likewise, the supposed difference between abstract theology and concrete religion has far-reaching results only if literary excerpts support the hypothesis.[108]

---

94 Brooke 1979, 248; King 1980, 142.
95 Beker 1978, 110; Byrne 1979, 230. Cf. Dahl 1978, 155.
96 McNamara 1979, 73.
97 Horbury 1979, 117.
98 Op. cit., 116–17.
99 Caird 1978, 540; Horbury 1979, 117; Jacques 1979, 898.
100 Horbury 1979, 117. Cf. Sandmel 1978, 159.
101 Brooke 1979, 247. Cf. King 1980, 143.
102 Brooke 1979, 247–48; Dahl 1978, 155.
103 Meeks 1980, 27–41. Cf. Dahl 1978, 155; Gaventa 1980, 43.
104 Brooke 1979, 247–48; Hagner 1979, 26; Murphy-O'Connor 1978, 123.
105 Sanders 1977, 33–418.
106 See Gundry 1985, 2. Cf. Dunn 1983, 99.
107 Gundry 1985, 4.
108 Op. cit., 5.

Hence, it turns out that the sources read and analyzed by Sanders do not necessarily need supplementary material. It remains to resolve the question of whether he interprets his texts correctly.

As a rule, the reviewers have objected to the handling of the rabbinic (or Tannaitic) literature. Most vehemently, J. Neusner directs his criticism against the very dating of the rabbinic tradition. Sanders's procedure leaves much to be desired. Beyond a reasonable doubt, he seems to take the authenticity of the rabbinic sayings simply for granted. Whatever a rabbi has said according to tradition, that is accurately what he has said in reality. In addition, Sanders suggests that the much later theology of the Tannaitic ages characterizes the Palestinian Judaism in the first century AD.[109] He holds the diverse rabbinic sources (separated by more than half a millennium in two different countries) as homogenous and utterly overlooks the difficulty of harmonizing them.[110]

For all intents and purposes, Neusner's criticism is largely true. As is well-known, to him goes the credit for establishing criteria of authenticity for rabbinic sayings by use of his innovative form-historical analysis. He has definitely opened up a new field of research in Judaic studies.[111] Unfortunately, the change and shift of focus first came to pass in the 1970s.[112] Sanders did not have enough time or a real opportunity to take Neusner's work into consideration for his book that first appeared in 1977.[113] He did not truly realize the epoch-making turn in research. As a consequence, he relies somewhat thoughtlessly on the authenticity of the rabbinic tradition.[114]

Notwithstanding, Neusner's criticism does not hold in every respect. By no means does Sanders presuppose that Tannaitic literature, without further ado and in a completely reliable manner, portrays the Palestinian Judaism of the first century AD.[115] He rather presents his evidence in cumulative terms: Since not

---

109 Neusner 1984, 195–96; cf. also 1980, 58.

110 Neusner 1984, 196. See further Gaventa 1980, 39; King 1980, 142; Saldarini 1979, 300, 302.

111 Gaventa 1980, 39; King 1980, 142; Sanders 1980, 70. See also Neusner 1971, 1:1–10; 1980, 51.

112 Neusner 1980, 51; Sanders 1980, 70. Neusner's *The Rabbinic Traditions about the Pharisees before 70* (3 vols.) appeared in 1971.

113 Neusner 1980, 51; Saldarini 1979, 303; Sanders 1980, 70. Cf. King 1980, 142: "Sanders' work, though it has the merit of being both sympathetic and careful, is undermined by his failure to use what Neusner has achieved."

114 Sanders does not examine to what extent the supposedly Tannaitic texts are indeed Tannaitic. Often he quotes Tannaitic sayings deriving from various sources and interprets them together. Cf. his argumentation in 1977, 84–238.

115 Cf. Sanders 1977, 60: "I do not suppose that it [the Tannaitic literature] provides an accurate picture of Judaism or even of Pharisaism in the time of Jesus and Paul, although it would be surprising if there were no connection." Correctly, Oberforcher 1987, 214: "Aufhorchen läßt zudem die heute eher vernachlässigte Vorsicht des Autors [Sanders], rabbinische Belege in die Zeit vor 70 n. Chr. tendenziell zurückzuverlegen. Skeptisch ist

only the Tannaitic literature but also the Apocrypha, Pseudepigrapha (except 4 Ezra), and the Dead Sea Scrolls support and corroborate covenantal nomism, it seems very reasonable to think that Palestinian Judaism at the time of Jesus and Paul had a similar pattern of religion. It does not at all appear plausible that Palestinian Judaism in the first century AD would basically differ from the overall depiction of Judaism in the era of 200 BC to AD 200.[116]

Apropos, Sanders does not suppose or suggest that each Tannaitic saying is authentic. With reference to Neusner (!), he points out that the Tannaitic traditions that occur already in the Mishnah or Tosefta are generally more reliable than the traditions that appear first in the Tannaitic midrashim or in the two talmudic versions.[117] Besides, Sanders goes much further and represents a more nuanced and detailed hypothesis. He concludes that the Tannaitic literature sufficiently represents the Tannaitic religion, even though some uncertainty is attached to the authenticity of various Tannaitic sayings.[118] For example, he seems to mean that the Tannaitic data offers better evidence concerning the Tannaitic religion than the Amoraic dicta. Source criticism, even of the most radical type, can scarcely overturn his fundamentally sound reasoning. At any rate, the burden of proof (at least primarily) lies on Neusner. In order to prove a contrary position, he must himself distinguish the genuine Tannaitic material from the spurious and on that basis verify that the genuine Tannaitic material, unlike the supposed Tannaitic literature, does not represent a covenantal nomism.

It is exactly the dominant tendency in Sanders to discuss solely and exclusively the existence or alternatively the nonexistence of covenantal nomism which has prompted some questions about his methodology. Many reviewers strongly criticize his procedure. In the first place, J. Neusner and A. J. Saldarini point out that Sanders addresses neither the rabbinic nor the other Jewish texts from their own perspectives. His interest does not focus on the themes naturally arising from the sources. He very simply observes whether or not covenantal nomism is there.[119] Important subjects for covenantal nomism, such as election, covenant, obedience, and disobedience do not necessarily—since they are

Sanders gegenüber der Rekonstruktion der Positionen von Pharisäern und Sadduzäern zur Zeit Jesu."

116 Sanders 1977, 426–28. See further Räisänen 1986, 83.

117 Op. cit., 63–64.

118 Ibid. The discussion over the authenticity of rabbinic sayings began first and foremost with Neusner himself. The results are still pending. See particularly Alexander 1983, 237–46; K. Müller 1989, 551–87.

119 Neusner 1980, 49–50; Saldarini 1979, 300, 302. In particular, Best (1982, 72–73), Gaventa (1980, 40), and King (1980, 142–43) share Neusner's criticism. Further, Beker (1978, 108, 110), Brooke (1979, 248–49), Caird (1978, 539), Dahl (1978, 155), Drury (1978, 236), Hafemann (1981, 147), Horbury (1979, 116–17), McNamara (1979, 72), and Nickelsburg (1979, 173–74) have complained that Sanders overlooks the special features in the different forms of Judaism. Cf. further Klauck 1986a, 78; Snodgrass 1986, 77.

mostly just taken for granted—make up the core of any Palestinian Jewish text under consideration.[120] For instance, in no place do the Tannaitic sages divert the halakah concretely from the covenant. They regard the body of the Torah in and of itself as the main thing.[121]

Sanders defends himself against this criticism. He admits in his rejoinder that the specific features of the various forms of Judaism have not drawn sufficient attention in his survey. Rather, he has investigated the similarities instead of the diversities among the separate groups and sects in Judaism. He has worked out the common denominator based on covenantal nomism. It turns out to be the unifying factor in his diverse or distinct sources (with the exception of 4 Ezra). For example, the halakah indicates that a Jew should obey the God who chose Israel and handed over the Law on Sinai. But better not to push the thought too far: the overall theological pattern of covenantal nomism does not explain why some certain elements in the halakah are dealt with in detail but some others left aside with no interest, or why the authoritarian halakah of the rabbis differs from that of the Qumran community. Sanders endeavors to designate and delineate what position obedience as such takes in Palestinian Judaism. He is not keen on abundance of details.[122]

Additionally, Sanders finds an ambiguity in Neusner's review. On the one hand, they both accept the existence of covenantal nomism in the rabbinic texts.[123] On the other hand, Neusner comments that Sanders does not correctly sketch the rabbinic worldview of the Mishnah.[124] But the latter objection totally misses the point of discussion since Neusner fails to take into account that Sanders did not even intend to delineate the rabbinic worldview of the Mishnah. It is all about the existence of covenantal nomism and nothing else. All that matters is the relative importance of covenantal nomism in the whole system of Jewish theology.[125]

It is not easy to mediate between Sanders and Neusner. The debate between them just moves around the topic.[126] As a matter of fact, they are basically still at a standstill. It is truly difficult to reach a well-balanced mutual understanding.

120 Neusner 1980, 49. Cf. Brooke 1979, 248–49.

121 Saldarini 1979, 300.

122 Sanders 1980, 66.

123 Op. cit., 67. See Neusner 1980, 47, 49.

124 Neusner 1980, 49–51.

125 Sanders 1980, 67.

126 Neusner, for example, republished his review of Sanders's *Paul and Palestinian Judaism* in part or in whole in many publications. See 1978, 177–91; 1980, 43–63; 1984, 127–41; 1986, 80–82; 1986a, 17–24, 38–42; 1988, 405–19; 1988a, 11–25 (cf. already 3–6). Similarly, Sanders has republished his criticism against Neusner in many publications. See 1980, 65–79; 1985, xi–xii; 1990, especially 307–31.

To all appearances, Neusner has not wholly perceived the real subject and the actual purpose of the discussion. His review indeed contains an ambiguity. However, he is not the only one to blame. Sanders is as well. He creates, as shown, a certain confusion by his aim to compare religions in their entirety instead of their soteriological patterns of religion.[127] His unclear definition of the task derailed the discussion from the outset. Neusner cites what Sanders explicitly states in the introduction. Next, Neusner underlines that Sanders does not achieve what he promises, namely, the comparison of religions in their entirety.[128] Surely, if the "whole" of Palestinian Judaism should be juxtaposed with the "whole" of Paul for their comparison, it becomes necessary to sketch the rabbinic worldview of the Mishnah. Rightly, Neusner affirms that covenantal nomism does not cover all of the themes in rabbinism (to say nothing of Palestinian Judaism). Yet he does not deny that the Tannaitic literature represents a pattern of religion such as covenantal nomism.[129]

The fierce dispute between Neusner and Sanders goes back in large part to the imprecise exposition of task in *Paul and Palestinian Judaism*. They correctly criticize each other but paradoxically, at the same time and all the time, talk past each other! Neusner underlines what Sanders, based on his introduction, should have compared, and Sanders underscores what he, based on his survey, did compare. The attempt to disentangle the knotted threads of debate looks like a Sisyphean task. Still, the positive result remains that both Neusner and Sanders concede the existence of covenantal nomism in the rabbinic texts. Their shared consensus ought not become buried under their mutual polemics.[130] In several of his later publications, Neusner has then much more strongly confirmed and corroborated the occurrence of covenantal nomism in the rabbinic literature and even for the Palestinian Judaism of the first century AD.[131]

For further clarification, two succinct remarks, of which the first supports Sanders's response and the second the criticism raised by Neusner and Saldarini.

1. Sanders's procedure to examine the Tannaitic literature from the perspective of how to get into the covenant and stay there squares well with his definition of pattern of religion. As already shown, the comparison of patterns of religion confers an advantage of not examining all of the individual motifs. Attention is drawn rather to certain central motifs and particularly their place in the soteriological pattern of religion.[132] Therefore, it is methodologically

127 See 3.3.1.

128 Neusner 1980, 48–49.

129 Op. cit., 48–50.

130 See Davies 1980, xxix; Dunn 1983, 100 n. 16; Räisänen 1986, 83–84; 1987, xxvi–xxviii.

131 Neusner 1985, 9–34.

132 See above 3.3.1.

permissible not to analyze the rabbinic and Jewish texts in general or in their entirety but to concentrate on the salient characteristics of the pattern of religion within rabbinism and Palestinian Judaism.[133]

2. On the other hand, Neusner and Saldarini carry conviction that the covenant and the election—although central to rabbinic thought—do not form the core of the Tannaitic or rabbinic literature.[134] Sanders does not sufficiently take into consideration that the covenant and the election are hardly found (or just mentioned) in the Mishnah or in the other halakic documents.[135] He has to suppose and imagine as if they were there.[136] In fact, it is much more about the reaction of the devout Jews to the action

133 Best 1982, 69; Gundry 1985, 3–4; Klauck 1986a, 78; Nickelsburg 1979, 173; Westerholm 1979, 131–32. Cf. moreover Hartman 1980, 105, and his sketch on Jewish "Bundesgedankenmuster" (op. cit., 106–7). Notwithstanding, C. Wolff (1986, 423) underlines that several divergences between the various forms of Judaism "are clearly highlighted" ("deutlich herausgearbeitet werden") by Sanders.

134 Sanders (1980, 72) maintains: "I do not think that Saldarini can be right that the Rabbis did not connect the halakah with the election." However, Saldarini in no place asserts that the rabbis would not connect the halakah with the covenant. He affirms that the Tannaitic sources do not concretely derive the halakah from the covenant.

135 Correctly, Sanders avows that "rabbinic discussions are often at the third remove from central questions of religious importance" (1977, 71), but he does not lay great importance on this. See further King 1980, 143: "He [Sanders] is probably right on the gratuity of the covenant, although I am far from certain that the notion of covenant is quite so central to Rabbinic thinking as Sanders claims [. . .]." Similarly, Snodgrass 1986, 77.

136 Interestingly, N. A. Dahl (1978, 155) and N. King (1980, 143) ask how to verify or falsify covenantal nomism as the characteristic of the rabbinic pattern of religion, particularly since the covenant takes no central place in the rabbinic texts. Afterward, Sanders (1980, 70–73) corroborates his position with three arguments:

1. The Mishnah does not assert explicitly that Jews after the destruction of the temple should fast and repent in preparation for the Day of Atonement, nor even that they still observe the feast at all. Instead, it is simply taken for granted that the Jews celebrate the Day of Atonement with fasting and repentance. Direct and distinct exhortations are found first in the Sifra. For sure, Yom Kippur implies a relationship (a covenant) between God and his people (1980, 70–72).

2. The Mishnah assumes that each Jew recites the Shema and Amidah daily. Without a doubt, the rabbis attach great importance to the set of beliefs included in the Shema and Amidah (e.g., the covenant), even if they do not address those dogmatic issues in more depth and detail (1980, 72). Sanders repeats the argument in his later publications (1985, xi–xii; 1990, *passim*).

3. Such themes as covenant and obedience come into view particularly in polemical literature (such as Jubilees, the Dead Sea Scrolls, or the Pauline epistles), where the constitutive elements of covenantal nomism are either supported or opposed. The rabbis dig into the relevance of their theological beliefs (e.g., the covenant) especially in their commentaries as the Old Testament texts give occasion for it (1980, 72–73).

The three preceding arguments may satisfy Dahl and King. With Sanders's argumentation, cf. Segal 1985, 53–62.

of their God—in other words, what they should do in response to what he has done.[137] In basic terms, the indicative comes in the shadow of the imperative. Without a doubt, the relationship between divine grace and human works in rabbinic and Jewish texts deserves increased interest and not just passing attention.[138]

Sanders has drawn strict criticism not only for his use of the Jewish sources but also for his treatment of the Pauline epistles. Supposedly he discusses especially such themes as interest the exegetes, for example, the relationship between the juristic and the participatory categories, soteriology, or the Law of Moses. Accordingly, B. R. Gaventa points out that the focus lies on improper issues. She underscores that the urgent questions from the Pauline perspective do not come into view.[139]

By no means does this disapproval of Sanders's exegetical analysis and interpretation seem at all reasonable. It is simply not true that he and the majority of New Testament scholars are interested in totally irrelevant issues concerning Pauline theology. At least justification (the juristic categories), incorporation in Christ (the participatory categories), salvation through faith (soteriology), and the Law of Moses must be seen as most relevant for Paul himself.

As a result, Sanders's overall use of the Palestinian Jewish and Pauline writings is convincing in the main. However, his comparison of Palestinian Judaism and Paulinism is not necessarily in essence equally convincing. He arrives at two fundamental conclusions in his *Paul and Palestinian Judaism*:

1. Within Palestinian Judaism (with the exception of 4 Ezra) and Paulinism, salvation ultimately depends on the grace of God.[140]
2. Paul criticizes Jewish soteriology only because of his Christology. In other words, he remonstrates with the Jews since they do not believe in Christ as their Messiah.[141]

On the whole, Sanders starts with his understanding of the pattern of Palestinian Judaism and then proceeds to his understanding of the pattern of Paulinism. Finally, he concludes with the resulting theory for the absolute break between Palestinian Judaism and Paul. All three main aspects of his reasoning should undergo a critical assessment in the following.

137 Caird 1978, 539; Gundry 1985, 5–6.
138 See below, chapter 5.
139 Gaventa 1980, 41–42.
140 Sanders 1977, 543.
141 Op. cit., 442–47, 474–75.

Without going further into the specifics, Sanders deals with the question of how to get into the covenant in the context of Palestinian Judaism.[142] First and foremost, he strives to demonstrate that the Jews have not earned the covenant because of their good works. Obedience to the Law rather strengthens the mutual relationship between God and Israel.[143] In his survey of the Tannaitic literature, Sanders then asserts in passing that the Gentiles enter the covenant through their acceptance of the Torah.[144] He notices that one born a Jew naturally belongs to the covenant from birth or through circumcision.[145] Similarly, in his perusal of the Qumran texts, he provides very scanty explanations. Succinctly, he points out that the Gentiles and even those born as Israelites should get into the covenant by means of remorseful repentance of their sins[146] and unconditional commitment to the sectarian halakah.[147] As to the other Palestinian Jewish writings, he offers no data nor information about the possible conditions for "getting in."

Bizarrely enough, Sanders includes in his structural description of covenantal nomism[148] no answer to the question of how to get into the covenant. His defective presentation in *Paul and Palestinian Judaism* calls for urgent completion. In consideration of the pattern of Palestinian Judaism, one must—at least for rabbinism and the Qumran community—thirdly add: a Gentile (or an outsider in general) gets into the covenant through accepting the Law.[149] In this manner, the description of the pattern of Palestinian Judaism coincides well with the definition of the pattern of religion: the entrance into the covenant takes place by the acceptance of the Law. In this fashion, the comparison of Palestinian Judaism and Paulinism strikes a balance as well: the acceptance of the Law matches faith in the Gospel, the Pauline criterion of entrance.[150]

Although God established the covenant with Israel by his sovereign grace, a Gentile and a renegade (according to the view of the Qumran community, even

142 The question of how a person gets in a religion is missing from Sanders's Index of Subjects. The question of how a person stays in a religion he places under the heading of "Status-maintenance" (with reference to "Obedience," "Repentance," and "Righteous").

143 Sanders 1977, 419–24.

144 Op. cit., 85–86, 206–7, 211. Cf. Sanders 1980, 67–68: "[. . .] when the Rabbis did discuss how one gets in, they saw it in terms of accepting the election and the commandments." For more on this, see below 5.1.

145 Sanders 1977, 270. For more on this, see below 5.1.

146 Op. cit., 262, 270.

147 Op. cit., 264, 270.

148 See above 3.2.

149 See the examples in Sanders (op. cit., 85–86, 206–7).

150 Cf. Sanders 1983, 207–8, where he concludes: "The [. . .] point at which the break [between Paul and the Jews] is especially clear is his [sc. Paul's] insistence that it is through faith in Christ, not by accepting the law that one enters the people of God." The contrast between faith in Christ and acceptance of the Law comes into sight from the quotation.

a born Israelite) do not necessarily enter the covenant by his sovereign grace. Entrance can still depend on human abilities at their disposal.[151] For certain, no one earns the covenant through accepting the Torah. But he might still by his readiness to accomplish the Mosaic Law attain his entrance into the covenant. At least it seems that Sanders himself thinks along similar lines. He directly and promptly concedes that admission to the group of the elect rests upon the power and decision of the novice and the apostate. Their eternal fate lies in their own hands.[152] In all logic, it no longer follows that salvation in Palestinian Judaism comes about by mercy. Apparently, Sanders has not demonstrated his main thesis. He has not dealt with relevant anthropological dimensions within the comparison of patterns of religion in depth and detail. They demand further reflection.

With great expertise and diligence, Sanders deals with the question of how to stay within the covenant in the context of Palestinian Judaism. He succinctly concludes that Jews maintain their status as the chosen people through their obedience to the Law. Their good works are strictly the *conditio sine qua non* for the preservation of salvation.[153] Only in passing does Sanders add that their submission to the Torah comes about by their own strength. He frankly points out that they must and they can live in accordance with the divine will.[154] Considering such a condition of salvation, it is no longer indisputable that God alone works out the final salvation. Rather, he seems to demand and require a very active role on the part of his chosen people. Therefore, Sanders's overall analysis does not unmistakably support his characterization of the Palestinian Jewish pattern of religion. He does not sufficiently take anthropological dimensions into account.

Likewise, Sanders's wide-ranging sketch of the Pauline pattern of religion as a whole remains a torso. He does not thoroughly deal with or delve into the anthropological preconditions of how to "get in" and "stay in" Christ, in other words, the anthropological premises for faith and good works. If faith is something Christians press out of themselves and good works are something they do in their own power, their salvation falls back at least in part on human capacity. It does not then depend on divine grace alone. Although, for instance, Rom. 3:24 announces that all shall be saved without any merits, there is no guarantee that it is really so. What Paul writes here in theory does not yet prove that

151 An illustration from the Christian side can be taken from Pelagianism. Certainly, the Pelagians did not directly deny the grace of God. They (as all Christians) put their trust in the vicarious death of Christ for their sins. Yet they asserted that everyone must attain entrance into the (new) covenant in order to enjoy the divine mercy and benevolence there. Cf. Cooper 1982, 127–29. He refers to medieval nominalism as an example.

152 Sanders 1977, 261–68 (see further 114–15, 177 n. 155, 206–7).

153 Op. cit., Index of Subjects, s.v. "Status-maintenance."

154 Op. cit., 114–15, 261–70.

he in practice also sticks to his soteriological principle. Who knows if he shows any strict coherence or stringent consistency in his thinking?[155] It is precisely for that reason that it is necessary to examine the matter.

Neither does Sanders's extremely radical theory about Paul's break with Judaism rest on ample and abundant evidence. On closer reflection, his line of reasoning seems arbitrary. Without discussing the question of human capacity, Sanders cannot with full justification renounce Bultmann's interpretation that Paul abolishes the Jewish soteriology because of his profound anthropological insight into the depravity of the whole humankind. Still less can Sanders embrace his own categorical interpretation that Paul abandons the Jewish soteriology because of his exclusive Christological persuasion and solely afterward attempts to vindicate his abandonment through his description (or exaggeration) of humanity under the power of sin and death. Apparently, the argumentation amounts to an obvious *petitio principii*.

Sanders himself may know that an anthropological dimension appears not irrelevant for the Pauline pattern of religion. He explicitly speaks here of the soteriological pattern of religion.[156] As known, the concept of soteriology in line with his own definition implies *inter alia* the doctrine of original sin.[157] Despite his disgust for the systematic theological use of language, he still discusses Pauline soteriology for more than twenty pages![158] Nonetheless, the question of human capacity does not come into view. For sure, Sanders remarks in passing that he does not intend to examine once again different anthropological terms or expressions in Pauline theology. He emphasizes that others have already addressed those issues and exhaustively dealt with them.[159] Indeed, there is no need to repeat what they have done. Yet apart from—or, rather, because of—the relevant results of the previous exegetical studies, the plain and simple fact remains that one should at least pay attention to or make allowance for anthropological perspectives in order to shed more light on the Pauline pattern of religion.[160]

By and large, Sanders does take up one aspect in Pauline soteriology that entails the notion of the depravity of humankind. He puts his emphasis on those passages in which the focus lies on the demonic dominion of sin (for example,

155 Cf. Räisänen 1983, 184–86. In his footnote 117, he succinctly maintains: "[. . .] obviously, it is impossible to teach a 100 per cent *sola gratia* doctrine except in theory." Even more strongly, F. Watson 1986, *passim*. See further Snodgrass 1986, 82.

156 Sanders 1977, 423.

157 Op. cit., 17–18.

158 Op. cit., 447–74.

159 Op. cit., 508.

160 See above 3.3.1.

Rom. 3:9; 5:12–7:23; Gal. 3:22).[161] In one special respect, his otherwise very innovative interpretation falls short. For some reason, he, for all intents and purposes, ignores the pessimistic anthropology that the submission under the evil powers implies.[162] His interest primarily rests on the development of his own thesis that the apostle to the Gentiles thinks "backward," or from solution to plight.[163]

In summary, Sanders draws some conclusions that he is unable to prove completely or sufficiently. He does not validate that salvation is really by grace in Palestinian Judaism and in Paulinism. Neither does he verify that Paul, so to say, thinks "backward" from solution to plight. His argumentation fails to carry conviction since he for the most part overlooks the question of human ability.[164]

Finally, some uncertainty exists about diverse Palestinian Jewish writings, concerning whether they really demonstrate and substantiate the presence of covenantal nomism. A closer look at them follows next. Only short remarks are in order here.

N. A. Dahl perceives a crucial and radical shift in covenantal nomism within the sectarian community in Qumran. He points out that the Dead Sea Scrolls regard repentance and expiation as conditions for admission and entrance into the covenant and not only as a requirement for remaining in it.[165] His (in itself right) notion does not have a direct bearing on the structural pattern of Palestinian Judaism. As shown and made known, Sanders's description of it falls short. He leaves it open how one truly gets into the covenant.[166] Hence, the Qumran sect cannot contravene against the covenantal nomism of his provenance. Besides, the sectarians consider all but themselves as "Gentiles" (or "heathen outsiders") and for their entrance require a ritual baptism with confession of sins and penance.[167] Later, at least rabbis posit quite similar rites for the Gentiles who desire to become proselytes and full members in the people of Israel.[168]

A. J. Saldarini asks skeptically whether the apocalyptic book of 1 Enoch can really represent a pattern of religion similar to that of the Tannaitic literature.[169]

161 Sanders 1977, 453, 468, 470, 486–87, 498–502. Cf. further Brooke 1979, 249; Dahl 1978, 156.

162 See below 4.1.2.

163 See my summary above 3.2.

164 Cf. Sanders 2009, 49–52, and how slightly he deals with the question of anthropology (or human ability). He reduces it to a short and shallow discussion about the relationship between grace and works. (His contribution was reprinted in 2016, 77–80.) For a similar criticism of his position, see above 3.3.1.

165 Dahl 1978, 155.

166 See above.

167 See, e.g., Sanders 1977, 242–57.

168 See, e.g., Moore 1948–50, 1:332–35, 529; Sanders 1977, 206–7.

169 Saldarini 1979, 302. Cf. Beker 1978, 110.

To all appearances, his criticism would make a hit only if the concept of pattern of religion relates to the holistic description of a religion.[170] Yet Saldarini supplies no concrete arguments as to why 1 Enoch should not represent the same soteriological pattern of religion as the rabbinic texts.[171]

H. Räisänen emphasizes that Sanders carries the legalism in 4 Ezra too far. The radicalization of the Law's demands should only serve the theodicy of the author. In contrast to all evidence (for example, the destruction of the temple), God has remained true to his covenant. The Jews have themselves to blame for their national catastrophe.[172] Räisänen's argument seems to hold up, but appears somewhat imprecise. Does he mean that 4 Ezra does not depart from covenantal nomism at all or not to the extent that Sanders thinks?[173] The case remains open.

Further, Räisänen points out that *Pseudo-Philo*, a writing disregarded by Sanders, persuasively corroborates covenantal nomism.[174] In all probability, it originates in Palestine during the time before the fall of the temple. On the whole, it deals with "the history of the covenant." The concept of covenant takes a key position. *Pseudo-Philo* represents "a religion of the heart" that quite closely resembles the piety of Deuteronomy. There is no trace of a formalistic or legalistic mentality.[175] Räisänen primarily depends on C. Perrot's interpretations.[176] Assuming their accuracy and validity, *Pseudo-Philo* is to be esteemed as a representative of covenantal nomism. In any case, Sanders's conclusions do not depend on them. His arguments are based on other texts.

In a sense, Sirach is lacking covenantal nomism since the author does not link obedience to the Law with the covenant.[177] Yet Sanders contends that this specific feature does not detract from the overall picture of covenantal nomism. He justifies his position as follows:

170 See above 3.3.1.

171 Gundry 1985, 4 n. 9.

172 See Räisänen 1983, 180–91. Sanders assumes that the radicalization of the demands of the Law in 4 Ezra arises from the disappointment over the destruction of Jerusalem and the temple (1977, 427–28). Differently, J. C. Beker (1978, 110). He maintains that a great part of the Tannaitic material originates from the era after AD 70. Nonetheless, it preserves covenantal nomism. Beker does not take into account the plain and simple fact that the same historical event can produce different reactions in different people. The history of religions examines what the given reactions were, not what they should have been (Gundry 1985, 5).

173 Byrne (1979, 230) deliberates that "the 'works-righteousness' aspect of *IV Ezra*—only *one* aspect, to be sure—may be more 'typical' than Sanders is prepared to allow."

174 Räisänen 1983, 180 n. 92. Cf. already McNamara 1979, 68.

175 Ibid.

176 Ibid.

177 Sanders 1977, 333, 420.

1. Sirach addresses only Jews.[178] Apparently, the covenant and the election are self-evident truths for them and need no particular mention.
2. Sirach does not reckon with reward and punishment in a coming world but rather limits himself wholly to the present world. Therefore, he is not interested in the question of who really stays in the covenant and will be saved.[179]

For sure, these two explanations illuminate why Sirach does not link obedience to the Law with the covenant. However, they still do not remove the fact that Sirach does not link obedience to the Law with the covenant as such. In consequence, his pattern of religion does not exactly coincide with the structural framework of covenantal nomism since Palestinian Judaism (including 4 Ezra) combines submission to the Torah with the given reality of the Sinaitic pact between God and his people.

Astonishingly, Sanders shows—surely contrary to his own intention—that Sirach ultimately repeals covenantal nomism. As already made known, covenantal nomism embraces faith in eternal life,[180] while Sirach denies life after death.[181] Hence, he unavoidably diverges from Palestinian Judaism in general.

On the basis of the predominant exegetical research, it turns out that a great proportion of the Old Testament, along with Sirach, would lack covenantal nomism, if the idea of eternal life should belong as an essential element to the pattern of Palestinian Judaism. Consistent with the current conventional knowledge, it is the latest traditions of the Old Testament that first *expressis verbis* demonstrate faith in the bodily resurrection inclusive of the world to come. In that case, for instance, the five books of Moses absurdly would not involve covenantal nomism. In all probability, the academic discussion goes on and the results might change.[182] Yet it instills more trust to speak of the eternity aspect

178 On the one hand, Sanders (1977, 333) doubts if Sirach addresses only Jews: "[. . .] presumably only Jews are addressed [. . .]." On the other hand, Sanders has no doubts that Sirach addresses only Jews: "This [the fact that Sirach does not link fulfillment of the Law with the covenant] is doubtless to be explained by two facts: 1. He [Sirach] addressed only Israelites [. . .]" (op. cit., 420). The notion of the Mosaic Law as including all wisdom and the general character of several exhortations in Sirach (op. cit., 329–33) rather belies Sanders's position.

179 Op. cit., 420. Although Sanders does not say it explicitly, he evidently presents these two points to clarify why Sirach lends support to covenantal nomism despite specific theology. Otherwise he could not assert two pages later that 4 Ezra is the only writing to lack covenantal nomism (op. cit., 422).

180 See Sanders's outline of covenantal nomism above 3.2.

181 Sanders 1977, 333–37.

182 Without a doubt, the thought of bodily resurrection on the Last Day was not common in the Old Testament. Indeed, it was not easy to understand anything like that before the bodily resurrection of Christ (cf. Mark 9:9–10). However, the idea of revenge and retaliation in death and directly after death suggests itself more often (see, for instance,

as a nonessential element of the pattern of Palestinian Judaism, especially as the Sadducees (perhaps the majority in the Sanhedrin) denied life after death.

In conclusion, the outcomes obtained once again fall into two groups listed below, the first are points of agreement, and the second are points of disagreement between me and Sanders:

I 1. Sanders's research is based on sufficient source material, which does not necessarily need to be supplemented.

2. The dating of the rabbinic materials by Sanders turns out to be correct in the main.

3. It is plausible and relevant on the basis of the Jewish sources to pose the questions of how one gets into the covenant and how one stays there.

II 1. Sanders does not consider it necessary to explain more in-depth why the halakic texts, a large portion of the rabbinic literature, hardly deal with such themes as election and covenant.

2. In his structural pattern of covenantal nomism, Sanders does not answer his methodological question of how one enters the covenant.

3. Likewise, Sanders neglects the question of human ability and the inquiry of what significance it has for the pattern of religion. Nonetheless, his conclusions assume such anthropological premises.

4. Sirach—contrary to what Sanders supposes—falls short of covenantal nomism since the author does not relate obedience of the Law to the covenant.

5. In contrast to the structural pattern of Palestinian Judaism by Sanders, the notion of life after death does not belong to covenantal nomism as an inalienable element.

As a result, there is every reason to complete Sanders's line of reasoning. A critical assessment of his conclusions by covering the question concerning human ability is urgently needed. Since a broad consensus reigns among scholars on the main points of Jewish anthropology, it will suffice to outline them briefly and summarize the most relevant specifics. The Pauline anthropology requires more effort, because much confusion and uncertainty exist there.

Num. 16:29–35 or Psalm 73). The difference between the two perspectives deserves more attention in the academic discussion. In addition, Jesus himself found the thought of bodily resurrection in the self-presentation of God as the God of Abraham, the God of Isaac, and the God of Jacob (Mark 12:26–27)!

4. ANTHROPOLOGICAL PRESUPPOSITIONS OF THE JEWISH AND PAULINE PATTERN OF RELIGION

4.1. Human Freedom

4.1.1. Judaism

The common and standard set of beliefs in Judaism embraces a generally and widely accepted notion of human free will.[1] The first thought-out formulation probably appears in Sirach (15:11–20 NETS) by the year 200 BC.[2] He writes as follows:

> Do not say, "On account of the Lord I fell away," for what he hates, he will not do. Do not say, "It was he who led me astray," for he has no need of a sinful man. Every abomination the Lord hated, and it is not beloved to those who fear him. It was he who from the beginning made humankind, and he left him in the hand of his deliberation. If you want to, you shall preserve the commandments, and to keep faith is a matter of good pleasure. He has set aside for you fire and water; to whichever you want, you shall stretch out your hand. Before humans are life and death, and whichever one he desires will be given to him, because great is the wisdom of the Lord; he is mighty in dominance and one who sees everything. And his eyes are on those who fear him, and he will know

1 Hayman 1984, 21–22; Maier 1971, 84–115, 325–50; Meyer 1937, 69–74; Moore 1948–50, 1:453–59; Nissen 1974, 135–42; Odeberg 1980, 49; Schechter 1975, 285–89; Urbach 1979, 255–85. See also below. Cf. Jervell 1960, 26–29, 61–62, 87–89. He tries to show that only Israelites are human beings in the true sense and carriers of the *imago Dei*, whereas the Gentiles were not spoken of as images of God (op. cit., 31–37, 41–46, 81–84, 87–96, 104–7, 112–21). His whole reasoning has faced hard and heavy criticism. See especially Nissen 1974, 138–39; M. Smith 1968, 315–26.

2 Maier 1971, 85.

> every human deed. He did not command anyone to be impious, and he did not give anyone leave to sin.

Likewise, the Psalms of Solomon (9:4–5 NETS) attest around 50 BC:

> Our works are in the choosing and power of our soul, to do righteousness or injustice in the works of our hands, and in your righteousness you visit human beings. The one who practices righteousness stores up life for himself with the Lord, and the one who practices injustice is responsible for the destruction of his own soul, for the judgments of the Lord are in righteousness for each man and household.[3]

After the destruction of the temple, 4 Ezra (8:55–58) also postulates human free will:

> Therefore ask no more concerning the multitude of them that perish; for having received liberty they despised the Most High; scorned his Law, and forsook his ways: Moreover his saints they have trodden under foot; and have said in their heart that there is no God [. . .].[4]

At about the same time, the Syriac Apocalypse of Baruch (54:15, 19) asserts:

> For though Adam first sinned And brought untimely death upon all, Yet of those who were born from him Each one of them has prepared for his own soul torment to come, And again each one of them has chosen for himself glories to come. [. . .] Adam is therefore not the cause, save only of his own soul, But each of us has been the Adam of his own soul.[5]

Later on, Baruch (85:7) affirms:

> And let all those things aforesaid be always before your eyes, Because we are still in the spirit and the power of our liberty.[6]

The rabbinic literature maintains the same central tradition. J. Neusner contends that the whole Mishnah (ca. AD 200) is based upon free will. To quote his very own words:

> So, stated briefly, the question taken up by the Mishnah is, What can a man do? and the answer laid down by the Mishnah is, Man, through will and deed, is master of this world, the measure of all things.[7]

Neusner remarks further:

> Stated simply, at the center of the Mishnaic system is the notion that man has the power to inaugurate the work of sanctification, and the Mischnaic system states and restates that power.[8]

---

3 Cf. Gray in Charles 1964, 642.

4 Translation according to Box in Charles 1964, 598.

5 Translation according to Charles 1964, 511–12.

6 Translation according to Charles 1964, 525.

7 Neusner 1988, 271.

8 Op. cit., 275.

In the Mishnah, Rabbi Akiba (Avot 3:15) puts the concept of free will in plain words:

> Everything is foreseen; and free choice is given. In goodness the world is judged. And all is in accord with the abundance of deed[s].[9]

In the rabbinic tradition, the basic Old Testament references are Deut. 11:26–28; 30:15–20.[10] The first reads:

> See, I am setting before you today a blessing and a curse: the blessing, if you obey the commandments of the LORD your God, which I command you today, and the curse, if you do not obey the commandments of the LORD your God, but turn aside from the way that I am commanding you today, to go after other gods that you have not known.

The second says:

> See, I have set before you today life and good, death and evil. If you obey the commandments of the LORD your God that I command you today, by loving the LORD your God, by walking in his ways, and by keeping his commandments and his statutes and his rules, then you shall live and multiply, and the LORD your God will bless you in the land that you are entering to take possession of it. But if your heart turns away, and you will not hear, but are drawn away to worship other gods and serve them, I declare to you today, that you shall surely perish. You shall not live long in the land that you are going over the Jordan to enter and possess. I call heaven and earth to witness against you today, that I have set before you life and death, blessing and curse. Therefore choose life, that you and your offspring may live, loving the LORD your God, obeying his voice and holding fast to him, for he is your life and length of days, that you may dwell in the land that the LORD swore to your fathers, to Abraham, to Isaac, and to Jacob, to give them.

Sifre on Deut. 11:26 (par. 53) ascribes free will to man. The commentary explains:

> See, this day I set before you blessing and curse [. . .] (Dt. 11:26–30): Why is this passage stated? The reason is that, since it is said, "Life and death I have placed before you, a blessing and a curse" (Dt. 30:19), perhaps the Israelites might say, "Since the Omnipresent has placed before us two ways, the way of life and the way of death, let us go in whichever way we choose." Accordingly, Scripture says, "Choose life" (Dt. 30:19).[11]

Mek. on Exod. 15:26 comments in agreement:

> ". . . saying, If you will diligently hearken": In this connection sages have said, "If one has obeyed one commandment, he is given the opportunity to obey many commandments, as it is said [in Lauterbach's translation], 'If you begin

9 Translation according to Neusner [1984a], 114.
10 Moore 1948–50, 1:453, 455; Stiegman 1979, 524.
11 Translation according to Neusner 1987, 1:175.

> to hearken you will continue to hearken.' If one has forgotten one religious duty, he is made to forget many religious duties, for it is said, 'And it shall be, if you begin to forget that you will continue to forget' (Dt. 8:19)."[12]

It depends on man to become righteous, although God may render him help.[13] Rabbi Hanina (around AD 225) declares:

> And R. Hanina said, "Everything is in the hands of heaven except fear of heaven. For it is said, 'And now, Israel, what does the Lord, your God, require of you but to fear' (Deut. 10:12)." (See BT Berakhot 33b and further Megilla 25a or Niddah 16b.)[14]

He further takes an illustrative example in support of his thesis:

> The angel who is appointed in charge of conception is called "night," and he takes a drop of semen and sets it before the Holy One, blessed be He, and says to him, "Lord of the ages, as to this drop of semen, what will be its fate? Will it produce a strong man or a weak man, a sage or a fool? A rich man or a poor man?" But it does not ask whether it will be a wicked man or a righteous man! That is in accord with what R. Hanina said. For R. Hanina said, "Everything is in the hands of Heaven except for the fear of Heaven [. . .]." (See BT Niddah 16b.)[15]

All told, free will is denied in no place in the rabbinic literature.[16]

In line with the Tannaitic midrash on Deuteronomy (see above), Philo (from ca. 25 BC to ca. AD 40) meditates:

> And therefore it is reasonably held that the mind alone in all that makes us what we are is indestructible. For it is mind alone which the Father who begat it judged worthy of freedom, and loosening the fetters of necessity, suffered it to range as it listed, and of that free-will which is His most peculiar possession and most worthy of His majesty gave it such portion as it was capable of receiving. For the other living creatures in whose souls the mind, the element set apart for liberty, has no place, have been committed under yoke and bridle to the service of men, as slaves to a master. But man, possessed of a spontaneous and self-determined will, whose activities for the most part rest on deliberate choice, is with reason blamed for what he does wrong with intent, praised when he acts rightly of his own will. In the others, the plants and animals, no praise is due if they bear well, nor blame if they fare ill: for their movements

12 Translation according to *Mekhilta*, 1:238.

13 Particularly Schechter 1975, 265–66, 278–22, 341–43. He writes nicely: "But man has to show himself worthy of this grace, inasmuch as it is expected that the first effort against the *Evil Yezer* should be made on his part, whereupon the promise comes that *Yezer* will be finally removed by God." See also Moore 1948–50, 2:212–14; Nissen 1974, 139–40; Odeberg 1980, 71; Sanders 1977, 178; Urbach 1979, 273–74.

14 Translation according to Neusner 1984, 240.

15 Translation according to Neusner 1990, 1:83.

16 Hayman 1984, 21–22; Jervell 1960, 87–88; Meyer 1937, 69–74; Moore 1948–50, 1:456; Nissen 1974, 135, 140–41; Odeberg 1980, 49.

> and changes in either direction come to them from no deliberate choice or volition of their own. But the soul of man alone has received from God the faculty of voluntary movement, and in this way especially is made like to Him, and thus being liberated, as far as might be, from that hard and ruthless mistress, necessity, may justly be charged with guilt, in that it does not honor its Liberator. And therefore it will rightly pay the inexorable penalty which is meted to ungrateful freedmen. Thus God "had it in His mind and bethought Him" not now for the first time, but ever from of old—a thought that was fixed and steadfast—"that He had made man," that is He thought of what nature He had made him. He had made him free and unfettered, to employ his powers of action with voluntary and deliberate choice for this purpose, that, knowing good and ill and receiving the conception of the noble and the base, and setting himself in sincerity to apprehend just and unjust and in general what belongs to virtue and what to vice, he might practice to choose the better and eschew the opposite. And therefore we have an oracle of this kind recorded in Deuteronomy. "Behold, I have set before thy face life and death, good and evil; choose life" (Deut. xxx. 15, 19). So then in this way He puts before us both truths; first that men have been made with a knowledge both of good and evil, its opposite; secondly, that it is their duty to choose the better rather than the worse, because they have, as it were, within them an incorruptible judge in the reasoning faculty, which will accept all that right reason suggests and reject the promptings of its opposite. (*Quod Deus sit immutabilis* 10.45–50)[17]

The historian Josephus (born AD 37/38) characterizes on three occasions the most significant religious parties in the Palestinian Judaism of his day (see *De bello Iudaico* 2.119–66; *Antiquitates Iudaicae* 13.171–73; 18.11–25). Every time, he differentiates among the Essenes, the Pharisees, and the Sadducees preponderantly according to their concept of free will. A similar and historically quite reliable picture comes into sight:

The Essenes refer everything, including even the evil and the doing of evil, back to divine determination and predestination. In contrast, the Sadducees relate good and evil merely to human free will to the exclusion of divine involvement. As a compromise, the Pharisees disregard both extreme conceptions. They ascribe all things to "fate" or, rather, divine providence. But to do right or wrong depends on human efforts or free will, although "fate" also cooperates in every matter.[18]

In summary, it turns out that human free will in a soteriological context (or in the spiritual matters) from Sirach until the Babylonian Talmud was *opinio*

17 Translation according to Colson and Whitaker 1968, 3:33, 35, 37.

18 Particularly Maier 1971, 1–20.

communis in Judaism.[19] Presumably, one exception proves the rule: the Qumran community in all probability represents an absolute fatalism.[20]

Because of free will, man has not only the ability to always choose good instead of evil, he also has the power to always do good (cf. the quotations above).[21] Apparently, everyone has an inborn propensity but no hereditary compulsion to disobedience. It is fully conceivable to obey the Law in its entirety to the very end.[22] Otherwise God would in fact bear at least to some extent responsibility for sins committed, since he would have created his creation and creatures incomplete and defective. Hence, the dogma of human freedom and sincerity in a soteriological context becomes self-evident in Judaism.[23]

Moreover, the freedom of human will conforms to the purity of the human soul. The moral decision to obey the commandments stems from a pure soul. Exactly for that reason, everyone in his inner being necessarily towers over all

---

19 See especially Westerholm 2006. He goes through a great amount of Palestinian as well as Hellenistic Jewish texts and confirms the presence of human freedom in all of them (with some reservation and modification in regard to the Dead Sea Scrolls, which "occupies a half-way position" between Paul and the rest of Judaism). Cf. further Sprinkle 2013. He states that "a full-scale treatment of the anthropology was lacking until Timo Laato published his dissertation, *Paul and Judaism: An Anthropological Approach*." Then he avows that many opponents of the New Perspective "have taken Laato's conclusion at face value." Rather, they have merely "assumed that Laato's study ended the discussion, hammering the proverbial nail in the coffin" and that "Laato's study is proof enough" (op. cit., 126–27). Next, Sprinkle asks if Laato's work should be "the final word on anthropology" and correctly writes that "there is much more to be said" (op. cit., 127). He refers to S. Westerholm's important studies. For sure, "Westerholm arrives at a conclusion similar to Laato's" (ibid.). Thus Sprinkle sets himself the laudable task of examining "the soteriological structure of Paul and Judaism" more closely. However, in the end he only examines the soteriological structure of Paul and the Dead Sea Scrolls (op. cit., 28). He concludes that the anthropological view is more pessimistic in Qumran than in Judaism in general (op. cit., 125–44). All in all, his conclusion is in full agreement with the results of the studies by Laato and Westerholm! They simply bring forth well-known facts which are generally recognized—now also by Sprinkle himself, correctly. T. R. Schreiner 1998, 156 n. 17.

20 For the fatalism of the Qumran community, however, see particularly Sanders's important contribution in 1977, 257–70. He provides some good reasons for his deviating conclusions: "Yet despite this emphasis on the eternal and irresistible grace of God as the basis for entrance into the community of the elect, the sectarians did not understand this in such a way as to exclude man's ability to choose which of two ways he would follow. The idea of God's electing grace was not formulated in opposition to man's freedom of choice, and in this sense it is anachronistic to speak of 'predestination'" (op. cit., 261). Similarly, Nissen 1974, 146–49. By contrast, e.g., Maier 1971, 206–63. He subdues the notions of free will under those of predestination in Qumran: human decisions are themselves already preordained. Cf. Braun 1959, 8–9.

21 Epstein 1960, 215–17; Jervell 1960, 51, 86–92; Lindeskog 1938, 83–84; Nissen 1974, 135 and n. 156; Odeberg 1980, 51–52.

22 Hayman 1984, 17; Lindeskog 1938, 83; Nikolainen 1943, 32–33; Nissen 1974, 137–38; Odeberg 1980, 52; Sanders 1977, 114–15.

23 Moore 1948–50, 1:454–55, 482–83.

depravity.[24] BT Berakhot 60b corroborates this. The passage bears witness to a traditional benediction which every Jew should recite on awakening. Instantly, he gives his thanks for the purity of the soul:

> When someone gets up, he says, "My God, the soul that you put in me is pure. You formed it in me. You breathed it into me. You keep it in me. You will take it from me one day but restore it to me in the time to come. So long as the soul is in me, I thank you, Lord my God and God of my fathers, master of all ages, lord of all souls. Blessed are you, Lord, who restores souls to dead corpses."[25]

We do not know exactly where the benediction originally stems from and when it initially took shape. It does not begin with the customary formula: ברוך אתה. The present version (at any rate in its main features) was possibly formed before each petition was provided with the same style. To all appearances, the praise אלהי נשמה (in its essential content) goes far back to ancient times.[26] The insertion of it in the daily liturgy of the morning service shows the impressive importance of it. The Babylonian Talmud does not here revolve around a single saying by an individual rabbi. Rather, the emphasis lies on a fundamental principle of rabbinism (resp. Judaism in general).[27]

In consequence of its divine origin, the soul has a constant character or a stable essence. Sins can "taint" its purity temporarily, but never definitively corrupt.[28] The unchanged uprightness of human nature should not be misused for a moral slackness. Instead, each and every one has to bring his outer behavior into harmony with his inner being.[29] Notwithstanding, sins do not originate from the material body where the "immaterial" soul stays during its earthly visit. God formed the body out of the dust of the soil, and indeed for the help of the soul (Gen. 2:7). When someone acts against the Law, the whole person sits in the dock or is on trial. Any kind of Hellenistic dualism between body as the bastion of evil and the soul as the bastion of good does not occur in Judaism.[30]

---

24 See already Perles 1903, 131–32: "Die Anschauung [concerning free will] der Rabbinen ist am klarsten in dem Gebete ausgesprochen, das bis heute jeder Jude des Morgens zu sprechen hat: 'Mein Gott, die Seele, die du in mich gelegt hast, ist rein.'" Similarly, Odeberg 1980, 66–68. Sjöberg (1944, 111) asserts the same aspect (although more warily with a small shift in focus): "Däremot synes det mig ovisst, om man kan sammankoppla fariseismens tro på människans egen förmåga med tanken på själen som gudagnistan i människan *så nära* som Odeberg gör" (italics mine). Cf. further Dahl 1944, 135–36. For the purity of the soul in Hellenistic Judaism, see Dihle 1973, 630–33.

25 Translation according to Neusner 1984, 407. For the soul as "divine being," see Meyer 1937, 49–61. Cf. Billerbeck 1924, 437–38; Odeberg 1968, 172–73 n. 1.

26 Hedegård 1951, introduction, 35; cf. 15–16. Cf. further Stiegman 1979, 552.

27 Odeberg 1980, 68.

28 Odeberg 1980, 67.

29 Ibid.

30 Bacher 1903, 279, 417; Meyer 1937, 33–45, 60–61, 64–65; Moore 1948–50, 1:446–48; Nissen 1974, 136; Odeberg 1980, 68; Sjöberg 1944, 111; Stiegman 1979, 515–21.

The freedom of human will and the purity of human soul did not perish on account of the fall into sin by Adam and Eve. Their primeval disobedience worked neither a total loss nor a partial limiting of their original integrity and veracity. Before and after eating from the tree of knowledge, they still had the same ability to obey God. Human nature went through no restriction of essence by sin.[31] Genesis 3 does not describe what ever after must come to pass, but rather what now and then (or maybe in this case: then and now) can take place. The rebellion in Paradise only serves as one (but typical) example of transgression.[32]

Therefore, it turns out that mankind has been led astray from the very beginning through occasional, common, and concrete wrongdoings. But sin did not through the (primordial) fall attain to a demonic reign of terror in the whole world. The wide gulf to the Pauline line of thought appears totally unbridgeable (see the following section).[33]

4.1.2. Paul

In contrast to the common Jewish understanding, the apostle to the Gentiles does not recognize free will in a soteriological context. With exceptional emphasis, he expresses and explains the human incapacity to do good or even only to choose the right.[34] In the first place, he avails himself of the concept of ἁμαρτία to portray the wretched state of humankind. It does not primarily stand for the multitude of different and distinct, certain and common transgressions. Sin appears more like a demonic power. Particularly in Romans 5–7, it exerts a transsubjective reign of terror over the whole cosmos:

Sin came into the world through the fall of Adam (5:12) and gained dominion there (5:21). Now, man is enslaved to it (6:6, 17–23) and surrenders to slave service under its authority (6:13). Sin renders the salary of death to the sinner (6:23). It takes occasion by the Law to stimulate evil desire in man, to deceive and to kill him (7:8, 11, 13). The "I" is sold under sin (7:14). It dwells and acts in him (7:17, 20).[35]

31 In the first place, see Hayman 1984, 17; Moore 1948–50, 1:474–76, 479; Nissen 1974, 135–36, 138–39; Stiegman 1979, 527–29; Urbach 1975, 421. Similarly, Billerbeck 1926, 227–28.

32 Epstein 1960, 220; Hayman 1984, 17; Odeberg 1980, 67. Cf. Nissen 1974, 135–36, 138–39.

33 Cf. Hayman 1984, 21–22.

34 See, e.g., Schottroff 1979, 497–502.

35 See the presentations in Becker 1989, 415–16; Bornkamm 1987, 143; Brandenburger 1962, 160; Bultmann 1984, 245; Conzelmann 1987, 216; Lohmeyer [1954], 80–81; Schottroff 1979, 498–99. Kaye (1979, 30–57) and Röhser (1987, 103–81) disagree here. They deny that the concept of ἁμαρτία stands for a demonic power in Pauline theology. Such a linguistic usage rather originates in a rhetorical style or metaphorical figure of speech. See further Räisänen 1983, 99–100 n. 29. The Achilles' heel of Kaye and Röhser is Rom. 7:7–13, where the concept of ἁμαρτία obviously takes on a demonic character: sin represents the serpent (devil) in Paradise. It or he deceived and killed Adam and Eve

Paul calls the fallen and sin-bound human being σάρξ. Literally, it means "flesh." In Greek, the concept has two main meanings. On the one hand, σάρξ designates humankind in distinction from God. It refers to the human infirmity and mortality.[36] On the other hand, σάρξ denotes humankind in contrast to God. It relates to human impiety and depravity.[37] The latter sense extends over the ordinary usage in Old Testament texts. It does not appear in the later Jewish and Gnostic writings.[38] Moreover, σάρξ (just as ἁμαρτία) has attained to a demonic power.[39] It also exerts a transsubjective reign of terror over the whole cosmos:

The flesh has its own works (Gal. 5:19) and actions (Rom. 8:13), passions and desires (Gal. 5:24). It has a mind, hostile to God, and for that reason does not submit to his Law (Rom. 8:6–7). The flesh lusts against the Spirit and hinders the Christian from doing good (Gal. 5:17). The Christian incessantly runs the risk of becoming anew "debtor" of the flesh (Rom. 8:12) and throwing the gates wide open for it (Gal. 5:13).[40]

Hence, the ironhard *circulus vitiosus* of sin and flesh surrounds and encloses the whole humanity (*orbis terrarum*). It is not in man's power to escape from here. It does not belong to him who is walking to direct his steps too. Freedom of choice vanishes.

As a continuation of his pessimistic anthropology, Paul further underlines, contrary to Jewish and Hellenistic convictions, that the soul (ψυχή)[41] does not

(cf. 2 Cor. 11:3; see also below 4.2.3.4 and even Röhser 1987, 180). In the continuation of the chapter, ἁμαρτία is hardly permitted a "dis-demonization" since sin acts in the "I" (see especially vv. 17 and 20). Likewise, Rom. 5:12–21 explains the fall. In consequence, ἁμαρτία should maintain its demonic character also there. Hence, Paul's vivid language does not merely fall back into rhetorical style or a metaphorical figure of speech.

36 Baumgärtel 1966, 106; Bornkamm 1987, 143–44; Conzelmann 1987, 198; Lohmeyer [1954], 102–3; Ridderbos 1987, 93. See also Moo 2018, 45 n. 43.

37 Bornkamm 1987, 144; Conzelmann 1987, 198; Lohmeyer [1954], 102–3; Ridderbos 1987, 93; Schweizer 1966, 131–34.

38 Bornkamm 1987, 144; Bultmann 1984, 235–37; Conzelmann 1987, 198; Lohmeyer [1954], 102–3; Ridderbos 1987, 94 n. 8; Schweizer 1966, 132–34.

39 Dunn emphasizes that the tension in Romans 7 is to be understood not so much in anthropological categories as in eschatological terms of being caught between the two epochs of Adam and Christ. The "I" is split not because of (creation and) fall but mainly as the result of redemption (1988, 394–96). Yet the ontological dimension of the concept "flesh" cannot be separated from the salvation-historical perspective. Paul speaks about a "mindset" of the flesh (Rom. 8:7), as well as the works or lusts of the flesh (Gal. 5:19, 24). Moreover, he says, e.g., that the flesh "desires" (Gal. 5:17). See below. Accordingly, there is an anthropological component involved in that kind of usage. See T. R. Schreiner 1998, 354. Cf. Seifrid 1992a, 330. Burgland (1997, 169–70) and Garlington (1990, 231) uncritically refer to Dunn.

40 Bornkamm 1987, 144; Bultmann 1984, 244–45. Cf. Conzelmann 1987, 216.

41 The word ψυχή in Paul primarily renders the Hebrew term נפש. The Septuagint too translates נפש with ψυχή. See, e.g., Bultmann 1984, 204–5.

form the noblest and best part of man. Rather, he affirms that human corruption also affects it. The soul does not rise above depravity. 1 Cor. 2:14 explicitly asserts that the "natural" man (ψυχικὸς ἄνθρωπος) does not comprehend or consent to "the things of the Spirit of God" (τὰ τοῦ πνεύματος τοῦ θεοῦ). He simply rejects them as foolishness. Sin has penetrated even to the depths of the inner essence of each and every one. As a consequence, no one relies on the Gospel by his own initiative or because of his own reasoning. Conversion takes place only through divine benevolence and omnipotence.[42]

However, at times Paul does not seem entirely consistent in his pessimistic anthropology. The most relevant passages are Romans 2; 5:12; 7:14–25. In the next part, they will be dealt with in order and more in-depth. The argumentation in this section may be further developed.

4.2. Is Paul Consistent in His Pessimistic Anthropology?

4.2.1. Romans 2

4.2.1.1. The View of H. Räisänen

Most of all, H. Räisänen maintains that the argumentation in Romans 2 leaves much to be desired. Paul is neither convincing nor consistent. He considerably overdoes and unjustifiably generalizes. In the end, he completely fails to prove his point that all stand under sin (3:9).[43] Räisänen justifies his view as follows:

(1) In sharpest contradiction to 1:18–32, chapter 2 (see particularly vv. 14–15 and 26–27) asserts that some Gentiles truly fulfill the Law. They no longer appear as malicious malefactors. Besides, the argumentation goes even more astray when the Jews on their part infringe against the Law in every respect. It seems completely impossible that they only fulfill any of the commandments in the slightest degree.[44] Obviously, Paul is simply interested in demonstrating their guilt. To achieve his tendentious purpose, he contrasts the sin-laden Jews with the Law-abiding Gentiles. As a consequence, God's people become wholly guilty. But thereby, 2:14–15 and 26–27 fall in conflict with 1:18–32 and 3:9. Evidently, Paul did not notice his logical failure. He was obsessed by his own reasoning.[45]

42 Barrett 1968, 76–77; Grosheide 1980, 73; Odeberg 1944, 71–72; Wendland 1978, 30.

43 Räisänen 1983, 97–109. See already 1980b, 308–11. For example, Sanders (1983, 123–35) agrees with Räisänen. Similarly, Snodgrass 1986, 76.

44 Räisänen 1983, 101–3.

45 Op. cit., 106.

To be sure, the portrayal of the moral condition of the Gentiles in 2:14–15, 26–27 forms a more credible impression than that in 1:18–32. In his polemical zeal, Paul exaggerates very strongly in the first chapter. He sets forth the pagan world as thoroughly *massa perditionis*. For instance, they are all homosexuals or idolaters. No doubt, the empirical facts do not support the gigantic generalization.[46]

(2) Besides, Paul exaggerates in his description of the moral condition of the Jews. He likewise sets them forth as thoroughly *massa perditionis*. In 2:1–3, the Jews are supposed to be guilty of all the same sins as the Gentiles.[47] Yet Räisänen makes his exegetical analysis more precise in a footnote. There, he adds that Paul must have the catalog of vices (1:28–31) in mind (rather than idolatry and homosexuality).[48] Later, in 2:21–24, the Jews are explicitly accused of many heinous sins. They commit robbery, adultery, and sacrilege. Once again, the empirical facts do not support the gigantic generalization[49] (cf. Phil. 3:6, where Saul as a former Pharisee is depicted as "blameless" according to the righteousness of the Law).[50] Surprisingly, Paul seems to halfway recognize that his argumentation limps quite badly. In 3:3, he remarks that merely *some* (τινες) of the Jews were unfaithful (cf. 10:2, where they do have a genuine zeal for God). However, it does not then follow that *every* man turns out to be a liar (3:4), and still much less the final conclusion that *all* are under sin (3:9).[51]

As a result of his reasoning, Räisänen further emphasizes that Paul in Romans 1–2 is speaking about grave offenses against the Law. Gross sins are put under fire. There is absolutely no talk of impure motives or the like.[52]

In order to take forward the discussion with Räisänen, each of his arguments will be dealt with in turn. First, the focus lies on the moral situation of the Gentiles according to 2:14–15, 26–27 and then moves on to the moral condition of the Jews according to 2:1–3, 21–24.

4.2.1.2. The Moral Situation of the Gentiles

From a methodological view, Räisänen's procedure seems quite precarious. He simply assumes that Rom. 2:14–15 and 26–27 must be explained together and in the same way. Given that a certain interpretation does not fit either the one or the other passage, he draws the conclusion that it cogently fits neither

46 Op. cit., 98–99.
47 Op. cit., 98.
48 Op. cit., 98 n. 26.
49 Op. cit., 98–99.
50 Op. cit., 106.
51 Op. cit., 99–100.
52 Op. cit., 98: "There is absolutely no talk of motives and the like; gross sins are put under fire."

the one nor the other passage.[53] Therefore, his argumentation remains a half measure with obvious shortcomings.[54] Accordingly, vv. 14–15 and 26–27 should be interpreted separately and not necessarily in the same way.

(1) Verses 14–15

On closer examination, vv. 14–15 do not confirm that some Gentiles really fulfill the Law. Räisänen fails to carry conviction with his view. The following objections are raised against his exegetical analysis:

(a) The Gentiles *per definitionem* would no longer be Gentiles if they fulfilled the whole Law.[55]

(b) In line with 1:18–32, Paul repeats in 2:12 that the Gentiles do sin. It seems hardly plausible that he contradicts himself already in 2:14–15 and avows something else.[56]

(c) In 2:15, Paul indeed emphasizes that the Gentiles do not even fulfill the "natural" law. He states that their thoughts (consciences) accuse them (for sins they committed).[57]

(d) The conjunction ὅταν (v. 14) does not exactly mean "when," but "whenever" or "as often as."[58] Thus it is not about the continual but the potential and momentary fulfilling of the Law by the Gentiles.[59]

(e) The expression τὰ τοῦ νόμου (v. 14) stands not for "the whole Law," even though the amount and extent of the commandments are not diminished. Paul does not define exactly what good the Gentiles do. Yet he absolutely denies that they fulfill all of the Law.[60]

---

53 The procedure of Räisänen comes out clearly in 1983, 104–5. There he tries to posit solely on vv. 14–15 that neither vv. 14–15 nor vv. 26–27 relate to the Gentile Christians. See further below. Cf. also Riedl 1965, 198–207, 217–29.

54 It may well be that vv. 14–15 and 26–27 must be explained separately and in different ways. Cf. my interpretation below.

55 Thurén 1986, 175.

56 Cf. Wilckens 1978, 1:133. He writes: "Paulus kann nach 1,18–32 und nach 2,12 nur Ausnahmefälle aus der *massa perditionis* der heidnischen Sünder meinen."

57 See already Schlier 1938a, 268n. He affirms: "Oft freilich wird der Gedankengang im Anschluß an V.13 so verstanden, als hebe Paulus hervor, daß die Heiden doch das Gesetz tun, und als wolle er den Juden die Heiden als Täter des Gesetzes gegenüberstellen. Es geht aber ganz deutlich sowohl in V. 14 als auch in V. 15 nicht um die Behauptung, daß die Heiden das Gesetz tun, sondern daß sie es kennen, bzw. daß es unter ihnen waltet."

58 W. Bauer 1988, s.v.

59 Riedl 1965, 222: "Als temporale Partikel wird man 'wenn immer' (ὅταν) in V. 14 nur von einer möglichen und öfter wiederkehrenden Handlung verstehen dürfen. [. . .] Mit Vorliebe wird es gebraucht von regelmässig wiederholter Handlung: sooft als, jedesmal wenn [. . .]." But alas, Riedle (op. cit., 227) finally reasons away his philological comment! See further Schmidt 1962, 47; Zahn 1925, 124–25.

60 Feine 1899, 116: "[. . .] vielmehr bedeutet τὰ τοῦ νόμου 'das, was zum Bereich des Gesetzes gehört'. Das ist nicht gerade die Summe desjenigen, was das Gesetz gebietet, 'das ganze Gesetz', aber die Erfüllung des Umfanges der Gesetzesgebote wird auch durchaus

(f) By their partial fulfillment of the Law, the Gentiles do not avoid the most serious kind of all sins, namely, ungratefulness toward God. They do not glorify him as they should (1:21, cf. 1:25; 2:17, 23–24, 29; 3:27; 4:2; 5:2–3, 11; 7:25; 9:5; 11:33–36).[61]

In sum, it follows that Räisänen is simply wrong. In no case does Paul contend that some Gentiles fulfill the Law. What does he mean then? Without a doubt, Räisänen rightly rejects the interpretations that vv. 14–15 only hypothetically speak of the Gentiles[62] or that they actually speak of Gentile Christians.[63] Besides, vv. 14–15 do not, according to him, suggest that some Gentiles now and then obey (some) commandments perfectly.[64] To be sure, he agrees that an interpretation of that kind would be adequate, especially on account of v. 14. But it would not do justice to vv. 26–27, since the expression τὸν νόμον τελοῦσα (v. 27) relates to the whole Law.[65] In the final analysis, Räisänen does not bring forth any further evidence.[66] His decisive argument falls short in this context.

---

nicht beschränkt." See further, e.g., Bassler 1982, 145–46; Käsemann 1980, 58; Murray 1982, 1:73; Stalder 1962, 261–62; Zahn 1925, 124. Räisänen (1983, 103 n. 51) follows Feine, without noticing that by the expression τὰ τοῦ νόμου this does not mean "the whole Law." Gaston (1987, 31, 105–6) and Walker (1960, 35) suppose that τὰ τοῦ νόμου designates the sins of the Gentiles (1:18–32)! In contrast, Flückiger (1952, 35) takes to himself the liberty of thinking that Paul is aiming at the Christian faith!

61 Cf. Thurén 1986, 177. See also Schlier 1938, 115–16, 123.

62 Räisänen 1983, 103–4. See also Althaus 1951a, 46; Flückiger 1952, 22; Joest 1951, 166; Snodgrass 1986, 73–74. Differently, Van Dülmen 1968, 77, 82; Thielman 1989, 92–96. Cf. Bornkamm 1970, 110.

63 Räisänen 1983, 104–5. See also Althaus 1951a, 46; Bassler 1982, 141–45; Bornkamm 1970, 107–10; Kuhr 1964, 252–61; Kuß 1954, 77–98; Snodgrass 1986, 73–75; Stalder 1962, 261. Opposingly Cranfield 1982, 1:155–56; Feine 1899, 122–26; Flückiger 1952, 26–39; König 1976, 53–60; Mundle 1934, 249–56; Souček 1956, 99–113; F. Watson 1986, 121–22. Maybe even Bruce 1982, 33. According to Räisänen (1983, 104 n. 55), Zahn as well supports the reading that vv. 14–15 speak of Gentile Christians, but in reality, he writes: "Dadurch ist so nachdrücklich wie möglich ausgeschlossen, daß Pl hier [. . .] Heidenchristen im Sinn habe" (1925, 123).

64 Räisänen 1983, 103. He directs himself above all against Nygren (1979, 128–32).

65 Räisänen 1983, 103. Cf. Riedl 1965, 227.

66 To be sure, Räisänen also tries to establish his view on the basis of vv. 14–15. He (1983, 103) underscores: "As for verses 14–15, the phrase ἔθνη τὰ μὴ νόμον ἔχοντα is analogous to ἔθνη τὰ μὴ διώκοντα δικαιοσύνην (9,30); Paul has an unspecified number of Gentiles in mind—whether many or few he does not indicate. Moreover, there is in the expression τὰ τοῦ νόμου nothing to suggest a limitation of the number of the precepts fulfilled. As a comparison with corresponding nominalizations shows, it means in general 'that which belongs to the scope of the law'; the quantity of the commandments fulfilled is not limited." However, the quotation does not demonstrate the impossibility of the interpretation that some Gentiles now and then succeed in observing what the Law demands. For the expression τὰ τοῦ νόμου, see above.

On the basis of v. 27, he cannot conclude that vv. 14–15 speak of some sinless Gentiles.[67] His conclusion conspicuously conflicts with the facts (see above).

Strictly speaking, vv. 14–15 do not indicate that some Gentiles sometimes fulfill certain commandments perfectly. Paul formulates v. 14 with insight. The phrase ὅταν γὰρ ἔθνη [. . .] τὰ τοῦ νόμου ποιῶσιν maintains that the Gentiles occasionally (ὅταν)[68] do such things as the Law commands (τὰ τοῦ νόμου).[69] It is not a matter of a perfect fulfillment of some (much less all) commandments.[70]

All said, vv. 14–15, taken as a whole, show that the Gentiles now and then to a certain extent fulfill some commandments.[71] Paul sets forth his train of thought from vv. 12–13. He tries to explain how those who do not have the Mosaic Law can anyway commit sin (v. 12),[72] as well as act as if they know the Mosaic Law (v. 13).[73] He then finds an original solution to his problem: the Gentiles are "a law to themselves" (v. 14) or "the work of the law" is written on their hearts (v. 15). In support of his notion, he appeals to the indisputable fact that they do at least a little good.[74]

(2) Verses 26–27

No doubt, vv. 26–27 emphasize that the uncircumcised (ἡ ἀκροβυστία) fulfill the Law. Still, it is anything but clear what the text ultimately means. Many

---

67 Räisänen further argues on the basis of v. 27: "In addition, the 'casual' interpretation does not match the polemical function of the verses. Gentiles fulfilling just a few requirements of the law could hardly condemn the Jew (as v. 27 states), for undoubtedly, he has fulfilled a few things as well!" The conclusion harks back simply and solely to the hypothesis that vv. 14–15 and 26–27 must be explained in the same way. Riedl (1965, 223–29) establishes his argumentation largely on the same hypothesis.

68 See above point (d).

69 See above point (e).

70 Käsemann 1980, 58; Kuß 1954, 90–91, 95–96, 98; Murray 1982, 1:73; Schmidt 1962, 47; Zahn 1925, 124–25. Cf. further Barrett 1967, 51; Schlier 1938a, 268–69; 1977, 77–78. For the meaning of the verb ποιεῖν, see below.

71 Cf. Barrett 1967, 51: "[. . .] and in any case to suggest that the Gentiles kept the moral law would make nonsense of Paul's thought as a whole, since in the next chapter he conducts a detailed argument to prove that all men without exception, Jews and Greeks, are 'under sin' [. . .]." Similarly, Murray 1982, 1:73. See also Moo 2018, 159 n. 307.

72 Cf. commentaries. Similarly, Barrett 1967, 51; Bornkamm 1970, 98–99; Murray 1982, 1:72; Schlier 1977, 77; Walker 1960, 304; F. Watson 1986, 215 n. 45. Cf. Käsemann 1980, 57–58; Kuhr 1964, 254; Stuhlmacher 1985, 96.

73 Cf. commentaries. See also Althaus 1966, 25; Barrett 1967, 51; Bassler 1984, 51–52; Bornkamm 1970, 98–101; Riedl 1965, 199; Schlier 1977, 77; Schmidt 1962, 47; Stuhlmacher 1985, 96; Zahn 1925, 122. Cf. additionally Cranfield 1982, 1:155; Flückiger 1952, 26; Kuhr 1964, 254; Kuß 1954, 88–90; Michel 1978, 117; Murray 1982, 1:72; Nygren 1979, 128; Synofzik 1977, 81.

74 Althaus 1966, 25; Käsemann 1980, 59–60; Kuß 1954, 88–90; Lietzmann 1971, 40–41; Michel 1978, 118–21; Murray 1982, 1:73–74; Nygren 1979, 128–31; Riedl 1965, 199–202, 223; Schlier 1938a, 268–70; 1977, 78; Schmidt 1962, 48; Wilckens 1978, 1:134; Zahn 1925, 126–27.

diverging alternatives open up. Exegetes disagree whether ἡ ἀκροβυστία refers to Gentiles[75] or to Gentile Christians.[76] Besides, some of them maintain that the Jews first stand in contrast with the Gentiles but then, beginning at either v. 27 or v. 29, rather more accurately with the Gentile Christians.[77] Considering the various alternatives, it appears at the present impossible to arrive at full consensus. At any rate, one evident fact remains. It turns out that the Pauline terminology in vv. 26–29 becomes conspicuously "Christian" (cf. τὰ δικαιώματα τοῦ νόμου in v. 26 with τὸ δικαίωμα τοῦ νόμου in Rom. 8:4; λογισθήσεται in v. 26 with Rom. 4:3–8; v. 27 with Rom. 7:5–6; vv. 28–29 with 2 Cor. 3:6–7; Phil. 3:3; Col. 2:11).[78] Indeed, one gains—as Räisänen himself concedes[79]—the impression that Paul is no longer aiming at the Gentiles as such. So it follows that he is aiming at the Gentile Christians. Further, since the "Christian" terminology begins already in v. 26, Paul should not first in v. 27 (much less in v. 29) contrast Gentile Christians with Jews. So it follows that he is contrasting Gentile Christians with Jews in the whole passage (vv. 25–29).[80] In sum, he does not maintain in the slightest that the non-Christian Gentiles fulfill the Law.

In consequence, 2:14–15 and 26–27 do not run counter to either 1:18–32 or 3:9. Räisänen's interpretation (particularly in reference to 2:14–15) proves quite artificial. He fails to carry conviction. Besides, one generally endeavors to keep one's thought consistent. Hence at least some sort of consistency ought to appear in Romans 1–2 also. It does not seem convincing that the passage overflows with pure nonsense. No wonder if that kind of interpretation does not stand up under critical examination.

Before moving on, one issue still needs to be addressed. When Paul depicts all the Gentiles in Romans 1–2 as *massa perditionis*, does he not overstate his case? In other words, does he suggest that every Gentile is, for instance, a homosexual and idolater? Certainly not! In another context, Räisänen emphasizes

75 Althaus 1966, 27–28; Barret 1967, 58–61; Bassler 1982, 141–45; Bornkamm 1970, 110; Kuhr 1964, 253–54; Michel 1978, 132–35; Nygren 1979, 138–41; Riedl 1965, 209–13; Snodgrass 1986, 81. Cf. Bassler 1984, 50; Schmidt 1962, 54–55.

76 Cranfield 1982, 1:173–76; Flückiger 1952, 39–41; Murray 1982, 1:86–90; Souček 1956, 103–5; Zahn 1925, 144–48. Cf. Stalder 1962, 263 n. 13.

77 From v. 27 on: see, e.g., Schlier 1977, 88. From v. 29 on: see, e.g., Käsemann 1980, 71; Synofzik 1977, 82–83. Cf. Räisänen 1983, 105 n. 64; Westerholm 1984, 235, 239; Wilckens 1978, 1:155–60.

78 Particularly Schlier 1977, 88.

79 Räisänen 1983, 105 n. 64.

80 Ibid. Schlier (1977, 88) writes with little logic in his comment on 2:27: "Unbewußt geht Paulus vom Heiden zum Heidenchristen über. Er sieht den Heiden im Licht des Heidenchristen. Die Terminologie seiner Darlegungen wird auffallend 'christlich'. Vgl. schon [. . .] 2,26 mit 8,4 [. . .]." But why should Paul *first* in v. 27 pass over from Gentiles to Gentile Christians even though his terminology becomes "Christian" *already* in v. 26? And why should he "unconsciously" pass over from Gentiles to Gentile Christians if his terminology is "conspicuously" Christian?

that Paul, in agreement with strong Jewish tradition, characterizes the outside pagan world as *massa perditionis*.[81] In the Jewish tradition (especially in the pseudepigraphic literature), there are indeed plenty of parallels to Rom. 1:18–32 (or more precisely to 1:29–31).[82] It suffices to quote one example from Wisdom of Solomon (that lies beneath the argumentative surface in Romans 1–2[83]):

> Then it was not enough to go astray concerning the knowledge of God, but though living in great strife through ignorance, they call such great evils peace. For whether performing ritual murders of children or secret mysteries or frenzied revels connected with strange laws, they no longer keep either their lives or their marriages pure, but they either kill one another by treachery or grieve one another by adultery. And all things are an overwhelming confusion of blood and murder, theft and deceit, corruption, unfaithfulness, tumult, perjury, turmoil of those who are good, forgetfulness of favors, defilement of souls, sexual perversion, disorder in marriages, adultery and debauchery. For the worship of idols that may not be named is the beginning and cause and end of every evil. For they either rave in a state of euphoria or prophesy lies or live unrighteously or readily commit perjury, for because they trust in lifeless idols, when they swear wicked oaths, they expect to suffer no harm. But on both accounts justice will pursue them: because they thought wrongly about God through devoting themselves to idols and in deceit swore unrighteously through despising holiness. For it is not the power of those by whom they swear, but justice for those who sin that always pursues the transgression of the unrighteous. (14:22–31 NETS)[84]

Wisdom of Solomon (respectively the traditional Jewish polemics) raises just as extravagant accusations against the Gentiles as does Rom. 1:18–32.[85] For sure, Paul and the other Jewish authors wished to include exceptionally gross sins in the catalog of vices. But none of them could have had in mind that every Gentile commits every iniquity named, but rather that all of the iniquities

81 Räisänen 1980, 308, 310; 1983, 110.

82 Billerbeck 1926, 75. See also Kuß 1954, 86; Schulz 1958, 164–66.

83 See below 4.2.1.3.

84 Cf. Holmes in Charles 1963, 558–59.

85 Cf. Eising 1959, 407: "Der Bilderdienst ist so sehr an der unbedingten Glaubensüberzeugung des Verfassers [that is, the author of Wisdom] gemessen, daß es auch hier nicht zu einem wirklichen Verständnis für den Gegner, sondern zu starker Schwarz-Weiß-Zeichnung kommt. Bei allen Götzendienern sollen 'ohne Unterschied' alle möglichen schlechten Taten herrschen (14,25)." Already Feldmann (1926, 101) does Wisdom of Solomon more justice: "Der Verf. hat die heidnische Sittenlosigkeit in einem erschreckenden Gemälde uns vorgeführt. Wer behauptet, er habe die Farben zu grell aufgetragen, übersieht, daß selbst Heiden (wie Seneca) die Verbundenheit von Götzendienst und Unsittlichkeit erkannt und mit harten Worten beklagt haben." Cf. further Ziener 1970, 96, 106.

named really occur among the Gentiles (cf. 1 Cor. 6:11: "And such were some of you.").[86] In brief, it is Räisänen's own argumentation that overstates itself here.[87]

4.2.1.3. The Moral Situation of the Jews

Without further explanation, Räisänen maintains that Paul already in Rom. 2:1 proceeds to demonstrate the sinfulness of the Jews.[88] Many exegetes are of the same opinion.[89] However, some additional clarification is needed here. In vv. 1–16, Paul speaks at least not directly to the Jews (cf. later v. 17). He writes explicitly ὦ ἄνθρωπε (vv. 1, 3) and πᾶς ὁ κρίνων (v. 1). Should one really understand those common expressions to mean only the Jews or the Jews at all? Before continuing the discussion with Räisänen, his basic assumption has to be dealt with more carefully.

Behind the Pauline polemics in Romans 1–2 obviously lies Wisdom of Solomon.[90] The points of contact are manifold. Both linguistic similarities and theological parallels are found (see below). In the first chapter, Paul sets forth in agreement with Wisdom of Solomon, for example:

(1) Creation bears witness to the Creator (Rom. 1:19–20; Wisd. of Sol. 13:1–19).

(2) Idolatry is based on pure folly (Rom. 1:21–23, 25; Wisd. of Sol., principally chapters 13–15).

(3) Idol worship leads to lewdness (Rom. 1:24–28; Wisd. of Sol. 14:12).

(4) Gentiles make themselves guilty of gross sins (Rom. 1:21–32; Wisd. of Sol. 14:23–31).

(5) They are without excuse (Rom. 1:20; Wisd. of Sol. 13:8).

86 See already Schlier 1938, 121: "Und natürlich sollen die aufgezählten Laster nicht jeden Heiden und nicht jede heidnische Gemeinschaft charakterisieren. Gerade die drängende und ungeordnete Fülle der genannten Übel verrät, daß es sich nur um einen Gesamtdurchblick durch das heidnische Leben handelt." Also 1977, 66. See further Thurén 1986, 177. Cf. Westerholm 1988, 158–59.

87 Similarly, T. R. Schreiner 1998, 97–98.

88 Räisänen 1983, 97–101. For sure, v. 1 is no marginal gloss. In contrast to Bultmann 1947, 200; Käsemann 1980, 50. Correctly, e.g., Bornkamm 1970, 95 n. 4; Schlier 1977, 68 n. 1; Wilckens 1978, 1:123.

89 Bornkamm 1970, 94–95; Lietzmann 1971, 37–39; Marcus 1989, 69; Michel 1978, 112–13; Murray 1982, 1:54–56; Nygren 1979, 119–25; Riedl 1965, 190–92; Sanday and Headlam 1920, 53–54; Stalder 1962, 259; Synofzik 1977, 80; F. Watson 1986, 109–10. Cf. also Wilckens 1978, 1:122–25. Flückiger (1954, 155–57) suggests that the discourse on the Jews begins already with 1:32! Gaston (1987, 122) strangely assumes that 1:18–3:20 (with the exception of 2:17–29) relates to the Gentiles alone.

90 Bornkamm 1970, 96; Caird 1978, 540; Cranfield 1982, 1:141, 144; Flückiger 1952, 19; 1954, 154–57; Käsemann 1980, 49; Langerbeck 1967, 96–99; Lietzmann 1971, 38–39; Lührmann 1965, 23; Nygren 1979, 119–23; Sanday and Headlam 1920, 51–52; Schmidt 1962, 42; Snodgrass 1986, 77.

(6) God passes righteous judgment (Rom. 1:32; Wisd. of Sol. 12:13).[91]

From the beginning of the second chapter, Paul astonishingly turns against this very Wisdom of Solomon as made known particularly in vv. 1–6.[92] On closer examination, his critical notions become apparent.

Wisdom of Solomon affirms the judgment of God over the Gentiles. Because of idolatry and all sorts of vices, they are with full justice forever condemned (chapters 11–19). Even though the Jews themselves sin, they are nevertheless not damned nor hindered from judging the Gentiles (ibid.). In the final analysis, the conclusion harks back to the given specific logic. Wisdom of Solomon brings forward that

(1) God's wrath falls exclusively on the Gentiles:

> For when they were tested, although they were being disciplined in mercy, they learned how the impious, being judged in anger, were tormented. For these you put to the test like a father giving a warning, but the others you examined like a stern king passing sentence. (11:9–10 NETS)[93]

(2) The Jews escape God's wrath because of their knowledge of him and his mercy:

> But you, our God, are kind (χρηστός) and true, long-suffering (μακρόθυμος) and ordering all things with mercy. For even if we sin, we are yours, knowing your might, but knowing we are considered yours, we will not sin; for to know you is perfect righteousness, and to recognize your might is the root of immortality. (15:1–3 NETS)[94]

(3) God in his wrath shows patience in order to give the Gentiles a chance to repent:

> You have mercy on all, because you can do all things, and you overlook the sins of human beings that they may repent (εἰς μετάνοιαν). (11:23 NETS; cf. 12:10–11)[95]

(4) The Jews should bear in mind the goodness or forbearance of God in their judging:

> While therefore you chastise us, you scourge our enemies ten thousand times more in order that, when we judge (κρίνοντες), we may think about your goodness and, when we are judged, we may look for mercy. (12:22 NETS)[96]

91 Cf. Langerbeck 1967, 96–99; Nygren 1979, 120; Sanday and Headlam 1920, 51–52.

92 Lietzmann 1971, 38–39; Nygren 1979, 121–23; Schmidt 1962, 42.

93 Cf. Holmes in Charles 1963, 552.

94 Cf. Holmes in Charles 1963, 559.

95 Cf. Holmes in Charles 1963, 554.

96 Cf. Holmes in Charles 1963, 555. For above remarks, see first of all Nygren 1979, 120–21.

In Romans 2, Paul takes on the task of correcting the former four assertions of Wisdom of Solomon. He strives to do nothing less than overthrow the Jewish confidence in God and turn it into a reprehensible, egocentric arrogance and bigotry. How does he achieve his goal? According to vv. 1–3, no one has the right to judge his fellow men if he commits the same sins himself. Since the Jews do similar things as the Gentiles, they are all without exception condemned. In contrast to Wisdom of Solomon (see above), Paul brings to light that

(1) God's wrath falls also upon the Jews:

> Do you suppose, O man—you who judge [κρίνων] those who practice such things and yet do them yourself—that you will escape the judgment of God? (v. 3)

(2) The knowledge of God and his mercy rather increases the guilt of the unrepentant Jews:

> Or do you presume on the riches of his kindness [τῆς χρηστότητος] and forbearance and patience [τῆς μακροθυμίας] [. . .]? (v. 4a)

(3) God in his wrath shows patience in order to give the Jews as well a chance to repent:

> [. . .] not knowing that God's kindness is meant to lead you to repentance [εἰς μετάνοιαν]? (v. 4b)

(4) The Jews should in their judging bear in mind the justice and impartiality of God, viz. his final frightful judgment of them:

> But because of your hard and impenitent heart you are storing up wrath for yourself on the day of wrath when God's righteous judgment will be revealed. He will render to each one according to his works. (vv. 5–6; cf. vv. 7–11)

In sum, the Jews should relinquish their haughty judging of the Gentiles and confess themselves to be condemned sinners as all others. Then they will turn to God through Christ and gain eternal life in faith.[97]

To top it off, the lexical similarities between Wisdom of Solomon and Rom. 1:18–2:5 (see above and the table below) corroborates the conclusion that the latter passage really takes a stand on the former pseudepigraphic writing.[98]

As shown, Paul goes already in Rom. 2:1 into his polemic rationale to substantiate and demonstrate the sinfulness of the Jews. He maintains that they are not better than all others. The basic assumption of Räisänen indeed holds true but must be put more precisely. Since Paul explicitly addresses "superior" people (vv. 1, 3), he hardly discusses matters only with Jews. Rather, they become some kind of deterrent archetypes representing all those (for instance, the Greek moral

97 Cf. Lietzmann 1971, 38–39; Nygren 1979, 121–23. Neither one satisfactorily confronts Rom. 2:1–6 with Wisdom of Solomon. Correctly, T. R. Schreiner 1998, 109–10.

98 Lietzmann 1971, 38–39; Nygren 1979, 123; Sanday and Headlam 1920, 51–52.

philosophers or members of rigorous religions) who raise themselves above others to judge them.[99] Paul knows perfectly well that at least the best among the Gentiles, to say nothing of Jews, do not consider themselves as wicked sinners or the same as malicious heathens (1:18–32). Only after further reflection (2:1–29) does he set up the whole world as *massa perditionis* (3:10–18).[100]

The analysis so far has prepared the ground for further confrontation with Räisänen. In accordance with his main argument, the focus will next move on to the critical question of whether Romans 2 overstates the sinfulness of the Jews and the foremost Gentiles for propagandistic aims. Does Paul really play with fire and get burned? In that case, he surely loses the debate with his antagonists. It is particularly worth noting that the emphasis does not lie on the actual sinfulness of each human being. At least Wisdom of Solomon shows that even the Jews do not consider themselves sinless.[101] Rather, the issue revolves around the unheard-of charge that ultimately the most excellent people commit sin just as all others. As made known, the crucial passages in Romans 2 are vv. 1–3 and 21–24.

(1) Verses 1–3

To begin with, Räisänen himself remarks that vv. 1–3 more likely relate to the catalog of vices (1:28–31) than idolatry and homosexuality (1:18–27).[102] His explanation seems adequate and reasonable.[103] As a consequence, in the following the Pauline text shall be investigated on that basis.

In agreement especially with the Stoic and Jewish traditions, Paul places the inner motives of outward actions in the foreground.[104] Both idioms—"*filled* (πεπληρωμένους) with all manner of unrighteousness, evil, covetousness, malice" and "*full* (μεστούς) of envy, murder, strife, deceit, maliciousness" (1:29)—include sinful acts as well as sinful intentions.[105] In addition, such things as slander, hatred (against God), brutality, arrogance, inventive ingenuity of evil doing, senselessness, faithlessness, lovelessness or unmercifulness (see 1:29–31)

---

99 See Althaus 1966, 22; Barrett 1962, 42–44; Bassler 1982, 135–36; Cranfield 1982, 1:142; Schlier 1938a, 263; 1977, 68; Schmidt 1962, 42; Snodgrass 1986, 80. Cf. also Käsemann 1980, 48–50; Michel 1978, 113.

100 See below.

101 See above.

102 Räisänen 1983, 98 n. 26.

103 Cf. Althaus 1966, 22: "[. . .] er [the one who judges] tut ja dasselbe, wie der, über den er sich aburteilend ergeht; wenn nicht gerade Götzendienst und widernatürliche Unzucht, so doch irgend etwas von dem in Kap. 1 Genannten [. . .]." Similarly, Barrett 1967, 43.

104 See, e.g., Lietzmann 1971, 35–36. Similarly, Käsemann 1980, 45–47; Michel 1978, 106–7; Schlier 1977, 64–65; Schmidt 1962, 40; Wilckens 1978, 1:111–14; Zahn 1925, 103–6. Cf. Barrett 1967, 40; Cranfield 1982, 1:129–33; Murray 1982, 1:50.

105 Above all Schlier 1977, 64. See also Cranfield 1982, 1:129–30; Käsemann 1980, 45–46; Michel 1978, 106–7; Murray 1982, 1:50; Sanday and Headlam 1920, 47; Schmidt 1962, 40; Wilckens 1978, 1:113; Zahn 1925, 103–5.

in no case exclude wicked states of mind.[106] In brief, the cursory perusal of the listed vices strongly contradicts the simple prejudgment that Paul does not speak about impure "motives and the like."[107] Certainly he does![108]

This said, the list of vices contains besides some "big" offenses also many "small" faults which a person does not necessarily do (such as greed, depravity, envy, malice, slander, defamation, hatred, or arrogance). In fact, Paul uses the verbs ποιεῖν (1:28, 32) and πράσσειν (1:32) respectively, without making a clear differentiation between thoughts, words, and acts. According to his summary usage of speech, the Gentiles also do evil when it is "merely" a matter of the mind or mouth.[109] His way of speaking might go back to Jesus himself (cf., e.g., Matt. 5:21–30; Mark 7:20–23).

Apparently, the verbs ποιεῖν and πράσσειν embrace the same meaning in 2:1–3. Therefore, the judgmental person (ὁ κρίνων, v. 1) does evil also when he carries it out "only" in word or thought. Even outwardly good works remain insufficient if they are inwardly contaminated by latent corrupt intentions. Truly good works originate from pure motives.[110]

As a result, vv. 1–3 point out that the judgmental person at least in his innermost self "does" the same as the Gentiles (1:29–31).[111] He might not be "*filled* with all manner of unrighteousness, evil, covetousness, malice" and "*full* of envy, murder, strife, deceit, maliciousness" (1:29), but he is hardly *entirely free* of them (or some other iniquities). For sure, he sometimes also does evil in concrete acts. The list of vices contains many such general misdeeds (for example, wickedness, strife, disobedience to parents, lovelessness), which none has avoided altogether. On the whole, it shows that vv. 1–3 do not shoot beyond the target.

(2) Verses 21–24

As to vv. 21–24, Räisänen simply asserts that here every Jew is insulted as a thief, adulterer, and temple robber. Yet he does not vindicate his categorical assertion. It is not based on good reasons or any reasons at all.[112] On closer

106 Barrett 1967, 40–41; Cranfield 1982, 1:129–33; Käsemann 1980, 45–47; Michel 1978, 106–7; Murray 1982, 1:50; Sanday and Headlam 1920, 47–48; Schlier 1977, 64–65; Schmidt 1962, 40; Wilckens 1978, 1:113–14; Zahn 1925, 103–5.

107 *Pace* Räisänen 1983, 98. Differently, Sanders 1983, 129: "The conclusion which would naturally follow from chapter 2 is 'repent and obey the law from the bottom of your heart, so that you will be a true Jew.' [. . .] surely what one should do is to examine one's motives to make sure they are pure, to be sure that observance of the law is not merely external [. . .]."

108 T. R. Schreiner 1998, 108 n. 4 (in reference to Laato).

109 See also my interpretation of Rom. 7:14–25 below.

110 See below particularly 4.2.3.3–4.2.3.5.

111 In contrast, Bornkamm 1970, 96: "In der Aufrichtung der 'eigenen' Gerechtigkeit (10,3) und im Sich-rühmen tut der Jude 'dasselbe' wie der Heide: er behauptet sich selbst frevlerisch vor Gott."

112 Räisänen 1983, 98–101.

examination, there are no direct statements. Instead, distinctive accusatory questions are set forth in vv. 21–24.[113] In formal respect, it is about an interrogation.[114] Definitely Paul, as public prosecutor, presumes that at least some Jews have to answer one or more questions affirmatively. But in no place does he suggest that every Jew without exception should answer all the questions affirmatively.[115]

Moreover, Räisänen misleadingly appeals to Rom. 3:3. He maintains that it comes into conflict with the second chapter because now only some (τινες) of the Jews appear as unfaithful.[116] On further reflection, his conclusion fails to carry conviction. It has to be taken into account that the context changes. Paul puts forth the urgent question of whether the unfaithfulness of some Jews annul the faithfulness of God. Here, he first and foremost speaks of their attitude toward the covenant promises which ultimately point to Christ. The focus lies on the consummation of the salvation history that happens through the proclamation of the Gospel. The faithfulness of God shows itself just there, while the unfaithfulness of the Jews culminates in their refusal of the apostolic preaching.[117] As a consequence, the qualification "some" (τινες) does not suggest that Paul "on another level of his consciousness at least" (Räisänen)[118] disputes the sinfulness of other, in this case faithful, Jews. Their actual and factual sinfulness becomes apparent as they, in contrast to the unfaithful Jews, believe in the Messiah, Savior of sinners (see, e.g., Rom. 3:21–26).

To be sure, many exegetes have found fairly fanciful solutions to why Rom. 3:3 speaks of some unfaithful Jews notwithstanding that in reality most of the Jews reject the Gospel (see especially Rom. 11:1–10).[119] In my opinion, the

113 Correctly, Althaus 1966, 26; Barrett 1967, 54; Bassler 1982, 150 and 263 n. 106; Bornkamm 1966, 77; Cranfield 1982, 1:136; Käsemann 1980, 64; Lietzmann 1971, 42; Michel 1978, 126; Murray 1982, 1:80; Riedl 1965, 207; Schlier 1977, 81–82; Schmidt 1962, 50.

114 Thurén 1986, 176. Wilckens (1978, 1:149) speaks of "anklagenden Fragen"; Michel (1978, 130) of "vorwurfsvollen Fragen" or "anklagenden Aussagen"; and Cranfield (1982, 1:167) of "accusatory rhetorical questions."

115 Thurén 1986, 176. Cf. already Schlier 1938a, 272: "Natürlich will der Apostel nicht von jedem Juden behapten, daß er das Gesetz in der Weise übertritt, wie er eben ausführte, so wenig wie nach seinem Urteil ein jeder Heide von den Lastern befleckt ist, die 1,29ff. genannt werden." Similarly, F. Watson 1986, 114: "Paul does not state in Rom. 2,21ff that all Jewish teachers of the law are immoral." In a footnote, he points out that Räisänen "exaggerates at this point" (op. cit., 214 n. 38). Rightly, Snodgrass 1986, 76; Westerholm 1988, 188.

116 Räisänen 1983, 99.

117 Cranfield 1982, 1:180; Hall 1983, 186; Käsemann 1980, 73–74; Michel 1978, 138; Murray 1982, 1:93–94; Nygren 1979, 143–44; Sanday and Headlam 1920, 71; Schlier 1977, 92–93; Schmidt 1962, 57. Cf. Kertelge 1967, 64–70.

118 Räisänen 1983, 107.

119 Cf. Althaus 1966, 29: "Schon klingen die Töne von Kap.11 an; dort wird Paulus zeigen, wie Gottes Treue waltet und siegt. Diese Treue steht für ihn so unverrückt über allem, daß er in ihrem Lichte schon der Frage ihre Gestalt gegeben hat: nicht Israel, sondern nur 'einige' in Israel stellt er als bundesbrüchig hin!" Käsemann 1980, 75: "Näher liegt

solution is very simple. The qualification τινες (v. 3) forms the contrast to the generalization πᾶς ἄνθρωπος (v. 4). Paul underscores that not even the unfaithfulness of all humankind could nullify the faithfulness of God. In the same vein, he underlines that even less does the unfaithfulness of some (albeit the majority) Jews annul the faithfulness of God.

Additionally, it is worth noting that Paul in Romans 1–2 does not endeavor to prove empirically the guilt of all the Gentiles and the Jews. He does not set out to demonstrate in concrete terms that they without exception sin even in their very inner being and in multifarious manners. Indeed, he never says anything like that in his judicious exposé of their moral failures.[120] Strictly speaking, Paul confirms in 3:9 that he indicted (προῃτιασάμεθα) Gentiles as well as Jews. He accused them. He brought charges against them.[121] Definitely he presumes that they cannot defend themselves against all of his indictments (1:19; 2:1). Thus he lets God pass judgment (3:10–18).[122]

To sum up, Räisänen's own argumentation once again goes beyond the mark. By contrast, Paul does not overstate his case. He accurately and appropriately reprimands the moral situation of the Jews.[123]

Lexical Similarities Between Romans 1:18–2:5 and Wisdom of Solomon			
1:18	ἀδικίαν, ἀδικίᾳ	11:15 12:23	ἀδικίας ἀδίκως
1:20	κτίσεως νοούμενα ἀΐδιος δύναμις θειότης	13:3 13:4 2:23 13:4 18:9	ἔκτισεν νοησάτωσαν (cf. 13:1) ἀϊδιότητος ἀϊδίου δύναμιν, δυνατώτερος θειότητος (*hapax legomenon* in LXX)
1:21	ἐματαιώθησαν διαλογισμοῖς ἀσύνετος	13:1 11:15	μάταιοι λογισμῶν ἀσυνέτων

es, τίνες aus der Antithese zur neuen, durch den Glaubensgehorsam bestimmten Welt zu verstehen." Michel 1978, 138: "Die Einschränkung 'einige' (τίνες) will nicht Menschen entschuldigen oder ihr Vergehen verkleinern, sondern dessen Begrenztheit und Gottes Überlegenheit zum Ausdruck bringen."

120 *Pace* Räisänen 1983, 99–100. Correctly, Thurén 1986, 176.

121 Ibid. Furthermore, see Barrett 1967, 68–69; Michel 1978, 141; Murray 1982, 1:102 n. 9; Schlier 1977, 98; Schmidt 1962, 61; Zahn 1925, 165.

122 Becker 1989, 378–79; Barrett 1967, 69; Käsemann 1980, 81; Murray 1982, 1:102–3; Thurén 1986, 177; Zahn 1925, 165. In contrast, Schlier 1977, 98; Michel 1978, 142.

123 With approval, T. R. Schreiner 1998, 133–34.

Lexical Similarities Between Romans 1:18–2:5 and Wisdom of Solomon			
1:23	ἀφθάρτου, φθαρτοῦ	14:8	φθαρτόν (cf. 15:8)
	ὁμοιώματι	13:14	ὡμοίωσεν
	εἰκόνος . . . ἀνθρώπου	13:13	εἰκόνι ἀνθρώπου (cf. 14:15, 17; 15:5)
	ἑρπετῶν	11:15	ἑρπετά (cf. 12:23–24)
1:27	ὀρέξει (*hapax legomenon* in NT)	14:2	ὄρεξις
		15:5	ὄρεξιν
		16:2	ὀρέξεως
		16:3	ὄρεξιν
	πλάνης	11:15	πλανηθέντες
		12:24	πλάνης, ἐπλανήθησαν
		13:6	πλανῶνται
		14:22	πλανᾶσθαι
		15:4	ἐπλάνησεν
		17:1	ἐπλανήθησαν
1:19	τὸ γνωστὸν τοῦ θεοῦ	13:1	θεοῦ ἀγνωσία,
1:21	γνόντες τὸν θεόν		οὔτε ἐπέγνωσαν
1:28	οὐκ . . . τὸν θεὸν . . . ἐν	13:3	γνώτωσαν
	ἐπιγνώσει	14:22	τὴν τοῦ θεοῦ γνῶσιν,
			ἀγνοίας (cf. 16:16)
2:1	ὁ κρίνων	12:22	κρίνοντες
2:4	χρηστότητος	15:1	χρηστός
	μακροθυμίας		μακρόθυμος (cf. 16:2, 5, 10)
	εἰς μετάνοιαν	11:23	εἰς μετάνοιαν (see also 12:10, 19–20)
2:5	δικαιοκρισίας τοῦ θεοῦ	12:13	οὐκ ἀδίκως ἔκρινας

4.2.2. Romans 5:12

4.2.2.1. The Problem

Rom. 5:12, rich in content, consists of the following main assertions:

(a) Just as sin came into the world through one man, (b) and death through sin, (c) and so death spread to all men (d) because all sinned.[124]

Paul's argumentation appears quite contradictory. On the one hand, he maintains that all die on the basis of Adam's fall (a–c), but, on the other hand, he adds that ultimately all die by their own sins (d). Particularly R. Bultmann perceives where the problem lies: Paul gets into conflict with himself "[. . .] because he still wants to view even the death of men following Adam as the punishment or consequence of their own sin."[125] But with consideration to the context, "[. . .] it would have been enough to mention Adam's sin; the sins of

124 Kirby (1987, 283–86, especially 284) understands οὕτως "so" (v. 12c) "in responsion to ὥσπερ" (v. 12a), in order to remove the apparent anacoluthon in v. 12. But καὶ οὕτως (v. 12c) should not be interpreted in the sense of οὕτως καί (see vv. 15, 18, 19, 21).

125 Bultmann 1984, 252: "[. . .] weil er doch auch den Tod der auf Adam folgenden Menschen als Strafe oder Folge ihrer eigenen Sünde angesehen wissen will."

other people need not have been discussed."[126] Further, Bultmann writes in respect to vv. 15–18:

> Thus through Christ nothing more has been procured than the possibility of ζωή, which, however, will become the certain reality for believers. [. . .] It then makes sense to say analogously that through Adam the possibility of sin and death has been procured for the adamic humanity that is only realized through the culpable behavior of the individual for which he is responsible. However, whether this should be understood as the actual thought of Paul must remain questionable; for him, in any case, the factual common fallenness of adamic humanity into sin and death remains beyond question.[127]

E. Brandenburger has dealt meticulously with the same problem. He carries on (largely following Pelagius in contrast to Augustine) *expressis verbis* the classical dogma of *liberum arbitrium*.[128] In his opinion, v. 12d notes unequivocally "the freely willed acts for which everyone is therefore accountable and culpable" ("das frei-gewollte und darum verantwortlich-schuldhafte Tun aller"). However, the act of sinning should likewise not be misunderstood as "a *possibility* that *remains* free for the individual" ("eine frei *bleibende Möglichkeit* des einzelnen"). Paul raises "a *reservatio*, a correction over against the underlying and schematic thought of a fate" ("einen Vorbehalt, eine Korrektur gegenüber dem der zugrunde liegenden Schematik eignenden Verhängnisgedanken"). His "broken" ("gebrochen") or "inharmonic" ("unharmonisch") formulation in v. 12d expresses exactly the very "brokenness at issue" ("die Gebrochenheit in der *Sache*").[129] Accordingly, it follows:

> Paul brings to bear the total, inescapable fallenness of man to the power of sin and death, without understanding this falleness as a fate justified traditionally or otherwise outside his existence. On the other hand, he can maintain man's responsibility for his fallenness to sin and death without having to speak of a free remaining *liberum arbitrium*.[130]

---

126 Ibid.: "[. . .] hätte es genügt, Adams Sünde zu erwähnen; von der Sünde der übrigen Menschen brauchte nicht geredet zu werden." See also 1959, 154.

127 Bultmann 1984, 253: "Durch Christus ist also nicht mehr beschafft worden als die *Möglichkeit* der ζωή, die freilich bei den Glaubenden zur sicheren Wirklichkeit wird [. . .]. Es liegt dann nahe, analog zu sagen: durch Adam ist für die adamitische Menschheit die *Möglichkeit* der Sünde und des Todes beschafft worden, die erst durch das verantwortliche schuldhafte Verhalten der Einzelnen realisiert wird. Ob man das als den eigentlichen Gedanken des Paulus ansehen darf, muß allerdings fraglich bleiben; für ihn steht jedenfalls die faktische allgemeine Verfallenheit der adamitischen Menschheit an Sünde und Tod außer Frage." See also 1959, 158. Cf. H. Müller 1967, 86.

128 Brandenburger 1962, 218–19.

129 Op. cit., 176.

130 Op. cit., 219: "Paulus bringt das totale, unentrinnbare Verfallensein des Menschen an die Macht der Sünde und des Todes zur Geltung, ohne dieses Verfallensein als tradiertes oder sonstwie außer seiner Existenz begründetes Verhängnis zu verstehen. Er kann andererseits an der Verantwortlichkeit des Menschen für sein Verfallensein unter Sünde

However, Brandenburger does not adequately establish his point of view. What does he actually mean by his saying that no one remains free? Probably he suggests that every man (not only the original man) has, by his own decision to sin, lost the innate freedom of the will.

Thus Rom. 5:12 seems to run counter to the extremely pessimistic framework of Pauline anthropology. Next, more clarification is needed.

4.2.2.2. Various Solutions

Many exegetes have sought in one way or another to show that no inherent contradiction is really found in Rom. 5:12. Each one of their attempts concentrates on the analysis of ἐφ' ᾧ πάντες ἥμαρτον in v. 12d.[131] In the following, the focus lies on the most important contributions:

(1) From Augustine onward, several commentators have interpreted the compound ἐφ' ᾧ in reference to "one man," Adam (v. 12a). Hence, they translate it with "in him." Their traditional translation goes back to the Vulgate (*in quo*). The text reads that the whole of humankind participated in Adam (cf. Heb. 7:9–10!) and even in his sin.[132]

The Augustinian interpretation is no longer sustained. Simply put, the expression ἐφ' ᾧ does not mean the same as ἐν ᾧ. The translation "in him" leads astray.[133] Besides, the antecedent "one man" is too far removed for the ἐφ' ᾧ to refer to it.[134]

(2) According to another interpretation, the relative ᾧ should rather relate to the word "death," θάνατος (v. 12bc). E. Stauffer maintains that the preposition ἐπί means "in the direction of" ("in Richtung auf") (cf. Phil. 4:10; 2 Tim. 2:14; Wisd. of Sol. 2:23). He then paraphrases the end of v. 12 as follows: "the death to which they fell, man by man, through their sinning" ("der Tod, dem sie Mann für Mann durch ihr Sündigen verfielen").[135]

On behalf of Stauffer's solution, the preposition ἐπί sometimes stands for "in the direction of" ("in Richtung auf"), In addition, the word θάνατος goes well as the antecedent of the pronoun ᾧ.[136] Nevertheless, the repetition of "all" in

---

und Tod festhalten, ohne von einem freibleibenden liberum arbitrium sprechen zu müssen." Cf. Patte 1983, 268–69, 289.

131 See Brandenburger 1962, 168–80; Cranfield 1982, 1:274–81.

132 On the interpretation of Augustine and the history of its influence, see, e.g., Cranfield 1982, 1:276.

133 Cranfield 1982, 1:276; Freundorfer 1927, 233–34; Käsemann 1980, 139–40; Michel 1978, 187; Murray 1982, 1:183; Schlier 1977, 162; Wilckens 1978, 1:316.

134 Cranfield 1982, 1:276; Freundorfer 1927, 233; Schlier 1977, 163. See also Danker 1968, 436. His own attempt "of construing the relative ᾧ with νόμος as its implied antecedent" (428) fails to carry conviction.

135 Stauffer 1945, 248–49 n. 176. Cf. Zahn 1925, 265–69. Schmidt (1962, 98–99) follows Stauffer.

136 Cranfield 1982, 1:275. Cf. Danker 1968, 436.

v. 12cd shows that v. 12d explains v. 12c, especially the reason why humans one after another have died.[137] It makes better sense to translate ἐφ' ᾧ with "because," as in 2 Cor. 5:4 and Phil. 3:12 (cf. also 4:10).[138]

(3) The majority of the scholars translate the clause ἐφ' ᾧ πάντες ἥμαρτον correctly with "*because* all have sinned."[139] However, some of them dispute that v. 12d applies to the sins people themselves committed after Adam. In support of their view, the following main arguments are presented.

Given that v. 12d relates to every person's own transgressions,

a. the line of thought in vv. 13–14 would be wholly incomprehensible: Why must humankind from Adam to Moses die, although sin is not reckoned when there is no Law (v. 13) and although they had not sinned after the similitude of Adam's transgression (v. 14)?[140]
b. v. 12d would come into conflict with the context: Paul constantly reminds the reader that sin, death, and damnation are imposed on humankind solely on the basis of one transgression of one man (see vv. 12a–c, 15–19).[141]
c. v. 12d would stand in contradiction with vv. 15–19: Paul draws from the analogy between Adam and Christ the logical conclusion that humankind, as they were made sinful without their own fault but only for Adam's sake, also without their own merits but only for Christ's sake are made righteous (v. 19).[142]

As a result, v. 12d suggests that sin and death entered the world "because all have sinned (in Adam)."[143] As a consequence, Augustine's interpretation (see the first alternative) turns out to be theologically correct, although ἐφ' ᾧ should not be read along with the Vulgate as "in him" but rather as "because."[144]

In line with the preceding interpretation, the close context of v. 12 certainly deserves to be taken into consideration. Yet in light of the wider context, it is equally worth noticing that elsewhere in Romans Paul uses the verb ἁμαρτάνειν where he exclusively speaks about the sins that people have themselves

137 Ibid. See also Murray 1982, 1:182.

138 Already Freundorfer 1927, 232–38. See further Brandenburger 1962, 171–72; Cranfield 1982, 1:269; Käsemann 1980, 140; Michel 1978, 184; Murray 1982, 1:178; Schlier 1977, 158; Wilckens 1978, 1:306. Cf. Nygren 1979, 220–21.

139 Ibid.

140 Freundorfer 1927, 247–54; Murray 1982, 1:183; Nygren 1979, 221–22; Ridderbos 1987, 96. According to Ridderbos, the conjunction οὕτως (v. 12c) further would be senseless, if verse 12d referred to everyone's own sins.

141 Freundorfer 1927, 241–47; Murray 1982, 1:183–84; Nygren 1979, 221; Ridderbos 1987, 97.

142 Freundorfer 1927, 240–41; Murray 1982, 1:184; Nygren 1979, 221; Ridderbos 1987, 97–98.

143 Freundorfer 1927, 254–55; Murray 1982, 1:186; Ridderbos 1987, 96. Cf. Nygren 1979, 221.

144 Brandenburger 1962, 172–73; Cranfield 1982, 1:275.

committed.[145] If he had wished to say that all humankind had sinned already in Adam, why does he not say so unequivocally?[146]

(4) Eminent exegetes have distanced themselves from artificial solutions of all kinds and accepted the text at hand "as it stands." The controversial clause ἐφ' ᾧ πάντες ἥμαρτον, going "because all (as individuals) have sinned," still does not clash with the context.[147] Truly, v. 12d emphasizes that people did not die for Adam's sake alone, without their own guilt. The sin which came into the world through one man (v. 12a) has dominion in the world for the very reason that people themselves sin (v. 12d).[148]

Of all the interpretations, the last one seems preferable and most unrestricted. The verb ἁμαρτάνειν obviously links the attention to sins committed by people themselves (see especially Rom. 3:23).[149] Hence, v. 12 expresses at the same time the resulting universal calamity of Adam's fall as well as the personal guilt of his wicked posterity. Both aspects should be taken into careful consideration.

In the final analysis, however, it looks as if scholars, in their urgency to clarify the alleged contradiction in 5:12, have jumped out of the pan and into the fire. Their solution of one problem has brought other burning issues with it:

(a) How does v. 12 fit into the context (vv. 13–19)? If people are jointly responsible for their own calamity (v. 12), why should Adam be seen as the only guilty one (vv. 13–19)? The arguments for the third alternative (see above) still require closer examination. On the whole, scholars have not paid enough attention to each of them. They have not taken the context at face value.[150]

(b) As a consequence, do vv. 12–19 collapse into two conflicting theories on how sin dominates the world? Does Paul, for example, in v. 12 speak out his primary view, and then in vv. 15–19 his secondary thought in which he strays in his zeal to set Adam and Christ in relationship to each other?

145 Brandenburger 1962, 173–76; Cranfield 1982, 1:279; Danker 1968, 436, 438; Schlier 1977, 162; Wilckens 1978, 1:317.

146 Ibid.

147 Cranfield 1982, 1:280; Jüngel 1963, 51–52; Käsemann 1980, 140–41; Schlier 1977, 162–63; Wilckens 1978, 1:316–17.

148 Käsemann 1980, 141; Schlier 1977, 163. Cf. Cranfield 1982, 1:278–281; Michel 1978, 186–87; Wilckens 1978, 1:316–17.

149 Brandenburger 1962, 173–76; Cranfield 1982, 1:279; Danker 1968, 436, 438; Jüngel 1963, 52; Schlier 1977, 161; Westerholm 1988, 180.

150 Michel 1978, 186–87; Schlier 1977, 159–64; Wilckens 1978, 1:314–17. In their interpretation, they mainly deal with vv. 13–14 in the context of v. 12. Cranfield (1982, 1:278–79) suggests that v. 12d (in the sense of the fourth alternative) does not stand in contradiction to vv. 15–19, since Paul does not set Adam and Christ in complete contrast to each other. It would be "surely enough for the justification of the analogy that in both cases the act of one man has far-reaching consequences for all other men [. . .]" (278).

(c) To what extent has Adam's fall caused the culpability of his descendants? Does v. 12 indicate an innate depravity transmitted from Adam[151] or maybe not?[152] At least the clear evidence for the dogma of *peccatum originis* is missing in the academic discussion of Romans 5 so far.[153]

Thus some puzzling problems still remain unresolved. A further discussion is needed. In the following, v. 12 will be more closely read and analyzed as to its place in context (points a and b above) and the relation between the fall of Adam and the guilt of his descendants (point c above).

4.2.2.3. The Relation Between Adam's Sin and Human Sinfulness

The argumentation in Rom. 5:12 culminates in the notion that death caused by Adam's fall has passed to every person.[154] Here, the Greek word θάνατος is commonly understood as the termination of earthly life or the annihilation of human existence.[155] It or its derivations certainly do bear such a meaning (for example, 5:6, 8, 10; 6:3, 9–10; 8:34; 14:9, 15 speak of the death of Christ on the cross; for instance, 5:7; 7:2–3; 8:36, 38; 14:7–8 speak of the death of other people). Still, there are further nuances. Sometimes the Greek word θάνατος refers to eternal death in contrast to eternal life (most clearly in 6:23). It also relates to the "sacramental" death in Baptism (see especially 6:2, 4–8; 7:4). None of the former connotations fits 7:7–13, which stands in close relationship to 5:12.

Rom. 7:7–13 reads in the first person and speaks of an anxious experience with the Law of God:

> [. . .] I was once alive apart from the law, but when the commandment came, sin came alive and I died. The very commandment that promised life proved

---

151 Cranfield 1982, 1:275, 278–79; Schlier 1977, 160–63, 179–83.

152 Barrett 1967, 111; Dodd 1947, 80; Michel 1978, 193–94; Wilckens 1978, 1:316–17. Cf. Murray 1982, 1:184–87. They find no evidence for a traditional interpretation of *peccatum originis* here.

153 Despite his extensive interpretation, Cranfield (see 1982, 1:278–79) brings in reality no arguments in support of his thesis that v. 12 would indicate the corrupt and from Adam inherited nature of humankind. Schlier's argumentation (1977, 159–63, 179–83) has much more going for it. He exegetes the Pauline personification of *hamartia*. In light of Romans 5, sin extended through Adam's fall to a demonic dominion in the world (op. cit., 181–82). However, it still remains to be demonstrated that human nature is thereby absolutely depraved. Neither does Schlier's analysis of the concept of θάνατος (op. cit., 160–61) affirm his thesis. Cf. my interpretations further below.

154 Cf., e.g., Bultmann 1959, 153: "Das eigentliche Interesse des Satzes ist nicht das, den Ursprung der Sünde aufzuzeigen, sondern den Ursprung des Todes als Folie für das eigentliche Thema des Abschnitts: den Ursprung des (neuen) Lebens." See further H. Müller 1967, 84–85; Schlier 1977, 163.

155 Barrett 1967, 111; Cranfield 1982, 1:274; Freundorfer 1927, 227–30; Michel 1978, 186–87; Murray 1982, 1:181–83; Wilckens 1978, 1:315.

> to be death to me. For sin, seizing an opportunity through the commandment, deceived me and through it killed me. (vv. 9–11)

Apparently, death does not designate bodily death here. The "I" still lives physically after his own death and reports of himself. His monologue—as will be shown later—retells and reinterprets the Old Testament story of the fall (Genesis 3). The commandment that brought death picks up the divine threat: "But of the tree of the knowledge of good and evil you shall not eat, for in the day that you eat of it you shall surely die" (see Gen. 2:17).[156] Certainly Adam and Eve did not die any bodily death on the day they ate from the tree of the knowledge of good and evil. Nevertheless, they died, shall we say, spiritually (cf. Hosea 13:1).[157] The divine threat was fulfilled directly, but in an unexpected way.

Conceivably, the Old Testament psalms of lamentation and praise have served as a model for the I-style in Romans 7.[158] They frequently portray Hades (or Sheol) as the place where devotion and thanksgiving to God are silenced (for instance, Ps. 6:6; 30:10; 88:11–13; 115:17).[159] Death overtakes man not only at the end of his days but rather besets and torments him throughout his life. The power of death manifests itself in illness and frailty, in the cunning and malice of violent enemies, in the want of justice, in anxiety or captivity, in other restrictions of human existence. Whenever the psalmist lands in such severe duress that he can no longer adore and exalt Adonai, he sinks into the abyss, deprived of breath. At that moment, the infernal underworld takes hold of the upper world, even though he still continues to live bodily and pleads for help from God (for example, Ps. 16:10; 30:4; 56:14; 86:13; 88:5–7).[160]

A similar concept of death is found in the Epistle to the Romans, where godlessness ultimately and utterly relates to human arrogance of neither honoring nor glorifying the one God (1:21, 25; 2:17–24, 29; 3:27; 4:2, 20). Hence, the

---

156 See my interpretation below in 4.2.3.4.

157 Cranfield 1982, 1:352: "Though he [the "I"] continues to live, he is dead—being under God's sentence of death (cf. v. 24b). Physical death, when it comes, is but the fulfilment of the sentence already passed." Likewise, Michel 1978, 228: "Gottes Gericht tötet den Menschen, auch wenn er leiblich weiter lebt." Wilckens 1980, 2:82: "Mein 'Sterben' bedeutet [. . .] den Verlust meiner Verfügung über mich selbst. Als 'Gestorbener' bin ich der Sklave der Sünde geworden (vgl. V 14)." See further Espy 1985, 169, 183 n. 50; Hübner 1982, 68; Osten-Sacken 1975, 200; Theißen 1983, 209. Cf. Barrosse 1953, 442–44; Gundry 1980, 233; Kümmel 1974, 53.

158 Käsemann 1980, 185; Schunack 1967, 113–16; Wilckens 1980, 2:77.

159 Kraus 1979, 207–9; Schunack 1967, 63–71; H. W. Wolff 1984, 161, 166–68. Cf. Barrosse 1953, 450–53.

160 Kraus 1979, 207–11; Schunack 1967, 58–62; H. W. Wolff 1984, 166–68. Cf. Barrosse 1953, 450–53. Certainly the godless is in a still worse position, since he cannot and will not trust in God at all.

godless stands under the authority and dominion of sin and death (3:9; 5:12–21; 6:20–23; 7:5–6, 7–13).[161]

Further, Rom. 4:19 speaks of death in a sense that benefits the reading of 7:7–13 (and 5:12). It states that Abraham's "body" (σῶμα) and Sarah's womb were dead. Obviously, death indicates here the notion of absolute incapacity to beget and conceive children.[162]

Similarly, it is about incapacity in Rom. 7:7–13 as well. When Adam and Eve died, they could no longer live in accordance with the will of their Creator. In the Old Testament, the transgressions against the commandments lead to curse and death, while the fulfillment of the commandments results in blessing and life (see, e.g., Lev. 18:5; Deut. 8:3; 30:19–20; Neh. 9:29; Ezek. 20:11; 37:1–14; Amos 5:4, 6; Hab. 2:4).[163] Later, the Qumran community maintained and continued the conventional Jewish usage of speech.[164] In the Epistle to the Romans, the same kind of language occurs: apart from 7:7–13, most clearly in 6:12–13.[165]

The death-bringing process in Paradise took its beginning with the "coming" of the commandment "You shall not covet" (Rom. 7:7–11). It actually refers to God's forbidding eating of the tree of the knowledge of good and evil (Gen. 2:17).[166] Yet Paul, as a Jew, finds an even deeper meaning in the Torah. He suggests that the command "You shall not covet" sums up all the transgressions against the Decalogue, especially the second table.[167] Covetousness is the opposite of love. If the latter makes possible the fulfillment of the whole Law (Rom. 13:8–10; Gal. 5:14), then the former makes it absolutely impossible and ushers in an overall disobedience with regard to the totality of the Mosaic legislation.[168] Hence, the story of the fall in Genesis 3 discloses that the transgression of Adam and Eve was ultimately directed against the entire Torah.

All told, the lack of gratitude toward God (the offense against the first table of the Decalogue) and the loss of love toward others (the offenses against the second table of the Decalogue) illustrate and characterize the death of Adam and Eve in Romans. They were dead long before they died bodily.

161 Becker 1989, 381–82; Thurén 1977, 14. Cf. Käsemann 1961, 376. For sure, the Pauline concept of death involves also traits not found in the Psalms. See, e.g., Bailey 1981, 87–91.

162 For example, Schlier 1977, 133; Wilckens 1978, 1:275.

163 Bailey 1981, 39; Hill 1967, 164–65.

164 Bailey 1981, 82–85.

165 See my interpretation below in 4.2.3.4. Cf. further, e.g., Eph. 2:1, 5; Col. 2:13; 1 Tim. 5:6. In all those passages, death refers to the incapacity to fulfill the commandments of God.

166 Cranfield 1982, 1:350–51; Michel 1978, 228; Schlier 1977, 224; Wilckens 1980, 2:79, 83. See further below 4.2.3.4.

167 Cranfield 1982, 1:349–51; Michel 1978, 226; Schlier 1977, 221–22; Wilckens 1980, 2:78–79. Philo expressly affirms that Adam knew the whole Mosaic Law (particularly Käsemann 1980, 188). See further below 4.2.3.4.

168 Cranfield 1982, 1:349; Schmidt 1962, 123–24.

Thus Paul explains the primordial story of the fall (Genesis 3) in both chapters 5 and 7 of his Epistle to the Romans. The content of 5:12ab includes the kernel of what is found in 7:7–11. The transgression of Adam brought death into the world.[169] Consistent with 5:12c, death has already penetrated (διῆλθεν in aorist tense as an expression of the accomplished consequences) humankind, although the now living have not yet died bodily. Later, vv. 18–19 enhance the line of thought more in-depth. They emphasize that all have been made (κατεστάθησαν) sinners through the disobedience of one single person.[170] Adam (in Hebrew: "Man") represents the whole of humanity. His fall determines their destiny. His story is their history. Everyone is entangled *nolens volens* in his corruption. Human sinfulness ultimately goes back to him.[171]

Particularly E. Brandenburger emphasizes that Rom. 5:12–19 and 7:7–13 cannot be harmonized. He suggests that the viewpoint in the former passage contrasts with that in the latter. Properly speaking, they interpret differently the story in Genesis 3. In chapter 5 (except in v. 12d), human depravity originates in Adam alone.[172] Yet in chapter 7 his fall should be understood simply "in a typical, archetypal sense" ("in einem typischen, urbildlichen Sinne"). In the end, everyone repeats through his own misdoings what his ancestor once did in Eden.[173] Brandenburger gives no arguments in support of his thesis.[174] Since 7:7–11 literally fits only Adam and Eve, there is indeed much more going for the reading that the story in Genesis 3 refers not only to a typical example of everyday shortcomings but rather to the entrance of sin and death into the world.[175] In my opinion, there is no reason to suppose any contradiction between Rom. 5:12–19 and 7:7–13.[176]

As a result, 5:12–19 and 7:7–13 agree in underscoring that Adam's primeval fall has plunged humankind into corruption and every sort of calamity. His fatal transgression in Eden brought about that death gained dominion in the world.

---

169 Espy 1985, 169–70. Cf. Dodd 1947, 81. He understands 7:7–13 autobiographically and fails to place 5:12 in clear relationship to the whole passage.

170 See, e.g., Cranfield 1982, 1:290–91; Schlier 1977, 174.

171 Especially Cranfield 1982, 1:274–81; Schlier 1977, 159–64, 179–83. Cf. Barrosse 1953, 454–55.

172 Brandenburger 1962, 175–78, 217.

173 Op. cit., 216. See further Modalsli 1965, 32.

174 Brandenburger (ibid.) expresses himself as follows: "Die Verwertung der Tradition von Gen. 3 bedeutet keineswegs, daß unter dem ἐγώ Adam oder gar die in ihm verkörperte Menschheit und unter der ἐντολή das Paradiesesgebot zu begreifen ist. Vielmehr wird hier das Adam-Geschehen in einem *typischen, urbildlichen* Sinne verstanden: als je eigene 'Urgeschichte' des unter den Nomos gestellten (nachmosaischen) Menschen, in der sein schuldhaftes Verlorensein vor Gott immer schon gründet." No supporting arguments are added.

175 Particularly Käsemann 1980, 186–88; Schlier 1977, 223–24. See also Gundry 1980, 242 n. 15.

176 In addition, cf. 1 Cor. 15:21–22, where Paul, to be sure, lays emphasis on bodily death.

Its reign of terror involves spiritual death (the depravity of the nature of *Homo sapiens*) that leads to the bodily and eternal death. In this sense, the traditional Christian dogma of *peccatum originis* is based on solid ground. It solves the problem of the relationship between Adam's sin and human sinfulness (the third question to be dealt with, see above).

It remains to examine the place of 5:12 in its context (vv. 13–19). Particularly v. 12d seems to stick out. Does it come into a severe conflict with the argumentation in vv. 13–14, and does it deprive the foundation for comparing Adam and Christ in vv. 15–19 (the first and second question to be resolved, see above)? On the whole, the following discussion will decide whether the exegetical analysis so far blends into the Pauline line of thought in chapter 5. In the best case, v. 12 does not reveal a rupture from its context.

The *crux interpretum* in v. 13 draws on the enigmatic phrase "sin is not counted [or verbatim: reckoned] where there is no law." Scholars who maintain that v. 12d does not speak of the self-committed sins of the people, but rather of their common guilt in Adam's sin (see the third alternative above), understand the "reckoning of sins" mainly as any kind of punishment for sins. Accordingly, God does not reckon (ἐλλογεῖται as *passivum divinum*) or punish sinners who unknowingly transgress his commands. Since death nevertheless is his retribution or a hard punishment for their transgressions, and since death "reigned from Adam to Moses" (v. 14) respectively already before the Mosaic legislation, v. 12d must reasonably mean that all have sinned in Adam.[177]

The previous argumentation makes the overall flow of thought in Romans by no means more consistent but rather less coherent on the whole. For certain, it allows a kind of harmonization in the reading of 5:12–14. Yet on a much wider scale, it comes into conflict with 1:18–32. Here, Paul reproaches the Gentiles for their over-the-top wickedness. He also pronounces God's strict judgment against them. But since the Gentiles do not even know the Mosaic Law,[178] and since sin is not "reckoned" (read: punished) where there is no Law, should they in that case not be punished at all, at least not for their own sins? Nevertheless, the focus lies on the plain fact that God delivers them up to shameful lusts as punishment for their godlessness (vv. 24–28) and that he directs his wrath from heaven against them (v. 18).[179]

Besides, those who lived from the time of Adam to the time of Moses did not escape the punishments of God. Just a fragmentary knowledge of the Old Testament suffices to make clear that the whole of humankind or some human

177 Especially Freundorfer 1927, 249–53; Ridderbos 1987, 96. According to Murray (1982, 1:188–89), Paul affirms in v. 13 that sin without the Law does not exist at all!

178 The natural law, known to the Gentiles (Rom. 2:14–15), is not to be placed on a par with the Mosaic Law.

179 Cf. Friedrich 1952, 524; Käsemann 1980, 141–42; Wilckens 1978, 1:319.

groups have brought down horrendous calamities upon themselves for their sins (cf. the accounts of the flood or of Sodom and Gomorrah in Genesis). It is implausible to presume that Paul in Rom. 5:12–14 should not have taken at face value what was formerly written in the Torah. Neither is it feasible to assume that he should have ignored what he himself had earlier written in chapter 1 of his letter.[180]

It seems more promising to interpret the phrase ἁμαρτία δὲ οὐκ ἐλλογεῖται μὴ ὄντος νόμου according to the literal sense of the saying. The verb ἐλλογεῖν ("reckon") means exactly "to write something on the account of someone" or "to set on the account" (cf. Phlm. 18). It functions as *terminus technicus* in the Jewish setting and relates to the "heavenly bookkeeping": God observes the acts of people and records in his register of iniquities what evil every single individual has committed and commits.[181] To this end, sins cannot be reckoned given that no formal Law exists against which one infringes. The Mosaic Law is first to define with precision what sin is, namely, a transgression against the divine legislation.[182] In close association with 5:13b, 4:15b makes the same point: "where there is no law there is no transgression."[183] Although sins were "merely" sins, they always lead to ruin. That is the reason why death reigned over those who lived before Moses and did not sin in the same way as Adam did through his rebellion against God's special command (v. 14).[184]

Thus the line of thought in Rom. 5:12–14 appears consistent. It reads as follows:

> Adam is the head of the entire humankind. He was the first to sin in history (v. 12a). His fall has brought about that death (in every respect) gained dominion in the world (v. 12b). Death came to all people (v. 12c), since they have all done wrong (v. 12d). Already before the Mosaic Law people sinned (v. 13a), but their sin was not precisely "reckoned" for lack of a law. Their sin was not a matter of an overt rebellion against law (v. 13b). In any case, the divine punishment remained for the sins committed. In consequence, death reigned from Adam to Moses, although people at that time—in contrast to Adam in Eden—did not become guilty of the transgression of a law (v. 14).

In vv. 15–19, Paul then depicts Adam and Christ (respectively the heads of the old and the new humanity) as opposites to each other whose influence

180 Friedrich 1952, 523–24; T. R. Schreiner 1998, 278; Stalder 1962, 273. Cf. Gundry 1980, 230–31; Westerholm 1988, 183–84. *Pace* Dahl 1952, 43–44.

181 Friedrich 1952, 525; Käsemann 1980, 141; Schlier 1977, 165; Stalder 1962, 274; Westerholm 1988, 183–84; Wilckens 1978, 1:319.

182 Ibid.

183 Käsemann 1980, 141; Schlier 1977, 164–65 (in contrast, Wilckens 1978, 1:218 n. 1059). Cf. Friedrich 1952, 523.

184 Nicely Cranfield 1982, 1:282–83; Friedrich 1952, 526; Käsemann 1980, 141–42; Schlier 1977, 165; Wilckens 1978, 1:319–20. Cf. further Jüngel 1963, 55–56.

extends throughout the history of the world on the whole. He delineates the contrast as follows:

> Through Adam's disobedience people were made (κατεστάθησαν) sinners, subject to death and damnation. But through Christ's obedience they will be made (κατασταθήσονται) righteous, free from their doomed existence.

The juxtaposition of Adam and Christ in vv. 15–19 does not suggest that v. 12d should read "because all have sinned (in Adam)." The corruption inherited by humankind from Adam works itself out in the life of each person concretely in evil actions (vv. 12d–14).[185] By analogy, the righteousness gained through Christ to humankind works itself out in the life of each Christian concretely in good works (cf. vv. 18–19).[186] As a consequence, the juxtaposition of Adam and Christ is suitable for the organic continuation from v. 12 just in the simple sense of "because all (themselves) have sinned."

To sum up, it appears that 5:12 does not break down the hard core of the very pessimistic and yet realistic anthropology of Paul as known and acknowledged otherwise in his letters. Rightly understood, the following context (vv. 13–19) corroborates the result.

4.2.3. Romans 7:14–25

4.2.3.1. Introduction

Back in his days, W. Bousset already perceived the chief problem arising from Rom. 7:14–25. He put it into the following noteworthy words:

> This reasoning in Rom 7 actually occupies a singular position within the Pauline thought world. Nowhere has the apostle made so many concessions for the natural "I" of man as here.[187]

---

185 Particularly Schlier 1977, 163; Käsemann 1980, 141. Cf. Luz 1968, 200–201.

186 With regard to the benefit of the salvific death of Christ, v. 18 affirms that "one act of righteousness leads to justification and life [εἰς δικαίωσιν ζωῆς] for all men." Accordingly, v. 19 asserts that "by the one man's obedience the many will be made righteous [δίκαιοι κατασταθήσονται οἱ πολλοί]." The Greek idioms are best understood eschatologically: God will proclaim the Christians righteous on the day of judgment, whereupon they will gain eternal life (rightly, Käsemann 1980, 148–49; Schlier 1977, 174–76, Schmidt 1962, 102; see further Bultmann 1959, 158–60, 162). However, proclaiming righteous and eternal life are not only in the future reality but also in the present (ibid.). God has already now justified the Christians through faith and given them the gift of a new life with a new understanding of existence. In other words, the righteousness won by Christ works itself out—as stated—in the good works of the Christian. The same theological emphasis often emerges in the Pauline epistles and sometimes more substantially than in Rom. 5:15–19 (see, e.g., Ridderbos 1987, 205–326).

187 Bousset 1967, 123: "Denn tatsächlich nimmt diese Ausführung von Rö. 7 eine singuläre Stellung innerhalb der paulinischen Gedankenwelt ein. Niemals hat der Apostel dem natürlichen Ich des Menschen so viel Konzessionen gemacht wie hier." In reference to Romans 7, Blank (1969, 170) similarly maintains that "dem Menschen zwar die

Besides, Bousset does not keep the door open for other possible interpretations. He maintains that Rom. 7:14–25 definitely does not describe the condition of the Christian existence. The conventional reading of the Lutheran Reformation receives no sympathy from him. In contrast, he harshly rejects it with the following words:

> Whoever actually believes that the apostle would describe the condition of the converted Christian with this picture of division and misery has still not understood him.[188]

Later, R. Bultmann carries his teacher's thesis further with equally categorical words:

> It seems to me, that these questions have been adequately discussed and that the answer cannot be doubtful: the situation of man standing under the law is generally characterized here [in Romans 7] and in the manner in which it appears to the eyes of the one who has been set free from the law through Christ.[189]

Until recently, most exegetes have over and over again supported the same interpretation, often with uncommon pathos.[190] Supposedly the discussion need not be carried on. H. Räisänen hits the nail on the head as he utters his contribution:

> It is hardly necessary to argue once more that the famous passage *Rom 7.14–25* is not intended by Paul as a description of the Christian. It can by now be taken for granted that he is speaking of man's existence under the law [. . .].[191]

Exegetes are almost unanimous in their conviction that Rom. 7:14–25 does not describe the condition of Christians but rather the situation of non-Christians struggling under the Law. Generally, they regard their interpretation (to be sure, with many variations) as *opinio communis* that goes back to W. G. Kümmel and the decisive breakthrough of his doctoral thesis *Römer 7*

Möglichkeit des guten Willens verblieb, doch fehlt es am Können, an der ungebrochenen Kraft zur Realisierung des Guten."

188 Bousset 1967, 123: "Wer wirklich glaubt, daß der Apostel mit diesem Gemälde der Gespaltenheit und des Elends den Zustand des bekehrten Christen schildern wolle, hat ihn noch gar nicht verstanden."

189 Bultmann 1932, 53: "Mir scheint, daß diese Fragen hinreichend diskutiert worden sind, und daß die Antwort nicht zweifelhaft sein kann: die Situation des unter dem Gesetz stehenden Menschen überhaupt wird hier [in Romans 7] charakterisiert, und zwar so, wie sie für das Auge des vom Gesetz durch Christus Befreiten sichtbar geworden ist."

190 Cf. modern standard commentaries. See further Althaus 1951a, 31–41; Beker 1980, 216; Bornkamm 1966a, 53; Braun 1959, 3; Ellwein 1955, 255–56; Hübner 1980, 446; 1982, 69–70; Kertelge 1971, 106; Lichtenberger 1985, 1:137, 174, 180, 293; Luz 1968, 160; Osten-Sacken 1975, 195; Räisänen 1976, 426–27; 1979, 85; Schnackenburg 1975, 283, 295–96; Theißen 1983, 181–82. In addition, cf. Deuser 1979, 421–22. For a short overview of previous interpretations, see Léon-Dufour 1973, 70–71.

191 Räisänen 1983, 109.

und die Bekehrung des Paulus (1929).[192] Since the great majority of prominent New Testament scholars do not call the continuing validity of his reading into question, it seems not worth the effort to resume the discussion. Yet it appears incorrect to close a further analysis of data on a matter of course for the following reasons:

1. In academic context, an open mind to reexamine the durability of even the most certain results on occasion contributes to remarkable progress in research and promotes the goal of critical evaluation.
2. Kümmel's interpretation enjoys much support in the German-speaking world.[193] In the English-speaking world, however, it hastens to increasing disapproval.[194]
3. Moreover, Kümmel's doctoral thesis turns out to be notably dated. Does it still, after one hundred years, make sense to accept the outcomes of his pioneering research without further ado? Apparently, a revision proves necessary. At least, it should not instantly fall into the danger zone of exegetical censure.

4.2.3.2. W. G. Kümmel's Argumentation

Kümmel furnishes the following main arguments in justification of his thesis that Rom. 7:14–25 is not speaking about the Christian.

1. The context of 7:14–25 shows that one should not identify the "I" with the Christian.

---

192 Althaus 1951a, 36; Bornkamm 1966a, 53; Bultmann 1932, 53; Ellwein 1955, 255–56; Hübner 1980, 446; 1982, 69–70; Kertelge 1971, 106; Lichtenberger 1985, 1:137, 174, 180, 293; Luz 1968, 160; B. L. Martin 1981, 39; Osten-Sacken 1975, 195; Räisänen 1976, 426; 1979, 85; 1983, 109 n. 84; Schnackenburg 1975, 283, 295–96; Theißen 1983, 181–82. Cf. Deuser 1979, 421–22.

193 Hübner 1987, 2668: "Nahezu die gesamte Diskussion um Röm 7 nach 1945 setzt WERNER GEORG KÜMMELs Dissertation 'Römer 7 und die Bekehrung des Paulus' voraus, indem sie entweder diese Arbeit nicht nur als Markstein, sondern als (fast) endgültige Antwort betrachtet—das gilt für fast die gesamte Forschung im deutschsprachigen Bereich—[. . .]." Similarly, Theißen 1983, 181 n. 1. But see Möller 1939, 5–27, 68–79; Stalder 1962, 284–307.

194 See, *inter alia*, Barrett 1967, 146–53; Bruce 1963, 150–56 (however, cf. 1982a, 244–45); Byskov 1976, 75–87; D. H. Campbell 1980, 57–64; Cranfield 1982, 1:344–47, 355–70; Dunn 1975, 257–73; Espy 1985, 173–75; Murray 1982, 1:256–73; Packer 1964, 621–27; Wenham 1980, 80–94. In Scandinavia, see Modalsli 1965, 34–37; Nygren 1979, 290–310, Thurén 1994, 129–41. Cf. Nikolainen 1975, 111–19; 1978, 313–24. See Hübner's appraisal of the state of contemporary research (1987, 2668). Gundry (1980, 228) sums up: "Despite announcements that W. G. Kümmel cut down once and for all the interpretation of Rom. 7:7–25, or at least 7:14–25, as both autobiographical of Paul and psychologically descriptive of his Christian experience, that interpretation is enjoying somewhat of a revival."

a. 7:1–6: The passage shows that Christians are free from the Law (see especially v. 6; cf. 6:14). The "I" in contrast stands under the Law.[195]

b. 7:7–13: Paul does not speak here of his own (Jewish) past, although he uses the first person.[196] Hence, he neither speaks of himself in vv. 14–25, although he even there uses the first person. The subject must self-evidently be the same in both pericopes.[197]

c. 8:1–11:[198] Chapter 8 deals more accurately with the new order of salvation. Christians are free from every condemnation since the Spirit has liberated them from sin and death. Therefore, they now walk according to the Spirit and not according to the flesh. On the other hand, the "I" is carnal and sold under sin. It must continue against his better will to obey his lusts and finds no escape from the despairing situation.[199]

2. 7:14–25 betrays too hopeless a trait to portray the inner emotions of Christians. The "I" is wholly carnal and sold under sin without any hope of escaping from his slavery. It further lacks the Spirit and the knowledge of the redemption.[200]

3. For sure, Paul regarded neither himself nor his fellow Christians as sinless (cf. Rom. 14:10; 1 Cor. 4:4; 9:26–27; 2 Cor. 5:10). Nevertheless, he does not appear conscious of any particular sin in the cadre of his apostolic activity. Paul even dares to maintain that he no longer walks according to the flesh (2 Cor. 10:3; 13:6). Other Christians have his example to follow (1 Cor. 4:16; 11:1; Phil. 3:17; 4:9).[201] Against the background of such evidence, Rom. 7:14–25 hardly exposes his own confession of sin.[202]

4. Not even does Gal. 5:16–18 suggest that Rom. 7:14–25 describes the situation of the Christian. According to the latter text, the "I" has neither Spirit nor power to fulfill the Law (see argument 2

---

195 Kümmel 1974, 97.

196 Op. cit., 76–84. Kümmel's argumentation is, in my opinion, convincing. Besides, it is generally accepted. I forego further reference here.

197 Op. cit., 9–10, 90, 97.

198 Kümmel (op. cit., 97–98) discusses the whole of chapter 8 in general terms.

199 Op. cit., 97–98. Kümmel holds 7:25a as a thanksgiving for the redemption happening to the Christian. The verse anticipates 8:1–2 (op. cit., 98).

200 Op. cit., 98, 104.

201 Kümmel suggests that neither Gal. 2:20 nor Phil. 3:12 relate to the sinfulness of Paul. The latter passage speaks "zweifellos nicht von sittlicher, sondern von religiöser Unvollkommenheit" (op. cit., 101–2). The former passage speaks of "life in the flesh" only as being "im irdischen Leibe" (op. cit., 103).

202 Op. cit., 101–3.

> above). According to the former text, Christians instead live "in the Spirit." They have the duty and the actual possibility to live "according to the Spirit." In effect, Gal. 5:17 asserts that man stands *either* under the power of the Spirit *or* under that of the flesh.[203]

From the arguments he presents, Kümmel draws the conclusion that Rom. 7:14–25 portrays man under the Law.[204] Paul employs the first person to express vividly "a common thought" ("einen allgemeinen Gedanken").[205] He makes use of the same rhetorical device frequently in his epistles (Rom. 3:5–7; 1 Cor. 6:12, 15; 10:29–30; 11:31–32; 13:1–3, 11–12; 14:11, 14–15; Gal. 2:18).[206] A similar style is found in ancient literature as well as in rabbinic texts.[207]

In consequence, 7:14–25 deviates from the Pauline anthropology in general. In no other place do we ever learn that the natural man consents to the Law of God, delights in it, and indeed wills to do it.[208] Kümmel notes in clarification that the passage depicts the struggle against sin and the search for redemption from a Christian point of view ("von dem Bewußtsein des Erlösten aus").[209] Hence, he suggests that some deviant features slip into the text.[210]

Besides, Kümmel points out that in 7:14–25 even "a peculiar shift of subject" ("eine eigentümliche Verschiebung der Subjekte") takes place. The "I" is wholly carnal and completely sold under sin in vv. 14–16 and 24, while a fine distinction between the "real I" ("mind" or "inward man") and the "flesh" ("members") emerges in vv. 17–23. Nevertheless, it deserves special attention that at the same time the action of the members as well as the will of the mind are, so to speak, "the wider concept of 'I' " ("dem weiteren Ich-Begriff") subordinated (cf. v. 19). The "I" does not consist of two different parts. In reality, νοῦς and σάρξ are "the same man from different points of view" ("derselbe Mensch in verschiedener Hinsicht"). The mind, even when it joyfully consents to the Law of God, does not cease to stand under the power of sin.[211]

It follows that 7:14–25 does not so much contradict the Pauline anthropology in general. There remains, however, a formal incongruity: apart from v. 22 it is nowhere indicated that the natural man consents joyfully to the Law of God (although he should do so).[212]

---

203 Op. cit., 105–6.
204 Op. cit., 117–18.
205 Op. cit., 124.
206 Op. cit., 121–23.
207 Op. cit., 126–32.
208 Op. cit., 118, 134–35.
209 Op. cit., 118.
210 Op. cit., 118–19, 138.
211 Op. cit., 135–36.
212 Op. cit., 136–37.

4.2.3.3. Text

Kümmel's argumentation mainly rests on the thesis that Paul in the Epistle to the Romans characterizes the Christian in a different manner from the "I" (see above 4.2.3.2., points 1a, 1c, and 2). It therefore seems reasonable to think that 7:14–25 portrays a non-Christian (or, more precisely, man under the Law). Despite the popularity of this reasoning, the line of evidence does not provide full coverage. The two most critical and relevant texts are Rom. 6:12 and 8:10. In general, neither passage is sufficiently taken into consideration.[213]

Rom. 6:12 reads as follows:

> Let not sin therefore reign in your mortal body [ἐν τῷ θνητῷ ὑμῶν σώματι], to make you obey its [αὐτοῦ] passions.

As made known, evil desires arising from the human body still harm Christians and try to exercise mastery over them. For sure, the genitive αὐτοῦ harks back to σῶμα ("body") and not to ἁμαρτία ("sin").[214] It is not about an ephemeral and transient condition that passes and never returns. No, evil desires are "the basis for the lordship of sin" ("die Basis der Sündenherrschaft")[215] in the Christian. They repetitively bring a lot of heat on him. They prepare him grave and grievous difficulties. He should constantly resist them. If not, through them sin can gain power over him anew. The temptations do not only amount to outward enticements which torment the Christian. Notably, his mortal body itself craves incessantly. For that reason, he always runs the risk of falling back into various vices.[216]

It follows that σῶμα in 6:12 does not primarily mean the physical body, but rather the person in entirety out of harmony and in contrast with God. The mortal body is like an independent subject which fundamentally stands at the disposal of sin. The Christian has to put up with troubles and harms caused by it. Between the two reigns an incompatible tension in never-ending hostility. In the course of time, their mutual tug-of-war does not diminish little by little. It remains as long as life continues.[217]

---

213 However, see D. H. Campbell 1980, 58–59; Cranfield 1982, 1:357, 366; Dunn 1975, 261, 263–64; Gundry 1980, 239; Räisänen 1976, 430; Wenham 1980, 85–86. Cf. Espy 1985, 173. There should indeed be much more focus on Rom. 6:12 and 8:10. See below.

214 The Western text (also P46) with the variant reading αὐτῇ (*pro* ταῖς ἐπιθυμίαις αὐτοῦ as *lectio difficilior*) polishes. See Cranfield 1982, 1:317 n. 2; Schlier 1977, 202 n. 22; Wilckens 1980, 2:20 n. 73.

215 Schlier 1977, 202. Wilckens calls lusts "die noch verbliebenen Agenten der Sünde" (1980, 2:20).

216 Cranfield 1982, 1:316–17; Fuchs 1949, 39; Michel 1978, 208–9; Ridderbos 1987, 116–17, 124, 127, 265; Robinson 1966, 29–30, 44, 73; Schlier 1977, 202; Wilckens 1980, 2:20. Cf. K-A. Bauer 1971, 152–55.

217 Robinson 1966, 29–30, 44, 73; Cranfield 1982, 1:317.

Similarly, 8:10 reads as follows:

> But if Christ is in you, although the body [τὸ σῶμα] is dead because of sin, the Spirit[218] is life because of righteousness.

Here, many commentators find an unmistakable allusion to chapter 6: in Baptism, the death of the body of sin ensues and the reception of the Spirit results, who creates true life and works out immaculate righteousness.[219] Apparently, the preposition διά is more likely to have the meaning of "in view of" instead of "for the sake of."[220] Käsemann accordingly paraphrases the verse as follows:

> The body is dead since baptism as far as sin is in question, but the divine Spirit which was given to us brings to life where righteousness is concerned.[221]

Quite the opposite, some other commentators raise objections against such an exegesis and insist that in Baptism not only does the corporal body of a man die but the whole "old man." Therefore, 8:10 in no case relates to chapter 6. It rather refers to the coming day of resurrection.[222] Obviously, this alternative interpretation does not hold true. It incorrectly assumes that τὸ σῶμα in 8:10, contrary to chapter 6, does not express more than just the physical existence. Notably, Paul affirms with emphasis that the body is already dead,[223] although Christians in Rome had not yet died bodily. Then he asserts that God will give life to their mortal bodies (v. 11). It is primarily about the resuscitation of the whole person, not solely of the resurrection of the "soulless" body.[224] A little later, Paul speaks of the body as if it were a person in itself, the actions of which Christians have to mortify (v. 13). He places the actions of the body in direct equation with the life according to the flesh.[225] In consequence, τὸ σῶμα means in 8:10 nothing else than the whole human being apart from God.

---

218 Namely, the Spirit of God, not that of man. Against NIV. See Barrett 1967, 159; K-A. Bauer 1971, 162; Bultmann 1984, 209; Cranfield 1982, 1:390; Käsemann 1980, 216; Lichtenberger 1985, 1:215; Michel 1978, 254; Murray 1982, 1:289–90; Osten-Sacken 1975, 153–54; Paulsen 1974, 68–69; Schlier 1977, 247–48; Schmidt 1962, 140. Cf. Fuchs 1949, 97.

219 Barrett 1967, 159; K-A. Bauer 1971, 162–63; Joest 1955, 291; Käsemann 1980, 216; Lichtenberger 1985, 1:215–16; Osten-Sacken 1975, 153, 237–39; Paulsen 1974, 70–76; Schmidt 1962, 139; Schlier 1977, 247; Wilckens 1980, 2:132. Cf. Bultmann 1984, 201, 209; Fuchs 1949, 97; Schmidt 1962, 139.

220 Käsemann 1980, 216; Schlier 1977, 247. Otherwise you must translate διὰ ἁμαρτίαν in a causative sense but διὰ δικαιοσύνην in a final sense, which I find doubtful. Cf. also Käsemann 1980, 216.

221 Käsemann 1980, 216: "Der Leib ist tot seit der Taufe, sofern die Sünde in Frage steht, der uns geschenkte göttliche Geist dagegen lebendigmachend, was Gerechtigkeit angeht."

222 Barrosse 1953, 446; Michel 1978, 254 n. 12; Wenham 1980, 85; Zahn 1910, 388.

223 The clause τὸ μὲν σῶμα νεκρὸν διὰ ἁμαρτίαν lacks the word ἔστιν. See Schlier 1977, 224.

224 The same thought is found in 1 Cor. 15:51: "Behold! I tell you a mystery. We shall not all sleep, but we shall all be changed." Cf. v. 52 and Phil. 3:21.

225 Bultmann 1984, 197–98; Ridderbos 1987, 117, 124, 201.

Notwithstanding, Rom. 8:10 does not (directly) relate to the event of Baptism:

(1) The preposition διά + accusative here hardly has the rare meaning of "in view of."[226] It primarily denotes "for the sake of," "on account of."[227]

(2) In chapter 8, Paul frequently sets death and life against each other (vv. 2, 6, 11, 13). In no instance does he deal with the problematics of Baptism. As a consequence, such does not appear in v. 10 either.[228]

(3) According to v. 11, God will vivify (ζωοποιήσει) the mortal bodies of Christians through his Spirit. No doubt, the future tense refers to the redemption on the day of judgment (v. 23). Then, v. 10a clarifies why (namely, because of sin) the bodies of Christians do not yet take part in the new life.[229]

(4) V. 11 underlines twice that God raised Christ from the dead (ἐκ νεκρῶν). The adjective νεκρός naturally points to the bodily dead. The same adjective cannot in v. 10 stand for those dying in Baptism.

In sum, 8:10 proves that the body of the Christian is subject to the power of death on account of its corruption and sinfulness. Yet the Spirit has transferred the Christian himself into the domain of life.

In the light of 6:12 and 8:10, the condition of the "I" becomes much more reasonable. The body is also a heavy burden to him:

> Wretched man that I am! Who will deliver me from this body of death [ἐκ τοῦ σώματος τοῦ θανάτου τούτου]?[230] (7:24)

Kümmel maintains that the "I" reported here is completely carnal and sold under sin (v. 14). In the deep pessimism of lamentation, he does not see a spark of hope burning.[231] However, he seems to overlook that v. 24 rather reveals the

226 Cf. Cranfield 1982, 1:389; Michel 1978, 254 n. 12; Murray 1982, 1:289; Zahn 1925, 389.

227 Bornemann and Risch 1978, 200 par. 197.5.

228 Barrosse 1953, 446. Admittedly, he argues his point quite weakly. He points out: "Further, in the context immediately preceding, life and death are *contraries*; they will hardly be used here [8:10] differently." As far as I know, no one has ever denied that life and death are contraries in 8:10.

229 Cf. Barrosse 1953, 446; Cranfield 1982, 1:389; Murray 1982, 1:289.

230 It is not here of greater importance whether τούτου belongs either to (1) τοῦ σώματος (Cranfield 1982, 1:367; Van Dülmen 1968, 118 n. 145; Schlier 1977, 235) or (2) τοῦ θανάτου (Gundry 1980, 239; Kümmel 1974, 63; Murray 1982, 1:268; Schmidt 1962, 133; cf. K-A. Bauer 1971, 160) or (3) τοῦ σώματος τοῦ θανάτου (Fuchs 1949, 80; Hommel 1961, 95; Käsemann 1980, 201; Lichtenberger 1985, 1:160; Michel 1978, 237; Möller 1939, 16; Wilckens 1980, 2:94 n. 388; Zahn 1925, 362–63 n. 19).

231 Kümmel 1974, 63–64, 135. On parallel petitions in extrabiblical sources, cf. E. W. Smith 1971, 127–33.

same dichotomy between the real "I" and the flesh which he found in vv. 17–23.[232] Despair ultimately overwhelms the "I" not because of his own person but more exactly on account of the body of death, *with* which it must live and *from* (preposition ἐκ) which it wishes to be redeemed.[233] Moreover, v. 23 strongly weakens Kümmel's position. He correctly points out that the "members" (v. 23) and the "body of death" (v. 24) are synonyms. The members, in which the "law" of sin works, indeed form the body of death.[234] It follows then that the tension between the real "I" and the members (v. 23) reigns likewise between the "I" and the body of death (v. 24). It is absolutely improbable that "a curious shift in subjects" ("eine eigentümliche Verschiebung der Subjekte") takes place at the end of chapter 7.

In addition, redemption from the body of death suggests that the "I" can follow its mind without any opposition on the part of its members. At that very moment, the contrast between will and action (vv. 15–23) ceases.[235] If the "I" (v. 24) were now completely carnal and sold under sin, it would also remain as sinful as ever after the longed-for deliverance. There would be utterly no change for the better! The text has then lost its scope entirely.

Many common traits link 7:24 with 6:12 and/or 8:10:

(1) The body hinders the Christian and the "I" from keeping the Law of God completely.

(2) The lusts and the wrongdoings of the Christian and the "I" actually have their origin in the body.

(3) Death still plagues the body of the Christian and the "I" because of constantly present sin.

(4) In fact, sin is, as it were, a demonic person which unceasingly torments the Christian and the "I" through the body.[236]

Concisely, both the Christian and the "I" face many problems of the same kind arising from the body. In consequence, the Christian has not become free from the body of death that troubles the "I." The reasoning in 6:12 as well as 8:10 prevents such a conclusion.[237]

In order to prove the diametrical opposition between the "I" and the Christian, Kümmel appeals particularly to 8:1–2. According to him, these verses answer the anxious question of the "I" (7:24). Both passages show "without

232 Kümmel 1974, 60–63, 135.

233 Cf. K-A. Bauer 1971, 160; Stalder 1962, 300, 305.

234 Kümmel 1974, 23, 63–64. See further K-A. Bauer 1971, 160; Fuchs 1949, 80; Robinson 1966, 30.

235 Without a doubt, the "I" in no case wishes for the end of the bodily life. See the majority of commentators (e.g., Schmidt 1962, 133; Wilckens 1980, 2:94–95). Similarly, Kümmel 1974, 63–64. Cf. Wenham 1980, 86.

236 To be sure, sin is not dealt with explicitly in 7:24. Nonetheless, vv. 17 and 20 show that it works also in and through the body of death.

237 *Contra* Kümmel 1974, 65, 68.

doubt" that the Christian is free from the law of sin and death. His situation looks different from that of the "I."[238]

On closer examination of the context, serious objections arise against Kümmel's exegesis (that certainly obtains broad support nowadays).[239] To be precise, the question in 7:24[240] is not exactly answered in 8:2. The former verse copes with the redemption of the "I" from the body of death, while the latter verse deals with the liberation of the "you"[241] from the law of sin and death. Simply, liberation from the law of sin and death serves no sufficient parallel to redemption from the body of death.[242] The law of sin and death relates rather to the law of sin which abides in the members (viz. in the body of death) and besets the "I" (7:23).[243] Then, 8:2 asserts that Christians indeed are already free from the law of sin and death, but not yet from the body of death where the law of sin and death oppresses as much as ever. A similar eschatological situation in severe tension appears a little more distinctly in 8:10 as well. There it turns out that the body of the Christian is dead because of sin. But he himself will paradoxically be freed from death (and from its cause, sin) since the Spirit brings about life on account of righteousness.[244]

Thus the question in 7:24 finds no answer in 8:1–2. Rather, the line of thought continues immediately in the next verse:[245]

> Thanks be to God through Jesus Christ our Lord! (v. 25a)

Here, it remains in doubt why or for what the "I" thanks God. Kümmel indicates that ultimately the "I" does not thank God at all. In appeal to 8:2 (see above), he assumes that in reality Paul thanks God for the liberation of the Christian from the body of death. The subject of 7:14–25 is carnal and sold under sin (v. 14).

---

238 Op. cit., 68.

239 See most commentators. Likewise, Lichtenberger 1985, 1:204; B. L. Martin 1981, 44; Paulsen 1974, 23, 31. Cf. Fuchs 1949, 82; Theißen 1983, 186.

240 Perhaps the question should be understood rather as a wish: "Oh, that God might deliver me from this body of death!" It could be a Hebraism. See Brockelmann 1956, par. 9.55c. He delivers some examples that show that wish-clauses in the Hebrew language are frequently set out as questions.

241 Most commentators consider σε (*pro* με) the original reading. See Cranfield 1982, 1:376–77; Van Dülmen 1968, 120 n. 150; Fuchs 1949, 84; Käsemann 1980, 207; Michel 1978, 249; Paulsen 1974, 30; Schlier 1977, 237–38; Wilckens 1980, 2:123–24.

242 Cf. Möller 1939, 25–26. He (op. cit., 26) writes: "Vom *Gesetz* der Sünde und des Todes ist der Christ durch Christus zwar befreit, aber außerhalb des Todes*leibes* befindet er sich nicht." See also Dunn 1975, 263. He writes: "Rom. 8,2 cannot denote complete liberation from the power of the flesh and of death—even men of the Spirit die (1. Thess. 4,13, 1. Cor. 15,26)."

243 Cranfield 1982, 1:375; Lichtenberger 1985, 1:204; Möller 1939, 26; Murray 1982, 1:276; Räisänen 1980, 113–14; 1983, 52–53 n. 46; Schlier 1977, 238. See further Patte 1983, 278.

244 See above. Cf. Cranfield 1982, 1:367–68.

245 Cf. Kümmel 1974, 64–65. Correctly, Barrett 1967, 151; Cranfield 1982, 1:367; Murray 1982, 1:269; Schlier 1977, 235; Wilckens 1980, 2:95.

He knows nothing of redemption. He has not the slightest certainty of a coming redemption. Altogether, he lacks every reason to thank God. As a result, Kümmel argues that the future ῥύσεται (v. 24) "cannot be completely real" ("nicht ganz wirklich sein kann"). Apparently, he means that the "I"—in consideration of the surrounding context—does not look forward to any approaching redemption, although the future tense easily creates such an impression.[246]

To all appearances, we are left with no reasonable choice but to take 7:24–25a as an exclamation of the "I" who gives thanks for the approaching (not yet accomplished) redemption. His monologue goes from v. 7 to the end of the chapter. Who of the readers (respectively listeners) in Rome would have conceived that the "I" in vv. 24–25, without giving any notice, engages in a short dialogue with Paul?[247] Moreover, Kümmel's hypothesis rests in the main on false premises. Since Christians in the light of 6:12 and 8:10 are not liberated from the body of death, Paul cannot somewhat abruptly thank God for their liberation from the body of death. Likewise, since the "real I" lives in tension with himself and distanced himself from sin, present in his members, his hope for a coming redemption (v. 24) and his gratitude for it (v. 25a) become entirely apparent. The future ῥύσεται must "be completely real" ("ganz wirklich sein") according to the context.[248]

Besides, 7:25a does not only affirm that the "I" thanks God for redemption through Jesus Christ but also that God will redeem (the implicit meaning of the verb ῥύσεται in v. 24) the "I" through Jesus Christ.[249] On the whole, Paul twice calls the Redeemer ὁ ῥυόμενος (Rom. 11:26; 1 Thess. 1:10). In both texts, he speaks of the parousia on the Last Day: Christ will soon return in order to remove godlessness from Israel (Rom. 11:26) and to save Christians from the coming wrath (1 Thess. 1:10). He stands out as the great Redeemer (ὁ ῥυόμενος).[250] Hence, God will redeem (ῥύσεται) the "I" from the body of death as soon as Christ (ὁ ῥυόμενος) returns. Redemption should not take place before that H-hour, because Christians themselves must wait for the redemption of their bodies until the fulfillment (Rom. 8:23; cf. 1 Cor. 15:50–57).[251]

246 Kümmel 1974, 65. On parallel thanksgivings in the extrabiblical sources cf. E. W. Smith 1971, 133–35.

247 V. 25b is no gloss. See below.

248 See further Barrett 1967, 151; Cranfield 1982, 1:367–68; Möller 1939, 9; Murray 1982, 1:269–70; Nygren 1979, 308; Packer 1964, 626–27.

249 Michel 1978, 249; Schlier 1977, 235; Schmidt 1962, 133; Wilckens 1980, 2:95.

250 For sure, Rom. 11:26 cites Isa. 59:20 (LXX), where ὁ ῥυόμενος naturally refers to God. Yet Paul has—like many rabbis as well—interpreted the text messianically (Laato 2021, 75–79). See further Michel 1978, 355–56; Wilckens 1980, 2:256–57, in contrast to Zahn 1925, 525–26, particularly n. 71. 1 Thess. 1:10 ascribes the epithet ὁ ῥυόμενος unambiguously to Christ (Bruce 1982b, 18–20).

251 D. H. Campbell 1980, 58–59; Espy 1985, 186 n. 70; Möller 1939, 26–27; Packer 1964, 626–27. For 1 Cor. 15:50–57, see below.

As a result, there appears a further common trait between the "I" and the Christian (see above), namely, the fifth, that God will redeem them both from the body of death first on the Last Day. Taking into account all those similarities, the big question more and more approaches the foreground, whether the situation of the "I" and that of the Christian differ from each other to any extent. In the following, a shift in emphasis ensues, and the focus will move on to the New Perspective.

To begin with, Kümmel considers the characterization in 7:14–25 as too pessimistic to illustrate the new life through faith. In particular, vv. 14–16 show easily that the "I" is fully carnal and sold under sin. It desires indeed to do good, but it continually does evil instead. In contrast, the Christian wishes to do and (at least) for the most part does good.[252]

Kümmel's argumentation fails to carry conviction. He does not explain why the "I"—although it wishes to do good—is wholly carnal and sold under sin. Besides, he finds in vv. 17–23 a clear distinction between the "real I" and the "flesh." Correctly, he maintains that vv. 17–20 no longer ascribe a single subject to the willing and doing. Now, the "I" indeed wills good, while the sin working in his flesh does evil. Instead, the "I" in vv. 15–16 allegedly turns out to suffer from his complete corruption or depravity.[253] Against Kümmel speaks out the fact that vv. 19–20a repeat vv. 15b–16a almost word for word. Actually, he suggests that an identical sequence of words entails "a curious shift in subjects." The odd implication of his explanation leaves the impression of breathtaking exegetical acrobatics.

Without doubt, Kümmel analyzes vv. 17–23 correctly. The "I" in his own defense explains that sin does evil (v. 17).[254] The very same words are shortly after repeated with emphasis (v. 20b). Altogether, vv. 15b–16a, 17, and vv. 19–20 therefore correspond to one another. Insofar as v. 20b serves to clarify vv. 19–20a, so by analogy v. 17 clarifies vv. 15–16.[255] Taken as a whole, vv. 15–17 indicate

252 Kümmel 1974, 58–61, 98–105, 135–36.

253 Op. cit., 59–61, 135–36. He (op. cit., 61) asserts as follows: "Dieses Ich [particularly in v. 18] nun, das nicht handeln, sondern nur wollen kann, muß ein anderes sein als das in V.15, wo ἐγώ das Subjekt von Wollen *und* Tun bezeichnet hatte."

254 Schmithals (1980) surprisingly interprets the pericope 7:17–8:29 as a compendium of Pauline theology which was written long before the epistle to the Romans A (!) and later included in it with slight modifications. Hübner (1982a, 817–19) rightly criticizes that kind of construction.

255 Cf. Kümmel 1974, 60. He maintains: "V. 17 folgert aus V. 15, daß nicht das Ich der Täter ist, sondern die in ihm wohnende Sünde, die hier zur Erklärung eingeführt wird. Demnach muß V. 17 mit einer folgernden Partikel angefügt sein, und aus diesem Grunde müssen νυνί und οὐκέτι logisch [but not in a temporal sense] gefaßt werden. Die Unterscheidung von Ich und Sünde war vorher nicht gemacht worden, und die Täterschaft des Ich wird logisch durch οὐκέτι aufgehoben." Among others, Espy (1985, 174) and Nygren (1979, 307) have taken the particle οὐκέτι as temporal. Cf. also Möller's remark (1939, 19): "Wie andere Zeitpartikeln können auch sie [νυνί and οὐκέτι] zur Bezeichnung nicht nur

that it is ultimately not the "I" but the sin working in his flesh which does evil. In consequence, the opposition between the real "I" and the flesh appears already in vv. 15–16.

To justify a shift in the subject, Kümmel still has 7:14 on which to rely. At first glance, it truly seems to prove that the "I" is wholly carnal and sold under sin.[256] But such a conclusion turns out to be inadequate. Apparently, v. 14 must be read in the light of the context. The confession of the "I" is matched by the harshness of his concession in v. 18a. They are verbatim almost one-to-one:

v. 14: οἴδαμεν γὰρ . . . ἐγὼ δὲ σάρκινος

v. 18: οἶδα γὰρ . . . ἐν τῇ σαρκί μου[257]

In addition, the echo of being "sold under sin" in v. 14 is heard in v. 18 as the total absence of goodness. The "I" emphasizes that no good dwells in him or, properly speaking, in his flesh (οὐκ οἰκεῖ ἐν ἐμοί, τοῦτ᾽ ἔστιν ἐν τῇ σαρκί μου, ἀγαθόν). As shown, vv. 19–20 then relate the absolute compulsion of not doing the good (ἀγαθόν) viz. of doing the evil (κακόν) explicitly to the indwelling sin (ἡ οἰκοῦσα ἐν ἐμοὶ ἁμαρτία). The similarity in terminology is evident (ἀγαθόν and οἰκεῖν), substantiating the linkage between flesh and sin. Their close relationship is also made known by use of some copulative conjunctions (γάρ, δέ, or ἀλλά), which join together the subsequent phrases in mutual dependence. Besides, vv. 19–20 illuminate v. 18 and reiterate word for word most of vv. 15b–17, which in turn elucidate v. 14. Hence, vv. 14 and 18 are parallel, explaining each other.[258]

Further, v. 18 differentiates between the "I" who *is* wholly flesh and the "I" who *has* flesh.[259] The "I" who speaks of "my flesh" has flesh. In contrast,

---

einer zeitlichen, sondern auch einer logischen Folge verwendet werden. Aber auch dann läßt der Zeitcharakter sich nicht von der Partikel ablösen, sondern weil und soweit die logische Folge mit der zeitlichen Folge zusammenhängt, kann die Zeitpartikel Ausdruck einer logischen Folge sein."

256 The words σάρκινος and σαρκικός are synonymous (see 1 Cor. 3:1–3). Rightly, Kümmel 1974, 59 n. 1. In contrast to Nygren 1979, 305.

257 Dunn 1988, 390. See also Hofius 2002, 138.

258 Cf. Dunn 1988, 390–92 and Seifrid 1992a, 326–29. For the structure of vv. 14–17 and 18–20, see especially Hofius 2002 136–38; Seifrid 1992a, 326–28. Cf. Garlington 1990, 210–11, 218.

259 See Thurén 1986, 171. Cf. Cranfield 1982, 1:360–61; Möller 1939, 11, 15; Stalder 1962, 304; Zahn 1925, 355. Similarly, Kümmel 1974, 61! Cf. already Möller 1939, 11, 15; Zahn 1925, 355. Here, it is not required to decide on the old controversial subject of debate whether τοῦτ᾽ ἔστιν in v. 18 has a defining or limiting sense (cf. various commentaries), though I myself opt for the latter interpretation. Against Wilckens (1980, 2:87–88), who ignores the fine nuance in v. 18. He postulates without further ado: "Aber es ist sehr zu beachten, daß Paulus 'in meinem Fleisch' im Sinne von V 14 so versteht, daß das Ich selbst Fleisch *ist*."

the "I" in whom no good dwells is "wholly fleshly."[260] It follows that the former "I" is at any rate not per se fleshly and sold under sin.[261] The odd complexity of the existential misery in chapter 7 does not allow a simple characterization. It turns out that v. 14 merely emphasizes one aspect, and the following phrases complete the description. The passage is composed of two parts (vv. 14–17 and vv. 18–20) which correspond to each other. Apparently, it is not quite easy for the "I" to put his struggle within himself into plain and easy words. His story evolves and advances during his monologue. It ends in v. 25 where the lethal coalition of flesh and sin occurs once more (see above). The "I" who delightfully serves the Law of God with his mind still has to serve (the present tense δουλεύω, indicating the continual activity) "the law of sin" with his flesh. The closing line in his self-portrait shows that isolating v. 14 from its context would not do justice to the content and progress of the story in vv. 15–25.[262]

In conclusion, vv. 14–25 testify thoroughly to the tension between the real "I" and the flesh in which sin dwells.

Against the backdrop of the critical confrontation with Kümmel, his thesis that Rom. 7:14–25 represents man struggling under the Law must be met with increasing skepticism.[263] As is widely known, Paul frequently underscores in his epistles that all people are by nature wholly fleshly and hostile to the Law of God.[264] Yet the "I" who has flesh (v. 18) is at least not wholly fleshly and according to his "inward man" (v. 22) not at all hostile to the Law of God.[265] Kümmel himself calls attention to the incompatibility of his own interpretation with Pauline anthropology in general.[266]

Chapter 8 strengthens the critical skepticism still more. V. 5 asserts that those who "live according to the flesh" set their minds on "the things of the flesh" (τὰ τῆς σαρκὸς φρονοῦσιν). Further, v. 7 affirms that the mind of the flesh (τὸ φρόνημα τῆς σαρκός) does not submit to God's Law, nor can it do so. In contrast, the "I" delights in the Law of God according to the "inward man" or in

260 See Varo (1984, 38–39) in reference to some church fathers: "La primera vez podría parecer que a todo el hombre, facultades superiores e inferiores, se aplica la debilidad significada por el attributo 'de carne'; pore so San Pablo especifica en el versículo 18c que no habita nada bueno 'en su carne,' no en todo el 'yo' sino solamente en la carne."

261 Thurén 1986, 171. Cf. also Gundry's remark (1980, 243 n. 30) on v. 14: "Strictly speaking, the fleshly 'I' in 7:14 is not a sinful 'I,' but an 'I' whose physical weakness and needs make it easy prey for sin [. . .]."

262 More for the content and progress of the story in Rom. 7:14–25, see especially Laato 2018a, 747–51.

263 Kümmel 1974, 117–18.

264 See above 4.1.2. and further below.

265 Packer 1964, 625–26. For the characterization of Christians as "fleshly" or tainted by the flesh, see Laato 2018a, 747–49.

266 Kümmel 1974, 118, 134–35, 137.

his own "mind" (νοῦς, 7:21–23).[267] Kümmel ignores the relevance of 8:5, 7. He discusses the context only up to v. 4.[268]

More accurately, the mindset of the "I" rather arises from the spiritual mind (8:6–7) which does not turn against the Law of God (see 8:3–17). For sure, the Spirit is not explicitly mentioned in 7:14–25.[269] However, a mere *argumentum e silentio* does not prove that the passage by no means presupposes his influence. Incidentally, the Spirit is not explicitly mentioned in chapter 6 either and yet definitely is taken for granted.[270] The larger context should be kept in mind. Otherwise the right track is lost. Accordingly, the positive attitude toward the "spiritual" Law (7:14) originates from the impact of the Spirit.[271] The "I" is no doubt spiritually minded. It yearns for fulfilling the divine will.[272]

Despite its positive attitude vis-à-vis the Law, the "I" does not succeed in doing what is good:

> For I do not understand (οὐ γινώσκω) what I do (κατεργάζομαι). For what I want to do I do not do (πράσσω), but I do (ποιῶ) the very thing I hate. (v. 15 according to my own translation)[273]

---

267 Modalsli 1965, 34; Packer 1964, 625–26.

268 See Kümmel 1974, Register der Bibelstellen. He (op. cit., 73) writes of 8:5ff.: "Da die abschließenden Verse 8,5–11 die Gedanken von 8,1–4 nur noch näher ausführen, indem sie die Unvereinbarkeit des fleischlichen Wandels mit dem Geistbesitz der Christen dartun, ist ein Eingehen auf sie hier nicht mehr notwendig."

269 Kümmel 1974, 104–6.

270 D. H. Campbell 1980, 59. He sarcastically points out: "There is, for that matter, no reference to the Spirit in ch. 6, yet no one seems to think that this precludes a description of Christian experience there." Similarly, Packer 1999, 80: "[. . .] the lack of reference to the Spirit in 7:14–25 proves nothing; not only because arguments from silence are intrinsically inconclusive, but because Paul's theme here, focused by his own question in verse 7, is sin's antipathy to God's law [. . .]." See also Leeste 1979, 93. Cf. Garlington 1990, 224; Möller 1939, 24–25.

271 Cranfield 1982, 1:356; Möller 1939, 24–25; Nygren 1979, 306–7. Besides, the words νοῦς (vv. 23, 25) and πνεῦμα are sometimes synonyms. See the commentaries on Rom. 11:34 and 1 Cor. 2:16. Cf. Cranfield 1982, 1;370; Dunn 1975, 263. Kümmel (1974, 27–28) also writes in view of the two verses: "Hier ist im Zitat aus Jes. 40, 13 vom νοῦς κυρίου die Rede, und im Anschluß daran redet Paulus 1.Kor. 2, 16b vom νοῦς Χριστοῦ, den die Gläubigen haben, so daß also hier νοῦς = πνεῦμα ist (vgl. Röm. 8, 9)."

272 Varo (1984) erroneously maintains that Rom. 7:7–25 should describe not only Christians but all human beings, e.g., their (uncorrupted) "razón" (pp. 31–32, 45–46, 49 *et passim*), "facultades propiamente humanas, racionales" (p. 36), "potencias superiores" (pp. 42, 45), "libertad" (pp. 43–47), "la facultad volitiva" (p. 45), "las facultades superiores del hombre" (p. 48). He seems to read into the text much of Roman Catholic doctrine and theology. In contrast to Rom. 8:5–8 and even without discussing the passage, he speaks about "la potestad de la voluntad cuya capacidad de querer el bien no quedó viciada como consecuencia del pecado original" (p. 43), concluding that "San Pablo en ningún momento pretende quitar el libre arbitrio [. . .]" (p. 47).

273 For parallels in ancient literature compare Hommel 1961, 106–12; Lichtenberger 1985, 1:192–201; Theißen 1983, 213–23; Thielman 1989, 104–6. For the confessions of sins in Qumran compare Braun 1959, 4–15 and Thielman 1989, 106–7.

Obviously, the verb γινώσκειν does not mean "to know" here. The "I" is well aware of its sinfulness and wickedness in doing evil against its better will. For instance, the German translation of the revised Luther Bible (1984) misses the point in speaking of "knowing" in v. 15. Rather, the phrase οὐ γινώσκω expresses the idea of "not understanding" one's own doings and not doings.[274]

Unfortunately, v. 15 does not explicitly point out which evil the pronoun ὅ hints at. Kümmel does not discuss the question at all. Apparently, he simply and tacitly takes for granted that transgressions of the Law are brought into focus.[275] However, his assumption needs to be clarified somewhat. He does not sufficiently deal with the context.

Parallel to v. 15, the verb κατεργάζεσθαι occurs later in v. 17 as well as in v. 20 (ultimately a word-for-word recurrence of v. 16a and v. 17). Here it is sin which, in fact, works the wickedness of the "I."[276] The same verb occurs already in v. 13. Also there, sin appears as the subject. Now, it "produced (κατεργαζομένη) death in me through what was good." Some commentators convincingly infer that in vv. 13 and 15 the object of the verb κατεργάζεσθαι must be the same, namely, death.[277] Still, they frequently disregard the fact that the same verb occurs already in v. 8. Even there, sin appears as the subject.[278] Now, it seized the "opportunity through the commandment" (v. 7: "You shall not covet") and "produced (κατειργάσατο) in me all kinds of covetousness." Hence, the object of the verb κατεργάζεσθαι in vv. 8 and 15 must be the same, namely, lusts of all kinds. In consequence, the pronoun ὅ has two antecedents. It harks back to πᾶσαν ἐπιθυμίαν (v. 8) and θάνατον (v. 13). Simply put, the "I" does not understand that sin has brought him death by calling forth lusts.[279]

In Romans 7, it is all about sinning against the commandment "Do not covet." Covetousness is the chief of sins, which most of the time remains out of sight, hidden in the depths of the heart, but which still contaminates everything that comes out of it with a taint of depravity.[280] Covetousness militates

274 Kümmel 1974, 59. See further Barrett 1967, 147; Cranfield 1982, 1:358–59; Hommel 1961, 96; Murray 1982, 1:261–62; Wilckens 1980, 2:87.

275 Kümmel 1974, 59.

276 See above.

277 Bornkamm 1966a, 63; Bultmann 1932, 60–61; Fuchs 1949, 70–71; Hommel 1961, 96 n. 8; Schlier 1977, 231–32; Wilckens 1980, 2:86–87. Cf. Käsemann 1980, 194.

278 But see Bornkamm 1966a, 63; Fuchs 1949, 70–71; Hommel 1961, 96 n. 8. Cf. also Seifrid 2011, 156: "There is no reason to suppose that he [Paul] now [in v. 15] has shifted his attention away from the prohibition of coveting that he has cited in v. 7."

279 For the meaning of θάνατος, see above 4.2.2.3.

280 Blank 1969, 167; Bornkamm 1966a, 54–55; Brandenburger 1962, 207; Bultmann 1940, 23–25; Van Dülmen 1968, 108; Espy 1985, 161–77; Fuchs 1962, 288–90; Hübner 1982, 63–65; Joest 1955, 285 and n. 51; Käsemann 1980, 186; Möller 1939, 76; Patte 1983, 265–66; Stalder 1962, 293–94; Theißen 1983, 207–8; Ziesler 1988, 47–52. By contrast Althaus 1951a, 87–88; Räisänen 1976, 434–35 (see nevertheless 1979, especially 90–94); Stendahl 1976, 12–15, 78–96. They assert that Paul did not consider lusts as such sin. On

against love. They rule each other out. Where the one holds sway, the other fades away. As the opposite of love, which is the fulfillment of the Law (Rom. 13:10; Gal. 5:14), covetousness then is the transgression of the Law. On occasion, it certainly engenders blatant and odious vices but conceals itself even behind seemingly blameless piety.[281] The "I" sins each and every time it does not do good from the bottom of the heart. An "outer" fulfilling of the Law without "inner" consent does not suffice. The commandment "Do not covet" always calls for an absolute perfection with renunciation of all evil desires. Nothing less is enough.[282]

By and large, it is in Romans 7 a matter not primarily of evil works. The accent falls in the first place upon impure motives. The commandment "Do not covet" bans all sins (see above). By transgressing that single commandment, the "I" is therefore transgressing the whole Law (cf. James 2:10). An all-inclusive and wide-ranging list of vices with an exact distinction between heinous acts, words, or thoughts is missing. The "I" sins where- and whenever it does not do good from the bottom of the heart.[283] As a result, it has to confess in v. 19:

> For I do not do the good I want, but the evil I do not want is what I keep on doing.

---

the other hand, Bultmann (1932, 53–62; 1940, 13–18) reads too much into Romans 7. He (1932, 60) proposes a puzzling "transsubjective" interpretation which "bezieht sich gar nicht auf die empirische Tat der Übertretung, sondern auf das Ergebnis des Tuns, das für die gesetzliche Existenz bei jeder Tat herauskommt: auf den Tod." Thus the "I" sins because it attempts to fulfill the commandments (and establish his own righteousness), not so much because it really has to transgress them. His error results from his "nomistic" desire. Of course, Bultmann deserved much credit for his interpretation among his followers. See Bornkamm 1966a, 54–57, 62–63; Braun 1959, 2–3; Hübner 1981, 70–71; 1982, 65–69; Osten-Sacken 1975, 202–9; cf. also Patte 1983, 275–77. They suggest similarly that Paul especially stigmatizes the "nomistic" lust (= the attempt to fulfill the Law). For biting criticism, see Althaus 1951a, 47–49; Ellwein 1955, 259–60; Hommel 1961, 96–97, 115–16; Kertelge 1971, 110–11; Räisänen 1979, 85–99; 1983, 111–12; T. R. Schreiner 1991, 238–41; Stalder 1962, 296–97 and n. 26; Theißen 1983, 210–11; Westerholm 1984, 237–38; Wilckens 1980, 2:80–81. Cf. Osten-Sacken 1975, 202–3.

281 Cf. Espy 1985, 161–88; Fuchs 1949, 71–72; Ziesler 1988, 47–52. See further Seifrid 1992a, 328 n. 45: What the "I" desires "to accomplish, is not a particular deed, but the moral perfection which is contained in the Law as a whole." Similarly, Osborne 2011, 35: "Still, the 'good' here means that which God requires, not just good deeds. One can perform good acts without truly being 'good' in a divine sense."

282 Differently, Kjær 2010, 136: "[. . .] and the motives of the 'I' are pure, because the 'I' wants to do the good, delights in God's law and hates the evil" (my translation). However, someone definitely can yearn to have pure motives and solely do what is good—only to realize that he is unable to change himself. So it goes in Romans 7. Furthermore, Kjær insufficiently takes into account the context, especially the object of the verb κατεργάζεσθαι in vv. 8, 13 and 15 (see above). As a result, he fails to discuss the problem of covetousness in the whole passage (see op. cit., 222–23). Neither does Kjær satisfactorily allow for the difference between the "I" who *is* "fleshly" and the "I" who *has* the "flesh" (v. 18), nor for their mutual agony (see below).

283 See Laato 2018a, 743–44. Rightly, T. R. Schreiner 1998, 391 n. 28.

Indeed, no one always does only evil and never good. Being so bad is out of the question.[284] The excessive pessimistic tone in the lamentation of the "I" originates from his total impotence to carry out the commandments (if at all) from pure motives. Despite earnest striving, it cannot attain the distant ideal of not coveting. Concupiscence constantly remains latent in his heart. At times also occasional lapses occur. As a result, an immeasurable defeatism or resignation accrues within himself, devoid of any alleviation of anxiety through himself. In view of the perfectionistic perspective, explicitly written in the Law, the "I"—as expected—always does evil and never good. What else could he do?[285]

Besides, here the verbs ποιεῖν and πράσσειν most likely express an actionism that is by no means manifested exclusively in works. In agreement with the usage elsewhere in Romans, man actually "does" evil also when he carries it out either in thoughts or words. The long list of vices in 1:28–31 includes along with various "large" offenses some "small" aberrations, even such as a person does not necessarily "do" (e.g., greed, depravity, envy, malice, slander, hatred toward God, and arrogance). At any rate, they are enumerated as the object of ποιεῖν (1:28, 32) and πράσσειν (1:32). No clear-cut division into thoughts, words, and acts appears appropriate. Evil is "done"—be that "merely" a matter of the mouth or mind.[286] In the Septuagint as well there are numerous exhortations to "do" (ποιεῖν)[287] the Law or, respectively, the Decalogue (see, e.g., Exod. 24:3, 7; Lev. 19:37; Deut. 5:1, 31–32; 6:1, 24; 28:58; 31:12), though one cannot fulfill every individual commandment through good works (e.g., to honor God, not to take God's name in vain, not to bear false witness against one's neighbor, or not to covet one's neighbor's house).[288]

In consideration of the tangible emphasis on coveting especially in Romans, it seems less convincing to maintain that Paul was simply a man of "a rather robust conscience," not being in accord with the so-called "introspection" of

284 Particularly against Räisänen's interpretation 1983, 109–11 (already 1980b, 310–11). See further Gundry 1980, 238; Sanders 1983, 74–81, 124–25. Cf. even Nygren 1979, 296–303. He suggests that the "I" (= the Christian) "verkligen och entydigt har sin lust i det goda" (298), but "i utförandet slår det ständigt fel" (300). For criticism, see Althaus 1952, 478. On the contrary, Kjær (see 2010, 170, 181–82, 223) tries to convince that the present form of some verbs in chapter 7 (as "I do" and "I will") is "iterative," designating only what occurs occasionally. Then he concludes that Christians sin now and then. Finally, the text is telling us nothing else! But do we really need such an extensive passage to tell us simply that? And how should the reader know when and why some verbs (but obviously not all) are "iterative"? In trying to solve one big problem Kjær actually engenders more troubles to himself.

285 Cf. further Ziesler 1988, 51. See also the discussion of the "radicalized" Law, introduced by Bruckner (1995, above all 104–8).

286 See my interpretation of Rom. 2:1–3 above. Cf. further Fuchs 1949, 71–72.

287 The verb πράσσειν appears only sometimes. See Ziesler 1988, 55 n. 25.

288 First and foremost, Ziesler 1988, 50.

Western Christianity ever since Augustine and in particular Luther.[289] On the contrary, the apostle appears to be conscientious at least vis-à-vis the unconditional demand of the divine Law. He thoroughly knows his total inadequacy as a consequence of the commandment prohibiting concupiscence in every form. To be sure, the heartrending or heartbreaking description in Romans 7 does not spring from the soul of "a rather robust" person. It is serious, not in the least theatrical.[290] Neither, for example, does the great, magnificent hymn of love (the opposite of covetousness) in 1 Corinthians 13 support any idea of moral pragmatism. Outward outstanding outcomes of superior behavior are nothing, if not done out of pure motives. Even the gifts of the Holy Spirit weigh nothing without an altruistic mindset. Indeed, all you need is love, real love which flows from God through Christ to you. In that context the notion of a "robust" conscience does not comport with the overall picture.[291]

Yet it would certainly not do justice to Paul—if not having a "robust" conscience—to portray him as holding something like an "introspective" mindset. The whole of his theology and missionary diligence rests on Christ alone, who has died for the fallen world and atoned for their sins. While passing judgment on Gentiles in general and Jews in particular (Romans 1–3), he is naturally not attempting to show the whites of their eyes and make them gaze

289 Stendahl 1963, 199–215, here in particular 200. It is highly symptomatic that Stendahl does not at all discuss the problem of coveting in Pauline writings but dwells chiefly on the Pharisaic past of the apostle; his later call to apostleship, which should not be misunderstood as his conversion; his apostolic ministry in sincerity; and his weakness in the course of the missionary work—but without any specific relation to his sin (see op. cit., 204–11). However, see Althaus 1951a, 87–88; Räisänen 1976, 434–35 (but cf. 1979, 90–94). They assert that Paul did not consider lusts as such sin. Yet see my arguments above. Rightly, Espy 1985; Ziesler 1988, 47–52. Similarly, already Möller 1939, 76. Cf. also Blank 1969, 167; Fuchs 1962, 288–90. Certainly because of Roman Catholic theology, Varo speaks here merely of *fomes peccati* (see 1984, 50 *et passim*), concluding: "[. . .] esos actos de la concupiscencia desordenada no son pecados mortales si falta la advertencia del entendimiento o el consentimiento de la voluntad" (op. cit., 41).

290 See Dunn 1975, 260–61. Later Dunn (1988, 394) writes: "The illogicality of arguing that the passage here expresses with Christian hindsight the existential anguish of the pious Jew—which as a pious Jew he did not actually experience and which as a Christian he still does not experience!—is not usually appreciated." Cf. Deuser 1979, 422. See further, e.g., D. H. Campbell 1980, 60; Gundry 1980, 229; Nygren 1979, 308; Packer 1964, 623; 1999, 74.

291 Like Paul, many of his contemporaries in the field of religion, philosophy, or culture were engaged in differentiating inner motives of people making moral decisions. For parallels in ancient Jewish and Greek literature, cf. Van den Beld 1985, 495–515; Braun 1959, 4–15; Burgland 1997, 163–76; Hommel 1961, 90–116; Krauter 2011, 1–15; Lichtenberger 2004, 177–86; E. W. Smith 1971, 127–35; Theißen 1983, 213–23; Thielman 1989, 104–7; Wasserman 2007, 793–816, and her more detailed monograph 2008. Most of all, see the critical remarks in Huggins 1992, 153–61. Similarly, Garlington 1990, 229 n. 140. Also, Dunn (1988, 389) speaks here of "significant differences" referring to the eschatological tension in Pauline theology.

into themselves. No, on the contrary, he is begging them to look away from themselves and focus on the cross of Calvary where they are freely forgiven. Truly, they are not to learn "introspection," or at least they do not have to stick to that attitude obstinately. Instead they are—in line with the Gospel—to be taught "Christ-spection" through faith. Nothing else will save them. I suppose neither Augustine nor Luther would disagree.[292]

Obviously, the "I" does not reckon with an immediate alteration in its existence. It speaks with resignation:

> So then, I myself (αὐτὸς ἐγώ)[293] serve the law of God with my mind, but with my flesh I serve the law of sin. (v. 25b)

Kümmel wonders why, after the thanksgiving for the redemption of the Christian (7:25a), Paul returns to the slavery of the "I" under sin (7:25b), and then once more harks back to the notion of Christian freedom (8:1ff). V. 25a seems very disturbing between vv. 14–24 and v. 25b. Perhaps Paul simply broke off dealing with his theme in chapter 7 and for an instant expressed his thanks to God. Judging by the content, his praise rather belongs to chapter 8.[294]

Kümmel's solution has hardly found approval among scholars.[295] Nowadays, most of them explain 7:25b as a marginal gloss that does not interfere with the original context.[296] Without a doubt, their hazardous hypothesis fails to carry conviction since all of the manuscripts speak in favor of the authenticity of v. 25b.[297] Kümmel is surely correct in warning "not to change anything in the

---

292 In addition, cf. Wengert 2013, 90: "[. . .] as interesting a thesis as Krister Stendahl's proposal in his brief article on the 'introspective conscience of the West' is, it is unfortunate that New Testament exegetes are willing to believe his unproven argument about fifteen hundred years of church history rather than employ the careful work of historians. And yet they would never allow a historian of biblical interpretation to write the definitive work on Paul in an equivalent fifteen-page essay—nor should they. That is, New Testament scholars simply need to stop using a meditative piece by Stendahl as the lens through which to judge all interpretations of Paul from Augustine through Luther to the present."

293 The expression means "I myself," not, e.g., "I alone (without Christ)." Against Kürzinger 1963, 272–73. Rightly, already Kümmel 1974, 66–67.

294 Kümmel 1974, 65–66.

295 See however Räisänen 1976, 431.

296 K-A. Bauer 1971, 159; Bultmann 1947, 198–99; Fuchs 1949, 82–83; 1962, 304; Käsemann 1980, 203–4; Lichtenberger 1985, 1:165–72; Paulsen 1974, 23–31; Schlier 1977, 235. Cf. Bornkamm 1966a, 66; Braun 1959, 3; Ellwein 1968, 160; Wilckens 1980, 2:96–97. Some commentators place v. 25b even behind v. 23. See the discussion in F. Müller 1941, 249–52; Lichtenberger 1985, 1:166–67; Paulsen 1974, 23–27; Schmithals 1980, 81–82. Rightly, e.g., Packer 1999, 79. On the history of the interpretation of verse 25b, see first and foremost Keuck 1961, 257–80.

297 Bruce 1963, 156; Cranfield 1982, 1:368–69; Dunn 1975, 262; Gundry 1980, 240; Möller 1939, 13–14.

text that has been handed without variant" ("an dem variantenlos überlieferten Text etwas zu verändern").[298]

My exegesis of v. 25a (see above) shows that v. 25b makes good sense in the original context. After crying for deliverance from the body of death and giving thanks to God for his impending help (vv. 24–25a), the "I" finally summarizes the enduring dichotomy by making a clear-cut existential distinction between serving the Law of God with the mind and serving the law of sin with the flesh at the same time (v. 25b). With resignation, it remarks that the current exhausting duel between the mind and the flesh does not end before the Last Day.[299] No spiritual renewal leaves off the tension between them. The "I" cannot extinguish his desires and cleanse his conscience from impure motives. It is and remains "slave" both of God and sin (δουλεύω, the present tense indicating the continuous activity).[300]

Consequently, the "I" does not live in harmony with itself. As a person, it is divided as if in two parts. With the mind it serves the Law of God; with the flesh, the law of sin.[301] In it and for it are, strictly speaking, two powers fighting. They are beside and against each other. Readiness for compromise is lacking: the flesh desires evil, the mind good; or, alternatively, the mind works against evil, but the flesh against good. Their continual tug-of-war in constant tension puts the patience of the "I" to sore trial. Its psyche falls incessantly under hard pressure. The "I" cannot be satisfied in regard to the mind with evil nor in regard to the flesh with good intentions. Besides, feelings of self-accusation overwhelm its very sensitive personality, because only 100 percent obedience would prevent the condemnation of the Mosaic Law.[302]

All told, vv. 14–25 as to both terminology and theology reflect on the Christian experience which stems from a conscientious encounter with the Mosaic Law. In light of 6:12 and 8:10, evil desires and lusts still reside in the body even after conversion and Baptism. They have not disappeared anywhere. Thus all Christians constantly come to sense the burden of the command "Thou shalt not covet" and the necessity of corruption in their own life. Despite the new eschatological situation, they have reason enough for a complaint such as 7:14–25 since the Torah imposes on them unattainable requirements for lily-white motives. The precise distinction between the "inward man" (only used of

298 Kümmel 1974, 67–68. Cf. further Byskov 1976, 84–85; Packer 1964, 625.

299 Byskov 1976, 84–85; Cranfield 1982, 1:368–69; Dunn 1975, 262–63; Möller 1939, 14; Packer 1964, 626–27.

300 Ibid.

301 Modalsli 1965, 33–34. Cf. Stalder 1962, 299–301. By contrast Bultmann 1940, 15–16.

302 The attempt to interpret the monologue of the "I" in terms of a theological "Handlungstheorie" (Bader 1981) or a psychoanalytical conception (Vergote 1973) in my opinion leads no further.

the Christian, see 2 Cor. 4:16; Eph. 3:16)[303] respectively the "mind" (sometimes a synonym for Spirit)[304] and the "flesh" respectively the "members"[305] shows the paradoxical reality of the "already now/not yet." The old era of sin, condemnation, and death has not ended abruptly and suddenly in the new era of grace, salvation, and eternal bliss.[306] The absolute upheaval first takes place on the Last Day. Then the final redemption of the body from its corruption and mortality (7:24) will come to pass (Rom. 8:23).

In particular, the consistent meaning of the word σῶμα (repeatedly overlooked in mainstream exegesis) should receive attention here. It obviously retains the same basic content in Romans 6–8. As shown, it relates to the physical body as representative of the whole person. Even Christians no doubt have their body after their conversion or Baptism. They are no ghosts! All this hardly needs corroboration. The interpretation of the "I" as Paul himself (or any Christian) indicates that σῶμα in 7:24 maintains the most natural meaning. He will be released from his body of death and sin on the Last Day. On the contrary, if the "I" depicts either the man under the Law or without the Law, then his release from the body of death stands for conversion in some metaphorical sense. Consequently, the body of death is brought to nothing already through faith! Moreover, a similar thinking pertains to 6:6 and 8:10 as well. Both texts are understood along the same lines (partially in order to be comported with 7:24).[307] This kind of reasoning seems, however, very arbitrary. In chapters 6–8, there are several occurrences where the word σῶμα retains its common meaning (see 6:12; 7:4; 8:11ff.). The body consists of members, and the word μέλη retains an equally concrete meaning (see 6:13, 19; 7:23). Who in Rome would ever have figured out that the author of the letter abruptly and recurrently moves from one sense to another in a totally chaotic manner? Supposing anything like that turns his mode of arguing topsy-turvy.[308]

Summa summarum: On account of the many common traits between 7:24–25a and 6:12 as well as 8:10, with regard to the positive mindset of the "I" and the Christian toward the Torah, and in consideration of their constant

303 Barrett 1967, 150; Byskov 1976, 78; D. H. Campbell 1980, 61; Cranfield 1982, 1:363; Dunn 1975, 262; Möller 1939, 68–69; Murray 1982, 1:265–66.

304 Cf. Rom. 11:34 and 1 Cor. 2:16 (see above).

305 The distinction is found in the whole pericope, not only in vv. 17–23 (contra Kümmel). See above.

306 Particularly Dunn emphasizes that the paradox "already now/not yet" in fact "underlies the whole of Paul's soteriology" (1975, 265). He produces a number of telling examples (op. cit., 264–73).

307 Here it is impossible to go at length into a detailed discussion. I only refer to Laato 2013, 117–18.

308 Cf. Garlington 1990, 231. He underlines: "In chaps. 6–7 this phrase [the 'body of death' in 7:24] is paralleled by 'body of sin' (6:6), 'this mortal body' (6:12), 'my flesh' (7:18), and 'my members' (7:23). [. . .] This is the body which is dead on account of sin (8:10)."

wrestling with the tormenting covetousness in their hearts, it turns out that vv. 14–25 cannot be describing man under the Law. The current consensus appealing to the prominent authority of Kümmel fails to carry conviction. His interpretation should be revisited. Indeed, Rom. 7:14–25 does not cover anything that does not fit the Christian, or—to put it simply—everything that Romans 7 covers fits the Christian alone.[309]

4.2.3.4. Context

For Kümmel, Rom. 7:14–25 turns into a disturbing alien pericope in the context, if it in fact describes the dilemma of Christian existence (see 4.2.3.2., point 1). In order to assess his point of view, I shall scrutinize the three passages under debate (7:1–6; 7:7–13; 8:1–11). To begin with, my study will resort to chapter 8 and mainly repeat what has already been told in relation to vv. 1–2, 5–11. Then the academic discussion will be continued in relation to vv. 3–4.

Indeed, vv. 1–2 spell out that Christians are free from the law of sin and death. Still, vv. 10–11 point out that they are for that reason not free from the body of death. Their definitive liberation does not come until the Last Day (vv. 22–23). That is why they have to hope to be redeemed from the body of death (7:24–25a) at the parousia of Christ.[310]

As shown, vv. 5–9 affirm that the carnal mind in contrast to the spiritual never submits to the Law of God. Because the "I" consents to the Law of God according to the inward man without grumbling (7:22), it must retain a spiritual mind and show a Christian identity.[311]

Finally, the focus lies on vv. 3–4:

> For God has done what the law, weakened by the flesh, could not do. By sending his own Son in the likeness of sinful flesh and for sin, he condemned sin in the flesh, in order that the righteous requirement (τό δικαίωμα) of the law might be fulfilled in us, who walk not according to the flesh but according to the Spirit.

The text raises a number of problems. It seems unnecessary to go through all of the details.[312] The most relevant issue concerns the question whether especially v. 4 supports Kümmel's interpretation of 7:14–25. In his judgment, Christians who live according to the Spirit cannot experience the anxiety of the "I" who struggles with the flesh.[313] Does his conclusion hold true?

---

309 For a similar argumentation, see Laato 2018a, 738–55.

310 See above 4.2.3.3.

311 See above 4.2.3.3.

312 See the commentaries *ad loc.* Kümmel rightly means that v. 3 "zu den umstrittensten des N.T. gehört" (1974, 70).

313 Kümmel 1974, 72–73.

Whatever one thinks about the likelihood of moral faultlessness or perfect sinlessness in Christian life,[314] the new mode of living in the Spirit does not indicate that the flesh abruptly or gradually ceases to exist.[315] The Christian must in himself sense and endure the continual wrestling of the flesh and the Spirit (for instance, Gal. 5:16–25; see further especially Rom. 6:12–13; 8:12–13). He is unable to follow his good intentions without the opposition of his evil compulsions.[316] He lives in tension with himself. All along the line, he fails to extinguish the lusts of his body or flesh (Rom. 6:12; Gal. 5:16–17). Instead, he comes under obligation to kill the deeds of his body or flesh (Rom. 8:13).[317] Thus his life according to the Spirit indicates that he (at his best) does not carry out his evil desires.[318] In any case, he does not do good from absolutely pure motives. Accordingly, the commandment "Do not covet" still threatens him and proves his depravity. Yet he has died to the Law and is free from its curse (7:1–6; 8:1–2).[319] Even so, he finds in himself an inward wickedness that plainly and frankly emerges in 7:14–25.

Besides, it deserves particular attention that Paul formulates the final clause (8:4: ἵνα) very carefully. He does not emphasize that Christians observe the Mosaic Law perfectly through their living according to the Spirit. Rather, his argument culminates in the thesis that "the righteous requirement (τό δικαίωμα)[320] of the law" might "be fulfilled" (πληρωθῇ, passive!) in them. How does that take place? Without a doubt, the righteous requirement of the Law amounts to love. It is, in contrast to concupiscence, "the fulfillment of the Law" (πλήρωμα νόμου, Rom. 13:10; see also Gal. 5:14).[321] Kümmel and many commentators in accordance with him underscore that Christians under the

314 See the summation of the discussion in Ridderbos 1987, 266–67.

315 Cf. Kümmel 1974, 25: "[. . .] und wenn der Christ Sünde tut, so ist auch bei ihm noch die σάρξ die Ursache (2.Kor. 10,3; Röm. 8,13)." And further, 26: "Im Christen ist bis zum Tode das psychische Leben zwar ebensowenig wie das sarkische aufgehoben [. . .]." Moreover, e.g., Bultmann 1940, 23–26; Wenham 1980, 81. Cf. Möller 1939, 16.

316 See, e.g., Ridderbos 1987, 265–72.

317 See also below.

318 Cf. Cranfield 1982, 1:385; Michel 1978, 251–52. To be sure, Christians did not always live according to the Spirit. At least now and then they rendered themselves guilty of the works of the flesh (see 1 Cor. 3:1–4; 5:1–2; 6:1–8; 8:9–12; 11:17–22).

319 On 7:1–6 see below. On 8:1–2 see above.

320 See the commentators.

321 Lichtenberger 1985, 1:152–53, 211; Paulsen 1974, 65–66; Westerholm 1986–87, 230, 232; Wilckens 1980, 2:128–29. Cf. Cranfield 1982, 1:384; Joest 1955, 285; Osten-Sacken 1975, 233. See, however, Hübner 1975, 240–48; 1982, 37–43, 76–80. He maintains that Gal. 5:14 (in contrast to Rom. 13:8–10) refers not to the Mosaic Torah, but rather to the "law of Christ" (Gal. 6:2). For further discussion, see Räisänen 1983, 27–28 n. 72; Sanders 1983, 96–97.

guidance of the Spirit can really follow the Law in their self-sacrificing love.[322] Here, the main focus falsely lies on human activity. Käsemann correctly maintains that a strong emphasis rests on the passive of the verb.[323] God's action comes to the fore.[324] He has already fulfilled the righteous requirement of the Law in Christians (ἐν ἡμῖν), namely, in that he poured out his (own) love[325] through the Holy Spirit (certainly by means of Baptism) in the hearts of Christians (ἐν ταῖς καρδίαις ἡμῶν, Rom. 5:5).[326] Thus the new covenant excels the old by far. Now God has written his Law in the hearts and minds of his eschatological people (Jer. 31:31–34). Absolutely Christians still have to carry out love, present in them thanks to the Spirit, by living according to the Spirit in various everyday situations and conditions. Rom. 7:14–25 reveals that their practice does not measure up to their high ideal.

Accordingly, it follows that Rom. 8:1–11 does not speak in favor of Kümmel's interpretation of 7:14–25, but rather against it.

In the framework of context analysis, chapter 7 is next in line. To begin with, the focus lies on vv. 1–6. Then the interest moves to vv. 7–13. The textual evidence in both passages strongly revolves around the problematics of the Mosaic Torah.

According to vv. 1–6, Christians "died to the law through the body of Christ" (v. 4). Consequently, they have been "released from the law" and serve (God) now "in the newness of the Spirit, and not in the oldness of the letter" (v. 6, my own translation). Here, Kümmel finds again a recognizable support for his own interpretation of vv. 14–25. He contrasts the Christian who is free from the Law with the "I" which stands under the Law.[327] Does his conclusion hold true this time?

---

322 Kümmel 1974, 72–73. He promptly suggests that v. 4 relates to "das sündlose Leben der Christen" (op. cit., 72). In contrast, many other scholars convey the principle of *posse non peccare* (at least) not *expressis verbis* (see, e.g., Van Dülmen 1968, 123; Murray 1982, 1:283–84; Osten-Sacken 1975, 149–50, 155, 233; Schlier 1977, 243–44; Stalder 1962, 405–6; Thielman 1989, 88–90; Wilckens 1980, 2:128–30). However, cf. Mauerhofer 1981, 117–29! Strangely, Dunn (1975, 263) asserts that "in 8,4ff. Paul does not contrast believer with unbeliever; rather he confronts the believer with both sides of the paradox, both sides of his nature as believer." Correctly, Räisänen 1976 n. 34.

323 Käsemann 1980, 210. See further Westerholm 1986–87, 236.

324 Ibid. Similarly, Lichtenberger 1985, 1:152, 211.

325 The Greek concept ἡ ἀγάπη τοῦ θεοῦ is without doubt *genetivus subiectivus*, not *genetivus obiectivus* (Barrett 1967, 105; Cranfield 1982, 1:262; Käsemann 1980, 127; Michel 1978, 181; Murray 1982, 1:165; Schlier 1977, 150–51; Wilckens 1978, 1:293). Yet it at the same time stands for "Gottes Liebesmacht" (Käsemann 1980, 127) and his "wirkende Kraft" (Bornkamm 1987, 222–23) in Christians (cf. Barrett 1967, 105; Schlier 1977, 150–51; Wilckens 1978, 1:293). See further, e.g., Rom. 15:30; 1 Corinthians 13; 2 Cor. 5:14; Col. 1:8.

326 Cf. Michel 1978, 252 n. 7: "Gottes Geist ist sachlich identisch mit der uns zugesprochenen Gerechtigkeit." Further, see Fuchs 1949, 90–93.

327 Kümmel 1974, 97.

Taken as a whole, Kümmel's argumentation does not have much in its favor. The "I" nowhere claims to stand under the Law.[328] His attention centers on his own inadequacy or failure in the face of the Law. Even if sinful passions are not allowed to "be at work in the members" (v. 5), strictly speaking, the overall picture of evil desires as a dreadful threat depicts nothing that belongs merely to the past or the time before conversion. It is simply not true that the new eschatological existence through faith falls outside the enticements provoked by them.[329] As already shown, Rom. 6:12 proves that covetousness arising from the human body still harms Christians and tries to exercise mastery over them. In that regard, there is absolutely no clear-cut contrast between the before and after of conversion. In any case, Baptism marks the great difference. The baptized are able to offer resistance to their heinous penchants. They are free not to carry them out. Now the demonic power of sin has definitely been broken. The plaint in 7:14–25 rises from the disillusionment that the sinlessness, required by the Torah on pain of death, is not attainable. Christians want to obey the Law from pure motives, but they know they cannot. They understand perfectly well that they suffer from their evil desires. They have died to sin, although sin has not died at that very moment. Hence, 7:1–6 hardly serves the slightest objection to their identification with the person of the "I."

In conclusion, the weight falls on vv. 7–13. From v. 7 onward, the "I" delivers his monologue and continues his speaking to v. 25. It first covers a historical event (vv. 7–13), and then the present situation (vv. 14–25).

Kümmel repeatedly emphasizes his conviction that the use of first person (vv. 7–25) as rhetorical device solely serves the purpose of making the story vivid.[330] In vv. 7–13, Paul in no way speaks of himself (of his Jewish past). Accordingly, neither does he speak of himself in vv. 14–25 (of his Christian present), for the subject must in both passages be the same.[331] To be sure, Kümmel points out that vv. 7–13 and 14–25 do not necessarily portray the same

328 Kümmel (1974, 97) writes as follows: "Nun ist aber das Ziel der Erörterung 7, 1–6, daß die Christen vom Gesetz frei seien, weil sie mit Christus gestorben sind [. . .]. Demnach kann Paulus in 7, 14ff. schwerlich von sich als einem Christen sagen, er stehe unter dem Gesetz [. . .]." Where does Paul then say the like? Being under the Law means the total dominion of sin and death over the person (cf. Rom. 6:14, 23a) See, e.g., Ridderbos 1987, 143–49. From the split existence of the "I" (see above, *passim*) one could—if that is what one wishes—draw the conclusion that the "I" sold under sin and bound to death (but in striking contrast to the real "I") stands under the Law. Cf. Stalder 1962, 304–5.

329 Dunn (1988, 371) writes on Rom. 7:5: "The description of what characterized their previous life 'in the flesh' provides the clearest echoes of the preceding exhortation, with almost every word or phrase paralleled in 6:12–23: 'sinful passions' (6:12), 'the law' (6:14–15), 'in our members' (6:13, 19), 'to bear fruit for death' (6:21). One difference is that what 7:5 refers to their preconversion state, 6:12 envisaged as still a possibility for the Roman Christians [. . .]." See above. Cf. Varo 1984, 29–30.

330 Kümmel 1974, 119–32.

331 Op. cit., 90. See further 9–10, 97.

situation or condition of the subject.[332] What exactly he means by that remains for rumination. Later, he offers the reader the following:

> The question of "Who is the subject?" proves to be misunderstood, because a person could formalize exaggeratedly: No one or everyone is the subject. So it is better to think of τίς as the subject.[333]

For certain, τίς aims at the non-Christian. But presumably vv. 7–13 and 14–25 do not describe the same situation of the subject. Strictly speaking, the former passage explains the entrance of a conscious knowledge and experience of sin through the Law.[334] That said, the latter passage further explicates "the curious event" ("das eigentümliche Geschehen") in relation to the enduring conflict between human will and action.[335] Still, chapter 7 deals throughout with the influence of sin on the individual through the Law merely theoretically. It points to no definite incident.[336]

Nevertheless, the narrative of the "I" appears very realistic and authentic. It hardly turns into a theatrical spectacle. Therefore, it must stand in relation to a definite incident.[337] Most exegetes interpret vv. 7–13 as a description of the fall into sin (Genesis 3).[338] Adam (the "I" in vv. 7–13) functions as the prototype of man under the law (the "I" in vv. 14–25).[339]

Kümmel has already known an interpretation like this. He discards it and brings forward principally the following arguments:

1. Paul quotes in v. 7 not the prohibition given by God in Paradise οὐ φάγεσθε (Gen. 2:17), but rather the last commandment (the

---

332 Op. cit., 90.

333 Op. cit., 132: "Die Fragestellung: 'wer ist Subjekt?' erweist sich als mißverständlich; denn man könnte überspitzt formulieren: niemand oder jedermann ist Subjekt. Doch ist es besser, sich τίς als Subjekt zu denken."

334 Op. cit., 48–49.

335 Op. cit., 57–58.

336 Op. cit., 132.

337 See, e.g., D. H. Campbell 1980, 60; Dunn 1975, 260–61; Gundry 1980, 229, 236; Packer 1964, 622–23; Stalder 1962, 294, 306. Cf. Deuser 1979, 422; Ellwein 1955, 260. They all warn of a "theatrical" interpretation of Rom. 7:7–25. In a similar way, see Thurén 2002, 430: "Summing up, if Paul spoke in first person singular excluding himself, but without giving any sign thereof, he must have assumed that his audience was well aware of such a technique. But evidence from ancient rhetoric shows that no such commonly known device existed." Cf. also Varo 1984, 11: "Ciertamente cuando Sa Pablo se sirve del pronombre 'yo' no miente: está hablando en nombre propio."

338 Cf. most modern commentaries. See further Espy 1985, 169; Lichtenberger 1985, 1:139–46, 173; Luz 1968, 166; B. L. Martin 1981, 43; Modalsli 1965, 32; Osten-Sacken 1975, 198; Schnackenburg 1975, 293–94; Sloan 1991, 51; Theißen 1983, 204–11; Ziesler 1988, 43–47.

339 Cf. the preceding note.

two last commandments) of the Decalogue οὐκ ἐπιθυμήσεις (Exod. 20:17; cf. Rom. 13:9).[340]

2. The command οὐκ ἐπιθυμήσεις summarizes the Mosaic Law. The prohibition "not to eat of the tree of the knowledge of good and evil" hardly fits as a summary, but by contrast the last commandment of the Decalogue.[341]
3. In vv. 7–25, Paul wishes to show that the Mosaic Law "was not a sin, but only a tool for sin" ("nicht Sünde, sondern nur eine Handhabe für die Sünde war"). Genesis 3 does not serve as proof, because Adam did not know the Mosaic Law at all.[342]
4. Paul in no place explicitly points out that "the reader should make Adam or the humanity in Adam the subject of the story, quite apart from the fact, that in 7:14ff. this meaning fails all the more" ("der Leser zum Subjekt des Geschilderten Adam oder die Menschheit in Adam zu machen habe, ganz abgesehen davon, daß in 7,14ff. diese Deutung erst recht versagt").[343]

I deal with the previous arguments in reverse order:

Kümmel seems not to have thought through his fourth argument. For certain, Paul in no place explicitly identifies the subject in vv. 7–13, but neither does he disclose that the first person would merely be a rhetorical device or style.[344] Furthermore, I find no explanation why the "I" in the light of vv. 14–25 could not symbolize, for example, the humanity living in Adam (without Christ).

Besides, Kümmel's third argument has little going for it. Rom. 5:13–14 compares Adam's transgression against the "law" in Paradise with transgressions against the Mosaic Law: he transgressed God's concrete commandment, as the Jews do when they sin.[345] Accordingly, Genesis 3 suffices, at least for the apostle to the Gentiles, to prove that sin—just as it once took advantage of the "law" in Paradise—now makes use of the Mosaic Law in provocation of evil works.

In fact, Kümmel's second argument merges into his first. Provided that Paul finds out from the prohibition οὐ φάγεσθε the deeper meaning of οὐκ ἐπιθυμήσεις as the quintessence of the Mosaic Law, then Gen. 2:17 in his view includes the quintessence of the Mosaic Law as well. Hence, the actual point of disagreement culminates in the question whether the commandment οὐ φάγεσθε assumes the deeper significance of οὐκ ἐπιθυμήσεις or not.

340 Kümmel 1974, 86–87.

341 Op. cit., 86.

342 Op. cit., 87.

343 Ibid.

344 First of all, Theißen (1983, 194–204) has convincingly objected to Kümmel's hypothesis of a purely fictive "I."

345 Osten-Sacken 1975, 200; Theißen 1983, 205.

The story of the fall itself associates covetousness and eating with each other. Eve ate from the tree of the knowledge of good and evil since it was נחמד, "lust-arousing," and תאוה, "desirable" (Gen. 3:6).[346] The verbs חמד and אוה ("to covet") occur also in the last two commandments of the Decalogue (Exod. 20:17; Deut. 5:21). In order to understand Rom. 7:7–13, a closer look at the Jewish tradition proves helpful.

In their thorough analysis of the contents of the last two commandments, many rabbis explain with precision the meaning of covetousness: The concept תאוה denotes the mere wish in the heart, while חמוד designates the human intention to bring the object of desire within one's control. Hence, חמוד indicates sin, which inevitably—insofar as circumstances permit—leads to transgression.[347] This is precisely how the fall took place: Eve ate from the tree of the knowledge of good and evil because she had immediately before doing so coveted it.

B. Shabbat 145b–146a (parallels: Jabmuth 103b and Avodah Zarah 22b) tells that the serpent approached Eve and inflamed (הטיל) her with covetousness (זוהמא). As a result of the fall, not less than all the world came under the control of covetousness. First at Sinai the Israelites (not the others!) liberated themselves from the control of covetousness when they received the Torah and obtained their status as the people of God. Ever since, no Jew has any longer had the inner compulsion to carry out his evil instincts.[348]

Thus the course of events in the fall (Genesis 3, particularly in the light of rabbinic explanations) corresponds exactly with the course of events in the monologue of the "I": commandment → desire → transgression → death (Rom. 7:7–13).[349] Indeed, it seems that Rom. 7:7–13 interprets and summarizes the story in Genesis of the episode in Paradise. In order to illustrate the data, I outline as follows the fall of Adam and Eve. In parenthesis, I show how Paul links up with the tradition of the Old Testament (and the rabbis):

(1) Once upon a time, Adam and Eve lived a life of full value (v. 9: ἐγὼ δὲ ἔζων) in Paradise. They could eat the fruit of the tree of life. (2) There was no Law to begin with (v. 9: χωρὶς νόμου ποτέ). (3) Later, God gave his specific commandment (v. 9: ἐλθούσης δὲ τῆς ἐντολῆς; cf. ἐνετείλατο, Gen. 2:16). (4) The commandment should help humankind to live (v. 10: ἡ ἐντολὴ ἡ εἰς ζωήν) or to secure free access to the tree of life. (5) But the serpent (tantamount to sin

346 Espy 1985, 163; Luz 1968, 166; Lyonnet 1962, 161; Theißen 1983, 206. Cf. Räisänen 1979, 92.

347 Billerbeck 1926, 234–37. Since the two verbs occur in the two last commandments of the Decalogue, they hardly differ from each other but function in a parallel fashion (as already in Gen. 3:6).

348 Lyonnet 1962, 161–62. See further Dochhorn 2009, 59–68. He discusses additionally some relevant and parallel passages in the Apocalypse of Moses.

349 Op. cit., 161.

in vv. 8–9, 11, 13) took advantage of the commandment (vv. 8, 11: ἀφορμὴν δὲ λαβοῦσα ἡ ἁμαρτία διὰ τῆς ἐντολῆς), (6) deceived Eve (v. 11: ἐξηπάτησεν; see further 2 Cor. 11:3, cf. ἠπάτησεν, Gen. 3:13), (7) and produced in her all kinds of desires, above all the specific desire to eat of the tree of the knowledge of good and evil (v. 8: κατειργάσατο ἐν ἐμοὶ πᾶσαν ἐπιθυμίαν; cf. Gen. 3:6). (8) Eve succumbed to temptation and ate of the tree of the knowledge of good and evil. As expected, also Adam ate (especially vv. 9–11). (9) As a result of sin, both met death (vv. 10–11, 13).

The brief outline may suffice to illustrate that Rom. 7:7–13 actually interprets and summarizes the story in Genesis of the episode in Paradise.[350] Apparently, Paul modified the prohibition οὐ φάγεσθε to the form οὐκ ἐπιθυμήσεις, since he (after the manner of later rabbis) considered Eve's initial sin in terms of covetousness. The scribe easily came to the conclusion that Gen. 2:17 even forbids desires, assuming that lusts necessarily lead to an "outer" transgression of the prohibition (cf. the concept of חמוד among the rabbis). Moreover, Paul has doubtless modified the prohibition οὐ φάγεσθε to οὐκ ἐπιθυμήσεις also on polemical grounds. He quotes the last commandment of the Decalogue in order to equate the command given in Paradise with the Law given on Sinai and thus to overthrow the Jews' trust in their own elevated status.[351] From his perspective, they have not liberated themselves from the control of covetousness through their knowledge of the Law. On the contrary, the Torah subordinates them under the slavish dominance of covetousness, for sin provokes the individual to "all kinds of lusts" (Rom. 7:8) as much through the Law of Sinai as earlier by the "law" in Paradise. A person can triumph over his desires and serve God "in newness of Spirit," if he simply dies to the Law (Rom. 7:5–6).[352]

Who, then, is the subject in vv. 7–13? The answer seems not so straightforward because some traits in the passage fit either Adam or Eve. For example, it was only Adam who originally lived without law; only he received the command from God not to eat of the tree of the knowledge of good and evil (see points 2

350 Recently, Gundry (1980, 229–32) denies that Rom. 7:7–13 refers to Genesis 2–3. For criticism see Ziesler 1988, 43–47.

351 Obviously, Paul does not share the Jewish notion of the Torah as eternal or the dating of the Torah back to Paradise. He attaches great importance to its secondary character (Rom. 5:20; Gal. 3:17). Nonetheless, he finds an analogy between the single commandment in Paradise and the many commandments at Sinai. See Theißen 1983, 205–6 n. 42. Cf. T. R. Schreiner 1998, 361. Rightly, he concludes: "Paul's own writings demonstrate that he did not follow Jewish tradition in the theory that Adam knew the Torah." Subsequently, Schreiner contends: "To sum up, the view that Paul refers to Adam is attractive, but it should be rejected since Adam did not encounter the Mosaic Law." Still, he does not make allowance for the notion that Paul speaks "of the law as a whole, seen archetypally in Gen 2:16–17" just as Paul speaks "of humankind as a whole, seen archetypally in Adam" (Dunn 1988, 385).

352 Cf. Lyonnet 1962, 162.

and 3 above; cf. Gen. 2:8–25). Similarly, it was only Eve who was deceived; only she desired to eat of the forbidden fruit (see points 6 and 7 above; cf. Gen. 3:1–3 or 2 Cor. 11:3 and 1 Tim. 2:14).[353] Since certain traits fit either Adam or Eve, the "I" cannot represent Adam or Eve alone.[354] On the other hand, if the "I" symbolizes both Adam and Eve, the choice of the subject appears strange. In the end, Paul chooses as the subject the ἐγώ. He avoids mentioning the names of both progenitors of the human race. Besides, there should be preserved some kind of consistency in chapter 7. For that reason, it fails to carry conviction that the "I" is Adam and/or Eve in vv. 7–13 but another person in vv. 14–25.[355]

Finally, Kümmel is right in his warning that the reader should not make "Adam [not to mention Eve] or the humanity in Adam as the subject of the narrative" ("zum Subjekt des Geschilderten Adam [not to mention Eve] oder die Menschheit in Adam"). Nevertheless, his conclusion that Rom. 7:7–13 does not relate to Genesis 2–3 is wrong.[356] How should one understand the apostolic line of thought?

In Rom. 7:7–13, there are evidently strong allusions to the primeval history of Genesis, but no particular mention of Adam and Eve. Yet they are implicitly found in the text.[357] Paul has by no means projected into Genesis 3 any spiritual crisis which, for instance, he himself (as a Pharisee) would have lived through. The "I" does not repeat the fall of Adam and Eve. Rom. 7:7–13 presupposes that it is about a unique incident.[358]

Despite the exceptional character of their fall, the transgression of Adam and Eve has nonetheless led to serious consequences. It resulted in the separation between God and the whole of humankind (Rom. 5:12–19).[359] In Rom. 7:7–13,

353 Gundry 1980, 230–32. Cf. Dochhorn 2009, 59–77. He takes notice of diverse Jewish texts in which the role of Eve is to some extent transferred to Adam. In particular, God's question "What have you done?" (Gen. 3:13) which was originally spoken to Eve turns into his question to Adam (op. cit., 68). For a further discussion, see Krauter 2010, 145–47. Cf. Busch 2004, 1–36.

354 Ibid.

355 Cf. Lichtenberger 1985, 1:141: "Trotzdem wäre es gleichwohl verfehlt, anstelle des 'Ich' 'Adam' einzusetzen [. . .]."

356 Kümmel 1974, 87.

357 Käsemann (1980, 197) asks in great confusion: "The only question is why Paul uses 'I' instead of naming Adam." To be sure, his question is a good one under the condition that Paul uses "I" only as a rhetorical device and in a fictive sense. Why not then speaking about the "one man" (as already in Rom. 5:12)? Why not directly refer to Adam (as already in Rom. 5:14)? The simple answer is that the "I" is Paul—but seeing his present existence in relation to Genesis 2–3. See below. *Pace* also Varo 1984, 12: "Ciertamente hay rasgos que presentan semejanzas con la narración del pecado del primer hombre, pero si el Apóstol hubiese querido referirse a nuestro primer padre parece lógico que lo hubiera indicado de algún modo más explícito."

358 Cf. my discussion with Brandenburger in 4.2.2.3 above.

359 See above 4.2.2.

the "I" reflects on his own existence as a descendant of Adam and Eve with the purpose of reading in Genesis 2–3 his original history, namely, that their primeval disobedience brought depravity upon himself. His participation in their fate means his identification with them, who together represent their posteriority (cf. Gen. 1:27; 2:21–24).[360] In brief, the fall of "Evadam" was the fall of the "I."

Without doubt, the subject in vv. 7–13 must agree with that of vv. 14–25 (*cum* Kümmel). If the "I" in the latter passage is identical to the Christian, then the "I" in the former passage cogently must be identical to the Christian (*contra* Kümmel). Yet vv. 7–13 and 14–25 do not depict "the same situation of the subject." The former passage explains the past of the Christian in "Evadam," while the latter passage, his present in the "body of death." The change of tense in the middle of the monologue (vv. 7–13: predominantly aorist; vv. 14–25: predominantly present) suggests that the line of thought moves from the past to the present.[361]

Thus Romans 7 does not principally establish an apology for the Mosaic Law.[362] More precisely, it portrays an indispensable supplement to chapter 6, emphasizing that the new eschatological situation has not totally broken through. For the time being, the tension persists. Truly, there is no room for an enthusiastic triumphalism. The ultimate victory is still to come. It does not in the slightest depend on doing the Mosaic Law. On the contrary, chapter 7 expounds that an adherence to the Mosaic Law hits a dead-end, making matters only worse (much worse indeed) and being no solution to the problem. Surprisingly, the opposite of transgression is actually not obedience. In reality, obeying divine commandments would end deeper in the predicament of wickedness. The story of Genesis 3 palpably confirms that sin (the serpent) can abuse the divine commandment to provoke transgressions. Exactly the same condition pertains to the Mosaic Law as well.[363] The power of covetousness is ultimately not broken by

360 Theißen (1983, 253–62) borrows from psychology the concept of "Rollenübernahme": "Das Ich übernimmt in Röm 7,7ff. die Rolle Adams und gestaltet sie im Lichte der eigenen Konflikterfahrung um" (op. cit., 205). The idea of a reforming of the story of the fall "im Lichte der eigenen Konflikterfahrung" obviously misses the mark. The "I" does not play the role of Adam. It identifies itself with him (and Eve). Cf. Käsemann 1980, 189.

361 B. L. Martin 1981, 43: "The switch to the present tense in v. 14ff. indicates that the Genesis story is no longer in view." Similarly, see D. H. Campbell 1980, 60; Dunn 1975, 261–62; Modalsli 1965, 34; Möller 1939, 7–9; Packer 1964, 622, 624, 626; Wenham 1980, 86–87. Quite the reverse, Kruyf 1978, 140: "Why not suppose that Paul, having made the change, goes on in the present tense, perhaps without even being aware [!] of the switch?"

362 *Pace* Kümmel 1974, 9, 74, 89 (and many commentaries in reference to him). See further Schnackenburg 1975, 292: "Der Abschnitt wird öfter überschrieben 'Apologie des Gesetzes'. Diese Kennzeichnung trifft sicher eine Intention des Apostels, erschöpft aber sein Anliegen nicht." Cf., e.g., Kertelge 1971, 109; Kruyf 1978, 141. Similarly, Hofius 2002, 110; Seifrid 1992a, 324.

363 The primeval era of Paradise and the entire epoch of the Mosaic Law are analogous, corresponding to each other (see Rom. 5:13–14). Accordingly, the Law "came in to increase

forbidding it. Rather, every single prohibition adds further fuel to human coveting. Therefore, the Mosaic Law will never set anyone free from the bondage of sin. The Jewish concept of the Torah as the best remedy for moral fallacies and faults verges on delusion.[364] Knowing is not following—principally as soon as the question of overwhelming evil desires and lusts is at issue. Consequently, chapter 7 explains why it is absolutely necessary to die to the Mosaic Law in order to live in the Spirit. Apologetic tendencies play only a subsidiary role in vv. 12–13.[365]

In conclusion, Rom. 7:7–13 does not speak in favor of Kümmel's interpretation either.[366]

Further, the disposition of the Epistle to the Romans puts Kümmel's position at least in doubt. Chapters 5–8 deal by and large with the relation of Christians to the powers of the old aeon: with regard to (God's) wrath (chapter 5), to sin (chapter 6), to the Law (chapter 7), and to death (chapter 8).[367] If 7:14–25 describes non-Christians, it turns into a long excursus not developing the relation of Christians to those powers of the old aeon (in this case to the Law). The obvious accuracy and precision of the structure in the Epistle to the Romans makes it unlikely that Kümmel is right in his interpretation.

4.2.3.5. Parallels

Kümmel further mentions as his argument that Rom. 7:14–25 stands as a description of the Christian in contrast to the other pericopes in the Pauline epistles (see above 4.2.3.2., points 3 and 4). He mainly bears upon 1 Cor. 4:4; 9:26–27; 2 Cor. 10:3; 13:6. They are supposed to show evidence for very high moral standards. To be sure, Paul did not consider himself sinless but reckoned with the possibility of guilt. Yet he was not aware of any particular sin, or at least did not say that he was.[368] Therefore, the extremely pessimistic confession of

---

the trespass" (Rom. 5:20), viz. the one and only trespass of Adam and Eve in Paradise long ago. *Pace* T. R. Schreiner 1998, 361. He writes: "[. . .] especially since Paul argues in 5:13–14 that the era of the law is to be distinguished from the time of Adam." Rightly, Dunn 1988, 276. Furthermore, I am not convinced by the tentative notion that the commandment in Rom. 7:9–13 should refer to "the commandment of Christian righteousness" (or "the commandment inherent to faith in Christ") as in an article written by Jervis (2004, 206). Correctly, Napier 2002, 20: "[. . .] with the coming of Torah sin would once again be 'in the likeness of Adam's transgression.' This is precisely what transpires in 7:7–12."

364 See especially Laato 1995; Stowers 1994, 200–202.

365 See also Laato 2013, 103.

366 For a similar argumentation, see Laato 2018a, 759.

367 Bornkamm 1966a, 51–52; Nygren 1979, 39. Cf. D. H. Campbell 1980, 57; Dunn 1975, 260. See further Dahl 1952, 40: "In fact, however, chapter 5 also deals with freedom from death, and 8 with freedom from condemnation just as much as with freedom from death." Cf. Schnackenburg 1975, 284.

368 Kümmel 1974, 103.

the "I" does not apply to a description of the present Christian state.[369] In order to evaluate the strength of Kümmel's arguments, each of his scriptural passages from the epistles to the Corinthians needs to be accounted for one by one.

On 1 Cor. 4:4, Kümmel writes that Paul is "not aware of any unfaithfulness in his office" ("irgendwelcher Untreue in seinem Beruf bewußt"), but presumes "in any case the possibility of conviction from God" ("jedenfalls die Möglichkeit der Schuldigsprechung durch Gott").[370] Yet it is hardly a matter of *posse non peccare* here. Paul maintains that he has administered his apostleship blamelessly (vv. 1–3; see 1 Cor. 9:15; 2 Cor. 7:2 and chapters 11–12; cf. Acts 20:18–35), without thereby refusing his sinfulness in general. His resolute rejection of any neglect of duty does not amount to any notion of his actual sinlessness.[371]

Kümmel laconically writes on 1 Cor. 9:27 that it reckons "with the possibility of being unapproved, before God" ("mit der Möglichkeit, ἀδόκιμος, d.h. vor Gott unbewährt zu werden"). Yet the passage does not deal with *posse non peccare* in the least. In light of the context, Paul subordinates his potential rejection by God to refusal of the Gospel and carelessness in his apostolic as well as Christian ministry. Ignorance of his own sinfulness does not emerge.[372]

On the contrary, 1 Cor. 9:27 forms a close parallel to Rom. 7:14–25. Paul talks about his body, which threatens to carry him into destruction. He has to prepare himself for a fight against it. However, nowhere does Paul say why he must ὑποπιάζειν ("strike under the eye") or δουλαγωγεῖν (literally: "enslave" or "bring into subjection") his own body. He was in no way a Gnostic who considered all material evil. Rather, 1 Cor. 9:27 bears on Rom. 7:14–25. Paul finds himself in the middle of the eschatological tension. Already free from sin and death, he lives in his mortal body, which still persists with sin and death. Sin works in his members bringing about death (Rom. 7:23–24). Despite the change of aeon, the old and the new prevail side by side (more exactly: side against side). Therefore, Paul tries very hard to restrain his body. Else he will not escape rejection.[373]

On 2 Cor. 10:3 and 13:6, Kümmel writes that Paul, alongside the consciousness of possible sin (see above 1 Cor. 4:4; 9:26–27), even dares to affirm that he

369 Op. cit., 101–4.

370 Op. cit., 101.

371 Donfried 1976, 105–6; Espy 1985, 163–64; Mattern 1966, 179–86; Möller 1939, 73; T. R. Schreiner 1998, 393; N. M. Watson 1983, 217. Cf. Synofzik 1977, 42–43. See further Althaus 1951, 96–97. He in fact does not differentiate between the "official" and the "private" life of the apostle.

372 See the commentaries. Cf. Espy 1985, 163: "Ultimately, Paul is no doubt fairly certain of the verdict concerning himself in the final judgment; but this does not mean that he is already free of agonizing private struggles with sin."

373 Cf. already Möller 1939, 74–75.

is free of all carnal behavior.[374] But once again, those passages do not deal with the opportunity of *(non) posse non peccare*. 2 Cor. 10:3 emphasizes that Paul and his coworkers do not struggle "according to the flesh" (οὐ κατὰ σάρκα), that is, they do not administer their office through impure motives or by human power (cf. vv. 1–6).[375] 2 Cor. 13:6 underscores that he and his coworkers are not "unfit" (ἀδόκιμοι), that is, without apostolic authority (despised by the Corinthians).[376] Moral sinlessness as such does not stand out.

Kümmel's argumentation loses even more credibility if one takes into consideration 1 Cor. 15:50–57,[377] a passage he completely ignores.[378] Without a shred of doubt, the passage portrays the condition of Christians before the parousia of Christ. The following illustration of their new life emerges:

The Christian is not definitively free from the power of death. His physical existence daily threatens to dissolve into nothingness. Death results from sin (v. 56). Because the Christian must die, he is also not definitively free of sin. Depravity and mortality[379] go together. Sin again has its power in the Law (v. 56).[380] Since the Christian must die on account of his sin, he is therefore also not definitively free of the Law. The redemption from the Law, sin, and death will be completed first at the Last Day with the parousia of Christ. Already now the awareness of the coming victory awakens gratitude in the Christian toward God (v. 57).[381]

The common traits between the Christian and the "I" are again obvious:

(1) The Christian and the "I" are not yet fully free of death.

---

374 Kümmel 1974, 101.

375 See, e.g., Barrett 1973, 250–51. Rightly, T. R. Schreiner 1998, 393.

376 See, e.g., C. Wolff 1989, 263. Similarly, T. R. Schreiner 1998, 393.

377 Many commentators have remarked on the close relationship between 1 Cor. 15:50–57 and Rom. 7:14–25. See Lietzmann 1969, 88; Wendland 1980, 158; C. Wolff 1982, 210. Cf. Barrett 1968, 383; Klauck 1984, 122. But insofar as I know, it was first Thurén (1986, 171–72) who dealt with the subject question in Rom. 7:14–25 in connection with 1 Cor. 15:50–57.

378 See Kümmel 1974, Register der Bibelstellen.

379 The words ἡ φθορά and τὸ φθαρτόν in vv. 50, 53–54 indicate both "depravity" and "mortality." Cf. Barrett's translation "corruption," "corruptible" (1968, 378).

380 For sure, v. 56 is no gloss. In contrast to Weiß 1910, 380, who agrees with Straatman. Lastly still Horn 1991. According to his interpretation, the suspicion of a gloss remains as "freilich eine subjektive [!] Überlegung des Exegeten ohne jeglichen textgeschichtlichen Anhalt" (p. 104). Rightly, e.g., Barrett 1968, 384; Conzelmann 1981, 361–62; Klauck 1984, 122; Räisänen 1983, 143 and n. 78; C. Wolff 1982, 209. Cf. further Hübner 1982, 182. Rather, v. 56 is to be understood as a Pauline interpretation of the given quotation (Hosea 13:14). Paul takes up—mark you—in other places likewise as rashly as in 1 Cor. 15:56 the problematics of the Law (see, e.g., Gal. 3:22–23; 5:18). Cf. Sloan 1991, 49–50).

381 See the commentaries.

(2) Death plagues the Christian and the "I," since they make themselves guilty of sin.
(3) On account of their depravity, the Christian and the "I" cannot fulfill the Law thoroughly.
(4) The Law binds the Christian and the "I" to sin, since the power of sin comes from the Law.
(5) Only on the Last Day will the Christian and the "I" be fully free of the Law, sin, and death.
(6) Then the Christian and the "I" will be redeemed from their mortal body (= the old man).
(7) Redemption takes place through Jesus Christ.
(8) The awareness of the coming redemption awakens gratitude toward God.[382]

Further, both passages close with an anticlimactic end. After thanksgiving (see the last point), a phrase follows establishing the state of affairs that still prevails at the moment (see Rom. 7:25b; 1 Cor. 15:58). The meantime means time for assiduous working in faith and love.[383] Additionally, in the context of both chapters the story of Adam and Eve is told (see Rom. 7:7–13; 1 Cor. 15:20–49).[384]

On the whole, Rom. 7:14–25 and 1 Cor. 15:50–58 match perfectly. The latter passage corroborates persuasively and compellingly that the former passage accounts for the eschatological tension. Freedom from the Law, sin, and death truly pertains to the Christian life by faith. However, as long as living in the mortal body continues, it is still totally lost under the Law, sin, and death. The transfer from the old aeon to the new does not yet take place wholly and completely. The definitive change comes only on the Last Day. Until then, gloom and shadows fall over the bright sunrise.

No change takes place—mark you—in the paradox of *sic et non* in the Christian existence if Rom. 7:14–15 does describe man as *sub lege*. In any case, 1 Cor. 15:50–57 describes it differently than Rom. 7:1–6 or 8:1ff. Kümmel tries—as I dare to assert—rather constrainedly to harmonize the argumentation in Romans 7–8 in order to show an extremely positive (from there so fascinating) portrayal of the moral situation in the congregations with the attainable

382 On the situation of the "I" see above 4.2.3.3.

383 Thurén 1994, 130.

384 Additionally, the confession of the "I" in Rom. 7:14 resembles the broad and more common statement in 1 Cor. 15:50. "Being fleshly" (Rom. 7:14b) denotes that "flesh and blood cannot inherit the kingdom of God" (1 Cor. 15:50a). "Being sold under sin" (Rom. 7:14c) indicates that corruption or the perishable does not inherit incorruption or the imperishable (1 Cor. 15:50b). Such being the case, the harsh announcement in Rom. 7:14 makes real sense in a Christian setting (see above).

ideal of sinlessness.[385] However, he does not notice the absolute impracticability of his own designs. For the most part, the Christian existence cannot be painted in bright and rosy colors. Both Rom. 7:14–25 and 1 Cor. 15:50–57 demonstrably shed light on its dark sides.

Further, it is worth the effort to take into consideration 2 Cor. 12:7, although it does not truly compare to Rom. 7:14–25. At any rate, diverse remarkable features emerge through a closer comparison. They uncover an exceptional and distinctive illustration of a Christian condition which extends beyond all the ordinary.

To begin with, 2 Cor. 12:7 shows that Paul does have problems with his body. He has "a thorn" in his flesh. It relates to the "messenger of Satan" who torments him. This extremely peculiar thought is because of the fact that Paul over and over again strives to restrain his arrogance but simply fails in all of his endeavors. He has to admit that the evil desire of haughtiness—on account of "the surpassing greatness of the revelations" he has been given—holds sway over him. He knows what he should do but cannot. The contrition pertains particularly to impure motives, a characteristic that absolutely does not fall under a "robust conscience" but rather attests to a diligent self-examination (see above). As the most striking detail that stands out here is the announcement that the messenger of Satan (ultimately given by God: ἐδόθη as *passivum divinum*) in the end paradoxically fulfills the divine intention! Without a doubt, he causes much harm, and yet he finally prompts humility. Paul plainly says that he needs "harassment" (whatever it means), lest he "[become] conceited." He repeats the phrase in order to put more emphasis on it. The repetition simultaneously suggests that arrogance tempts and provokes him not only once but many times (if not all the time).[386]

By and large, 2 Cor. 12:7 comes quite close to Rom. 7:14–25. In both passages, wrestling with evil desires is ongoing, depravity utterly resides in the flesh, and as a result inability to fulfill what God wills emerges. Moreover, one common denominator might be added. As far as sin in Rom. 7:7–25 represents the serpent in Paradise (devil in disguise, see above), it is consonant with the messenger of Satan in 2 Cor. 12:7. They inhabit the flesh, intruding upon the new life in faith. But they do not absolutely reign over the whole person (neither the "I" nor Paul). Their power is at present strongly restricted.

---

385 Cf. Kümmel 1974, 108: "Und wenn die Einsicht in den Text von Röm. 7 uns zwingt, den Text als Schilderung des Nichtchristen zu verstehen, zugleich aber wir unsere eigene sittliche Lage darin wiederfinden [. . .], so kann die Frage nicht lauten: 'paßt Röm. 7 etwa auch oder in erster Linie auf den Christen?', sondern vielmehr: 'wie ist es zu erklären, daß unser Christentum von dem paulinischen soweit abweicht, daß wir uns im Bilde des paulinischen Nichtchristen wiederfinden?'"

386 See commentaries, in the first place Harris 2005, 851–59; R. P. Martin 1986, 410–16. Cf. Middendorf 1997, 180–81.

However, despite all the similarities, 2 Cor. 12:7 does not, in contrast to Rom. 7:14–25, depict every Christian, but Paul and maybe him alone! This time his situation seems much worse. The messenger of Satan beats and buffets him, who has died to sin, who has been set free from death, and who currently serves Christ, the Lord. Indeed, this would be hardly believable—if it were not clearly written down in the text.

Such being the case, 2 Cor. 12:7 sheds some new light on Rom. 7:14–25 and makes it easier to understand the passage as a portrayal of the Christian existence.

Finally, Kümmel discusses Gal. 5:16–17. In his view, the passage confirms "the ability of the Christ to fully overcome the σάρξ" ("die Fähigkeit der Christen, die σάρξ vollständig zu überwinden")[387] with the help of the Spirit. By contrast Rom. 7:14–25 shows the incapacity of the "I" while trying to obey the Law and ward off sin without the Spirit. As a result, the two passages obviously speak about different circumstances in different cases.[388]

However, upon closer examination, Galatians 5 does not assert a complete and conclusive triumph over the flesh anywhere. V. 16 exhorts: "Walk by the Spirit, and you will not carry out (τελέσητε) the desire (ἐπιθυμίαν) of the flesh."[389] In other words, Christians have to hinder the fulfillment of their desires. Anyhow, they cannot extinguish the desires themselves.[390] V. 17 founds (conjunction γάρ used to express cause) the exhortation on the remark that the flesh relentlessly desires (ἐπιθυμεῖ, present tense used to express ongoing action) what is contrary to the Spirit just as the Spirit desires what is contrary to the flesh. The tension goes on and on without interruption. No, deliverance follows gradually, bit by bit. In their struggle, Christians, to be sure, gain the upper hand over their wickedness by living in the Spirit, not doing the manifest works of the flesh (vv. 18–21) but crucifying the flesh with its passions and desires (v. 24). Even so, they know that their lusting flesh is not yet to be disarmed.[391]

On purely formal grounds there is a remarkably close similarity among these three passages:

Gal. 5:17d: ἵνα μὴ ἃ ἐὰν θέλητε ταῦτα ποιῆτε
Rom. 7:15: οὐ γὰρ ὃ θέλω τοῦτο πράσσω
Rom. 7:19: οὐ γὰρ ὃ θέλω ποιῶ ἀγαθόν[392]

387 Kümmel 1974, 106.

388 Op. cit., 105–6.

389 My own translation.

390 Beyer 1972, 47: "Wandelt der Christ aber im Geiste, dann ist damit das Begehren des Fleisches, des natürlichen selbstsüchtigen Ich zwar nicht ausgetilgt—es bleibt im Menschen, und eben deswegen ist der Aufruf, im Geist zu wandeln und nicht im Fleisch, nötig-, aber es wird nicht mehr zur Tat (Röm. 8,13)." See further, e.g., H. D. Betz 1988, 474–75.

391 Ibid. Further Mußner 1974, 377–78; Ridderbos 1981, 203–4; Schlier 1971, 249–50. On a syntactical problem in v. 17, see, e.g., Lichtenberger 1985, 1:279–81; Oepke 1979, 174–76.

392 Althaus 1951, 17; Lichtenberger 1985, 1:282.

By and large, Gal. 5:16–17 and Rom. 7:14–25 relate closely to each other in content. Because of their flesh opposing the Spirit, the Galatians cannot do what they sincerely wish. They have to continue their struggle against evil desires. In that respect they remain in their depravity. There is for the time being no way out of it despite the fact that they are able to hold sway over their flesh by the power of the Spirit. Admittedly, Gal. 5:13–26 underscores far more the positive idea of not fulfilling evil desires but serving one another in love. This is not so in Rom. 7:7–25, where the "I" describes his total incapacity to obey the commandment "Do not covet." The shift of perspective causes the illusion that the two passages speak about two different circumstances, such as the condition before and after conversion. Still, despite distinct emphases, the truth is that in both cases a depiction of the Christian existence occurs.[393] Neither Galatians nor the "I" really get done what they to all intents and purposes want as long as their flesh desires. Therefore, a sort of pessimism, respectively resignation, endures in them until the end. They must live in tension with themselves and within themselves. On account of their impure motives (and occasional lapses) they never attain moral perfection.[394] The overall picture does not change in the least, although Gal. 5:16–17 in contrast to Rom. 7:14–25 explicitly mentions the Spirit. Nonetheless, a similar line of thought emerges.[395]

On the whole, three palpable parallels to Rom. 7:14–25 stand out, namely, 1 Cor. 9:26–27; 15:50–57; Gal. 5:16–17. The most distinct similarities are found among the two latter passages. Besides, 2 Cor. 12:7 shows the dark side of Christian existence in very gloomy colors.[396]

4.3. Conclusions

To sum up the main evidence, it turns out that the anthropological presuppositions of the Jewish and the Pauline pattern of religion differ from each other in essence far and wide. The former is based on human free will, while the latter is founded on human depravity. Paul seems never to have given up his pessimistic anthropology. Neither in Romans 2 nor in 5:12 nor in 7:14–25 does

393 *Pace* Oepke 1979, 175–76. He affirms that Paul in no way explains the conflict between Spirit and flesh as "irgendwie normal," but wishes to urge "vielmehr zur Überwindung desselben durch völlige Hingabe an den Geist" (p. 176).

394 See above. Similarly, Modalsli 1965, 30. *Pace* Das 2007, 209 n. 14. In confrontation with me, he wonders that I "incomeprehensibly" affirmed "a deep pessimism" in Gal. 5:16–17. As to the question of eradicating wholly the evil desires of the flesh, there is indeed no other choice left (v. 17). A triumphant optimism pertains to the ability of stopping "sinful desires from expressing themselves in action" (v. 16) in line with the fine formulation of Das (op. cit., 209).

395 Cf. Althaus 1951, 17–18 (!); Möller 1939, 69–70.

396 For a similar argumentation, see Laato 2018a, 759–63.

he veer aside. No question, one could continue thorough analyses *ad infinitum* and examine a host of other passages. However, the extension of examination hardly brings much new data. The outline of the study appears evident: the common anthropological optimism in Judaism runs counter to the anthropological pessimism or realism in Paul, who consistently and firmly holds on to his diverging thoughts.

Notwithstanding, far-reaching perspectives have opened up. If especially Rom. 7:14–25 does indeed depict the situation of the Christian in his confrontation with the Mosaic Law, the inventive interpretation of that kind overturns the contemporary consensus and should call forth a reevaluation of Pauline theology in many basic points.[397] Still, because of lack of space it is impossible to focus on the issue in detail here.

Later, more attention is drawn to Sanders's theory that Paul thinks "backward," that is, he supposedly deduces his anthropology from his soteriology.[398] However, my chief interest is not turned to the genesis of a way of thinking but rather to the comparison of patterns of religion as related to their respective anthropological presuppositions.[399]

Accordingly, considering Jewish and Pauline anthropology, the following chapter will examine Sanders's central thesis that salvation in the context of both the Jewish and Pauline pattern of religion takes place by grace.

397 See especially the interpretation of Rom. 7:14–25 by Käsemann (1980) and my own evaluation of it (2018a, 764).

398 See below, chapter 7. In reference to Sanders 1977, 442–47, 474–75, 481–82, 499. Räisänen (1983, 108 n. 79) shows that P. Wernle already presented a similar thought. Likewise, G. F. Moore (see above 2.2.1).

399 Cf. Gundry 1985, 21: "In the end, however, it does not matter whether in Paul's mind universal sinfullness came before justification by faith or vice versa, or whether the two occurred to him simultaneously. The fact remains that he includes Jews with Gentiles as law-breakers in order to undermine legalistic dependence on the law and thereby support justification by faith." (See also p. 27.)

5. THE SIGNIFICANCE OF ANTHROPOLOGY FOR THE JEWISH AND PAULINE PATTERN OF RELIGION

5.1. The "Getting In"

Sanders deals with the how of "getting in" Judaism particularly in relation to the Tannaitic notions on the election of Israel.[1] To begin with, he directs his interest to some pivotal excerpts in which the entrance into the covenant precedes the fulfillment of the Law. They should show that the Israelites have not merited their covenant, but, instead, God has initiated it by his grace.[2] Obviously the conclusion holds true at least in the main points.[3]

Consequently, Sanders collects three explanations for God's election of Israel from the Tannaitic literature. They are:

(1) God offered the covenant (or the Torah associated with it) to all people, but only Israel consented to it.

(2) God redeemed Israel from Egypt on the basis of a certain merit which was on the part of the patriarchs or in the generation of the exodus or on the condition of future obedience.

(3) God elected Israel for the sake of his own name.[4]

---

1 Sanders 1977, 84–101.

2 Op. cit., 85–87.

3 In line with Schechter 1975, 61: "This suggests that even those Rabbis who tried to establish Israel's special claim on their exceptional merits were not altogether unconscious of the insufficiency of the reason of works in this respect, and therefore had also recourse to the love of God, which is not given as a reward, but is offered freely." See further Hruby 1966, 173; Nissen 1974, 118–30.

4 Sanders 1977, 87–88.

None of the rabbinic attempts at interpretation pretends to depict a dogma or component of systematic theology. Each of them only offers a model of clarification.[5]

At times, Sanders seems to identify the election of Israel entirely with her entrance into the covenant.[6] To that extent, his analysis apparently misses the mark. It should be corrected. The first point above underscores the fact that Israelites achieved their entrance into the covenant by accepting the Torah and not disregarding any of its commandments. It is worth taking a closer look at the tradition in question.

The haggadah on offering the Torah to the different nations of the world before establishing the covenant with Israel appears quite old. It is found in both schools of the second century, namely, of R. Aqiba and R. Jischmael. It might even go back to a common (oral) source.[7]

The most fundamental evidence for offering the Torah to the nations of the world in the Tannaitic literature is found in Mek. Exod. 20:2 and Sifre Deut. 33:2 (par. 343).[8] The first passage reads like this:

> Therefore the nations of the world were approached [to accept the Torah], so as not to give them an excuse to say, "If we had been approached, we should have accepted responsibility [for carrying out the Torah]." Lo, they were approached but did not accept responsibility for them, as it is said, "The Lord came from Sinai" (Dt. 33:2). [. . .] First of all he came to the children of the wicked Esau. He said to them, "Will you accept the Torah?" They said to him, "What is written in it?" He said to them, "'You shall not murder' (Ex. 20:13)." They said to him, "The very being of 'those men' [namely, us] and of their father is to murder, for it said, 'But the hands are the hands of Esau' (Gen. 27:22). 'By your sword you shall live' (Gen. 27:40)." So he went to the children of Ammon and Moab and said to them, "Will you accept the Torah?" They said to him, "What is written in it?" He said to them, "'You shall not commit adultery' (Ex. 20:13)." They said to him, "[The very essence of fornication belongs to them (us)], all of us are the children of fornication, for it is said, 'Thus were both the daughters of Lot with child by their father' (Gen. 19:36)." So he went to the children of Ishmael and said to them, "Will you accept the Torah?" They said to him, "What is written in it?" He said to them, "'You shall not steal' (Ex. 20:13)." They said to him, "This is the blessing that was stated to our father; 'And he

5 Op. cit., 99–101.

6 Most clearly in op. cit., 424: "Speculative differences on the time and nature of the end are not, to repeat, constitutive of different types or patterns of religion. This becomes clear once one focuses on the pattern of getting in (election) and staying in (obedience)." Cf. pp. 87–101.

7 Childs 1974, 379; Moore 1948–50, 1:277; Schoeps 1950, 188–89; Sjöberg 1939, 17 n. 1; Stiegman 1979, 507. Cf. pre-rabbinic evidence for offering the Torah to the nations of the world in, e.g., 4 Ezra 3:32–36 and sBar 48:38–40 (see Nissen 1974, 63 and n. 126). Cf. further Gal. 3:19–20; Heb. 2:2.

8 Sjöberg 1939, 17 n. 1.

> shall be a wild ass of a man' (Gen. 16:12). 'For indeed I was stolen away out of the land of the Hebrews' (Gen. 40:15)." But when he came to the Israelites: "At his right hand was a fiery law for them" (Dt. 33:2). They all opened their mouths and said, "All that the Lord has spoken we shall do and we shall hear" (Ex. 24:7). "He stood and measured the earth, he beheld and drove asunder the nations" (Hab. 3:6).[9]

The accepting of the Torah by Israel alone, in contrast to all foreign peoples, serves as apt and outstanding explanation of her special status in the world. The other ethnic groups—for example, the descendants of Esau, Ammon, Moab, or Ishmael—have only themselves to blame for their own misery or miscarriage from beginning to end. God offered the Torah to them also. But since each one of them in succession discarded his offer, the covenant simply did not come into force in their case. Finally, Israel effectuated it by voluntary submission to the yoke of the kingdom of heaven as a whole. The sharp distinction between the Israelite tribes and the pagan multitudes demonstrably culminates in their relationship to the Law. Willingness to obey all of the prescriptions, without exception, utterly determined who in reality became the people of God.[10]

For certain, acceptance of the Torah involves not only a theoretical persuasion of the grandeur and magnificence of the Mosaic Law. It also implies an earnest attempt to obey the very specific commandments in practice (with a view to different circumstances). Indeed, the heathen peoples disregarded the Torah accurately because they did not want to give up murder, adultery, stealing, or any other detestable vices.[11] Good will would already have sufficed. As shown, consistent with rabbinic conviction, appropriate actions always result from right intentions—if possible, in favorable conditions.[12] In an exemplary manner, the Israelites uttered their readiness to do all that their God had spoken. Here, they differed from the Gentiles.[13]

In order to enter into the covenant, the proselyte must, just as the generation of the exodus once at Sinai, accept the Torah out of free will. Otherwise he cannot really convert to Judaism (T Demai 2:5; Sifra Lev. 1:2). He remains a Gentile. Acceptance of the Torah demands absolute submission to the Law. Conscientious obedience shows that a genuine and sincere conversion has taken place.[14]

---

9 Translation according to *Mekhilta* 2:68–69.

10 Childs 1974, 379–80; Davies 1980, 64–65; Hruby 1966, 179–86; Nissen 1974, 128–30; Patte 1983, 103; Schechter 1975, 88, 98; Sjöberg 1939, 17; Stiegman 1979, 507; Urbach 1979, 531–32.

11 In particular Urbach 1979, 532.

12 See above 4.1.1.

13 Nissen writes aptly: "Denn die Gnade Gottes bei der Erwählung hebt die verantwortliche Tat des Menschen nicht auf, sondern setzt sie frei und fordert sie" (1974, 127).

14 Sanders 1977, 206–7; Urbach 1979, 400.

A born Jew and Jewess self-evidently belong to the covenant from birth.[15] Still, he or she must later consciously take up the yoke of the kingdom of heaven.[16] The common custom of reciting the Shema (Deut. 6:4–5) three times a day[17] offers a continual profession of Jewish religion.[18] With it, the covenant members bind themselves for their part to love their God with all their heart and soul and might.[19]

In light of the previous traditional haggadah, it is obviously incumbent on the heathen or the Jew respectively to acquire or renew their entrance into the covenant by their own free will. Salvation requires human cooperation. It does not rest per se on God's grace.

As is well known, Paul does not demand the acceptance of the Torah as a condition of entrance. He maintains that one enters communion with God as a consequence of the approval of the Gospel. Faith in Christ effects the new, eschatological existence (see, e.g., Galatians 3 *et passim*).[20] Here, the exegetical consensus already comes to an end. There are two main diverging alternatives. On the one hand, some New Testament scholars assert that faith originates in the human capacity of decision. In order to be saved the sinner must summon so much out of himself that he puts his trust in the divine benevolence. Once this has been done, God will bestow his grace.[21] On the other hand, some New Testament scholars in contrast affirm that faith does not in the slightest validate human ability of free choice or craving for recognition in spiritual issues. The

15 Sanders 1977, 260, 284, 372–73; Vermes 1961, 190.

16 Cf. already Hruby 1967, 33: "Wir haben bereits auf die Bedeutung hingewiesen, die der Sinaioffenbarung als Kollektiverfahrung zukommt. Das schließt allerdings nicht aus, daß es den einzelnen Israeliten auch weiterhin freisteht, die Gottesherrschaft anzuerkennen oder sie abzuschütteln."

17 Neusner (1971, 235; 1988, 86) considers the recitation of the Shema as a constituent component of Judaism already before the destruction of the temple. Later, the rabbis would merely have standardized the practice already in place. See also Hruby 1965, 245.

18 Moore 1948–50, 2:173: "'The yoke of the kingdom of Heaven' is the acknowledgement of God's sole sovereignity and of the obligation to love him with mind and soul and substance, which man makes when he recites the Shema (Deut. 6:4)—the daily renewed profession of his religion." Cf. op. cit., 1:465. Similarly, Hruby 1969, 47; Neusner 1984, 101; Schechter 1975, 66–67; Sjöberg 1939, 18–19; Stiegman 1979, 534; Urbach 1979, 400.

19 Moore 1948–50, 2:173; Schechter 1975, 66–67; Stiegman 1979, 534.

20 Rightly, Kietzig 1957, 901: "'Umkehr' und Eintritt in das Reich Gottes ist jetzt nur möglich auf dem Weg des im Glauben angenommenen Sterbens Jesu." Already Mundle 1932, 114–40. Faith undoubtedly belongs closely together with Baptism. See Kertelge 1967, 172–73; Kietzig 1957, 902; Lohse 1978, 113–14.

21 See, e.g., the expositions of Friedrich 1982, 109; Nygren 1979, 75–76. For sure, they do not take sufficiently into account that not all exegetes understand faith necessarily as "Vorleistung," although definitely a condition for justification. Cf. Bornkamm 1987, 151; Bultmann 1984, 317. The meriting character of faith has been brought forward in particular by Bormann (1965, 159–200); Kuß (1963, 196–200); Mundle (1932, 99–111). Cf. W. T. Hahn 1937, 163–72; Kertelge 1967, 173–75; Lohmeyer 1929, 125–33; Siegert 1985, 144–48.

proclamation of the Gospel converts or transforms the sinner and engenders in him trust in the divine compassion. God demands no preparations for his grace.[22] The whole conflict culminates in the discussion of Rom. 1:16 that portrays the apostolic kerygma as "the power of God for salvation to everyone who believes."[23] Does Paul here point out faith in the Gospel as an achievement par excellence or sort out the intimate correlation between faith and the Gospel without weighing the part of God and that of man in salvation?

The controversy in question cannot be resolved solely on account of Rom. 1:16. Other relevant passages must be taken into consideration as well. Especially 2 Cor. 4:6 serves the purpose and deserves attention. In his scriptural reading, Paul explicitly qualifies Christian faith as a result of the new creation (*creatio ex nihilo*). He finds the following parallel: "For God, who said, 'Let light shine out of darkness,' has shone in our hearts to give the light of the knowledge of the glory of God in the face of Jesus Christ." As a consequence, the analogy between the primeval time and the present time shows that God acts in a creative manner through the Gospel and calls forth faith out of nowhere.[24] His divine action demolishes human activity in terms of synergistic cooperation.[25] Similarly, 1 Cor. 1:28 underscores in a soteriological context that God has elected "things that are not" (cf. further Rom. 4:17[26]). The previous "nonexistence" of the believers in Corinth implies that their faith does not originate in themselves. Instead, they have only their gracious Creator to thank for it (see also 1 Cor. 2:4–5).[27] Rom. 10:17 brings forth more of the same.[28] It substantiates that faith comes from hearing the Gospel, in other words, that the

22 Becker 1989, 438–39; Binder 1968, 64, 68–74; Bornkamm 1987, 151, 155; Deissmann 1925, 132–33; Friedrich 1982, 109–12; Klein 1988, 56 n. 39; Michaelis 1927, 116–38; Nygren 1979, 76–80; Ridderbos 1987, 171–72, 231–36; Stuhlmacher 1966, 81–83 (cf. 1966a, 341–46). Cf. further Limbeck 1972, 101–7.

23 Nygren 1979, 75–76. Cf. Siegert 1985, 148.

24 Hughes 1980, 132–34; Klauck 1986, 44; Odeberg 1944, 390; Ridderbos 1987, 234–35; Wendland 1980, 187; Windisch 1970, 138–41. Cf. Bornkamm 1987, 169. See further Bultmann 1976, 111. He suggests, however, that the Greek phrase ἐν ταῖς καρδίαις ἡμῶν refers "nur auf Paulus selbst, bzw. auf ihn und seine Mitarbeiter." Barrett (1979, 134–36) follows Bultmann.

25 The tradition of *creatio ex nihilo* naturally originates in the Jewish common property. Yet in 2 Cor. 4:6 Paul is not applying it to cosmology, but ecclesiology. See, e.g., Klauck 1984, 26.

26 In all probability, the Greek expression ὡς ὄντα in Rom. 4:17 has a consecutive meaning: so that the nonexistent becomes existent. Accordingly, it is not a comparison ("as that which is"). Rightly, Cranfield 1982, 1:197, 244–45; Käsemann 1980, 116; Schlier 1977, 132; Wilckens 1978, 1:275 n. 891.

27 See particularly Conzelmann 1981, 60 (in reference to v. 18): "Aber der Glaube ist kein Akt des freien Willens; er entsteht durch dieses Wort selbst." Cf. Bornkamm 1987, 169; Ridderbos 1987, 235; Strobel 1989, 55–56; Wendland 1980, 23–24.

28 Rom. 10:17 should not be taken as a marginal gloss of a reader. Rightly, Cranfield 1981, 2:536–37; Schlier 1977, 318; Schmidt 1962, 181; Wilckens 1980, 2:229. *Contra* Bultmann

preaching of the Gospel engenders faith (cf. 1 Cor. 4:15).[29] Finally, as if this were not enough, Phil. 1:29 explicitly distinguishes faith as a gift of God's grace (cf. 3:12b).[30] Accordingly, it follows from the big picture that the Christian has not entered the new Israel on his own initiative. Rather, he belongs to it after having been reborn as a member in it.[31]

The Pauline doctrine of justification furthermore corroborates the diametrical conflict between faith and every sort of merits. The righteousness of God equates with righteousness through faith, and both stand in opposition to righteousness by works (*passim*).[32] Faith is not one work of the Law which in contrast to numerous works of the Law earns salvation.[33] Justification does not result because of (existing) faith.[34] No, the believer has surrendered his previous self-reliance (including his alleged freedom of choice and capability of decision in spiritual matters). He has nothing to add to his redemption.[35] Justification always takes place by faith without any human contribution at all.[36]

As a final point, the Pauline anthropology affirms that not even the first phase of salvation lies at human disposal.[37] By nature, no one is his own master,

---

1947, 199; Michel 1978, 334. Cf. Käsemann 1980, 285. Besides, F. Müller (1941, 252–54) attempts a transposition of the verse.

29 See Friedrich 1982, 107–9; Lohse 1977, 156; Ridderbos 1987, 234–35. Cf. Cranfield 1981, 2:536–37; Käsemann 1980, 285; Schlier 1977, 318; Stuhlmacher 1966, 82; Wilckens 1980, 2:229. *Contra* Binder (1968, 66–67), who contests in his interpretation of Rom. 10:17 that "die Entstehung der *pistis* von der Predigt des Evangeliums abhängig ist." Rather, the verse attempts to say that "es die Predigt nur gibt, weil es die *pistis* gibt." Accordingly, Binder offers an artificial translation: "Folglich (wird) die *pistis* von (ihrer Selbst-) Kundgabe her (deutlich), diese Kundgabe aber (wird vernehmlich) durch (die) Christusverkündigung."

30 Friedrich 1976, 106; 1982, 111; Stuhlmacher 1966, 81. See also G. Barth 1979, 38; Gnilka 1968, 100; Lohmeyer 1956, 78.

31 See further Laato 2008, especially 45–68 (pertaining to the overall outline of the Pauline view of justification by faith).

32 Becker 1989, 440; Bultmann 1984, 280–85; Friedrich 1982, 111–12; Ridderbos 1987, 173. Cf. Wißmann 1926, 30–33, 89–91. To be sure, he speaks of a contradictory coexistence of grace and faith (op. cit., 33).

33 See, e.g., Becker 1989, 440; Bornkamm 1987, 151; Cranfield 1982, 1:90; Friedrich 1982, 110; Goppelt 1939, 164–65; Michaelis 1927, 121–22; Wilckens 1978, 1:89. Cf. Ridderbos 1987, 233–34.

34 Correctly, Bornkamm 1987, 151; Friedrich 1982, 98–99, 109–12; Michaelis 1927, 116–24, 134–38; Nygren 1979, 76–80; Ridderbos 1987, 171–72, 233–36; Stuhlmacher 1966, 82.

35 See Bornkamm 1987, 151, 155; Bultmann 1984, 280–85, 300, 315–18; Conzelmann 1987, 190; Friedrich 1982, 110; Michaelis 1927, 121–22; Ridderbos 1987, 171–72, 231–36. Nevertheless, Bultmann appears to contradict himself in characterizing faith (the radical surrender of *all* human achievements) as "freie Tat der Entscheidung" (op. cit., 317). Similarly, Patte 1983, 268–69, 289, in comparison with 281–86. Cf. already W. T. Hahn 1937, 168–72.

36 Particularly, Laato 2008. See further Becker 1989, 438–39; Friedrich 1982, 98–99, 109–12; Michaelis 1927, 116–24, 134–38; Nygren 1979, 76–80; Ridderbos 1987, 171–72; Stuhlmacher 1966, 82.

37 Nygren 1979, 79–80.

but instead is like a slave delivered up to the brutal terror and tyranny of the flesh and sin in the fatal reign of death.[38] Neither the Jews nor the Gentiles take up a neutral, to say nothing of a positive, attitude toward the Gospel. Much to their own detriment, they simply discredit the message of the cross as scandalous foolishness (1 Cor. 2:14; see further 1:18, 23).[39] Excited by their carnal mind, they burn with enmity (ἔχθρα, in the active sense[40]) against God (see Rom. 8:7).[41] It is beyond their power to overcome their negative attitude against the Gospel. They are transformed only if the Creator creates a new creature (2 Cor. 5:17) and makes them his people.[42]

In the light of the preceding juxtaposition, a fundamental difference shows itself in the question of "how to get in" between the Jewish and the Pauline pattern of religion. In the first case, it is based on the human decision by the power of free will but, in the second case, on the divine action by the power of the Gospel through faith.

In the next section, the other main question of "how to stay in" will be taken up.

5.2. The "Staying In"

In his summary of the Palestinian Jewish and Pauline patterns of religion, Sanders briefly and succinctly describes the how of "staying in":

> *Salvation is by grace but judgment is according to works; works are the condition of remaining "in," but they do not earn salvation.*[43]

In his later writing, Sanders explains his position as follows:

> In both cases [in Judaism and in Paul] [. . .] salvation is by the grace of God, while works (in Judaism, observance of the Mosaic Law; in Paul, producing the Fruit of the Spirit) are the condition of remaining "in."[44]

38 See above 4.1.2.

39 Barrett 1968, 77; Fascher 1975, 129; Grosheide 1980, 73; Odeberg 1944, 72; Strobel 1989, 72.

40 In the first place, Käsemann 1980, 211; Schlier 1977, 245; Schmidt 1962, 138. See also Cranfield 1982, 1:386–87; Michel 1978, 252–53; Wilckens 1980, 2:130. Cf. Paul's Pharisaic past!

41 In particular, Cranfield 1982, 1:386–87; Käsemann 1980, 211–12; Michel 1978, 252–53; Nygren 1979, 327–28; Schlier 1977, 245; Schmidt 1962, 138–39; Wilckens 1980, 2:130.

42 Hughes 1980, 201–4; Wendland 1980, 206. Cf. Kietzig 1957, 901. Klein (1988, 56) writes nicely: "Denn der Glaube ist paulinisch überhaupt keine Bewegung menschlichen Handelns, sondern Stigma göttlichen Handelns am Menschen."

43 Sanders 1977, 543 (original with italics).

44 Sanders 1983, 449.

On closer examination, the previous quotations clarify in kernel the relation between *causa efficiens* and *conditio sine qua non* in the Palestinian Jewish and Pauline patterns of religion. Hence, the former expression ("efficient cause") shows the moving cause of religious behavior, while the latter expression ("condition without which not") shows the condition (or conditions) of salvation within a particular religion. Sanders himself uses the term *conditio sine qua non* in this sense.[45] However, he does not *expressis verbis* employ the term *causa efficiens*. Nonetheless, both concepts appear to come to bear, since according to Aristotelian philosophy *causa efficiens* and *conditio sine qua non* require each other.[46] As a result, a harmonious picture arises:

In Sanders's concluding summaries, obedience to the (Mosaic) Law in Palestinian Judaism and the fruit of the Spirit in Paulinism stand for the *conditio sine qua non* of salvation. In both cases, the new life is based on God's grace (tied with the covenant resp. Christ). This constitutes then the *causa efficiens* as their common denominator.

Accordingly, Palestinian Judaism in general shares with Paul the traditional teaching that salvation is by grace, but judgment is according to works. In all logic, the result can be divided in two theses:

(1) As a rule, salvation in Palestinian Judaism does not depend on works. They rather effect "remaining in" the covenant.

(2) With regard to the relationship between grace and works, Palestinian Judaism in general does not differ from Paulinism.

In order to take forward the discussion with Sanders, I raise two pertinent questions. The one aims at the first thesis; the other, at the second. They are:

(1) Strictly speaking, on what does salvation in Palestinian Judaism depend?

(2) Is obedience to the Law in Palestinian Judaism to be placed on the same level with the fruit of the Spirit in Paulinism?

First, I shall cope with the first question. Second, I shall deal with the second question.

Here and there, Sanders's argumentation gives evidence of a very confused quality: He often uses the expression "salvation" in a restricted sense. It means either (1) the salvific historical action of God in the past (the establishment of the covenant on Sinai resp. the death of Christ on the cross) or (2) the present state of salvation (belonging to the covenant resp. participation in Christ), but

45 See, e.g., Sanders 1977, 141: "Obedience, especially the intention to obey ('confessing') is the *conditio sine qua non* of salvation, but it does not *earn* it."

46 Routila 1969, 81–82.

not precisely embracing (3) the final redemption (eternal life).[47] As a result, it remains uncertain who, then, will finally be redeemed. Apparently, Jews and Christians must, after their salvation already won, still exert themselves on behalf of their future salvation. After all, they might forfeit it at any time. Rightly, the ancient proverb says: All's well that ends well (and not before).

From the perspective of eternity, belonging to the covenant as well as fulfilling the Law are no doubt necessary conditions for salvation in Palestinian Judaism. For sure, the basis of salvation does not under any circumstances falter: God's faithfulness to his covenant in all compassion prevails in every situation, even in the worst possible.[48] Notwithstanding, the Jew still comes under

---

47 Sanders uses the word "salvation" in the first quotation (see above, p. 144) in two (!) distinct meanings. In the first part of the sentence ("salvation is by grace but judgment is according to works"), it refers to final redemption. In the context, Sanders remarks that the aspect in question occurs, with the exception of 4 Ezra, in the whole of Palestinian Judaism (see 1977, 543). Indeed, 4 Ezra teaches that the righteous must merit final salvation by an extreme and perfect fulfilling of the Law without regard to God's incessant mercy (cf. op. cit., 420: "Thus salvation in the dialogues of IV Ezra is constructively by works—one must be perfectly obedient to be saved [. . .]." And later (422): "It is in IV Ezra that it is clearly said that the righteous *merit* redemption and do not require mercy [. . .]."). Nonetheless, in the second part of the sentence ("works are the condition of remaining 'in,' but they do not earn salvation") the same word "salvation" cannot refer to final redemption. In the context, Sanders remarks that the aspect in question occurs throughout Palestinian Judaism, even in 4 Ezra (see op. cit., 543). It is now rather a matter of the salvific historical action of God in the past. Also 4 Ezra maintains the formal relationship between the covenant and the Law: obedience to the Law effects the retention of one's place within the covenant but does not as such merit God's grace (op. cit., 420).

In addition, Sanders uses the word "salvation" in the second quotation (see above, p. 144) once again in a narrower sense, probably with the meaning of "the present state of salvation." In the context, he speaks of good works and indeed as the *consequence* of salvation (see 1982, 449).

In other places as well, Sanders uses "salvation" or "save" in a rather narrow sense. The following two quotations should suffice as illustration: "Thus repentance is not a 'status-achieving' activity by which one initially courts and wins the mercy of God. It is a 'status-maintaining' or 'status-restoring' attitude which indicates that one intends to remain in the covenant. To use other language, one is already 'saved'; what is needed is the maintenance of a right attitude toward God" (1977, 178). Or: "Their [the rabbis'] legalism falls within a larger context of gracious election and assured salvation. In discussing disobedience and obedience, punishment and reward, they were not dealing with how man is saved, but with how man should act and how God will act within the framework of the covenant" (op. cit., 181).

48 Dramatically, e.g., after the destruction of the temple. Cf. Räisänen 1983, 180–81, with reference to 4 Ezra: "It is so profoundly marked by the crisis caused by the fall of Jerusalem [. . .]. The radicalized view of the obedience required of man would seem to be a device that is intended to serve the author's theodicy and that alone: contrary to all appearance God *has* remained faithful to his covenant; it is themselves men have to blame for what has happened. God is reliable and will carry out his salvific plan in the future."

obligation to carry out the Law from his free will.[49] Without his contribution, he will indeed lose his place in the future world. Everyone must do his own part as God has already done his own part.

Although Sanders has rightly criticized the Weberian caricature of Jewish religion,[50] he seems in his pioneering monograph *Paul and Palestinian Judaism* (1977) to have gone to the other extreme. A more well-balanced interpretation is called for. Free of anti-Semitic polemics of every sort, one must frankly acknowledge that not a little importance is attached to works in Jewish soteriology. In fact, the Jew does work for his place in the future world.[51] His obedience to the Law is truly *conditio sine qua non* for salvation.[52] To be sure, God's grace does not devolve on forgetfulness in the overall religious framework. The redemption as a whole is based to a greatest degree on his constant faithfulness to the covenant. Even so, the Jew has not mere divine grace to thank for his acquittal on the Last Day. He must contribute through his own works in the process of salvation.[53]

Such being the case, the next pertinent follow-up question of equating obedience to the Law in Palestinian Judaism with the fruit of the Spirit in Paulinism becomes more urgent.

---

49 See above 4.1.1.

50 See above, chapter 2.

51 Sanders argues similarly with regard to 4 Ezra, although it does not, in agreement with the rest of Palestinian Judaism, isolate obedience to the Law from membership in the covenant (1977, 420). The author, however, demands not less than perfect piety in contrast to the widely accepted view of common human sinfulness. In this respect, he strongly differs from the general approach (op. cit., 413–16, 418, 421–22). Thus it seems that one merits his salvation through his own works only in the context of an extremely rigorous soteriology. But the Jew does not need to do *everything* in order to do *something* for his salvation!

52 In agreement with many reviewers. Especially, Byrne 1979, 230: "Whatever be the fundamental case in *theory*—that is, that the covenant and God's mercy overarch the whole pattern of progress to salvation—if works are a condition of remaining 'in' the covenant community and if exclusion from that community means loss of salvation, then in *practice*—that is, from the point of view of one on the road from election to salvation—works *are* a means of gaining salvation." Cooper 1982, 129: "[. . .] Palestinian Judaism [. . .] grounded *ultimate* salvation on imperfect obedience brought as an appeal to God's mercy in the context of a gracious covenant relationship." Westerholm 1979, 133. This time, he expresses himself in Swedish: "Men eftersom villkoret för individens fortsatta ställning inom förbundet var, att han visade allvar i sitt försök att hålla lagen, så kan det ändå sägas att laggärningar spelade en viss roll i hans slutliga frälsning. Frälsningen *förtjänades* inte genom laggärningar, men i viss mån kunde den ändå anses vara beroende av dem." See further 1988, 147–50. Cf. Cooper 1982, 123–30, 137; Gundry 1985, 19, 36; Hafemann 1981, 148. For the soteriology of the Qumran community, see Garnet, who argues similarly (1980, 19–23, 31). Here, it ought not be forgotten that the Jew (in general) desires to fulfill the Law from the highest motives, not, e.g., from the crass intention of gaining particular merits before God. See Nissen 1974, 181–82, 201–19; Odeberg 1980, 31–33; Sanders 1977, 183–98; Sjöberg 1939, 23 n. 2. Cf. above 2.2.

53 See also Moo 2018, 233–37.

Many New Testament scholars disagree with Sanders, who suggests that the fruit of the Spirit constitute the *sine qua non* of salvation in the Pauline letters. It rather depends from beginning to end on faith alone (Rom. 1:17; 11:20–23; 2 Cor. 1:24; 13:5–7; cf. also the whole Epistle to the Galatians, particularly 2:20).[54] Good works effect by no means remaining in Christ. Instead, they show that one has entered communion with God by grace.[55]

Now and then, Sanders gives the impression that he might partially agree with the foregoing criticism. He seems to consider faith as the only condition for final salvation in the Pauline pattern of religion and therefore—cogently and logically—as the only means for remaining in Christ.[56] The harsh break with the Jewish pattern of religion in that case remains unbridgeable.

Notwithstanding, Paul at the same time underscores that judgment will take place according to works or that gross sins draw after them loss of salvation (cf. Rom. 2:12–16; 6:15–23; 8:12–13; 11:22; 14:10; 1 Cor. 3:10–13; 4:2–5; 5:1–5; 6:9–10; 10:1–13; 2 Cor. 5:10; Gal. 5:19–21; etc.).[57] Palpably, he ascribes considerable importance to the new life in Christian context. How does his call for love and charity relate to the Jewish demand for obedience to the Law? The question has not lost relevance. It still remains to be seen if or how the apostolic parenesis squares with the principle of *sola gratia per fidem*.

With the juxtaposition of his theological explanations and his practical exhortations, Paul does not at all strive for a partition between the divine and human work, something in the sense that the indicative would stand for the part of God and the imperative for that of man within the process of salvation. The close and strong intertwining of call for trust in divine kindness and call for action in human kindness should not be replaced by a loose and vague relation

54 Cooper 1982, 137–38; Gundry 1985, 8–10, 34–35. Cf. Caird 1978, 542; Dunn 1983, 118.

55 Gundry 1985, 11, 35. He concludes as follows: "It appears, however, that for Paul good works are only (but not unimportantly) a sign of staying in, faith being the necessary and sufficient condition of staying in as well as of getting in" (op. cit., 35).

56 Cooper 1982, 138, with reference to Sanders 1977, 446, 492, 551. Cf. Lohse 1977, 156: "Der christliche Glaube, der sich in den Worten des Bekenntnisses ausspricht, steht am Anfang des Christ-Seins und bestimmt den gesamten Lebensvollzug des Christen." See further 1978, 114–15.

57 Sanders 1977, 515–18; 1983, 113–14. Without launching myself into a detailed discussion, I refer especially to my own 2018 article and the comprehensive works of Mattern (1966) and Synofzik (1979). In addition, see further Donfried 1976, 103–10; Heiligenthal 1983, 165–217; Hooker 1982, 48–50; Joest 1951, 165–68, 185–88; Jüngel 1963, 70–74; Limbeck 1972, 98–99; Snodgrass 1986, 72–75, 79–87; Stuhlmacher 1966, 228–36; N. M. Watson 1983, 209–21. In his profound exegetical analysis of the relevant source material, Volf (1990, 83–154) draws the false conclusion "that Paul does not think Christians' ethical failure results in exclusion from final salvation" (op. cit., 157). In my opinion, his thesis needs no refutation (but see, e.g., Räisänen 1983, 185 n. 116).

between them, as if they merely remain side by side or in a successive row.[58] That kind of odd foul-up would lead to a fatal distortion and have as a consequence a new form of legalism.[59] If the missionary preaching provokes no good works among the congregation members, Paul does not urge them to do their best just as God has given his best by reconciling the world in Jesus Christ. More exactly, he rather argues for the new life that depends on the Gospel reviving the dead faith.[60] Living faith works then incessantly by love (Gal. 5:6).[61]

This being so, Paul does not understand salvation as a long and drawn-out process which is divided into a divine and a human part. In contrast, he rather thinks in theocentric terms and in a holistic manner: "I am sure of this, that he who began a good work in you will bring it to completion at the day of Jesus Christ" (Phil. 1:6; see also 1 Cor. 1:8; 10:13; 2 Cor. 1:21; 1 Thess. 5:24). Later, he clarifies more his assertive thinking: "Therefore, my beloved, as you have always obeyed, so now, not only as in my presence but much more in my absence, work out your own salvation with fear and trembling, for it is God who works in you, both to will and to work for his good pleasure" (Phil. 2:12–13; cf. 1:11; 1 Cor. 12:6b, 11).[62] It is worth noticing that Christians should not work *for* their salvation. Instead, they should work *out* their salvation (τὴν ἑαυτῶν σωτηρίαν κατεργάζεσθε) since God works *in* them (ἐνεργῶν ἐν ὑμῖν) in order that they

58 Here, the original German text of *Paul and Judaism* reads idiomatically as follows: "Das enge Mit- und Ineinander von Zu- und Aufruf darf nicht durch ein loses Neben- und Nacheinander ersetzt werden."

59 Bornkamm 1987, 162, 207–9; Bultmann 1984, 334–35; Conzelmann 1987, 320; Käsemann 1961, 369–74; Ridderbos 1987, 225. Cf. Becker 1989, 459–60; Goldhahn-Müller 1989, 117–18.

60 Cf. Goppelt 1980, 541: "Würde Paulus von den Früchten der Gerechtigkeit das sagen, was Jakobus von den Werken sagt? Paulus würde Jakobus in der Negation zustimmen. Selbstverständlich wird ein Glaube, der sich nicht in einem entsprechenden Verhalten auswirkt, nicht zur Gerechtigkeit gerechnet (1 Kor 6,9; 10,5–13). Paulus würde freilich dieses Versagen des Gehorsams nicht als Glauben ohne Werke bezeichnen, sondern fragen, ob da, wo der Gehorsam fehlt, überhaupt Glaube vorliege (2 Kor 13,5). Er würde nicht fordern, daß zum Glauben das Werk hinzugefügt werde, sondern daß der Glaube lebendig werde."

61 See, e.g., Becker 1976, 62; Bornkamm 1987, 162–63; Bultmann 1984, 316–18; Mußner 1974, 351–54; Ridderbos 1981, 190–91; Schlier 1965, 234–35.

62 Glombitza (1959, 103) reads an awkward sense in v. 12. He combines (in light of Gal. 4:18, hardly convincing) the negation μή with the verb κατεργάζεσθε: "Darum meine Geliebten, da ihr ja immer gehorsam wart, *schaffet*—wie in meiner Anwesenheit allein, sondern jetzt viel mehr in meiner Abwesenheit [strictly speaking, an illogical construction]—*nicht* mit Furcht und Zittern eure Seligkeit" (italics mine). Even so, Glombitza translates v. 13 "normally" as follows: "Denn Gott ist es, der in euch wirkt das Wollen und das Vollbringen für das Wohlgefallen." Räisänen (1983, 185) cites only v. 12 (similarly, see already Mundle 1932, 101) and consequently summarizes: "Bearing this in mind, it would be possible to claim that Paul actually teaches salvation (or at least reward) by works!" (op. cit., 186).

will and work (τὸ θέλειν καὶ τὸ ἐνεργεῖν) according to his purpose.[63] Taken as a whole, the message in Philippians substantiates the simple truth that whatever progress Christians make in their spiritual maturity they can never fulfill the Law by their own firm decision and power. In faith, they have put themselves completely outside the field of human action. Now they act only because God, in fact, acts in them. His activity does not reach the highest point at the outset of their conversion and then gradually cease in the course of time as they slowly become better and better. No, it truly starts in their conversion and then continues in their life from that time on to the end as strongly as ever.[64]

Hence, the apostolic parenesis does not merely count for the important notion of the interaction between indicative and imperative or grace and works as it is found in Judaism as well.[65] In the deepest sense, the focus centers on the indicative or—more to the point—on Christology: Christians live in Christ (ἐν Χριστῷ), and he lives in them.[66] Gal. 2:20 eloquently clothes the radical and innovative way of thinking (or believing) in accurate words: "I live, yet not I, but Christ lives in me; and the life which I now live in the flesh I live by faith in the Son of God, who loved me and gave himself for me" (my own translation). Faith resp. Baptism creates a "mystical" communion with Christ (see Romans 6; 7:4; 1 Cor. 6:15–17; 12:12–13; 2 Cor. 5:17; 13:5; Gal. 3:27–28; Phil. 3:9 *et passim*).[67] The fulfilling of the Law arises from the eschatological participation in Christ.

---

63 See the important discussion in Hansen 2009, 170–76.

64 Correctly, K. Barth 1928, 9, 15, 68–69; Bornkamm 1987, 208; Friedrich 1976, 138–40, 155–56; Gnilka 1968, 46–47, 53, 149–50; Gundry 1985, 9–10; Lohmeyer 1956, 19–21, 34, 103–5; J. J. Müller 1976, 41–42, 47, 91–92; Pedersen 1978, 1–2, 20–31; Ridderbos 1987, 254–55; Stuhlmacher 1966, 234–35; Volf 1990, 33–47; Westerholm 1988, 168–69. Volf (1990, 228) points out very fittingly: "For Paul salvation is exclusively by God's sovereign and unconstrained grace from start to finish. God is and God remains the sole and gracious subject of salvation."

65 For the interaction between grace and works in Judaism, see particularly Räisänen 1983, 178–79. Cf. Nissen 1974, 181–82.

66 First and foremost, Thurén 1986, 183. See further Bornkamm 1987, 163–65; Conzelmann 1987, 324–25; Davies 1980, 217–21; Flückiger 1952, 22–24, 38–39; Friedrich 1976, 140; Goldhahn-Müller 1989, 115–16; Goppelt 1980, 475; Heiligenthal 1983, 196–97, 206–7; Käsemann 1961, 370–74; Kietzig 1957, 902; Modalsli 1965, 27; J. J. Müller 1976, 47; Odeberg 1980, 93–100; Ridderbos 1987, 222–23, 232, 254–55. In the same breath, Paul often emphasizes that Christians live in the Spirit and he lives in them (see, e.g., Davies 1980, 195–96). Except for the messianic age, the Jews do not trace ethical conduct back to the Holy Spirit (but to human free will). See Davies 1980, particularly 208–26; Foerster 1962, 117–22, and Hill 1967, 269–70. Cf. further Willi 1972, 110–16. Davies (1980, 220) summarizes the result as follows: "In any case it is probably right to contrast Rabbinic Judaism and Pauline Christianity not so much in that the one made the Spirit the reward for good works while the other made it the source of good works, but rather in that the one can only have had a faint awareness of the activity of the Spirit while the other was dominated by the conviction that the Age of the Spirit had come." For a different kind of thought in Qumran, see Foerster 1962, 122–34; Willi 1972, 116.

67 Or with the Spirit (see Rom. 8:5–17; 1 Cor. 6:19; Gal. 5:16–18, 25 *et passim*).

He has already fulfilled the Law as he once lived his life on earth, and he continues to fulfill it now as he lives in those who believe in him. This very exceptional understanding shows where the exact emphasis lies in Pauline disapproval of Jewish self-righteousness and fleshly boasting.

Besides, Sanders himself rightly lays great weight on the participatory categories.[68] If only he had drawn the proper conclusion from them! In view of them, it appears indisputable that the how of "staying in" the Jewish pattern of religion does not at all respond or correspond to Paul's reorientation after his conversion from his Pharisaic past to his Christian present. No longer did he put his trust in his own strength and his own ability to obey the Law. Now he understood that his new life is Christ and is found in Christ. Indeed, it is Christ who does the good works of Christians. He acts in them. Sanders's focus on the participatory aspects in Pauline theology should have led him to this kind of reasoning. But he completely misses the crucial point. Unfortunately, he tragically fails to take advantage of his basically sound argumentation. He then turns a deaf ear to the pertinent anthropological differences between the Jewish and Pauline patterns of religion.

For sure, everyone sometimes trespasses against the commandments of a given religion although he earnestly tries to follow all of them. It is therefore still necessary to deal with the Jewish and Pauline conceptions of repentance and forgiveness of sins. The following section will in brief serve to address that issue.

5.3. Repentance and Forgiveness of Sins

Both repentance and the forgiveness of sin are included as key concepts in covenantal nomism. In a religion which calls frail man to a conscientious obedience to the Law, they understandably have an extremely high status.[69]

Sanders directs himself sharply against the long-established misinterpretation that in the main originates in the mind sensitized by Lutheranism for centuries. He discards the common notion that repentance within Judaism on closer inspection turns into meritorious compensation for transgressions committed. In fact, the original sources reveal not a hint of any compensatory reckoning.[70] For certain, God compels no one to an obedient and repentant thinking. Insofar,

68 In particular, cf. the positive assessments of many reviewers and scholars: Brooke 1979, 249; Dahl 1978, 156; Hooker 1982, 48, 52–53; Murphy-O'Connor 1978, 125. Cf. Best 1982, 73; Caird 1978, 540–41.

69 Moore 1948–50, 1:116–17, 226; Sanders 1977, 175.

70 Sanders 1977, 176–77.

repentance indeed functions as a fundamental requirement for his mercy.[71] Yet feelings of remorse do not cause God's solidarity toward Israel. He forgives all their sins from his sovereign loyalty to the covenant. They are released from his retribution solely on that basis. Repentance shows not a "status-achieving" activity, but rather a "status-maintaining" and a "status-restoring" mentality on the part of Jews.[72]

Evidently, Sanders's correction holds good in the broad outlines. He demonstrates that the old-style interpretation results from a fatal narrowing of perspective. The general Jewish practice of repentance does not arise from an anxious need for self-redemption.[73] God forgives sins because he is "merciful and gracious, slow to anger, and abounding in steadfast love and faithfulness" (see Exod. 34:6). He has given the promises to the patriarchs and established the covenant on Sinai out of his own free will. They ensure his compassion and enhance progress in the process of salvation.[74]

Yet not even Sanders denies that conversion, despite the covenantal ideological context, indicates an absolute prerequisite of salvation.[75] It falls into two fundamentals: the turning away from transgressions of the Law with trust in acquittal and the re-turning to the fulfilling of the Law in constant obedience.[76] Both of them are incumbent upon the Jew. He remains under his obligation to practice repentance by the power of his own free will,[77] if also often with God's kind help.[78] As soon as he is really ready for conversion, he, so to say, actuates

71 Op. cit., 177: "Repentance was considered to be the condition on the basis of which God forgives. God did not force one to maintain an obedient and repentant attitude against his will."

72 Op. cit., 177–78.

73 Already Moore (1948–50, 1:507–34), Schechter (1975, 313–43), and Sjöberg (1939, 125–53) speak and argue for a similar view as Sanders. Cf. Dietrich 1936, 388–405. Sjöberg maintains, nonetheless, that the idea of repentance as a merit occurs a number of times in the Tannaitic literature (op. cit., 154–69). See further Nissen 1974, 131–32.

74 Correctly Montefiore 1904, *passim*; Moore 1948–50, 1:535–45; Nissen 1974, 131–34, 146–49; Sanders 1977, 175–79; Schechter 1975, 293–312; Sjöberg 1939, 144–48.

75 Sanders 1977, 177. Moreover, see Moore 1948–50, 1:512, 520; Nissen 1974, 133–34, 142–49; Schechter 1975, 324; Sjöberg 1939, 148–53; Stiegman 1979, 530.

76 Behm 1942, 992; Dietrich 1936, 350–67; Moore 1948–50, 1:509–14; Sjöberg 1939, 149; Urbach 1979, 464–65. Cf. Cooper 1982, 137 and n. 45; Nissen 1974, 144–45.

77 In particular, Braun 1953, 248; Cooper 1982, 137; Dietrich 1936, 400–401; Hruby 1969, 59–60; Montefiore 1904, 222–23, 230; Nissen 1974, 133–34, 142–49; Schechter 1975, 324; Sjöberg 1939, 151–53; Stiegman 1979, 530. Cf. Odeberg 1980, 67.

78 In a liturgical context, one mostly encounters petitions for the enabling and outworking of conversion by God (see Nissen 1974, 143 and n. 197). The activity of God and that of sinners often intermingle, without ever becoming equally balanced. Cf. Dietrich's well-adjusted summary (1936, 405): "Die Umkehr wird also nach der einen rabbinischen Ansicht vom Menschen gewirkt, nach der anderen von Gott, aber so, daß das menschliche Handeln dabei nicht radikal ausgeschlossen wird, sondern vielmehr ein zwangloses Nebeneinander besteht." See further Hruby 1969, 56–60; Nissen 1974, 143–44.

expiatory means. In a sense, the grace provided by the covenant does not function properly earlier. It is there, but it is not fully charged. The sinner must first act. Then God acts. They interact. God's favor is activated by the sinner's self-humiliation. At long last, everyone determines his future salvation or condemnation through his present repentance or impenitence.[79]

In his comparison of the Jewish covenantal nomism and Pauline participatory eschatology, Sanders emphasizes that the position and function of repentance vary greatly in the respective patterns of religion. He maintains that it no longer plays any central role in the latter case. The alteration makes a big difference.[80] In the Pauline letters, only seldom or occasionally does the exhortation occur that Christians would repent for their failure to observe the Law. Remorse does not characterize their mentality.[81] There is practically no reflection upon the theme.[82] Even though Paul accordingly makes use of the juristic categories, they in effect show a quite "defective" quality. The core of his theological thinking consists rather of the participatory categories, and they do not actualize the question of repentance at all.[83]

In fact, Paul uses the verb μετανοεῖν once (2 Cor. 12:21),[84] the noun μετάνοια twice in 2 Cor. 7:9–10 and once in Rom. 2:4, and further the adjective ἀμετανόητος once in Rom. 2:5.[85] Thus he speaks of repentance altogether more frequently than Sanders has noted. Although the term μετάνοια does not occur so often in the Pauline epistles as תשובה in the Palestinian-Jewish texts,[86] it goes too far to assert that—with the exception of one passage (2 Cor. 12:21)—the conception itself does not even emerge.[87] A simple statistical analysis puts a damper on the assertion! Moreover, since Paul in his missionary proclamation

79 Rightly, Behm 1942, 992–93; Dietrich 1936, 400–405; Hruby 1969, 54, 59–60; Moore 1948–50, 1:512, 520; Nissen 1974, 113–14, 145–49; Schechter 1975, 324; Sjöberg 1939, 148–53; Stiegman 1979, 530.

80 Sanders 1977, 546. See already Knox 1950, 141–59.

81 Sanders 1977, 503, 513.

82 Op. cit., 470.

83 Op. cit., 502–4.

84 Has Sanders taken into consideration only the occurrence of the verb? Or has he merely the transgressions of Christians in view? Cf. his line of reasoning (1977, 500): "There is one passage on repentance dealing with *Christian* sins (II Cor. 12:21), but otherwise his response to *post*-conversion transgression is to tell his readers not to do it, but to live according to the Spirit" (italics added). At any rate, Sanders (op. cit., 503) draws his conclusion in a hurry: "Paul's juristic language is 'defective,' lacking a discussion of repentance and forgiveness (except for II Cor. 12,21 [. . .])." With regard to Rom. 2:4–5 and 2 Cor. 7:9–10, however, the juristic categories are not so "defective!" See below.

85 Merklein 1981, 1029. See further Cooper 1982, 132; Gundry 1985, 33; Moule 1967, 399.

86 Behm 1942, 1000; Gundry 1985, 33.

87 *Contra* Sanders 1977, 500 (cf. above). Correctly, Horbury in his convincing criticism: "[. . .] it is hardly consistent when Professor Sanders claims to find repentance implicit in the Scrolls (pp. 305, 316), yet attributes the comparable rarity of the word in St. Paul to the unimportance of repentance in the Pauline understanding of response to the Gospel"

has frequently rebuked and condemned gross sins (1 Cor. 6:9–11; Gal. 5:19–21; 1 Thess. 1:9; cf. also Rom. 1:18–3:20), he obviously suggests the necessity of penitence.[88]

The relatively rare use of the term μετάνοια is explained best by the fact that the thought itself or the same comprehension has taken on new forms. Repentance is contained in πίστις, the central expression of the apostolic doctrine of salvation. As a result, believers have crucified their flesh with all its passions and desires in order to walk according to the Spirit (Gal. 5:24–25).[89] Moreover, Paul seems to replace the traditional Old Testament terminology by his own specific and characteristic language and emphasis (especially the "mystical" unity or life with Christ: the death of the old man and the resurrection of the new man).[90] Apparently, he puts the whole of his theology into fresh words. At another place, Sanders himself appears to follow that kind of reasoning![91]

Taken as a whole, Paul has definitely departed from the Jewish doctrine of repentance. He nowhere emphasizes that God atones for sins only after the conversion of the sinner. The apostolic kerygma proclaims in contrast that Christ has already—before the sinner converts!—atoned for sins (cf. Rom. 3:21–26; 5:10; 1 Cor. 15:3; 2 Cor. 5:19; Gal. 1:4 *et passim*).[92] One then personally receives forgiveness by faith that has its origin in the creative power of the Gospel.[93]

To sum up: the question of repentance initiates a sharp contrast between the Jewish and the Pauline way of thinking. In the former case, it becomes a

---

(1979, 117). Gundry (1985, 32) argues in a similar way. Cf. Byrne 1979, 231; Räisänen 1983, 187 n. 122.

88 Goldhahn-Müller 1989, 115–56. See also Becker 1981, 450; Cooper 1982, 132; Friedrich 1957, 979–80. Cf. Moule 1967, 399–400.

89 Behm 1942, 1000; Bultmann 1984, 317–18, cf. 287; Hoffmann 1963, 724; Merklein 1981, 1029; Moule 1967, 400, 405–6; Poschmann 1940, 21.

90 Behm 1942, 1000; Hoffmann 1963, 724; Kietzig 1957, 900–901; Moule 1967, 400–401, 405–6. Cf. Byrne 1979, 231; Schubert 1967, 372–74.

91 Sanders 1977, 501, in basic agreement with Andrews 1935, 125. She maintains: "May not Paul's emphasis on Spirit, commonly called his mysticism, furnish the key to his neglect of the idea and technique of repentance? When he made possession of the Spirit the *sine qua non* of salvation as well as of a worthy ethical life, repentance was excluded by the simple expedient of being replaced by something more effective." Sanders explicitly quotes the last sentence and then concludes: "I would say not *only* more effective, but something which responds more to the plight of man as Paul perceived it: bondage" (italics mine).

92 Enslin 1982, 42. Cf. also Sanders 1977, 499–500: "He [i.e., Paul] has the opportunity to speak of man turning to God in repentance and being forgiven, but he twice—almost explicitly, it seems—rejects it. In Rom. 3:25 he writes that God 'passed over former sins'—without mentioning repentance or any of the prescribed means of atonement; and in II Cor. 5:19 he speaks of God 'not counting their trespasses against them,' this time on the basis of God's work in Christ. There is still no reference to man's repentance."

93 See above 5.1.

human task. In the latter case, it remains a divine gift. An anthropological difference leads to a soteriological divergence.

5.4. Conclusions

In consideration of anthropological presuppositions, obvious differences prevail between the Jewish and the Pauline patterns of religion. They directly relate to soteriology. On further reflection, God's grace does not receive the same position in both cases. The Jewish pattern of religion shows a strong synergistic purpose and meaning:

God has once in the past established a covenant with Israel, he now daily forgives sins out of his infinite mercy, and he will finally at the Last Day redeem his people into eternal life, but Jews nonetheless must and can through their own works cooperate with him in the process of salvation.

The Pauline pattern of religion, in contrast, shows a strong monergistic purpose and meaning:

Christians must indeed believe in the Gospel, repent, and continuously produce the fruit of the Spirit, but God works in them both to will and to do so. He initiates and completes all this through faith which he creates in them through his powerful word of grace.

Conclusion: salvation in the Jewish pattern of religion depends partly on human good works, whereas in the Pauline pattern of religion it depends on divine benevolence and mercy alone.

In consequence, a clear-cut correlation between anthropology and soteriology stands out. The difference between the anthropological premises (Jewish optimism versus Pauline pessimism) leads to the difference between the soteriological principles (Jewish synergism versus Pauline monergism).[94] Ultimately, Sanders himself indirectly confirms this result: he equates the relation between grace and works in the Jewish and Pauline patterns of religion while he ignores the question of human ability.[95]

With the serious intention of engaging in the dilemma of the current Jewish-Christian dialogue from the ground up, we must bear in mind that the discrepancy between the Jewish and the Christian pattern of religion is conditional upon their respective obstinate standpoints. It lies in the distant future to

94 For the concept of synergism in Judaism, see Moo 2018, 235: "In practice, then, Jews were saved through a combination of grace and works—what we appropriately can label synergism." Later, he (op. cit., 355 n. 197) concludes (in reference to me): "Indeed, Paul's pessimistic view of human beings trapped under sin's power played a key role in establishing differences between his theology and that of Judaism generally [. . .]." Similarly, Schreiner 1998, 174. Cf. Nissen 1974, 142.

95 See above, chapter 3.

mediate between the two opposite positions. It indeed seems hard to overcome the disagreement altogether as it now stands. The Jewish side seizes the absolute integrity and perfection of creation. Sifre Deut. 32:4 (par. 307) warns against every attempt to improve on God's action or by any means to shove the guilt for evil off on to him. Should anyone dispute free will in the area of soteriology, he according to rabbinic logic also destroys in a blasphemous way the doctrine of בריאה. The Christian side (insofar as it takes heed of Paul), in contrast, seizes the primordial fall into sin. In Augustinian terms, the absolute constraint of *non posse non peccare* exists since then. Should anyone acknowledge free will in the area of soteriology, he according to apostolic logic runs after a deceptive utopia under the spell of a naive, humanistic ideal. How could we in this controversy help ease some of the tension between synagogue and church? Certainly silence about the subject matter of the antagonism serves no purpose.

Thus it is worth taking a closer look at the ardent confrontation that the theological conflict between the synagogue and church already from the very beginning initiated. In the following chapter, the interest will focus on Paul's criticism of his mother religion. Since in Judaism works play a certain role in the process of salvation (see above), the question arises whether the inclusion of those works has consequently caused a self-complacent boast among the Jews. The question to what extent the apostle to the Gentiles was right in his analysis will not be the primary interest.

6. PAUL'S CONFLICT WITH THE JEWISH PATTERN OF RELIGION IN THE LIGHT OF HIS ANTHROPOLOGY

6.1. Material

In consideration of Paul's conflict with the Jewish pattern of religion, the following passages (in chronological order) prove most relevant: the Epistle to the Galatians; Rom. 3:27; 4:2–5; 9:30–10:3; and Phil. 3:3–9.[1] A closer examination of them will take place after a brief presentation of the material.

Frequently, the given passages, with the exception of the Epistle to the Galatians, are held to characterize (negatively) Jewish soteriology.[2] H. Räisänen suggests that even the Epistle to the Galatians characterizes (negatively) Jewish soteriology.[3] Neither of the two premises wholly stands up under critical examination. The following clarifications are necessary:

(1) The Epistle to the Galatians directs itself not against Jewish soteriology but rather that of Judaistic prevalence.[4] However, Paul draws

1 Sanders 1983, 17–48 and 57 n. 66. Cf. B. L. Martin 1989, 93; Räisänen 1980a, 68; 1983, 169.

2 First and foremost, Sanders 1983, 29–48.

3 Räisänen 1983, 162–63. He (op. cit., 162) emphasizes: "In a number of key texts in Galatians and Romans Paul suggests that the law is a rival principle of salvation. To be sure, he never sets out to give a sustained account of the Jewish religion, and a great many of his comments on the law are made with regard to Christian 'Judaizers.' *Nevertheless*, Paul's comments *at least imply* the notion of the Torah as the Jewish gateway to salvation or righteousness, [. . .]" (italics mine). Räisänen in no place gives grounds for his thesis that the Epistle to the Galatians delineates (and even falsely) Jewish soteriology.

4 See, e.g., Sanders 1983, 18–20; Thurén 1986, 183–84. For the expressions "Judaizer" and "Judaistic," see Schlier's remark: "Wer sind diese in die paulinischen Gemeinden in Galatien eingedrungenen fremden Missionare? Es nützt natürlich nicht viel, sie mit diesem oder jenem Sammelnamen zu benennen, etwa mit dem lange Zeit üblichen, der

such conclusions that relate to his conflict with Jewish soteriology.[5] Thus his argumentation must be taken into account.

(2) It is Paul (and not the Jews) who weighs faith against works in Rom. 3:27 and 4:2–5. Neither of the two passages deals with Jewish soteriology for itself.[6]

(3) In contrast, Rom. 9:30–10:3 contends with Jewish soteriology per se.[7]

(4) In Phil. 3:3–9, Paul distances himself from his Pharisaic past. It is primarily a representation of himself, not an open conflict with the whole of Pharisaism (much less with the whole of Judaism).[8]

Next, the passages under debate are discussed one at a time according to the same schema, like this:

At the outset, each text from the Pauline letters, with the exception of the Epistle to the Galatians, will be set forth in Greek. Then follows a review, set in italics, of the arguments of the exegetes (E. P. Sanders and H. Räisänen[9]), who (particularly against R. Bultmann) regard only the Christological criterion as the decisive distinction between the Pauline and Jewish pattern of religion. Finally, an alternative reading and a different interpretation in regular typeface show an optional interpretation.

'Judaisten,' d.h. Judenchristen pharisäischer Herkunft [. . .]. Eine solche Etikettierung vereinfacht den geschichtlichen Sachverhalt zu sehr" (1971, 19). Equally, Mußner (1974, 14–15) warns of a simplifying labeling of the opponents of the apostle in Galatia. Tyson again swims against the stream of overflowing pedantry. In my opinion he rightly maintains: "There is no reason to suppose that Paul's difficulties in Galatia sprang from more than one group of opponents, and we may as well call these 'Judaizers'" (1968, 250; see also 252). Similarly, Howard 1979, 19; Lührmann 1965, 68.

5 Sanders 1983, 46. First, Sanders asserts that the Epistle to the Galatians does not in the slightest shed light on the conflict of Paul with Jewish soteriology (op. cit., 19–20). Later, he contradicts his own assertion (op. cit., 46). Cf. further Hübner 1986, 24: "Natürlich ist 'Judaism in view.' [. . .] Insofern ist es berechtigt, von 'Paul's rebuttal of Judaism' zu sprechen, als für den Christen die Existenz unter dem Gesetz und folglich die Existenz als Jude per definitionem ausgeschlossen ist!"

6 Thurén 1986, 185.

7 Ibid. See also Sanders 1983, 30–36.

8 Ibid.

9 Hübner 1984, 71. In view of Rom. 9:30–10:4, he affirms: "Es scheint aber, als ob sich ein gewisser Trend abzeichnet, an dieser Stelle in Auseinandersetzung mit der Theologie *Bultmanns*, dann aber vor allem mit mir, an diesem Punkte das übliche Paulusbild energisch zu modifizieren. Vor allem sind in diesem Zusammenhang die beiden neuesten Monographien über Paulus und das Gesetz zu nennen: *E. P. Sanders*, Paul, the Law, and the Jewish People, und *Heikki Räisänen*, Paul and the Law, beide 1983 erschienen." The same tendency shows itself in other passages under discussion as well. See below. In addition, Sanders (1983) and Räisänen (1983) depend on each other. Furthermore, they have read each other's manuscripts. See Räisänen 1983, preface, v. Thus it seems necessary to examine the argumentation of both exegetes at the same time.

6.2. The Epistle to the Galatians

Right from the beginning, Sanders suggests that the Epistle to the Galatians does not deal with the issue of whether one could merit righteousness with the support of his good works. It is rather a matter of whether the Gentiles ought to accept the Jewish Law in order to enter the people of God.[10] *On the one hand, the Judaizers had explained to the Galatians that they are able to enter the people of God only through circumcision and unconditional acknowledgment of the Torah. On the other hand, Paul contends that no other conditions but faith have any bearing.*[11] *As a result, he drifted into an indirect conflict also with Palestinian Judaism, which likewise required circumcision and acknowledgment of the Torah.*[12]

The controversy between Paul and the Judaizers does not—mark you—concern precisely the question of how one remains in the people of God. Both parties underscore in agreement that the Christian maintains his status among the elect with the help of his good works.[13]

In addition, Räisänen points out that polemics of every kind against human boasting are completely and wholly missing in the Epistle to the Galatians. Strictly, the Law and Christ are set in opposition (2:21), but apparently not boasting and faith.[14] *The thematic of boasting occurs only in chapter 6 (see vv. 4, 13–14). A thorough reading and analysis of the text shows that the renunciation of glory before God by no means belongs to the self-understanding of true believers. Instead, they simply focus on doing what is good.*[15]

The dispute about the bone of contention between Paul and the Judaizers appears to have no end.[16] In my opinion, a new phase in the debate opened with P. Borgen's article "Observations on the Theme 'Paul and Philo': Paul's Preaching of Circumcision in Galatia (Gal. 5:11) and Debates on Circumcision in Philo," which he published in 1980.[17] His theses deal with the problematics of the Epistle to the Galatians and give occasion for further reflections and a critical evaluation of the ongoing discussion.

10 Sanders 1983, 18.

11 Op. cit., 19–20.

12 Op. cit., 46.

13 Op. cit., especially 17–20 and further 7–10, 112–13.

14 Räisänen 1983, 169.

15 Ibid.

16 See, e.g., the brief history of research in Borgen 1980, 92–93, and in Tyson 1968, 241–42. Howard (1979, 1–7), Mußner (1974, 14–25), and Rohde (1989, 14–21) outline fairly extensively the different attempts at resolution.

17 Cf. also Borgen's article "Paul Preaches Circumcision and Pleases Men" (1982) and his book *Debates on Circumcision in Paul and Philo* (1987).

Borgen sets out primarily from Philo's writings. He analyzes passages such as *De migratione Abrahami* 86–93 and *Quaestiones in Exodum* 2.2.[18] They display that a Gentile could occasionally be accepted or recognized as a proselyte without being physically circumcised. Instead, he was still in need of so-called ethical circumcision. In order to be ethically circumcised, he had to renounce idolatry and other gross vices. After having entered the people of God, he then was obligated as a Jew to be physically circumcised.[19]

In addition, there were some very marginal and radical groups in the Judaism of that time which entirely rejected physical circumcision in favor of ethical circumcision. In their fanaticism, they allegorized the covenantal commandment of circumcision. It allegedly symbolized that one should merely eliminate the lusts and desires of the inner self.[20] Accordingly, physical circumcision became utterly futile or superfluous. It no longer served any purpose.[21] An allegorization of that kind naturally raised the criticism of most Jews (*inter alia* Philo). They insisted that the ethical circumcision should not abrogate the physical.[22]

For certain, the academic discussion about the conditions and obligations of proselytism in Judaism will continue. It will have important impacts on the big picture.[23] Yet the emphasis here rests explicitly on the textual evidence

18 Borgen 1980, 86–89.

19 Op. cit., 86–88, 90–91. See also Friedländer 1905, 81, 282–87; McEleney 1974, 328–29. *Pace* Belkin 1940, 47–48; Wolfson 1948, 2:369–71. They distinguish between uncircumcised (inferior) and circumcised (superior) proselytes, although Philo does not recognize such a distinction.

20 Op. cit., 86–88. Similarly, the literal observance of the Sabbath or the Old Testament feasts was disregarded. The seventh day of every week symbolized that "God was the active creator and creation was passive in relation to him" (op. cit., 86). The celebration at the temple posed as "man's joy and thanksgiving to God" (ibid.).

21 Ibid. For the "radical" allegorists, see further Amir 1983, 46–51, 74–75; Goodenough 1935, 83–84, 236; Hay 1979, 47–51; Heinemann 1932, 103, 454–55, 463–64; Wolfson 1948, 1:66–71.

22 Ibid. Sanders (1983, 131, 135 nn. 48 and 49) supports Borgen's argumentation.

23 In the first place, Nolland (1981) tries to show that "none of the texts brought forward stand scrutiny as firm evidence for a first-century Jewish openness to the possibility of accepting as a Jewish brother a convert to Judaism who felt unable to undergo circumcision" (194). Without going into specifics, some short relevant remarks are needed:

(1) Nolland admits that according to *De Migr. Abr.* 89 the radical allegorists did not practice physical circumcision (op. cit., 175). Cf. above.

(2) As to *Quaest. in Ex.* 2.2, Nolland writes that "we should not attempt to read out of the passage Philo's answer to the question: do proselytes need to be circumcised?" (op. cit., 174). Then he abruptly adds that "since this is not Philo's question, it will not yield up his answer to that question, that therefore the presumption remains that Philo would expect a proselyte to be circumcised." Wholly differently argues Borgen (1980, 87–88): "The most probable view is that Philo here gives an answer to the question: When does a person receive status as a proselyte in the Jewish community and cease to be heathen?" Since *Quaest. in Ex.* 2.2 besides compares proselytes to uncircumcised Israelites in

for the complementary relation or contradictory tension between the ethical and physical circumcision (whether or not ethically circumcised persons are counted among the proselytes without being physically circumcised).[24] It makes it easier to delve into the serious conflict in Galatia and look into the vehement argumentation in Galatians.

The question of ethical and physical circumcision sheds light on the content in the Epistle to the Galatians. Many hitherto loose pieces of the puzzle fall in place and start to form a sharp picture:

During his missionary journeys to Asia Minor, Paul had preached the Gospel and proclaimed that Gentiles must abandon idolatry and other vices. Instead, they should bring forth the fruit of the Spirit (see especially Gal. 5:19–23). The Judaizers who followed a little later did not directly or right away reject the Christian message, but rather accommodated it through their intensive reinterpretation in agreement with their own theological tendencies. How did they outfox the converts in Galatia? They contended that Paul, with his missionary proclamation, indeed had intended for ethical circumcision. Now it is finally time to go further than that and perform his deepest purpose. He himself preaches (physical) circumcision (5:11) as a second stage. Therefore, Christians in Galatia must be physically circumcised (see, e.g., 5:2–3; 6:12–13). They should also live according to the Jewish calendar of festivals (4:9–10). Only then do they do what they are obliged to do. As told, Paul is of the same mind. He (allegedly) consents to that kind of Judaistic fanaticism.[25]

Egypt, Philo seems to suggest that Gentiles could at least occasionally convert to Judaism renouncing physical circumcision.

(3) In addition, Nolland does not define the exact problem sufficiently. He points out: "We must conclude therefore that Philo is not concerned [. . .] to oppose circumcision of proselytes" (op. cit., 179; cf. also pp. 174–79). Bialoblocki (1930, 15) deals with the problem much more precisely: "Unzweifelhaft muß sich der Proselyt der Beschneidung unterziehen. Fraglich ist nur, ob diese Pflicht *seinem Judesein entspringt* und er also wie jeder Jude zur Beschneidung verpflichtet ist oder aber ob die Beschneidung *eine Voraussetzung seiner Aufnahme* ins Judentum ist, deren Erfüllung ihn erst zum Proselyten macht." He tends (in concert with Borgen) toward the first solution (op. cit., 15–31).

(4) Even if entirely detached from the question of proselytism, the textual evidence for the differentiation between ethical and physical circumcision still remains. It sheds more light on the conspiracy of the opponents and their falsification of the Gospel in Galatia. They spared no efforts to convince their supporters that Paul is "still preaching circumcision" (5:11) despite his vehement denial of their lies (see below). Hence, they (as most Jews) strongly criticized the hasty fabrication of ethical circumcision as sufficient in order to practice physical circumcision as well.

24 Borgen (1980) does not make this reservation. Therefore, he fails to carry full conviction.

25 Op. cit., 89–92. Cf. Josephus's story of Izates and Ananias (*Antiquitates Iudaicae* 20.40–42).

Mußner (1974, 358–59) asserts that the particle ἔτι in the εἰ-clause in 5:11a has an additive ("hinzufügende") meaning ("besides, moreover, furthermore"). He writes: "Paulus stellt vielmehr aus zorniger Erregung heraus in dem εἰ-Satz einen schlechthin

The Epistle to the Galatians originated as a protest against the deliberate and malevolent anti-mission of the Judaizers. No doubt, Paul resolutely opposes their reinterpretation of his Gospel. Against their wishful thinking, he does not support any kind of a preparatory ethical circumcision. Instead, he once again points out that Gentile Christians should neither be circumcised nor live according to the Jewish calendar of festivals in order to maintain their new status as members in the people of God (2:3–5, 11–14; 4:8–11; 5:2–6; 6:12–15 *et passim*). As they well know, they have received the Spirit neither by (an ethical) circumcision nor by other works of the Law. No, only the Gospel has conveyed him to them (3:1–5). The Spirit (no one else or nothing else) effects the new obedience. His work can neither be supplemented nor completed by human merits. Even less can it be replaced by them (3:1–5; 5:13–25). Consequently, it is not the Jewish righteousness in accordance with the Law, but rather the Christian existence in the Spirit which forms the opposite of heathen wickedness. If Galatian Christians either fall back into heathendom or are caught under the Law, they lose their freedom from sin and death. Then they have stepped out of the people of God. Only one who constantly trusts in the Gospel, who has crucified his flesh with its passions and desires and walks in the Spirit (5:24–25), has taken part in the eschatological exodus and belongs to the true Israel.[26]

On the whole, Sanders seriously errs in his exegetical analysis of the Epistle to the Galatians. Indeed, he seems to have missed the entire point. As it has already been shown, it is not a matter of whether Christians must accept the Jewish Law in the intention of entering the people of God. Rather, it is about whether they should subordinate themselves to Jewish customs with the intent of staying in the people of God.[27] The heated debate especially concerns (physical)

---

unwirklichen Fall als wirklich hin, *um auf die Konsequenzen dieses 'Falles' aufmerksam machen zu können*" (op. cit., 359 n. 112). Similarly, already Merk 1969, 103–4, particularly n. 105. See also Rohde 1989, 223. In my opinion, Mußner perpetrates a considerable word-splitting at the cost of the text. How does he actually know that Paul takes "einen schlechthin unwirklichen Fall als wirklich"? The εἰ-clause in 5:11a has a grammatically "real" sense. Cf. Borgen 1980, 89 n. 15. Besides, Paul uses the particle ἔτι here twice. No doubt it has a temporal meaning ("still") in the question clause of 5:11a (see even Mußner 1974, 359 and n. 115). The same particle hardly has a deviate ("additive") meaning in the conditional clause. Hence, the Judaizers actually tried to convince the Galatians that Paul still preached (physical) circumcision. *Contra* Mußner already Weder 1981, 193–95. The commentators rightly (if also completely consternated) wonder on what basis the perfidious suspicion rested (see Oepke 1979, 161–62; Schlier 1971, 238–39). Borgen is first to offer a satisfactory solution.

26 Borgen 1980, 91–92, 98–101.

27 Hübner 1986, 241: "Sanders Argumentation, im Gal ginge es nur um die Frage nach dem Wie des Eintritts in das Gottesvolk, ist also Ausdruck einer enormen Perspektivenverengung." Similarly, Deidun 1986, 46–47. Gundry (1985, 11) writes to the point: "Paul did not dispute with the Judaizers because he thought they taught that believing Gentiles had to be circumcised and start keeping the rest of the law as means of getting in, then. In *PPJ* Sanders himself showed that, strictly speaking, not even

circumcision and different Old Testament festival days, since they had not so far been observed at all.

Many factors in the Epistle to the Galatians confirm that there Paul truly answers the question of staying in the people of God. His use of language reveals his focus. Here, a few relevant examples suffice. Paul wonders in 3:3: "Are you so foolish? Having *begun* by the Spirit, are you now being *perfected* by the flesh?" (italics mine). Later, he resumes a similar wondering in 4:9: "But now that you *have come to know* God, [. . .] how can you turn *back again* to the weak and worthless elementary principles of the world, whose slaves you want to be *once more*?"(italics mine). In chapter 5, he finally exhorts: "For freedom Christ has set us free; *stand firm* therefore, and do not submit *again* to a yoke of slavery. [. . .] You are *severed* from Christ, you who would be justified by the law; you have *fallen away* from grace. [. . .] You *were running* well. Who *hindered* you *from* obeying the truth?" (vv. 1, 4, 7, italics mine).[28]

The Judaistic position as expressed in the Epistle to the Galatians stands very close to the Jewish pattern of religion. As is well-known, covenantal nomism includes that the Jew stays in the covenant through obedience to the Mosaic *nomos*. His submission under the Law comes about freely and willingly because of human free will.[29] In the light of the Epistle to the Galatians, there is no doubt why Paul discarded covenantal nomism. His ardent confrontation with the Judaizers indicates a fervent confrontation with the Jews. Both groups overlook the fact that obedience to the Mosaic Law depends on the action of the Spirit.[30]

After all, there is even more. It gets worse. Paul turns against the Judaistic position further on and points out that it closely hangs together with boasting (see particularly 6:13–14). For sure, Räisänen categorically (and rhetorically) asserts that there are no polemics against human boasting in the Epistle to the Galatians. But a little later, he has to admit that the idea of boasting nonetheless occurs in 6:4 and 13–14![31] What does the passage (the text in view of the context) mean?

---

non-Christian Palestinian Judaism represented such a view [. . .]. We can hardly suppose, then—and Paul gives us no reason to suppose—that the Judaizers in the church taught that believing Gentiles had to be circumcised and start keeping the rest of the law to get in; on the contrary, he battles against circumcision and keeping the rest of the law as necessary to stay in [. . .]."

28 Dunn 1983, 121; Gundry 1985, 8–9. Later on, see Moo 2013, 20.

29 See above 4.1.1.

30 For the question of staying in Judaism and in Paul, see above 5.2.

31 See Räisänen 1983, 169: "[. . .] in this letter, where Paul mounts his most vehement attack on the way of the law there is absolutely no polemic against man's boasting and the like. Paul does not criticize the Galatians for giving room for boasting [. . .]. The theme 'boasting' only occurs in Galatians in 6.4,13,14." In his article of 1980a, Räisänen still completely sidesteps 6:13–14 (see p. 69).

According to v. 4, the Christian has reason for boasting (καύχημα), insofar as he scrutinizes his own actions to the utmost and reaches a positive result in his honest self-examination. Yet two reservations must be made at the same time: he will have reason for boasting *first* in the eschatological tribunal (ἕξει, future) and *only* in view of himself (εἰς ἑαυτὸν μόνον).[32] The limitations on Christian boasting already presuppose that the Galatians should not exceed them by carnal boasting.[33]

In v. 4, Paul does not yet confront the Judaizers directly. Rather, he creates the conditions for his relentless assault in vv. 13–14.

According to v. 13, the Judaizers boast *already now* and *also* in view of others (in comparison with religious achievements). They try by the "flesh" of the Galatians (an allusion to circumcision)[34] to gain reason for boasting particularly among the Jews. By contrast, Paul boasts—as v. 14 carries on—solely in the cross of Christ, by which the world is crucified to him and he to the world.[35] Obviously, behind his strong use of language lies the unspoken conviction that God really approves of such boasting, even though it is spoken already now.[36] In the context, the harsh reproach is thrown in the very faces of the Judaizers that they were unwilling "to suffer persecution" for the cross of Christ (v. 12b). That is why they were unwilling to boast in the cross of Christ. Hence, they pride themselves on vain things and from low, reprehensible motives.[37]

Apparently, Paul in chapter 6 blames the Judaizers for their unjustified boasting. He strongly avows that they boast in their persistent and prosperous zeal to carry out the Torah. The polemical tone aims not only against their unbelief or, more accurately, against their false belief in Christ (*contra* Räisänen). Rather, conflict is occurring on two fronts. The Judaistic zeal necessarily brings about contempt for the cross of Christ and, by implication, the renunciation of righteous boasting. As a result, Christians in Galatia are threatened by a double danger. They run the continuous risk of exchanging Christ for the Law

32 Hübner 1982, 82–88, under (partially critical) reference to other exegetes.

33 Bosch 1970, 258–59.

34 Lührmann (1978, 101) hardly goes wrong when he finds in the concept of σάρξ also an allusion to human efforts in general. It is a phrase with double meaning. See also Weder 1981, 204–5.

35 The Greek word κόσμος includes "all das, was mit dem Gesetz zusammenhängt" (Lührmann 1978, 101). See further Ridderbos 1987, 210: "The expression 'the world' here represents everything in which a man would wish to 'boast,' that is to say, on which in a religious sense he would suppose himself able to depend, as, for example, the law and circumcision (cf. v. 13)." Correctly, H. D. Betz 1988, 538; Oepke 1979, 202–3; Mußner 1974, 414; Schlier 1971, 281–82; Weder 1981, 207 n. 328.

36 Bosch 1970, 225–28. Cf. also Liebers 1989, 74: "Damit beinhaltet V. 14a gerade keine Abrogation alles 'Ruhmes,' sondern belegt die Existenz eines auch für den Apostel legitimen 'Sich-Rühmens.'" See also the commentators.

37 Hübner 1982, 88–91. See also Weder 1981, 205–11.

and deceiving themselves through self-sufficient arrogance. The two perils lurk simultaneously since a person expresses his deepest and most fundamental understanding of existence in praise.[38] Whoever trusts in his own works also boasts of his own action. Yet whoever in sincerity puts his faith in the crucified Christ and who himself is crucified with him boasts in the cross of Christ and not in the dead deeds of the dead self.

In order to corroborate his contrary interpretation, Räisänen refers to H. Hübner.[39] That indication, however, leads astray. It is not correct. Namely, Hübner does not contest that vv. 13–14 deprecate the Judaistic boasting. He expresses his thoughts in a clear and understandable way:

> Paul will then say—otherwise the relationship between v. 14 and v. 13 would be unintelligible—: Man should not boast for what he has done according to the law; because these are mere external achievements, only "flesh." Man ought to—and therein lies the paradox—boast in the cross. In other words, man ought boast of that which is not the product of his own accomplishment.[40]

Strictly speaking, Hübner contends that even in Gal. 6:4 Paul permits boasting (with the two reservations above), but later on, especially in Rom. 4:2, prohibits it.[41] His tentative analysis will be dealt with below.[42]

Besides, here Räisänen takes no notice of 3:28, although Paul indirectly but nonetheless problematizes Jewish (and Judaistic) boasting there.[43] The text reads that all believers, Jews and Gentiles, free and bond, men and women are one in Christ. The utterance recalls the traditional eulogy of the Jewish free man that he even today recites every morning.[44] BT Menahot 43b teaches as follows:

> It has been taught on Tannaite authority: R. Judah says, "A person must recite three blessings every day: 'Praised are you, O Lord, who has not made me a gentile,' 'Praised are you, O Lord, who did not make me a boor,' and 'Praised are you, O Lord, who did not make me a woman.'" R. Aha bar Jacob heard his son

38 Käsemann 1980, 125.

39 Räisänen 1983, 169 n. 46.

40 Hübner 1982, 90: "Paulus will dann sagen—andernfalls würde das Verhältnis von V.14 zu V.13 unverständlich—: Man soll sich nicht dessen rühmen, was man für das Gesetz getan hat; denn das ist als bloß äusserlich Erreichtes nur 'Fleisch'. Mann soll sich—und darin liegt die Paradoxie—des Kreuzes rühmen, 'sich' also dessen rühmen, was gerade nicht Produkt eigenen Schaffens ist." Also, against Liebers 1989, 73–75.

41 Op. cit., 81–91.

42 See below 6.4.

43 *Pace* Hübner 1982, 81: "Im gesamten ersten polemischen Teil des Briefes, in dem das mosaische Gesetz als Bereich der Unfreiheit deklariert wird, findet sich das Ruhmmotive nicht. Nur im letzten Kapitel läßt Paulus es anklingen." Cf. Sanders 1977, 482–84. He (op. cit., 482) mainly argues *ex silentio*: "We must first note that in Galatians, the reason for not keeping the law which Bultmann adduces (that keeping it is itself sinning, because it leads to sin: boasting before God) is notably not in evidence."

44 Lietzmann 1971, 24; Loewe 1966, 52–53; Oepke 1979, 125–26; Witherington 1981, 594; Zahn 1922, 188–89 n. 62. *Contra* Paulsen 1980, 85.

> reciting the blessing, "Praised are you, O Lord, who did not make me a boor." He said to him, "Arrogance—to such an extent . . . !" He said to him, "Then what blessing should one say?" ". . . who has not made me a slave." "But that is in the same category as a woman anyhow!" "A slave is worse."[45]

The eulogy stands for the reasoning that the Jewish free man as compared to the Gentiles, bondmen, and women can better live up to the divine will. He knows—in contrast to the Gentiles—the Torah. He has—in contrast to bondmen—freedom to follow it. He also has—in contrast to women—even the duty of obeying all the commandments. In order not to misunderstand BT Menahot 43b, we must take into consideration particularly the following facts:

(1) The petitioner thanks God and not himself.

(2) An affected gratitude or an intentional hypocrisy or any sort of disgusting pretense lies far from the eulogy. The petitioner reckons with truly praiseworthy prerogatives. He rejoices in them. His knowledge of the Torah ultimately goes back to God's sovereign revelation on Mount Sinai, as Israel achieved a particular status in contrast to the other nations. His fulfillment of the commandments in absolute freedom means that he follows his own and one Master's voice. His full-service obedience results in divine benignity and blessings in all areas of his human life. In consideration of his lucky lot, he expresses his joy to be able to enjoy the promised favors in the richest abundance through his most careful devotion and piety possible.[46]

(3) Further, the expectation of rewarding merits or the demand for compensatory submission or any sort of claim for earning divine distribution of justice lies far removed from the eulogy. The petitioner has indeed been born as a Jewish free man! He has by no means gained his innate privileges through his own occupation or pursuit. God has so determined. He is the Creator. Good gifts come from him.[47]

On closer reflection, the Jew demonstrably does not recite a bad doxology. Rather, his adoration of God sounds very pious. It indeed seems quite surprising or even odd that Paul dissociates himself from it. As a Christian, he no longer professes the eighteen petitions of the Amidah prayer (at least not all of them) as he once did as a Pharisee. What, then, goes wrong with the Jewish morning

---

45 Translation according to Neusner 1991, 2:29–30. In addition, see T Berakhot 7:18 and JT Berakhot 13b. No one exactly knows when the blessings in question originated. In all likelihood, Paul was acquainted with them, since he seems to formulate Gal. 3:28 in direct contrast to BT Menahot 43b. The resemblance is evidently no coincidence. See below.

46 Cf. Odeberg 1980, 33–34.

47 See ibid.

devotion? Certainly, Paul finds it impossible that anyone in his inner being might reverence God without simultaneously trusting in the Son of God.[48] Still, the Jewish doxology hardly miscarries exclusively in Christological dogma. The root cause lies much deeper. In the light of Galatians 6, Paul presumably does not accept Jews comparing themselves with others (in this case with Gentiles, bondmen, and women), since he knows perfectly well that their (typical human) comparison with others produces insolence and hubris (see vv. 4 and 13–14 above). He is familiar with their arrogance by his own experience (see especially Gal. 1:13–14; Phil. 3:3–9; cf. 2 Corinthians 10–13). Honestly, the Jewish free man reads an ominous ranking list in his doxology. He is—praised be the Lord—better than one and sundry. His comparison with those others reveals that his religious vanity emerges unhindered even in the midst of prayer. Ultimately, he *nolens volens* exalts himself under the mask of praise to God.[49]

Hence, the derogatory Jewish boasting (tantamount to characteristic human attitude) bothers the apostle. He brings it to naught in his programmatic proclamation in 3:28.[50] With regard to Christian unity, he withdraws from his fellow countrymen their precedence over Gentiles, bondmen, and women. The differences between the various groups now belong to a superseded past.[51] There are no longer any acceptable reasons for demeaning comparisons and the resulting religious bigotry. The Jew learns to praise his God in all humility and with pure motives once he sees himself crucified with Christ and his eyes entirely closed to the world, including others (see 6:14 above). Only at that moment does his doxology become finest Christology.

In conclusion, Paul seems to think that Jewish or non-Christian religiosity in general—in no matter what outer forms it conceals itself—is necessarily perverse. For the carnal man is σάρξ also (and particularly) in his relation to God until the Spirit through the Gospel brings about a radical change.

48 Cf. Sanders 1983, 35.

49 Oepke (1979, 202–3) underscores with regard to Gal. 6:13–14: "Paulus beleuchtet hier blitzartig ihren [i.e., the Judaizers] ungebrochenen theokratischen Stolz [. . .]. Je mehr Heiden (messiasgläubige) Juden werden, desto mehr tritt die Einzigartigkeit Israels und des in der Thora festgelegten Leistungsprinzips ans Licht. [. . .] Das [the crucifixion of the world and the I] bedeutet für den vorliegenden Fall die völlige Entwurzelung jenes theokratischen Stolzes, den Paulus als das innerste Motiv des Judaismus aufgedeckt hat."

50 Oepke 1979, 126; Witherington 1981, 594.

51 H. D. Betz 1974, 83; 1988, 333–47; Lührmann 1978, 65–68; Mußner 1974, 264–66; Oepke 1979, 125–26; Paulsen 1980, 74–95; Rohde 1989, 164–65; Schlier 1971, 174–75.

6.3. Romans 3:27

> Ποῦ οὖν ἡ καύχησις; ἐξεκλείσθη. διὰ ποίου νόμου; τῶν ἔργων; οὐχί, ἀλλὰ διὰ νόμου πίστεως.

Both Sanders and Räisänen argue that Rom. 3:27 in the light of 2:17, 23 does not at all relate to human boasting on account of one's own merits. Rather, it excludes Jewish boasting on the basis of the special or unique status of Israel in God's history of salvation. Paul's further argumentation in the following context goes in the same direction. He asserts that God is God not only of the Jews but also of the Gentiles (v. 29) and that both Jews and Gentiles are justified in the same way, namely, by viz. through faith (v. 30; cf. also vv. 21–25).[52]

It goes without saying that Rom. 3:27 refers to 2:17–23.[53] Sanders and Räisänen are thus far fully justified in linking the two texts with each other. It still remains to analyze what kind of boasting Rom. 3:27 exactly excludes in the light of 2:17, 23. How do they precisely relate to each other? To begin with, the discussion continues with Sanders and Räisänen as their exegetical explanations are critically addressed. If their interpretation fails to carry conviction, then a better solution is to be found.

Taken as a whole, Räisänen does not really mean that 3:27 excludes the special status of Israel once and for all.[54] He remarks that the boasting about the Law and God as such has validity in 2:17, 23. But since the Jews transgress their Law and thereby dishonor their God (see the context), their braggy boasting backfires.[55] Strictly speaking, Räisänen thus means that 3:27 excludes the special status of sinful Israel once and for all. Elsewhere, however, he maintains that the apostle does not consider the whole of Israel sinful.[56] As a logical consequence, he must then oddly presume that 3:27 in that case does not exclude the boasting of sinless Israel. They can still truly boast in God (2:17) and the Law (2:23)! Obviously, the deduced interpretation no longer conforms to the actual interpretation of Räisänen. As a result, his argumentation leads to a dead end. It cannot stand up to critical examination.

At large, it does not make much sense to suggest that Paul would renounce the special status of Israel in 3:27 whereas he at least indirectly still supports it

52 Räisänen 1983, 170–71 (cf. already 1980a, 70); Sanders 1983, 33. Their exegesis has found widespread approval. See Liebers 1989, 46–47, 69–71; F. Watson 1986, 133–34. Cf. Dunn 1983, 118.

53 See, e.g., Cranfield 1982, 1:219; Heil 1987, 25; Liebers 1989, 46, 70; Michel 1978, 154–55; Murray 1982, 1:122; Nygren 1979, 170; Schlier 1977, 116; Thompson 1986, 521–25; Wilckens 1978, 1:244–45. *Pace* Hübner 1985, 895: "Auf keinen Fall kann 3:27 im Horizont von Kap. 2 ausgelegt werden."

54 Räisänen 1983, 170–71.

55 Op. cit., 170. For criticism see already Klein 1988, 53.

56 Op. cit., 97–101, 106–9 *et passim*.

in 2:17, 23. In addition, the Septuagint—as especially J. S. Bosch shows with the massive text material he brings forward—allows Israel to boast in God and in the Law.[57] Why would Paul in 3:27 argue against what was for him authoritative Scripture? In his Epistle to the Romans, he elsewhere notoriously affirms with emphasis the special status of Israel in agreement with the Old Testament (see particularly 3:1–2; 9:4–5; cf. 11:16–24 and the formula "to the Jew first and also to the Greek").[58]

Accordingly, it turns out that 3:27—in the light of 2:17, 23 and in view of the Epistle to the Romans as a whole—does not precisely say what Sanders and Räisänen claim. Despite their good intention, they do not take the context sufficiently into consideration. In order to present an alternative and more plausible interpretation, it is necessary to analyze chapter 2 more in-depth.

In Romans 2, Paul tries primarily to attain two goals. He wants to show that

(1) the Jews are not better than the Gentiles but sin just as they and similarly fall prey to the wrath of God.

(2) the Jews as sinners have therefore no right to judge the Gentiles.[59]

In consequence, it then follows that the Jew—from the Pauline perspective—thinks in a contrasting way. He supposes that

(1) he does not sin like the Gentiles and therefore does not fall prey to the wrath of God.

(2) he as a guardian of justice has the right to judge the Gentiles.

---

57 Bosch 1970, 64–78, 112–13, 120–22.

58 For the privileges of Israel in Rom. 9:4–5, see especially Laato 2021, 37–41. Similarly, see Aageson 1987, 59; O. Betz 1978, 10–11, 15; W. S. Campbell 1981, 28; Haacker 1982, 68; Liechtenhan 1946, 64; Lübking 1986, 30–34, 53–57; Luz 1968, 269–74; Marquardt 1971, 4–7, 63–64; Rese 1975, 215–19 (also 1988, 209, 213); Schmitt 1984, 19–23, 72–77; Vischer 1950, 86–88; Zeller 1973, 85–87. Cf. Käsemann 1961, 376. *Pace* Räisänen 1987a, 2896. He asserts that all (!) of the privileges of Israel (Rom. 9:4–5) are right away denied (see already 1986, 73–74). Cf. already Bosch 1970, 137–40. He maintains that Paul, against the Septuagint, in practice denies the Old Testament preference for Israel. The argumentation goes as follows: "Cabría hasta preguntarse si una 'gloria', que se apoyaba en Dios y en su palabra (2,17.23) pudo llegar a ser excluida por Dios mismo [. . .]. Responderíamos que, aun sin destruir los fundamentos concretos de aquella 'gloria' [. . .], Dios les privó de la *categoría* de "motivos de 'gloria'", cuando—en virtud de las nuevas realidades salvíficas—la situación del judío dejó de ser una situación envidiable (¡gloriosa!) respecto de la situación del gentil" (op. cit., 138). In order not to fall into contradiction, Bosch later argues accordingly. He emphasizes out of necessity that χαύχησις "no significa el vicio—o la actitud vital—de gloriarse, sino algo que da 'motivos' para ello" (op. cit., 150). Taken as a whole, the argumentation of Bosch fails to carry conviction. In all likelihood, Paul understands by καύχησις (3:27) boasting as such and not the ground for it, to say nothing of "la *categoría* de motivos de gloria." See most commentaries. Cf. further how quickly Bosch (1970, 148–49) deals with 3:1–2 and moves on. Räisänen (1983, 70 n. 52) among others depends on Bosch.

59 See above 4.2.1.3.

Against the background of Wisdom of Solomon (which lies behind the Pauline argumentation in Romans 1–2 both in a positive and negative sense[60]), the Jew does in fact pursue that kind of thinking. His religious-philosophical set of beliefs shows ideological contours that usher in a rigorous moralism:

The Gentiles succumb to idolatry and other gross sins. With full justice, God pours out his fervent wrath upon them. He will punish and destroy them since they do not repent but remain as accursed evildoers of the worst kind. Only the people of Israel stand out as a righteous nation. They put trust in the one God and flee from idolatry. To be sure, Wisdom of Solomon does not try to cover or obscure that also a Jew may now and then sin. In contrast to the Gentiles, he still knows the truth through his knowledge of the Torah and hence will acknowledge his possible offenses in confession of his trespasses and in confidence of divine forgiveness. Loyalty to the Sinaitic covenant ensures that God's wrath does not fall on Israel. He encounters his people with clemency and leniency. Sometimes his paternal correction is needed and helps them to become obedient in their choices and decisions. In order to recompense the debt of gratitude for God's solidarity, Israel acts in solidarity with him. They—just as he—encounter heathen people with complaint and judgment, bearing in mind his readiness to forbearance.[61]

At large, the Jews do not let themselves be lulled into the illusion that under the protection or compassion of God they might go unpunished for sins. Their salvation within the covenant does not just happen as if automatically. Wisdom of Solomon categorically disputes that their present and eternal fate would differ from that of other people for some arbitrary reasons. Jews have access into the heavenly kingdom only under the condition that they neither on purpose foster the pagan vices nor without repentance ask forgiveness for their own sins (see above). They must take their religion most seriously.[62] Therefore, Wisdom of Solomon sets forth human freedom in order to underline human responsibility and divine justice.[63] In a sense, the Jews work out their own fortune if they want to do good and do what they want. Accordingly, the Gentiles work out their own misery if they want to do evil and do what they want. The two different

60 See above 4.2.1.2. and 4.2.1.3.

61 See above 4.2.1.3. Cf. Nissen 1974, 161.

62 See above all Clarke's commentary on Wisd. of Sol. 15:2–3 (1973, 98 and even 8–12). Similarly, Feldmann 1926, 102; Fichtner 1938, 55; Reese 1983, 19–21; Ziener 1970, 97–98.

63 Clarke 1973, 10–12 and his Index, s.v. "incorruption"; Reese 1983, 19–20; Winston 1981, 58. Cf. further Eising 1959, 400: "Nach Meinung des Verfassers [i.e., Wisdom of Solomon] gehört also die Gotteserkenntnis irgendwie zur natürlichen Fähigkeit des Menschen." See p. 397 as well.

outcomes are like the two sides of the same coin. On the one hand, God will then reward the Jews. On the other hand, he will also punish the Gentiles.[64]

Further, it turns out that Wisdom of Solomon exactly squares with Jewish self-understanding in general. In his comprehensive research, Sanders finds not a single Jewish writing that perverts covenantal nomism into covenantal libertinism. Israel stays in the covenant provided that they do not put off the "yoke of the kingdom" by forsaking the Mosaic Law. In their status as the people of God, they bind themselves to obey his will as diligently as possible.[65] Obedience comes to pass on the basis of human freedom in accordance with a doctrinal common property of covenantal nomism.[66]

In consideration of Wisdom of Solomon against the background of covenantal nomism, Romans 2 falls into place. The chapter does not suggest that the Jews disregard the grace of God and earn eternal life on the basis of their own meritorious works (cf. the Weberian position[67]). No, it rather tells a completely different story. In harmony with Wisdom of Solomon, v. 4 urges not to misuse the divine goodness, forbearance, and long-suffering through unrepentance.[68] Nor does Romans 2 suggest that the Jews would be short of their special status as the chosen people (cf. Sanders and Räisänen[69]). In harmony with Wisdom of Solomon, vv. 17–20 exalt the privileges of Israel (the Torah and the monotheistic creed) not with a note of irony, but in a tone of sincerity.[70] In addition, vv. 21–24 raise the reproach that the Jews themselves by their transgressions despise their Old Testament heritage or deride the name of their God. In other words, they should appreciate and esteem their solemn legacy even more![71]

Given the wide background data in Romans 2, Paul makes there from beginning to end a huge effort to attack the brazen absurdity that the apparent "smaller" sinners compare themselves with the others and condemn the apparent "greater" sinners. His perspective forms an exceptionally sharp contrast with Wisdom of Solomon.[72] To begin with, vv. 1–5 uncover the cardinal failure

64 Cf. Ziener 1970, 31–33, 44–46, 116–18.

65 Sanders 1977, 419–23.

66 See above 4.1.1.

67 See above 2.1.

68 Cf. in particular Cranfield 1977, 1:144–45; Käsemann 1980, 51; Schlier 1977, 71.

69 Räisänen 1983, 170–71; Sanders 1983, 33.

70 See above all Cranfield 1977, 1:164; Käsemann 1980, 64; Liebers 1989, 64; Michel 1978, 127 n. 1; Murray 1982, 1:81; Schlier 1977, 82; Schmidt 1962, 51; Wilckens 1978, 1:148. Cf. Stalder 1962, 263.

71 See above 4.2.1.3.

72 See above 4.2.1.3. and below. Sanders (1983, 123–35) treats Romans 2 as an anomaly in the *corpus Paulinum*. The chapter "deals directly with salvation and makes salvation dependent on obedience to the law" (op. cit., 132; see further in particular pp. 128–29). In clarification of the anomalous character, he develops the hypothesis that "in Rom. 1:18–2:29 Paul takes over to an unusual degree homiletical material from Diaspora

of Israel in relation to heathen peoples. The complaints can be paraphrased as follows: The Jew, despite his own countless offenses, pursues after the phantom of surpassing the Gentiles in piety. Indwelling arrogance comes out in humiliating condemnation. Behind the negative attitude lies the disgusting supposition that the "pious" himself through his hidden hypocrisy escapes the judgment of God.[73] Next, vv. 6–16 extend the polemical tone and explain the last judgment as God will judge humankind according to their works without respect of persons (= impartially).[74] Then, vv. 17–24 actualize the problem whether the undisputed prerogatives of Israel confer a certain numinous legitimation to their feelings of superiority. When anyone calls himself a Jew (the noble name of Israel), possesses the Law (the infallible divine revelation), and boasts in God (monotheism), when he has the instruction of the Law and knows the will of God in order to approve "what is excellent" (τὰ διαφέροντα), when he is a guide for the blind and a light for those who are in the dark, when he is an instructor of the foolish and a teacher of the young (vv. 17–20), does it not necessarily follow that he towers above the *massa perditionis*?[75] Wisdom of Solomon answers the question in the affirmative.[76] Hence, the Jew brings out his prerogatives to raise himself alongside God and to lower the Gentiles at the side of himself. No doubt, his religious superiority has a thick layer of gilding on account of his ethical prominence. This naturally invokes objections from the apostle to the Gentiles. He simply turns the complacency in Wisdom of Solomon upside down. Instead of rendering a guarantee of Israel's hegemony, the Torah shows that the Jews do not stand at the pinnacle of the hierarchy. Precisely because of their knowledge of the Law (vv. 18, 20), they should comprehend that they in more ways than one exceed the limits of decency and hence in no way excel the others in piety (vv. 21–23).[77] What is even worse, they for the same reasons blaspheme the name of their God (v. 24). Finally, vv. 25–27 assert that Israel's confidence in circumcision does not provide any guarantee of their hegemony either (cf. Deut. 10:16; 30:6; Jer. 4:4). Their transgressions—as the very biting sarcasm runs—rather turn the circumcised into uncircumcised ones.[78] In conclusion, vv. 28–29 set a barrier before the Jewish attempt at boasting. The true "inward" Jew experiences

---

Judaism" and that "he alters it in only insubstantial ways" (op. cit., 123; see further in particular pp. 129–32). As a result, Sanders means that Hellenistic Judaism at least normally, but Paul exceptionally, teaches the salvation of man by obedience to the Law. Does the apostle to the Gentiles then not have sufficient grounds to criticize the legalism of the Jewish soteriology at least occasionally? For the relation between faith and works in Paul, see above 5.2.

73 See above 4.2.1.3.

74 See the commentaries.

75 Cf. Heil 1987, 21.

76 Cf. above 4.2.1.3.

77 See above 4.2.1.3.

78 See, e.g., Ridderbos 1987, 335.

(eschatological) praise (the meaning of "Judah" in Hebrew; cf. Gen. 29:35; 49:8)[79] not from men, but from God (v. 29).[80]

As a result, Romans 2 on the whole succinctly overthrows the religious-philosophical system of Wisdom of Solomon.[81] In the Jewish praise of God in Rom. 2:17 and 23, there is mixed much praise of self. That kind of *tout ensemble* sounds like the discordant noise of an out of tune orchestra. The combination of high and low motives excites disgust. True praise of God is awakened only out of an utterly selfless heart.[82] Especially with reference to Wisdom of Solomon, the Jews remain far behind the noble ideal. In effect, they defame and denigrate the Gentiles under the cloak of the doxology (see Gal. 3:28 above). Despite the Mosaic Law or paradoxically because of it, they fail to get rid of their religious vanity. A real transformation of mind does not depend on their hard work or better trying. This is a lesson they should learn.

Against the background of Rom. 2:17, 23, boasting (καύχησις) in 3:27 relates to Jewish hubris over heathen peoples in recourse to the salvific historical

79 For the eschatological praise, see 1 Cor. 4:5 with a similar emphasis. Correctly, Cranfield 1978, 1:175–76; Käsemann 1980, 72–73; Wilckens 1978, 1:158. Cf. also Michel 1978, 135; Schlier 1977, 90.

80 Cranfield 1978, 1:175–76; Michel 1978, 135; Murray 1982, 1:89–90; Schmidt 1962, 55. Cf. Käsemann 1980, 73.

81 *Pace* Hübner 1982, 93–94. He maintains: "Der Vorwurf des Apostels geht vielmehr ganz dahin, daß [. . .] der Jude auf dem mosaischen Gesetz ausruht, gleich als ob schon der bloße Besitz desselben ein Verdienst wäre. Dann erhebt aber Paulus an dieser Stelle gerade *nicht* den *Vorwurf* der *Werkgerechtigkeit*! [. . .] Die Absicht des Paulus dürfte also am ehesten so richtig verstanden sein: Die Tatsache, daß die Torah Israel gegeben worden ist, verführte und verführt dieses dazu, sie als 'Besitz' zu mißbrauchen. Paulus prangert demnach nicht ein Sich-Rühmen mit Gesetzes*werken* an, sondern gerade umgekehrt ein Sich-Rühmen mit dem Besitz des Gesetzes *ohne* Gesetzeswerke." Here, Hübner evidently raises an unjustified reproach against the Jews. I indeed know of no Jewish writing in which the mere possession of the Law were a human merit rather than an expression for the divine love! In any case, Romans 2 does not state that Israel misuses the Law as a possession ("Besitz"). The chapter denounces boasting with qualitatively and quantitatively insufficient works of the Law. To be sure, the Jews do many outwardly good works. In their delusion, they then condemn the most sinful Gentiles (vv. 1–3). In his reproach, Paul emphasizes that the Jews think too highly of themselves. Strictly speaking, they do no really good works and sometimes make themselves guilty of gross sins (vv. 1–5, 17–23). In consequence, their boasting turns into the opposite: it degenerates to a farce (vv. 23–24). In addition, cf. B. L. Martin 1989, 137: "Romans 2 asserts that the Jews think they obey the law but do not really obey it." For Pauline criticism in Romans 2, see above 4.2.1.3.

82 Bultmann 1938, 649; Cranfield 1982, 1:163–70; Käsemann 1980, 64–67; Murray 1982, 1:80–85; Nygren 1979, 137–38.

signa of Israel.[83] Especially it denotes covert haughtiness which unveils itself in the midst of "devout" doxology in divine ceremony. O. Michel puts it into words:

> One should not thereby overlook that a particular form of prayer and hymnody can be a manner of praising oneself (Rom. 2:17, 23).[84]

By closer reflection, 3:27 does not devalue the special status of Israel. Rather, it renounces the misuse of the special status of Israel in self-praise. Under the precondition of their covenant, Jews have risen to their prominence because of their ethical superiority. They distinguish themselves by their diligence in works of the Law.

Now (οὖν), 3:27 announces that Jewish boasting is once and for all excluded (ἐξεκλείσθη).[85] The passive stands no doubt for God himself (viz. *passivum divinum*).[86] He has disqualified self-praise. He has brought it and every sort of humblebrag to naught "by the law of faith" (διὰ νόμου πίστεως). Here, the word "law" (νόμος) might have the meaning of "norm," "principle," or "rule."[87] At any

83 Cf. Haacker 1982, 66: "Daraus ergibt sich: Für ein Überlegenheitsgefühl, wie es der jüdische Lehrer von 2, 17–24 gegenüber den *gojim* an den Tag legte, ist kein Platz mehr (3, 27)." See further Theobald 1981–82, 146: "Gesetzeserfüllung führt zur Verdrängung der radikalen Verfallenheit an die Macht der Sünde und infolge dessen zu Überhebung und Abgrenzung von den Heiden [. . .]." Similarly, Miguens 1971, 604; Murray 1982, 1:122; Rhyne 1981, 67; Schlier 1977, 116; Stuhlmacher 1985, 97.

84 Michel 1978, 155–56: "Man darf dabei nicht übersehen, daß eine bestimmte Form des Gebetes und des Hymnus zum Selbstruhm werden kann (Röm 2,17.23)."

85 Räisänen (1983, 170–71) reads pretty much into the aorist ἐξεκλείσθη: "The aorist form of the predicate verb in 3.27 [. . .] is to be noted. 'Boasting' has been excluded by a once-and-for-all act of God. The exclusion is thus an objective event. But then 'boasting,' too, must refer to something more concrete than man's general attitude—such an attitude was hardly shut out once and for all through the 'principle' [. . .] of faith. The reference must rather be to the special status of the Jews which caused them to boast over the law." I cannot follow the analysis of Räisänen. Frankly speaking, he seems to maintain that boasting does not relate to "man's general attitude," but rather to the "Jew's general attitude" (*sit venia verbo*). But does the aorist ἐξεκλείσθη express so fine a nuance?

86 Above all Räisänen 1980, 110–11, against, for example, Hübner 1982, 119 and 1987, 2688–89. See also Cranfield 1977, 1:219; Michel 1978, 155; Osten-Sacken 1989, 29; Schlier 1977, 116; Wilckens 1978, 1:244. Cf. further Käsemann 1980, 96–97.

87 Until the middle of twentieth century, there dominated almost with no exception the trend to interpret νόμος in many passages (particularly Rom. 3:27; 7:21–25; 8:2) in a general, figurative or improper sense (see Räisänen 1980, 101–3). Cf. the above attempts at translation. Since then, many exegetes have contended that νόμος in 3:27 (especially Cranfield 1977, 1:219–20, 374–78; Friedrich 1954, 401–7; cf. Berger 1966, 64–65; Furnish 1968, 160; Liebers 1989, 46–47 n. 33, 70 n. 60; Rhyne 1981, 67–71; Theobald 1981–82, 163) or also in 8:2 (especially Fuchs 1949, 85; F. Hahn 1976, 37–38, 40–41, 47–49; Schmidt 1962, 73–74, 136; Stuhlmacher 1985, 97, 99–100 n. 18, 103) or even in 7:21–25 (Lohse 1973, 279–87; B. L. Martin 1989, 26–32; Osten-Sacken 1975, 209–12, 226–30, 233–34, 245–47; 1989, 9–33; Schnabel 1985, 285–90; Wilckens 1978, 1:245–47; 1980, 2:89–97, 122–24; cf. further Hübner 1980, 464–66; 1982, 95–97, 118–29; 1987, 2682–89) refers to the Torah. See already Fuchs 1949, 84–87. The still ongoing debate should have no greater relevance in this context. In any case, Räisänen (see 1980, 105–17; 1983, 50–52) tries to put an end to the new orientation. See also Bergmeier 1985, 162–72;

rate, the somewhat peculiar expression in Greek denotes the new order of salvation in faith: the total sinful man (v. 23) is justified freely by the grace of God on account of redemption in Christ Jesus (v. 24), which defines or determines his existence to the exclusion of boasting.[88] Since justification and the resulting transformation takes place without the works of the Law, the Jewish self-complacency has ceased and come to a definitive end forever.

Directly in vv. 29–30, Paul draws from the monotheistic creed of the Old Testament (Deut. 6:4) conclusions which make his doctrine of justification by faith without works of the Law (v. 28) acceptable—in fact, necessary. His rhetorical questions (v. 29) culminate in the theological axiom or liturgical acclamation εἷς ὁ θεός (v. 30a). The one and only God justifies Jews and Gentiles exactly in the same way, namely, by and through faith (v. 30b). He does not save humankind by different means (Israel by dint of the Law and other peoples by dint of the Gospel). On that account, the founder of the old covenant would not be the founder of the new covenant. Moreover, the one and only God does not restrict salvation to Israel. In that case, he would be the Savior of the Jews but not of the Gentiles. Thus the universalism of the monotheistic creed conflicts with the particularism of the Mosaic Law. While the former implies a uniform people of God recruited from all peoples, the latter differentiates between Israel as God's people and the whole rest of the world as god-less peoples.[89] As a consequence, both Old Testament aspects do not fit together. The Torah contains a serious tension.[90] Sharply, the monotheistic creed actually "prophesies" the end of the Law. The prophecy is fulfilled in Christ. For the very first time in history, he creates a uniform people of God from Jews and Gentiles in accordance with the monotheistic creed.

Simply, Paul hopes in vv. 29–30 that the Jews do not disown their special status recited by them daily in the Shema. Rather, they should on the basis of their monotheistic faith believe in Christ as the end of the Law (Rom. 10:4)! But they did not. It remained for the apostle to the Gentiles a great mystery—and misery at the same time.

Lichtenberger 1985, 1:205–7; Vollenweider 1989, 358–59, 366–70; Westerholm 1988, 123–26. Cf. Jones's significant impulse to further discussion (1987, 122–29).

88 Above all Räisänen 1980, 110–13.

89 Dahl 1977, 178–91. See further Caird 1978, 542–43; Cranfield 1982, 1:222; Giblin 1975, 543–45; Gräßer 1981, 201–5; Käsemann 1980, 97–99; Michel 1978, 156; Murray 1982, 1:123–24; Nygren 1979, 174; Rhyne 1981, 70–71; Schlier 1977, 118; Theobald 1981–82, 164–68; Thurén 1986, 185; Wilckens 1978, 1:248; Zeller 1973, 161. *Contra* Demke 1976, 475: "Nicht um Partikularismus oder Universalismus geht es. Nicht die Behauptung, daß es nur einen Gott gibt, ist hier entscheidend."

90 Thurén 1977, 40–42.

In summary, Paul denies neither in 2:17–24 nor in 3:27–30 the special status of the Jews. By contrast, he reproaches them there for their self-pride and self-praise before God.

6.4. Romans 4:2–5

(2) εἰ γὰρ Ἀβραὰμ ἐξ ἔργων ἐδικαιώθη, ἔχει καύχημα, ἀλλ᾽ οὐ πρὸς θεόν. (3) τί γὰρ ἡ γραφὴ λέγει; **ἐπίστευσεν δὲ Ἀβραὰμ τῷ θεῷ καὶ ἐλογίσθη αὐτῷ εἰς δικαιοσύνην**. (4) τῷ δὲ ἐργαζομένῳ ὁ μισθὸς οὐ λογίζεται κατὰ χάριν ἀλλὰ κατὰ ὀφείλημα, (5) τῷ δὲ μὴ ἐργαζομένῳ πιστεύοντι δὲ ἐπὶ τὸν δικαιοῦντα τὸν ἀσεβῆ λογίζεται ἡ πίστις αὐτοῦ εἰς δικαιοσύνην·

Sanders and Räisänen regard the argumentation in Romans 4 as a direct continuation and extension of the previous chapter 3. Paul presents Abraham as an illustration of his assertion that Jews and Gentiles have the same access to salvation (3:27–30). His polemics focus on national pride.[91] *The story in Genesis 15 shows that the progenitor of Israel was justified by faith without circumcision (v. 3). For certain, his justification forms a paradigmatic type: God always justifies man by faith without circumcision. The circumcised have no advantage over the uncircumcised (see, e.g., vv. 9–12, 16).*[92]

In chapter 4, Paul in no place disregards righteousness by the Law because it allegedly pretends to call forth arrogant boasting on account of one's own achievements. Rather, he harshly criticizes the salvation-historical notion of Israel's special status. His criticism culminates in v. 14: "For if it is the adherents of the law who are to be the heirs, faith is null and the promise is void" (cf. above).[93] *Besides, vv. 2 and 4–5 do not imply that righteousness by the Law necessarily leads to boasting in one's own achievements. Also here it is about the equality of Jews and Gentiles. On close reflection, v. 2 underscores that Abraham did not boast in the special status of Israel (Sanders) or in the Mosaic Law (Räisänen). Further, vv. 4–5 assert that God justifies the godless through faith apart from the works of the Law. Therefore, Jews and Gentiles have one and the same basis for salvation.*[94]

Surely, Sanders and Räisänen for good reason contend that the Pauline line of thought follows unbroken from Romans 3 to the next chapter.[95] For that

91 Räisänen 1983, 171 (see already 1980a, 70); Sanders 1983, 33–34 (also 1977, 489).

92 Räisänen 1983, 171–72 (see already 1980a, 70); Sanders 1983, 33–35 (also 1977, 489–91).

93 Ibid.

94 Räisänen 1983, 171 (see already 1980a, 70); Sanders 1983, 33, 35.

95 See Berger 1966, 65; Cranfield 1982, 1:224; Käsemann 1969, 140, 143; 1980, 100; Klein 1963, 429–30; 1964, 677–79; Michel 1978, 160; Van der Minde 1976, 68; Murray 1982, 1:127; Nygren 1979, 175; Osten-Sacken 1989, 32–33; Rhyne 1981, 30–32, 71–74; Schlier 1977, 121; Schmidt 1962, 75–76; T. R. Schreiner 1991, 232; Sutherland 1982, 165–66, 169–71; Wilckens 1978, 1:258; Zeller 1973, 99–100.

very reason, their interpretation of 4:2–5 raises grave suspicions if—or, rather, since—3:27–30 goes in another direction.[96] So what is the way ahead? What is the Old Testament story of Abraham all about?[97]

The conditional phrase in v. 2a implies the following syllogism:[98]

(1) In the case that a man is justified by works, he has καύχημα (= ground for boasting[99]).

(2) Abraham was justified by works.

(3) Therefore, Abraham had καύχημα.[100]

Already at first glance, it appears unquestionable that καύχημα refers to works. No doubt, v. 2a provides no other ground for boasting.[101] Neither does the context focus on any other ground (cf. below). Therefore, καύχημα cannot relate, for example, to the Law or the special status of Israel.[102] On the whole, Paul does not participate in the Jewish speculation[103] that the Torah has existed

---

96 See above 6.3.

97 It is unnecessary here to deal with the question of the continuity between Abraham and the believers. In particular, Klein (1963, 1964, 1966) and Wilckens (1961, 1964) have discussed that matter. Besides, see Berger 1966, 75–77; O. Betz 1978, 1–2; Käsemann 1969, 151–55.

98 Precisely, v. 2a can be taken in either a real or unreal sense. Schlier (1977, 123) illustrates well the difference between the two alternatives: "Wenn Abraham nämlich aus Gesetzesleistungen gerechtfertigt ist, wie ihr [that is, the Jews] annehmt, oder gerechtfertigt worden wäre, wie ich [that is, Paul] sage, dann hat oder hätte er Grund zum Ruhm."

99 W. Bauer 1988, s.v.; Bosch 1970, 282; Käsemann 1980, 100; Murray 1982, 1:130; Schlier 1977, 115.

100 Murray 1982, 1:130; cf. Nygren 1979, 177.

101 Berger 1966, 65; Bosch 1970, 166–67; Cranfield 1982, 1:227; Lohse 1978, 109–12; Luz 1968, 174–75; Michel 1978, 162; Van der Minde 1976, 69 n. 5; Murray 1982, 1:129–30; Nygren 1979, 176–78; Rhyne 1981, 77–79; Schlier 1977, 122–23; Schmidt 1962, 77; T. R. Schreiner 1991, 234–36; Stalder 1962, 270; Westerholm 1988, 166, 170; Wieser 1987, 58–59; Wilckens 1961, 115–16; 1978, 1:261. Cf. Heil 1987, 26.

102 Räisänen (1983, 171) arbitrarily reads the Law into v. 2. He paraphrases: "Had Abraham really been justified by *works*, then he would have had a reason to boast about the *law*" (italics mine). Räisänen unjustifiably substitutes boasting in works with boasting in the Law. A slight correction in the foregoing quotation brings it into harmony with the Pauline thought: "[. . .] them [*pro* the Law]." Correctly, Berger (1966, 65). He writes: "Vom Gesetz ist hier nicht die Rede, denn 1. handelt es sich ja um das Beispiel Abrahams, der vor dem Gesetz liegt, und 2. geht es um die grundsätzliche Frage (nach V.31), ob das Gesetz aus Glauben oder aus Werken erfüllt wird, d.h. auf welchem der beiden Wege die Gerechtigkeit erlangt wird. Nicht die Frage Glaube-Gesetz wird am Beispiel Abrahams entschieden, sondern: Glaube oder Werke, freilich so, daß dem Gesetz bis zu Jesus Christus hin die Werke zugeordnet sind. Ganz abgesehen vom Gesetz wird an der Gestalt Abrahams das Verhältnis von Glauben und Werken im Verhältnis zur Gerechtigkeit grundsätzlich erörtert." In reference to Laato, see T. R. Schreiner 1998, 218. See further, e.g., Liebers (1989, 73 n. 72; cf also 31–40, 71–73). He agrees with Räisänen's exegesis.

103 See in particular Billerbeck 1926, 204–6.

from all eternity. He affirms in agreement with the Old Testament that God has not revealed the Law earlier than 430 years after Abraham (Gal. 3:17 and Exod. 12:40–41; cf. further Rom. 4:9–12; 5:13–14, 20).[104]

Further, v. 2b concisely asserts that the second premise in the syllogism (see above) stands in contradiction with the biblical history.[105] The reference to Gen. 15:6 in v. 3 corroborates the assertion. It appears that Abraham was declared righteous by faith. His justification depended not in the slightest on works. Hence, every basis for boasting vanished.[106]

Next, vv. 4–5 expose Gen. 15:6 in more detail or depth. The verb λογίζεσθαι joins the clarification with the scriptural citation.[107] To begin with, v. 4 makes appeal to the common practice that the worker (ἐργαζόμενος) receives his salary not from grace (κατὰ χάριν) but strictly according to achievement (κατὰ ὀφείλημα). The participle ἐργαζόμενος refers here to one who lives ἐξ ἔργων. The expressions κατὰ χάριν and κατὰ ὀφείλημα again relate to divine mercy and human merits. The figurative speech affirms that Abraham did not gain righteousness with the help of his works.[108] Withdrawing from the image, v. 5 sets forth the doctrine of justification in explicit terms. It might even encompass an antithetical "battle formula" that reads something like "God justifies the godless."[109] All the same, a double adjustment proves crucial or necessary here. The godless will be justified only on the condition that he does not put his trust in works (μὴ ἐργαζόμενος) or, seen from the other side, that he has his faith (πιστεύων) in God. Thus it easily turns out that God counted (λογίζεται, *passivum divinum*)[110] to the godless Abraham the faith for righteousness.

As a result, it is clear from the beginning that Paul in 4:2–5 attacks boasting in one's own achievements.[111] He does not say a single word against the special

104 H. D. Betz 1988, 285–86; Lührmann 1978, 62; Oepke 1979, 113; Schlier 1965, 147.

105 Klein 1963, 430; Räisänen 1983, 171; Wieser 1987, 58.

106 Cranfield 1982, 1:228–30; Käsemann 1980, 100–104; Murray 1982, 1:130; Nygren 1979, 177–78; Rhyne 1981, 78–79; Schlier 1977, 123–24; Schmidt 1962, 77–78; Sutherland 1982, 173–75; Wieser 1987, 58–59.

107 Michel 1978, 162–63; Wilckens 1978, 1:262.

108 Cranfield 1982, 1:231–32; Michel 1978, 162–63; Murray 1982, 1:132; Schlier 1977, 124–25. See further Van der Minde 1976, 69.

109 Haacker 1975, 15; Michel 1978, 163. Cf. Käsemann 1969, 148–49.

110 Cranfield 1982, 1:231–32; Käsemann 1980, 104–5; Michel 1978, 162–63; Van der Minde 1976, 69; Murray 1982, 1:132–33; Schlier 1977, 124–25; Schmidt 1962, 78; Wieser 1987, 59–60; Wilckens 1978, 1:262–63.

111 Especially on the basis of Rom. 4:2, Hübner concludes that "der Ruhmverzicht vor Gott wesenhaft zum Selbstverständnis des an Christus Glaubenden gehört" (1982, 91 with emphasis; cf. futher 93–104). In contrast, Gal. 6:4 does not yet disqualify "einen echten Anspruch des Christen auf Ruhm aufgrund eines gerichtsrelevanten Lebenswerkes" (op. cit., 87–88). Apparently, in the Epistle to the Galatians the later thought of the Epistle to the Romans is missing (op. cit., 81–91). Hübner's analysis is not very convincing. Even in the Epistle to the Romans, Paul boasts of his apostolic mission (15:17). See,

status of Israel. In truth, Räisänen himself admits that v. 4 does not shut out "all overtones of the idea of anthropocentric legalism." He thinks that the apostle may have found "some tendency toward smugness and self-righteousness in the Jewish way."[112] Sanders makes a similar admission at least in principle. But he then draws the attention from the apparent anthropocentric legalism to the special status of Israel and lays no sufficient value on the former perception.[113] As a whole, it seems that Räisänen and Sanders themselves undermine their interpretation of 4:2–5 to a certain extent.

In the light of relevant Jewish material, the Pauline polemics become much more tangible. Various apocalyptic and rabbinic sources postulate that Abraham was declared righteous on the basis of his works. He gained great honor and fame not only among men but with God as well.[114] The justification of Abraham forms no exception. It is out of the question to imagine that the forefather of Israel has acquired righteousness in view of his exceptional piety but that a "common" Israelite could not achieve righteousness on account of his "ordinary" piety. There is absolutely no evidence for that sort of distinction. Rather, the justification of Abraham forms a paradigm for all of his descendants. As shown, Sanders himself emphasizes that Jewish righteousness always amounts to righteousness by works. He affirms that צדק means to obey the Torah to the full extent of human capacity and to repent of possible transgressions with the whole heart. In short, everyone is righteous who remains in the covenant through obedience and whose broken relationship with the covenant is restored through repentance and means of expiation.[115]

---

e.g., already Bultmann 1938, 650–53. Renunciation of self-praise (4:2) is formulated with almost the same words! It evidently deals with the question of justification. But Gal. 6:4 refers to boasting before the eschatological judgment of God (see above 6.2.). Many other places (see, e.g., 2 Cor. 1:14; Phil. 2:16; 1 Thess. 2:19) affirm that the Christian then truly has a valid reason for boasting. See Becker 1989, 392–93.

112 Räisänen 1983, 176. See also 1986, 82.

113 Sanders 1983, 34: "If one looks only at the phrase 'law of works' (3:27) and the participle 'the one working' (4:4) it may appear, as Hübner proposes, that what Paul attacks is achievement. But one must note the other terms which characterize those whom Paul criticizes: 'Jews' (3:29); 'the circumcision' (3:30; 4:9, 12); those 'of the law' (4:14, 16)—all phrases which focus on status, not religious attitude or behaviour."

114 Billerbeck 1926, 186–87. He cites passages from the Apocrypha, pseudepigraphic writings, and rabbinic sources. See also in particular Wieser 1987, 165–71. Rightly, Cranfield 1982, 1:227–30; Käsemann 1980, 100–101; Lohse 1978, 108–9, 111–12; Luz 1968, 178–79; Michel 1978, 161–62; Nygren 1979, 175–77; Rhyne 1981, 78–79; Schlier 1977, 122–23; Schmidt 1962, 77; Wieser 1987, 58–60; Wilckens 1978, 1:261. *Pace* Thielman 1989, 98: "Neither in Galatians nor here [Rom. 4:1–25], therefore, does Paul attack *Judaism*, rather in both places he argues against *Jewish Christian missionaries* [. . .]."

115 See Sanders 1977, Index of Subjects, s.v. "The Righteous" and "Righteousness," particularly pp. 198–205, 544–46. Cf. Moore 1948–50, 1:494–95; 1948–50, 2:89; Schechter 1961, 270–71; Urbach 1975, 483–86.

Taken as a whole, Paul does not in vv. 2–5 fight without any purpose.[116] His polemic against boasting and righteousness by works assails living Jewish traditions. He defends the truthfulness of his Gospel. Now, he corroborates and substantiates his crucial thesis that no one will be justified before God through the works of the Law (3:20 in connection with Ps. 143:2).[117] Chapter 4 demonstrates that not even the most pious of all people, Abraham, achieved righteousness by his own works. In that case, much less can common people—whoever they may be—achieve righteousness by their own works.[118]

From v. 9 onward, Paul expands and enlarges his soteriological perspectives. He aims to spell it out that nothing else but precisely his Gospel fulfills the Old Testament visions. Now it is explicitly about the promises in Genesis (17:5; 18:18; 22:17–18). They inform that Abraham and his seed will inherit the earth (v. 13) and that he himself becomes the father of many nations (vv. 17–18). They indeed open wide horizons for him. The divine prophecies tend to a universal scope. On the other hand, the Mosaic Law insists on a very particularistic perspective. It shuts all the Gentiles as *massa perditionis* out of Israel. On the condition that οἱ ἐκ νόμου will turn out as the legal (and legalistic!) heirs, the promises to Abraham are really brought to naught. He would remain the father only of the Jewish people, but not the father of many peoples (v. 14).[119] The Old Testament visions amount only to a utopia and delusion in a remote never-never land if they are not followed by the tangible reality that takes concrete form through the Gospel. It welcomes the Gentiles and includes them within Israel. Therefore, the promises stand firm. Abraham becomes the father not only of the Jewish people but truly the father of many peoples and ultimately of all the believers (see v. 16; cf. already vv. 11–12). His abundant legacy does not rest on the Mosaic legislation.[120] Moreover, v. 15 reminds in passing that the Law defines sin as transgression and makes it a deliberate offense or high treason against the King of kings. Hence, it intensifies his wrath (ὀργή, cf. 2:12; 3:20–21)

116 *Pace* Murray 1982, 1:130: "It is apparent, however, that the apostle is not making a suggestion or supposition that has any reality in fact and he is not making a suggestion that allows for the entertainment of the possibility that Abraham might have been justified by works. It is simply an hypothesis for the sake of argument, an argument which is immediately directed to the refutation of the hypothesis."

117 Cranfield 1982, 1:198; Käsemann 1980, 83; Michel 1978, 144; Nygren 1979, 150; Schlier 1977, 100; Schmidt 1962, 62; Thurén 1986, 177; Wilckens 1978, 1:173.

118 Cf. Berger 1966, 65–66; Käsemann 1980, 99–101; Murray 1982, 1:127; Nygren 1979, 175–76.

119 Particularly, Berger 1966, 69–74, 77; Käsemann 1969, 154–57; Zeller 1973, 102–4.

120 Ibid. See also Nygren 1979, 180–87.

against the promise. It is then more than clear that there is no other way out of the impasse and dead end but the apostolic Gospel (cf. 5:20).[121]

Truly, Paul strongly argues for the equal status of Jews and Gentiles in chapter 4 (*cum* Sanders and Räisänen). Surprisingly and paradoxically, his polemics do not turn against the special status of Israel (*contra* Sanders and Räisänen). Instead, he plainly confirms that God has made the forefather of Israel "the father of many peoples."[122]

In summary, Rom. 4:2–5 continues the line of argument from 3:27–30. Both passages accuse Judaism of an egocentric legalism that does not square with the theocentric Gospel.

6.5. Romans 9:30–10:3

(9:30) Τί οὖν ἐροῦμεν; ὅτι ἔθνη τὰ μὴ διώκοντα δικαιοσύνην κατέλαβεν δικαιοσύνην, δικαιοσύνην δὲ τὴν ἐκ πίστεως, (31) Ἰσραὴλ δὲ διώκων νόμον δικαιοσύνης εἰς νόμον οὐκ ἔφθασεν. (32) διὰ τί; ὅτι οὐκ ἐκ πίστεως ἀλλ᾽ ὡς ἐξ ἔργων· προσέκοψαν τῷ λίθῳ τοῦ προσκόμματος, (33) καθὼς γέγραπται· **ἰδοὺ τίθημι ἐν Σιὼν λίθον προσκόμματος καὶ πέτραν σκανδάλου, καὶ ὁ πιστεύων ἐπ᾽ αὐτῷ οὐ καταισχυνθήσεται.** (10:1) Ἀδελφοί, ἡ μὲν εὐδοκία τῆς ἐμῆς καρδίας καὶ ἡ δέησις πρὸς τὸν θεὸν ὑπὲρ αὐτῶν εἰς σωτηρίαν. (2) μαρτυρῶ γὰρ αὐτοῖς ὅτι ζῆλον θεοῦ ἔχουσιν ἀλλ᾽ οὐ κατ᾽ ἐπίγνωσιν· (3) ἀγνοοῦντες γὰρ τὴν τοῦ θεοῦ δικαιοσύνην καὶ τὴν ἰδίαν [δικαιοσύνην] ζητοῦντες στῆσαι, τῇ δικαιοσύνῃ τοῦ θεοῦ οὐχ ὑπετάγησαν.

Sanders and Räisänen both warn of the imminent risk of rushing to any hasty conclusions on 9:30–10:3. At first glance, it seems that the text really ascribes guilt to Judaism for an egocentric legalism and arrogant hubris (9:30–32a; 10:3). But on closer reflection, it turns out that the factual "stone of stumbling" is Christ (9:32b–33).[123] *Hence, Jewish unbelief rests principally (so Räisänen) or exclusively (so Sanders) on Christological grounds.*[124] *The clause* οὐκ ἐκ πίστεως ἀλλ᾽ ὡς ἐξ ἔργων *(9:32a) simply states that the Jews do not believe in Christ.*[125] *Immediately, chapter 10 reiterates the same reproach against them. It does not read there that they in their detestable boasting strive after salvation by some meritorious achievements. In effect, Paul accepts their zeal for God. He does not blame it as such (v. 2). Strictly speaking, the Jews find themselves on the false path since in their lack of*

121 Cranfield 1980, 1:240–41; Michel 1978, 169–70; Murray 1980, 1:143–44; Schlier 1977, 130; Schmidt 1962, 83–84; Wilckens 1978, 1:270–71. See further Berger 1966, 69–70; Dobbeler 1987, 137–38; Rhyne 1981, 84–86; Wieser 1987, 62–63.

122 Cf. Van der Minde 1976, 75: Romans 4 "bestimmt Abraham zum Vater beider Gruppen" (that is, of the Jews and the Gentiles). See further Luz 1968, 175.

123 Räisänen 1983, 174 (cf. 1987a, 2907); Sanders 1983, 36–37.

124 Räisänen 1983, 174; Sanders 1983, 37.

125 Ibid.

knowledge (οὐ κατ' ἐπίγνωσιν) *they do not search for the right (viz. Christian) kind of righteousness (v. 3).*[126] *The distinction between* ἡ τοῦ θεοῦ δικαιοσύνη *and* ἡ ἰδία δικαιοσύνη *does not relate to the contrast between human merits and divine mercy. The latter designates the righteousness that the people of Israel can acquire on account of their special status. The former denotes the righteousness that all peoples of the world can obtain without exception by their faith in Christ (v. 4; cf. vv. 11–13).*[127] *Taken as a whole, 9:30–10:3 simply affirms that the old covenant has now yielded to the new.*[128]

Oddly enough, first and foremost Sanders displays a striking alternative in his exegesis of 9:30–10:3. He maintains that Paul criticizes the Jewish soteriology—to put it simply—*either* for its anthropocentric *or* for its anti-Christological implication but not for both reasons at the same time. The two perspectives cannot be combined. One must choose between them.[129]

However, it turns out that 9:30–10:3 represents a combination of the two perspectives. Paul criticizes the Jewish soteriology *both* for its anthropocentric *and* for its anti-Christological implication. He does not actually go for any option of either/or.[130] Consistent with 9:31–33, the Jews stumble on the stone of stumbling because they overemphasize their own works. Consistent with 10:3, the Jews do not submit to God's righteousness because they pursue their own righteousness. In a sense, the anthropocentric and anti-Christological implications belong together, as cause and effect.[131]

---

126 Räisänen 1983, 174–75 (see also 1980a, 71); Sanders 1983, 37–38 (see also 1977, 482, 485, 550).

127 Sanders 1983, 37–38, and moreover 39–43. See further Räisänen 1986, 74–77 (cf. 1983, 174–75).

128 Räisänen 1983, 174. Cf. Sanders 1983, 36–43. Many exegetes subscribe to the interpretation of Sanders and Räisänen. See W. S. Campbell 1981, 34; Liebers 1989, 27–29, 55–58, 85–88, 226–28; Rese 1988, 211. Besides, cf. Gaston 1987, 139–41; F. Watson 1986, 164–68.

129 Cf. Hübner 1984, 71–72.

130 Aageson 1987, 61–62. He writes: "In the discussion in 9.30–33, the issue is not 'belief' versus 'unbelief.' It is 'faith' versus 'works.' Hence, when Paul claims that Israel has stumbled over the 'stone of stumbling,' he is not saying simply that it has refused to believe in Christ. Rather, Israel has not pursued righteousness according to 'faith' but according to 'works.'" In a similar way, Gundry 1985, 16: "We may agree that Paul blames Israel for lack of faith in Christ. But to make that lack displace rather than complement wrong dependence on one's own works fails to carry conviction." Hübner 1984, 72: "Aber gehorchen die Juden nicht gerade deshalb dem Gesetz nicht in korrekter Weise, weil sie nicht glauben? *Sanders* reißt auseinander, was im Zusammenhang der Theologie des Paulus notwendig zusammengehört." See further Deidun 1986, 51–52; Klein 1988, 53.

131 Käsemann 1980, 267–72; Kim 1981, 4, 298–99; Ljungman 1964, 83–84, 90, 104–5; Lohse 1978, 112; Lübking 1986, 80–84; Michel 1978, 320–26; Murray 1982, 2:42–49; Nygren 1979, 377–81; Schlier 1977, 306–10; Schmitt 1984, 88–92; Siegert 1985, 142–43; Stuhlmacher 1966, 91–93; Vischer 1950, 103–6; Wilckens 1980, 2:211–16, 219–21; Zeller 1973, 123–24, 189–92. Cf. Heil 1987, 70–71.

Yet astonishingly Sanders, strictly speaking, does not justify his reading at all that 9:32a aims only at the Jewish unbelief. He hastily jumps over the clause ἀλλ' ὡς ἐξ ἔργων, or more to the point, he reasons it out of the text by saying that the stone of stumbling in vv. 32b–33 refers to Christ![132] But how Sanders comes to his conclusion on the basis of his would-be argumentation remains obscure. He owes his readers an explanation. The evident scope of the passage is just too clear to be overlooked. Paul truly affirms that the Jews put their trust in their works. He says so explicitly in v. 32a. It cannot easily be dismissed.

Furthermore, Räisänen shows in his interpretation of 9:30–33 that he—despite his opposite intention—just does not manage to silence or turn down the polemical tone in the clause ἀλλ' ὡς ἐξ ἔργων. He avows that mainly Christological reasons lie behind Jewish unbelief.[133] If so, Paul then logically criticizes the Jewish soteriology not only for its anti-Christological but also for its anthropocentric implication. Obviously he does not put one off against the other. They are not mutually exclusive. They are rather complementary (see above). Finally, Räisänen himself closes his criticism against Bultmann with a similar broad look![134]

The polemical tone in chapter 9 continues in chapter 10. The two Greek idioms οὐ κατ' ἐπίγνωσιν (v. 2) and ἀγνοοῦντες (v. 3) hardly relate to mere "ignorance," "unknowing," or "lack of knowledge" of the Gospel or the apostolic message (against Sanders and Räisänen[135]). As a result of the fervent Christian mission, Israel has heard and understood the Gospel. But they (or most of them) have not been willing and ready to believe it (vv. 18–21). In their unbelief, it is more about a lack of the right insight. The Jews persevere in a false knowledge or in a mistaken comprehension. Their (in itself laudable) zeal (v. 2: ζῆλος)

---

132 Sanders (1983, 37) writes: "[. . .] the 'stumbling-stone' is Christ, and those who believe in him are not put to shame. The explanation of 'not by faith but by works,' *then*, is 'they did not believe in Christ,' not 'they incorrectly tried for righteousness and by trying achieved only self-righteousness'" (italics mine). The foregoing exegesis seems to me completely arbitrary. Further, Sanders writes on 9:31 as follows: "The context requires the last clause of 9:31 to be more general than *nomos* allows. Paul immediately specifies what Israel did not attain: the righteousness of God which comes by faith in Christ. To use *nomos* when one means 'righteousness by faith' is certainly curious [. . .]. Paul probably repeated the word *nomos* because it had just occurred and it seemed to make a balanced phrase" (op. cit., 42). Deidun rightly qualifies an exegesis of this sort "as the best class-room example of eisegesis in recent decades" (1986, 51–52).

133 Räisänen (1983, 174; see also 1980a 71 n. 47): "Verse 32a is, however, immediately followed and explained by 32b–33 which shows that the *main* reason for the Jews' unbelief is a Christological one [. . .]" (italics mine).

134 Räisänen 1983, 176.

135 Op. cit., 174; Sanders 1983, 37.

for their God is distorted.[136] Instantly, v. 3 explicates the cause for their biggest shortcoming. They try to set up their own righteousness, namely, with the help of their works of the Law (see above). There is indeed something very weird that the Jews as God's people have not submitted to God's righteousness. They should be the first in line to know and acknowledge what he has done for them. But now they rather prefer their own righteousness. They behave like a stubborn and obstinate people (v. 21).[137]

In addition, it is worth noting that Paul's approximative description and Sanders's meticulous depiction of the Jewish soteriology at least in general square with each other. Both emphasize by common consent that the Jews in actual fact search for righteousness by their works.[138] As already shown, צדק means explicitly to follow the Torah and to repent of possible transgressions.[139]

---

136 Conzelmann 1987, 278; Cranfield 1981, 2:514–15; Käsemann 1980, 270–71; Kertelge 1967, 95 and n. 160; Michel 1978, 325; Schlier 1977, 310; Siegert 1985, 143, 149; Vischer 1950, 105–6; Cf. also Ljungman 1964, 83, 94, 101–2; Van der Minde 1976, 107.

137 Ibid. See also Moo 2018, 652–54.

138 See Sanders 1977, 198–205, 494, 544–46, 551. *Pace* Luz 1981, 47: "Von hier aus wird deutlich, in wie hohem Maße der paulinische Gedanke der Werkgerechtigkeit vom jüdischen Gesetzesverständnis her ein Fremdkörper war. Daß der Mensch mit Hilfe des Gesetzes seine *eigene* Gerechtigkeit aufrichtet (Röm 9,30ff.)—welch unmöglicher Gedanke für den, der sich beim Joch der Gebote zugleich an den von Gott gewirkten Auszug aus Ägypten erinnert!" Mußner (1986, 41) joins this quotation. See already Reichrath 1967, 173. Wholly otherwise Liebers 1989, 86: "Verständlich erscheint diese Aussage [Rom. 9,31] erst, wenn man hier den jedem Juden geläufigen Gedanken anklingen sieht, daß die Tora 'Halacha', Weg (zur Gerechtigkeit) zu sein beansprucht." Cf. also op. cit., 28–29, 57. *Pace* Räisänen 1983, 178. He affirms: "Precisely this, however, is the problem: *Did* the Jews really look for 'righteousness' (in anything like the Pauline sense of the word) in the Torah? Here the answer must be a clear 'No.' In the words of Werblowsky: '. . . one thing seems to me fairly sure: It is not "righteousness" that the Jews look for in the Torah . . . One went to the Torah, because one wanted to live his life as a member of an elect community under God, in thankful acceptance of the guidance shown by him.' Sanders agrees: 'Being righteous is not the goal of a religious quest; it is the behavior proper to one who has accepted the covenant offered at Sinai and the commandments which followed the acceptance of God's kingship.'" For sure, the reference to Sanders leads astray. He does not actually deny that the Jews seek righteousness in the Torah. The passage quoted by Räisänen corroborates Sanders's thesis that "the question 'how can one *become* righteous?' is not asked" (see 1977, 205). However, the Jews seek righteousness in the Torah in order to maintain their status within the covenant (op. cit., 494, 505–6, 544–46, 551). Likewise, Werblowsky, strictly speaking, deals not with "righteousness," but with "justification" (see 1973, 159). Later on, Räisänen seems to have wheeled around. He (1986, 78) avers: "I concur that a Jew of Paul's day did seek righteousness if that means, in Sanders' by now well-known terminology, the *staying* in the sphere of salvation (into which one has got in another way)."

139 Sanders 1977, 198–205, 494, 544–46, 551. Later, he (2009, 52–54) repeats himself: "[. . .] thus a Jewish righteous person is *righteous by the law*." Further, he contends: "Jewish righteousness by the law comes by observing it [. . .]." Finally, he concludes: "Thus: Jewish literature speaks about people who are righteous by the law." (Reprinted in 2016, 81–82.) See also Nissen 1974, 154–58.

As a consequence, covenantal nomism forms a sharp contrast to the apostolic message that promotes the free gift of righteousness by faith in Christ.[140]

To conclude: Sanders's exegesis fails to carry through. Räisänen's exegesis rather supports my thesis that Paul criticizes Judaism for legalism. There is no longer any need to continue the discussion of Rom. 9:30–10:3.[141]

6.6. Philippians 3:3–9

> (3) ἡμεῖς γάρ ἐσμεν ἡ περιτομή, οἱ πνεύματι θεοῦ λατρεύοντες καὶ καυχώμενοι ἐν Χριστῷ Ἰησοῦ καὶ οὐκ ἐν σαρκὶ πεποιθότες, (4) καίπερ ἐγὼ ἔχων πεποίθησιν καὶ ἐν σαρκί. Εἴ τις δοκεῖ ἄλλος πεποιθέναι ἐν σαρκί, ἐγὼ μᾶλλον· (5) περιτομῇ ὀκταήμερος, ἐκ γένους Ἰσραήλ, φυλῆς Βενιαμίν, Ἑβραῖος ἐξ Ἑβραίων, κατὰ νόμον Φαρισαῖος, (6) κατὰ ζῆλος διώκων τὴν ἐκκλησίαν, κατὰ δικαιοσύνην τὴν ἐν νόμῳ γενόμενος ἄμεμπτος. (7) [Ἀλλ'] ἅτινα ἦν μοι κέρδη, ταῦτα ἥγημαι διὰ τὸν Χριστὸν ζημίαν. (8) ἀλλὰ μενοῦνγε καὶ ἡγοῦμαι πάντα ζημίαν εἶναι διὰ τὸ ὑπερέχον τῆς γνώσεως Χριστοῦ Ἰησοῦ τοῦ κυρίου μου, δι' ὃν τὰ πάντα ἐζημιώθην, καὶ ἡγοῦμαι σκύβαλα, ἵνα Χριστὸν κερδήσω (9) καὶ εὑρεθῶ ἐν αὐτῷ, μὴ ἔχων ἐμὴν δικαιοσύνην τὴν ἐκ νόμου ἀλλὰ τὴν διὰ πίστεως Χριστοῦ, τὴν ἐκ θεοῦ δικαιοσύνην ἐπὶ τῇ πίστει.

Sanders finds Phil. 3:3–9 of particular importance for the whole Pauline understanding of the Law.[142] *The passage does not claim that righteousness by the Law calls forth an offensive self-assertion and self-glorification. From the Pharisaic perspective, Saul has rather boasted of valuable and precious things, namely, his Jewish status and his living as a member of the Jewish people (with his own achievements and accomplishments). They became loss first in view of Christ (see vv. 5–6 with vv. 7–8).*[143] *Astonishingly, the passage does not claim that no one ever fulfills the Law faultlessly. Quite the opposite, it reads that Saul was indeed blameless (v. 6).*[144] *Moreover, v. 9 explicitly distinguishes between the two given sorts of*

140 Klein 1988, 56. F. Mußner (1977, 43–44) proposes a sort of "two-house" theory (a complementary existence of the synagogue and the church resp. the Jewish and the Christian set of beliefs). He emphasizes that Israel will attain salvation, "auch wenn es den Weg des Gesetzes weitergegangen ist und weitergeht und in dieser Zeit in Jesus Christus nicht seinen Messias zu erkennen vermag, sich vielmehr an 'dem Stein des Anstoßes stößt', den Gott in Sion hingelegt hat (vgl. Röm 9,32f.)." Similarly, Gager 1983, 197–264; Gaston 1987, *passim*; Stendahl 1976, 4. From the Pauline perspective, Mußner wholly misses the mark. See particularly Sanders (1983, 193–95); Gräßer (1981a, 411–29). They show the inadequacy of his theory. Cf. also Käsemann 1961, 376; Lüdemann 1983, 33–34.

141 See especially Gundry (1985, 16–19). He mentions a number of small defects and flaws in Sanders's argumentation. But I will not dwell on them here since a further discussion results in basically nothing new.

142 Sanders 1983, 43 (see also 1977, 505).

143 Op. cit., 43–44, 139–41.

144 Ibid.

righteousness. The one depends on the Law while the other rests on faith. Only and simply in comparison with the latter does the former appear reprehensible.[145]

Räisänen comes to similar conclusions.[146] *Besides, he emphasizes that in Philippians 3 Paul does not at all condemn his earlier zeal for the Law nor his fulfilling the Law.*[147]

In addition, Sanders and Räisänen refer to 2 Cor. 3:7–18 as a relevant parallel text. To begin with, Paul mentions that glory rules the ministry of Moses (see particularly v. 7). In what follows, he insists that surpassing glory gains sway by the ministry of the Spirit (v. 9). Finally, he concludes his train of thought and reaches the mind-blowing culmination that the former glory wholly pales in comparison with the latter (v. 10).[148]

It is an indisputable fact that, from the moment of his conversion, Paul renounces his previous Pharisaic righteousness in favor of the Christian faith. Therefore, it remains to ask with what theological arguments he afterward vindicates his decisive change. His personal account in Philippians 3 of his identity before and after shows where to start.

Pharisaic confidence (vv. 5–6) rests upon six utterances which can be outlined as follows:

A. Origin (the inborn prerogatives)
   1. circumcised on the eighth day (no proselyte)
   2. of the stock of Israel, of the tribe of Benjamin (no son of proselytes)
   3. a Hebrew of the Hebrews (the genuinely Jewish part of the people)

B. Attitude to the Law (the acquired prerogatives)
   4. according to the Law, a Pharisee
   5. according to zeal, a persecutor of the church
   6. according to the righteousness of the Law, (become, γενόμενος) without fault.

Pharisaic boasting culminates in the last expression.[149]

145 Op. cit., 43–45, 140 (see also 1977, 485, 505–6, 550).

146 Räisänen 1983, 175–76 (see already 1980a, 71 and further 1986, 67–71).

147 Ibid. Among others Liebers (1989, 58–60) and F. Watson (1986, 77–80) support the exegesis of Räisänen and Sanders. Cf. Gaston 1987, 78, 136.

148 Räisänen 1983, 176 (see already 1980a, 71); Sanders 1983, 137–41 (see also 1977, 484–85, 551).

149 Especially Thurén 1986, 175. See already Gnilka 1976, 188–91.

On closer reflection, vv. 5–6 sketch the Pharisaic ideal of Paul before his conversion as follows:[150]

As a man of the best conceivable origins (A 1–3), Saul had made considerable progress and gone further than most of his contemporaries among his own people. He subscribed to the strict and stern movement of the Pharisees and enjoyed great esteem because of his radical submission to the Torah (B 4).[151] In his extremism, Saul was zealous beyond measure for the habits and traditions of the fathers. As models, he took for himself, among others, Phineas (Numbers 25), Elijah (1 Kings 18), and Mattathias (1 Maccabees 2). They had once saved Israel by killing (in a sense a kind of exceptional expiation) as gross sins threatened the existence of the nation.[152] In the eyes of Saul, the Christian sect violated the Torah in ways just as dangerous as the Jewish people at Shittim or at the time of Ahab or the Maccabees. No wonder he, so to speak, "smoldered with wrath" against the Christians and their sacrilegious proclamation (B 5).[153] The bloody confrontation did not so much give evidence of a personal affect in Saul, but of a real postulate of his rigoristic Pharisaism. Unlike many of his contemporaries, he drew the logical consequence of his own religion.[154] Apart from a scrupulous obedience, faultlessness "according to the righteousness of the Law" (B 6) implied and actually still implies that Christians and their faith in the crucified Messiah should be rooted out.[155]

On the road to Damascus, Saul suddenly got to know that his ardent zeal for God had brought him into open conflict with God himself or with his church (see Gal. 1:13; 1 Cor. 15:9). Immediately, there fell, as it were, scales from the eyes of the orthodox Pharisee. He saw and realized with regret that faultlessness "according to the righteousness of the Law" had run into the worst sort of lawlessness. It would not ever satisfy God.[156] As a Christian, Paul considers all his earlier "gains" as σκύβαλα ("filth," "dung," "excrement," v. 8). Here, he employs a coarse street slogan or a slang expression of the common people in order to denote an extreme degree of disparaging contempt.[157] The word σάρξ

150 Cf. Kim 1981, 273–74.

151 G. Barth 1979, 58–59; Friedrich 1976, 160; Gnilka 1976, 190; Lohmeyer 1964, 130; J. J. Müller 1976, 110.

152 See particularly Haacker 1975, 7–10; Hengel 1961, 152–81; Kim 1981, 42–43. Similarly, G. Barth 1979, 59; Thurén 1986, 176, 187.

153 G. Barth 1979, 59; Thurén 1986, 176, 187.

154 Grundmann 1960, 268; Haacker 1975, 7–8; Lohmeyer 1964, 130. Furthermore, cf. G. Barth 1979, 59; Gnilka 1976, 190; J. J. Müller 1976, 110–11.

155 Thurén 1986, 176, 187. See also Grundmann 1960, 268. Cf. Lohse 1978, 102–5.

156 Gnilka 1976, 191; Grundmann 1960, 269–71; Kim 1981, 280–81, 287; Lohmeyer 1964, 132; Thurén 1986, 176, 187.

157 W. Bauer 1988, s.v. Besides, see K. Barth 1928, 94–95; Eriksson 1982, 124; Friedrich 1976, 161; Gnilka 1976, 193; Lohmeyer 1928, 135; Mengel 1982, 264–65.

that occurs thrice (vv. 3–4) has the same connotation.[158] No doubt, the vulgar figure of speech is evidence of a derisive condemnation of the past (*contra* Räisänen).[159] It goes without saying that from his new, Christian perspective Paul indeed regards his former persecutions of Christians as thoroughly reprehensible.[160] Phil. 3:3–9 asserts not only that—to speak in metaphors—the gleam of the stars (the Law with its commandments) disappears with the rising of the sun (the Gospel about the Messiah). Rather, the passage affirms that the brightness of the ultraorthodox Pharisee is simply darkness. How great must the darkness then be (cf. Matt. 6:23)![161]

Against his previous Pharisaic ideal of piety, Paul further argues that it rests upon the flesh (vv. 3–4) and includes self-righteousness (v. 9). What is he driving at with those reproaches?

The flesh (σάρξ) first and foremost refers to circumcision (or "concision" in v. 2).[162] Besides, it relates to all of the inborn and acquired prerogatives of Saul (listed in vv. 5–6).[163] His immaculate or impeccable piety functions as a shining example of fleshly confidence (v. 4).[164] Furthermore, the composite πεποιθέναι ἐν σαρκί stands in clear contrast to service by the Spirit of God and boasting in Christ Jesus (v. 3). The sharp antithesis articulates the discrepancy between the Pharisaic and the Christian ideal.[165] In consequence, Saul had not "served"[166] by the Spirit of God and not boasted in Christ Jesus. Quite the reverse, he had "served" by his own strength and boasted in his own achievements. The phrase πεποιθέναι ἐν σαρκί means nothing else but human self-confidence.[167] By his own power and by means of his own accomplishments, Saul with delight and

158 See Lohmeyer 1964, 128: "Zum dritten Male erscheint der Ausdruck 'vertrauen auf Fleisch'; dieses immer neue Wiederholen der gleichen Worte, die zudem ein deutlich verwerfendes Urteil in sich tragen [. . .]."

159 Räisänen 1983, 175–76.

160 See, e.g., Deidun 1986, 51; Grundmann 1960, 270; Stendahl 1976, 89–90. Cf. Caird 1978, 540.

161 Rightly, Thurén 1986, 176. See already K. Barth 1928, 93: "Nicht Null tritt an die Stelle des Plus, sondern das Plus selbst verwandelt sich in *Minus*." Similarly, Gnilka 1976, 191: "Es war kein Übergang vom Guten zum Besseren, auch nicht Preisgabe eines Besitzes. [. . .] In der Umwertung bemerkte er [Paul], daß die Dinge, die er bisher für Gewinn ansah, ihm in Wirklichkeit geschadet hatten, er bemerkte seinen Irrtum." See further Friedrich 1976, 160; Liechtenhan 1946, 59; J. J. Müller 1976, 112–13.

162 Eriksson 1982, 121; J. J. Müller 1976, 108.

163 G. Barth 1979, 57; K. Barth 1928, 90; Eriksson 1982, 121–22; Friedrich 1976, 159; Gnilka 1976, 187; Lohmeyer 1928, 127; J. J. Müller 1976, 108; Thurén 1986, 186.

164 Gnilka 1976, 188–89; Lohmeyer 1964, 129; Mengel 1982, 262; J. J. Müller 1976, 109.

165 See G. Barth 1979, 56; Friedrich 1976, 159; Gnilka 1976, 187–88; Lohmeyer 1964, 127–28; Mengel 1982, 262; J. J. Müller 1976, 107–8.

166 The participle λατρεύοντες (v. 3) lacks the object.

167 Bultmann 1984, 243.

pride assumed to have fulfilled the Law to perfection.[168] His sincere gratefulness for God's grace did not escape his memory. He made a big fuss about his membership in the covenant (cf. v. 5).[169] But still, Paul considers his former piety of no value and rates it as his own (filthy) righteousness (v. 9). Indeed, he became faultless thanks to his own study and learning, his own ardor and fervor, his own doing and obeying. Notwithstanding, he got help from his God. But it did not remove his carnal assurance and arrogance. His fleshly self-reliance persisted.[170] Therefore, his Pharisaism collapsed.

On this interpretation, Philippians 3 reveals an incomparable tragedy like no other. It is biting deep and hurting heart. Blinded in his fleshly mind, Saul lost his way, fell down, and sank in the muddy morass of self-righteousness, although he desired to reach the heights of heaven. But then suddenly and surprisingly, his horror story came to an unexpected turn. Because of his Damascus experience, he learned in time from all his past failures. Instead of human righteousness that depends on flesh and one's own power, he receives divine righteousness that rests on Christ and is freely given through faith (vv. 7–9). God alone has carried out the whole eschatological salvation from beginning to end. His action has totally counted out the Pharisaic notion of "achievements" or "accomplishments."[171] They had no place in the full amount of his mercy.[172] In lieu of them appears "the surpassing worth of knowing (τὸ ὑπερέχον τῆς γνώσεως) Christ Jesus" (see v. 8). The Greek idiom indicates not only intellectual knowledge but rather points, in the background of the Old Testament, to an intimate intercourse (exemplarily Gen. 4:1, where Adam "knew" his wife and she became pregnant).[173] Comprehensibly, v. 9 elucidates the line of thought by means of participatory terminology (cf. further v. 10). Paul hopes that he will be found in Christ. He looks forward to knowing Christ and "the power of his resurrection." Existence in Christ means to renounce one's own righteousness and to embrace God's righteousness.[174] Here, the "mystic-ontological" realism or the participatory perspective needs a theological boost through the forensic aspects or the juristic categories. They are tightly intertwined and belong closely

168 G. Barth 1979, 59; Gnilka 1976, 190–91; Lohmeyer 1964, 130–31; Thurén 1986, 186.

169 G. Barth 1979, 58; J. J. Müller 1976, 109. See further Hartman 1980, 107.

170 G. Barth 1979, 61; K. Barth 1928, 96–97; Friedrich 1976, 161; Gnilka 1976, 194; J. J. Müller 1976, 114–15; Thurén 1986, 186.

171 Sanders himself speaks of human achievements and accomplishments in Pharisaism. See 1983, 43–44, 139–41.

172 G. Barth 1979, 61; Friedrich 1976, 161–62; Gnilka 1976, 19495; Lohmeyer 1964, 137–38; J. J. Müller, 1976, 114–15.

173 Eriksson 1982, 124; G. Barth 1979, 60. Cf. Gnilka 1976, 193.

174 G. Barth 1979, 60–61; Friedrich 1976, 161; Gnilka 1976, 195; J. J. Müller 1976, 114–15. See also Stuhlmacher 1966, 99–101.

together for a better explanation of the apostolic proclamation.[175] By making a clean break with Pharisaic values and standards, they show the reason for boasting in Christ Jesus (v. 3).[176]

It is worth discerning and perceiving that the apostolic exhortations to fulfill the Law in love do not once again set up a new (but different) kind of legalism. Christians do good works not in reliance on their flesh. Instead, the Spirit produces fruit in them (v. 3).[177] God works in them (2:12–13). His action is all in all—all the time.[178]

Last but not least, it turns out that 2 Cor. 3:7–18 forms no precise parallel to Phil. 3:3–9. On close reflection, the former passage juxtaposes the ministry of Moses and that of the Spirit against each other, whereas the latter passage contrasts the Pharisaic and Christian piety with each other. As a result, there is no need to prolong the discussion.[179]

In conclusion, Phil. 3:3–9 sets forth four main arguments against Pharisaism.[180] It

(1) implies an open hostility against God and his congregation,

---

175 For the close interaction and correlation between the forensic and participatory terminology, see below, chapter 7.

176 G. Barth 1979, 60–61; Bultmann 1984, 243.

177 K. Barth 1928, 89; Eriksson 1982, 121; Friedrich 1976, 159; Gnilka 1976, 187; Lohmeyer 1928, 127; J. J. Müller 1976, 107–8. See also Stuhlmacher 1966, 100–101.

178 See above 5.2.

179 See Rissi 1969, 13: "Die neuere Forschung hat mehr und mehr erkannt, daß das dritte Kap. des 2. Korintherbriefes nicht eine theologische Abhandlung über das Verhältnis des alten zum neuen Bund oder des Judentums zum Christentum darstellt, sondern eine hochpolemische Auseinandersetzung des Paulus mit Irrlehrern, die der Korinthergemeinde lebensgefährlich geworden sind." Cf. Ulonska 1966, 385–88. He suggests: "Von einer Entwertung der Doxa des alten Bundes kann an unserer Stelle nicht die Rede sein, auch nicht davon, daß Paulus die Minderwertigkeit des mosaischen Gesetzes dartun wolle. Solche Interpretationen ignorieren die Situation, in die hinein er spricht. *Nicht Israel will Paulus treffen, sondern seine Gegner in Korinth*" (385). Similarly, Thielman 1989, 131–32.

180 Gundry (1985, 14) presents many details in Philippians 3 that should confirm the Pauline judgment against Pharisaic righteousness by the Law. To quote his own words here: "[. . .] a long list of items in Phil.3,2–11 points to the attitudinal sin of self-righteousness alongside the mistake of missing God's righteousness in Christ: (1) 'boast'; (2) 'have confidence'; (3) 'think [. . .] to have confidence'; (4) 'to me [. . .]' in connection with 'gain'; (5) 'I regard'; (6) Paul's setting out his past achievements as superior to the achievements of his opponents who boast in the flesh—as though there is a contest over who can boast the most; (7) his following denial that he now 'considers' himself to have arrived (vv. 12–16); and (8) his exhortation to be similarly 'minded [. . .]' (v. 15)." It seems that Gundry writes too briefly, with the result that the points listed do not particularly well serve the goal set. He keeps to himself how the first point differs from the sixth. The second and third points do not more closely concretize the bite or sting of polemics. The fourth point does not make clear sense. The fifth point seems completely incomprehensible. The sixth point hits the mark. The seventh point again does not make clear sense. The eighth point fails. Paul can well exhort the Philippians to unanimity even if in the beginning of chapter 3 he does not condemn righteousness of the Law.

(2) indicates confidence in flesh (the innate human abilities),
(3) involves boasting (in one's own achievements), and
(4) entails self-righteousness (on the basis of the preceding points).

As a Christian, Paul denounces his previous Pharisaic zeal for the Law and considers it as rubbish. Instead, he prefers his new righteousness in Christ as a gift from God through faith. Therefore, he engages himself for the Gospel.

6.7. Conclusions

In his work *Paul and Palestinian Judaism*, Sanders summarizes Paul's criticism of Judaism as follows:

> In short, *this is what Paul finds wrong in Judaism: it is not Christianity.*[181]

In his later work *Paul, the Law and the Jewish People*, Sanders clarifies his previous position in the following way:

> What is wrong with the law, and thus with Judaism, is that it does not provide for God's ultimate purpose, that of saving the entire world through faith in Christ, and without the privilege accorded to Jews through the promises, the covenants, and the law.[182]

As shown and made known, neither of the two summaries exactly—in juristic terms—gives the evidence for "the truth, the whole truth, and nothing but the truth." They are only half true. In reality, Paul reproves Judaism not only for not believing in Christ. He reproaches it also for self-righteousness and self-praise in the midst of self-satisfaction on account of the works of the Law. Hence, it turns out that the rejection of the Gospel and the retention of legalism are two sides of the same coin.[183]

By contrast, Räisänen frankly admits that the Jews, according to his analysis of the Pauline letters, indeed tried to attain righteousness by their own works.[184] For sure, he in his radical manner points out in the same breath that "Paul actually does give his readers a distorted picture of Judaism."[185] With the exception of this final judgment, his overall study of the basic data moves in the right direction but fails to carry conviction on closer reflection.[186]

So understood, the theological separation between church and synagogue to a wide extent goes back to the exclusive Christology and the pessimistic

181 Sanders 1977, 552.
182 Sanders 1983, 47.
183 Cf. Gundry 1985, 27: "It appears that the twin pillars of human weakness and salvation-history, not just salvation-history, uphold justification by faith alone."
184 Räisänen 1983, 187–88.
185 Op. cit., 188.
186 Cf. T. R. Schreiner 1991, 242.

anthropology of the apostle to the Gentiles. His soteriology functions as a kind of watershed or as a sort of milestone in this respect. In the final analysis, it seems that Bultmann in principle rightly underscores an anthropological approach as a solution to the problem.[187] Still, his constant recourse to the existential-philosophical concepts and ideas as a basis for his exegesis certainly leads down a blind alley.[188] Moreover, it is no longer plausible or even possible to return to the Weberian image of Judaism as he once did.[189] Paul criticizes covenantal nomism for self-praise and self-righteousness arising from human confidence in the works of the Law.[190] In his overall view, he does not miss the mark.

Last but not least, Sanders suggests that a considerable shift takes place between the Jewish and Pauline use of judicial terminology or their respective comprehension of the concept and content of righteousness. In the former case, the idea of being righteous means the staying within the covenant through obedience to the Law. In the latter case, it means the entrance into Christ through faith. Despite the difference in understanding, Paul maintains, in agreement with Judaism, that without correct conduct or behavior no one can remain within the group of those who will be saved.[191]

In consideration of Sanders's semantic analysis, the traditional Lutheran and Protestant view (represented also by Bultmann) gains much force with regard to the Epistle to the Galatians; Rom. 3:27; 4:2–5; 9:30–10:3; and Phil. 3:3–9. First, there is no doubt that Paul in fact turns his back on the Jewish understanding of righteousness. He teaches that righteousness rests not upon human activity in performing the works of the Law, but alone upon divine action in the redemptive work of Christ (see Ps. 143:2 as the scriptural basis in Rom. 3:10, 20 and Gal. 2:16; 3:11).[192] Second, there is no doubt that Paul likewise departs from the Jewish soteriology. He agrees with Judaism in the basic and common axiom

187 See Bultmann 1938, 648–50; 1940, 8–13; 1984, 239–46. In contrast, Klauck 1986a, 78–79: "So wird im Gefolge von Bultmann gegen S. [= Sanders] immer noch verteidigt, Paulus spreche vom legalistischen Mißbrauch des Gesetzes. Durch vorbildliche Gesetzeserfüllung wolle der Mensch seine eigene Gerechtigkeit aufrichten, anstatt sich auf Gottes Gerechtigkeit einzulassen, und das sei seine fundamentale Sünde. Mir scheint diese Position spätestens seit den Arbeiten von S. historisch und exegetisch obsolet geworden zu sein. Ich sehe nicht, wie man sie theologisch noch verteidigen will."

188 See especially Laato 2004, 343–53; 2021, 16–17.

189 See above, chapter 2.

190 Cf. Caird 1978, 542: "What we are led to expect is the thesis that the Judaism Paul rejects is not the spurious Judaism of Weber and Bousset but the genuine Judaism as expounded by Moore and Sanders."

191 Sanders 1977, 544–45.

192 Particularly, Dobbeler 1987, 135: "Erwählung und Rechtfertigung sind somit als Akte göttlicher Gnade nicht mehr grundsätzlich von einander geschieden. Wo die Tradition zwischen Erwählung und dem endgültigen Unter-die-Gerechten-Gerechnet-werden eine Phase der Bewährung sah, in der die Echtheit der Bekehrung erwiesen werden muß, kann Paulus unter dem Aspekt der Gnade beides in eins sehen."

that only the righteous will be saved. Therefore, the Jews acquire final salvation through their own works since those are a required part of their righteousness. In contrast, the Christians attain final salvation thanks to the grace of God. Good works are a result of their faith. In other words, Christ lives and loves in them. He has gained a perfect righteousness for them, and it amounts to their justification (their "entrance" into him). Since then, they show in their life and love what they got from him through faith.[193]

193 See above 5.2.

7. PAUL'S MINDSET: FROM SOLUTION TO PLIGHT?

ESPECIALLY R. BULTMANN and his pupils have taken anthropology (interpreted through existentialist philosophy) as the starting point of Pauline theology.[1] An exact analysis[2] of the human existence under flesh, sin, death, and Law leads through an act of faith to a new self-understanding before God and in relation to this world. The Bultmannian interpretation was in broad outline widely accepted. A shift took place, however, in 1977 when Sanders published his impressive monograph *Paul and Palestinian Judaism*, in which he developed a very innovative theory. According to this interpretation, Paul's thought moved "backward." He started with the solution (Christ is the Redeemer) and then identified the problem (human beings are sinful and need a redeemer).[3] The following reasoning should serve as evidence for his overall view:

Paul understands the relationship between grace and works in a way similar to the Jews in general. He maintains that redemption is by divine grace and that judgment is according to human works.[4] In that respect, he had not rejected the religion of his ancestors on the basis of an anthropological analysis. Bultmann was wrong.[5] In Pauline theology, justification means first and foremost sharing in Christ, namely, fellowship with the Kyrios, not predominantly justification through faith alone. Thus the focal point of the soteriological terminology

1 Bultmann 1984, 192. He writes the following classical words right at the outset of his investigation of Paul's theology: "Jeder Satz über Gott ist zugleich ein Satz über den Menschen und umgekehrt. Deshalb und in diesem Sinne ist *die paulinische Theologie zugleich Anthropologie*." In consequence, he avows: "Sachgemäß wird deshalb die paulinische Theologie am besten entwickelt, wenn sie als die Lehre vom Menschen dargestellt wird [. . .]" (ibid.).

2 Cf. the outline in Bultmann's *Theologie des Neuen Testaments* (1984).

3 Sanders 1977, 442–47, 474–75. See also above 2.2.2. and 3.2.

4 Op. cit., 543.

5 Op. cit., 442–47, 474–502.

amounts to the so-called participatory categories rather than the juridical.[6] The logical counterpart to the lordship of Christ is the lordship of sin. The idea that all human beings without exception are under the power of sin cannot possibly have its origin in Paul's Pharisaic background. He must have reached his conclusion on the basis of his soteriology: insofar as Christ exercises his lordship over those who believe in him, it follows inevitably that sin rightly exercises its lordship over those who do not believe in him.[7] As evidence functions the incontestable experience that all human beings sin.[8]

Sanders's theory regarding the backward movement of Paul's thought harks back to three main theses:

(1) The relationship between grace and works is the same in Pauline as well as in Jewish soteriology or pattern of religion. Anthropological pessimism does not serve as the reason for Paul's conflict with Judaism.

(2) Therefore, Bultmann's interpretation along those lines fails to carry conviction.

(3) The anthropological presuppositions in Paul (especially the un-Pharisaic idea of sin as a downright demonic lordship) are better explained as a deduction from his Christological soteriology (with a clear emphasis on "participatory categories").

Upon closer scrutiny, the first of Sanders's theses proves very problematic. As already shown, the relationship between grace and works is not the same in Pauline and Jewish soteriology.[9] Covenantal nomism as a category is not really an alternative to merit theology.[10] It does not represent a religion of "pure" mercy without synergistic tendencies. Especially the inclusion of anthropological perspectives shows that it does embrace self-righteousness and self-praise.[11]

---

6 Op. cit., 453–72, 502–8.

7 Op. cit., 499.

8 Op. cit., 499, 501, 503, 507.

9 See above, chapters 5 and 6.

10 Carson 2001, 544.

11 See above, especially chapters 5 and 6. Cf. Carson 2001, 545: "In other words, does it not appear that covenantal nomism has become a rubric so embracing that it includes within its capacious soul huge tracks of works-righteousness or merit theology?" It is quite easy to concur completely and unconditionally with his critical question. See Thurén 2000, 146–47. Here, he offers a two-front argument. On the one hand, he underlines against me, Seifrid, and Westerholm that the anthropological emphases in Judaism play a less prominent role than they do in our interpretation. On the other hand, he underscores correctly and in full agreement with us (!) that "a recurrent idea in Early Jewish texts is a 'synergistic' view of salvation, where the human factor in salvation is emphasized side by side with the divine action." What did we say that goes beyond this? With a sense of humor, it seems that at least a "derhetorized" Thurén is in agreement with us.

Furthermore, the second of Sanders's theses proves unfounded because, in his polemics against Bultmann, he ignores Paul's anthropological pessimism.[12] His argument evidently amounts to a begging of the question.

Only the third of Sanders's theses still remains. It deserves more attention here. Does Paul really give priority to participatory categories over against juridical categories? Did he derive his pessimistic anthropology from his Christological soteriology?[13]

In his interesting contribution to the debate, K. T. Cooper requests that Sanders give a precise answer to the following central questions: (1) why participation in Christ procures salvation and (2) how Christ has made it possible to be transferred from slavery under sin to freedom in fellowship with him.[14]

An exploration of the two previous questions readily leads to the conclusion that the juridical and participatory categories are closely interrelated. In the examples below, the first kind of statements (juridical) appear in **boldface** and the latter (participatory) in *italics*:

(1) Only Christ has shown himself to be righteous. He has fulfilled the whole Law (see, for example, Rom. 5:15–17). Human beings are then **justified**, when they are *incorporated in Christ.*

(2) Christ is made to be sin for our sake (2 Cor. 5:21). Through his death he is also justified from sin (Rom. 6:7: δεδικαίωται). Human beings are then **justified** from sin when they are *crucified with Christ* (and *resurrected with him*) in Baptism (see, for example, Romans 6).[15]

A sharp polarization of participatory and juridical terminology is at least in part artificial. Both ways to express the reality of salvation rather support and explain each other. Often they appear side by side in the same verse. In several instances, Paul in fact merges the juridical and the participatory categories. The following passages may serve as examples of his use of language. His participatory expressions have been presented in *italic* and juridical ones in **boldface**:

> 1 Cor. 1:30: Because of him you are *in Christ Jesus*, who became to us wisdom from God, **righteousness** and sanctification and redemption [. . .].
>
> 2 Cor. 5:21: For our sake he made him to be sin who knew no sin, so that *in him* we might become the **righteousness of God**.

---

12 Sanders 1977, 76–78. See further above 3.3.1. and 3.3.2.

13 I will here no longer dwell on the intense debate between Hübner (1980) and Sanders (1983, 5–6, 12–13 n. 15). They have been at loggerheads over the right understanding of the relationship between the juridical and participatory categories resp. terminology. In another context, I have taken my stance on the issue and presented my intermediate position (2004, 345–50). Cf. also below.

14 Cooper 1982, 136.

15 Cf. op. cit., 136.

> Gal. 2:17: But if, in our endeavor **to be justified** *in Christ*, we too were found to be sinners [. . .].
>
> Phil 3:9: [. . .] and be found *in him*, not having **a righteousness of my own** that comes from the law, but that which comes through faith in Christ, **the righteousness from God** that depends on faith.

Compare further the following similar passages:

> Rom. 3:24–25 (my own translation): [. . .] and are **justified** freely by his grace, through the redemption that is *in Christ Jesus*, whom God put forward as a propitiation by his blood [Gr. *in his blood*], to be received by faith for a demonstration of his (God's) **righteousness** [. . .].
>
> Rom. 8:1: There is therefore now no **condemnation** for those who are *in Christ Jesus.*
>
> 1 Cor. 6:11: But you were washed, you were sanctified, you were **justified** *in the name of the Lord Jesus Christ and by the Spirit of our God.*
>
> Gal. 3:24 and 26 (my own translation): So the law was our guardian (παιδαγωγός) to lead us to Christ that we might be **justified** by faith. [. . .] You are all sons of God through faith *in Christ Jesus.*[16]

Based on the examples above, in connection with his soteriology, Paul rather emphasizes the existence of Christians in Christ, but strictly speaking not the presence of Christ in Christians. That means he preserves the external feature of the salvific event. He does not change the objective nature of justification into a merely subjective experience. Justification always happens outside the believer. He is counted righteous in Christ. In addition, there is always a kind of "instrumentalism" or "sacramentalism" to justification. The participation in Christ and in his righteousness is fulfilled in the proclaimed and written Gospel (*passim*), in Baptism (Romans 6; 1 Cor. 6:11; Gal. 3:24–27), and in Holy Communion (1 Cor. 10:16–17; 11:23–29). It does not build on internal experience—although it surely has a connection to it.[17]

In consequence, it appears that Paul has made no (theological) distinction between the juridical and participatory categories. From different perspectives they both illustrate his soteriology. Understood rightly, they denote exactly the same point in his thinking. They are like two sides of the same medal. One does not exist without the other.[18] Hence, it does not make any sense to ponder over

---

16 Laato 2008, 63–64.

17 Op. cit., 64–65. Paul naturally applies participatory and judicial categories also in the area of ethics. They are then not to be mixed up with his teaching of justification (cf., e.g., Romans 1–4 and 6). This is where Dunn (cf. 2005, 80–86) makes a cardinal error!

18 In a different way, Kuula 1999, 37–41. Correctly, Dunn 2005a, 83–84 n. 354: "It is important at this point to avoid the polarisation of 'justification' and 'participation' encouraged by the well known assertion of A. Schweitzer [. . .]." Yet in the same context he does not recognize the need to distinguish between soteriological and ethical aspects. According to him, justification and sanctification blend together, and thus salvation is reduced to

which expresses the center of Pauline theology more authentically. Separated from the juridical categories, the participatory categories threaten to generate an enthusiastic interest in one's own inner life. On the other hand, independent of the participatory categories, the juridical categories run the risk of becoming nothing more than an empty doctrine. As a result, it is necessary to keep both aspects in view.

It is futile to speculate on the origin and the development of the juridical and participatory categories in Paul before the writing of his (preserved) letters. Such a research project could only bring meager insight (if any at all) into his spiritual maturation. An educated guess of his unknown past does not benefit a serious investigation. Based on the existing textual material, we already know that the juridical and participatory aspects together form the terminological and theological foundation for his soteriology.

Finally, the interpretations of Sanders and Bultmann should not be pitted against each other. They rather complement each other (without the one or the other having to be accepted with all its implications).[19] Sanders underlines the Christological criterion: Christ did not die in vain (Gal. 2:20). Thus we know that only he can justify. Bultmann, on the other hand, underscores the anthropological criterion: all human beings need Christ because of their sinfulness (Romans 1–3). Thus we know why only he can justify.

Moreover, Sanders himself approves Bultmann's position, although with the caution that Paul did not start out from an anthropological analysis.[20] Thereby he comes into conflict with himself. On the one hand, Sanders directly asserts that Paul exclusively criticizes Judaism on Christological grounds. On the other hand, he indirectly admits that Paul also criticizes Judaism on anthropological grounds.[21] Räisänen has correctly objected that Sanders can hardly back up his ambivalent position satisfactorily without interpreting Rom. 3:27; 4:2–5; 9:30–32; 10:3; and Phil. 3:4–9 in the same way as Bultmann. Nevertheless, in his exegesis of each of these verses, Sanders categorically deviates from Bultmann's interpretation. Accordingly, only one pericope remains to support him, namely,

---

"*a process of transformation* of the believer" (op. cit., 84). See above. Cf. Stuhlmacher 2002, 54: "Führende Vertreter der New Perspective propagieren aufs neue die uralte Zweiteilung der paulinischen Soteriologie in einen juridischen und einen partizipatorischen Teil [. . .]. Diese Aufteilung wird überflüssig, wenn man den von Paulus selbst klar herausgestellten Zusammenhang von Rechtfertigung, Sühne und Versöhnung beachtet und bedenkt, dass der Christus Jesus für den Judenchristen Paulus immer auch eine korporative Repräsentationsfigur ist [. . .]."

19 For disagreements with Sanders and Bultmann, see above. See further below.

20 Sanders 1977, 508–11.

21 Cf. already Beker 1978, 110; Dahl 1978, 156.

Rom. 7:14–25, a passage that he never analyzes.[22] Later, Sanders has corrected his ambiguity. Now he proceeds in an entirely "anti-Bultmannian" fashion.[23]

In a similar manner, Räisänen is also guilty of a contradiction. To begin with, he concurs with Sanders's theory regarding the backward movement of the Pauline thought. As he argues for it, he does not affirm the basis of Sanders's argumentation for such a movement, namely, the un-Pharisaic notion of sin as a demonic power and person.[24] That is where it becomes really bad. The whole thing seems to fall flat. Curiously, although Räisänen disputes the relevant aspect of sin as exercising demonic lordship for those under its dominion,[25] he still in another context refers to Sanders's *Paul and Palestinian Judaism* with approval. He writes:

> Paul argued, as E. P. Sanders has emphasized, "*backwards*." He tried, as it were, to define man's disease by analyzing the medicine which he knew to be wholesome and indispensable. "Paul actually came to the view that all men are *under the lordship of sin* [italics mine] as a reflex of his soteriology: Christ came to provide a new lordship for those who participate in his death and resurrection."[26]

In reality, Räisänen tries to provide a different explanation for the theory of the backward movement of the Pauline thought: Paul must think from solution to plight since his reflection on the Law "is full of difficulties and inconsistencies."[27] His numerous logical shortcomings serve as evidence of the secondary character of his anthropological analysis.[28] Initially, Sanders did not argue like this. Hence, the reference to his *Paul and Palestinian Judaism* above leads astray. But then in his later *Paul, the Law, and the Jewish People*, Sanders avails himself of a new argument for his theory of the backward movement of the Pauline thought. Now he, in reference to Räisänen, contends that Paul's anthropology would certainly betray more common sense and harmony if it were the starting point of his theology.[29]

A further qualification is necessary regarding the theory of the backward movement of the Pauline thought. According to Phil. 3:4–8 (cf. also Acts), the

22 Räisänen 1980, 72. He is not fully consistent in his argument. To begin with, he avows: "[. . .] without a Bultmannian interpretation of Rom 3:27; 4:2ff; 10:3; Phil 3. When Sanders interprets these passages [. . .]" (ibid.). In another context, he observes, however: "Rom 4:2–5 is not discussed at all by Sanders" (ibid., n. 55). See, nevertheless, the Index of Passages in *Paul and Palestinian Judaism* (1977).

23 Sanders 1983, 59 n. 77.

24 See above; cf. below.

25 Räisänen 1983, 99–100 n. 29. For a critique, see above 4.1.2.

26 Räisänen 1983, 108.

27 Op. cit., 264.

28 Op. cit., *passim*.

29 Sanders 1983, 70–91. However, even now his thinking does not seem compelling at all. One might as well conclude that Paul is simply an inconsistent or unsystematic thinker. In that case, the theory of the backward movement of his thought becomes superfluous.

historical (or autobiographical) interplay of cause and effect really moves "backward": the surprising encounter with Christ started a powerful process in Paul that had anthropological consequences. According to Romans 1–3, the theological (or theoretical) reflection, on the other hand, runs "forward": the anthropological analysis of the human existence under the lordship of sin points to the necessity of Christ's salvific death on the cross. In this sense, even Bultmann shares the theory of the backward movement of the Pauline thought.[30] He states:

> Therefore, Paul's theology can best be treated as his doctrine of man: first, of man prior to the revelation of faith and second, of man under πίστις. [. . .] Such a presentation presupposes, since theological understanding has its origin in faith, that *man prior to the revelation of faith is so depicted of Paul as he is retrospectively seen from the standpoint of faith.*[31]

Also, at an earlier time, Bultmann had made a similar judgment:

> One must distinguish between (1) human beings before the revelation of faith, and (2) human beings under faith. Thus, one must consider that *a human being's existence before faith can only be truly viewed and grasped from faith.*[32]

In a similar way, Bultmann explains from Philippians 3 and Romans 7 that, while historical cause and effect move "backward," theological reflection moves "forward." He writes:

> For just this is what his [Paul's] conversion meant: In it he surrendered his previous understanding of himself; i.e. he surrendered what had till then been

---

30 *Contra* Sanders 1977, 474 n. 1: "There is here a difficulty in understanding Bultmann's view of which should be noted, although we shall not attempt a full exegesis of his view. He argues at length that Paul's soteriology and his attitude towards the law, for example, are *based on* his view of man's plight [. . .]. It is this argument which is under criticism here. On the other hand, Bultmann did not view Rom. 7 as an autobiographical statement of how one moves from unfaith to faith, and thus would presumably have agreed with the view which is argued for here, that Paul saw man's plight from the point of view of one who is in Christ [. . .]. It is not clear precisely how he would hold together the view that Paul's conception of man's life depended on the Christ-event and the view that his conception of soteriology and his attitude toward the law depended on his analysis of man's plight." Correctly, Dahl (1978, 157 n. 2) observes: "I don't think that there is a real difficulty here, once one accepts Bultmann's distinction between faith in the kerygma and theology as an explication of the understanding of human existence. On that definition, human plight is the logical starting point for an analysis of Paul's *theology*, even though faith in Christ made Paul reach his assessment of human plight." Similarly, Beker (1978, 242) concludes: "I agree with Dahl's criticism of Sanders and his defense of Bultmann on this point: *faith in Christ* made Paul reach his assessment of the human life, whereas the human plight is the logical starting point for an analysis of Paul's *theology*." Later, see also Seifrid 1992, 54.

31 Bultmann 1984, 192 (italics mine).

32 Bultmann 1930, 1031: "Es muß also disponiert werden: 1. der Mensch vor der Offenbarung des Glaubens, 2. der Mensch unter dem Glauben. Dabei muß aber beachtet werden, *daß das Sein* des Menschen vor dem Glauben in seiner Wahrheit erst vom Glauben aus sichtbar geworden ist und verstanden werden kann" (italics mine).

> the norm and meaning of his life, he sacrificed what had hitherto been his pride and joy (Phil. 3:4–7). His conversion was not the result of an inner moral collapse (which it is frequently assumed to have been on the basis of a misinterpretation of Rom. 7:7ff as autobiographical confession). It was not rescue from the despair into which the cleavage between willing and doing had allegedly driven him. His was not a conversion of repentance; neither, of course, was it one of emancipating enlightenment. Rather, it was obedient submission to the judgment of God, made known in the cross of Christ, upon all human accomplishment and boasting. It is as such that his conversion is reflected in his theology.[33]

Many other exegetes have understood the historical and theological aspects in line with Bultmann.[34] Hence, the backward movement of the Pauline thought does not stand out as a really new theory in New Testament scholarship. On the contrary, it appears as the same old story that has been told for a long time.

Accordingly, Bultmann was fully right when he considered the anthropological analysis as the starting point for the Pauline theology. Yet it goes without saying that more can and must be said about his existentialist interpretation and exegetical details.[35]

33 Bultmann 1984, 189.

34 Cf. Räisänen 1983, 108 n. 79.

35 Sanders (1977, 510) correctly observes: "[. . .] one could now also object to some other elements of Bultmann's description, especially the consistent transformation of Paul's categories into those of existentialism, which now seem somewhat shopworn." For example, Bultmann's existentialist philosophy has fatal consequences for his definition of faith. On the one hand, believers have surrendered their self-confidence, including their presumed ability to choose (1984, 280–85, 300, 315–18). On the other hand, faith, as the total surrender of *all* human accomplishments, is also described as "the free deed of obedience" or "decision" (1984, 317). Because of his existentialist philosophy, Bultmann is also misguided in his interpretation of the concept of sin. Since the error of the entire humanity amounts to self-confidence, consequently even the best attempt to *fulfill* the Law must be regarded as the very sin (1932, 53–62). This interpretation of "nomistic" desire has obvious connections with M. Heidegger's speculative analysis of humanity.

8. SUMMARY

IT WOULD BE superfluous here to summarize the main results in detail since they are recurrently presented to the reader in the course of the investigation. In the following, it will suffice to recall the most important conclusions.

The main task of this work was to compare the Pauline and Jewish religion starting from the state of research arrived at through the impact of E. P. Sanders on the current exegetical discussion. In order to delimit the extensive theme, the emphasis was placed on the relationship between divine grace and human works in a soteriological context.

The history of research (chapter 2) verified that F. Weber's description of Judaism (or the Weberian position in general) that dominated until the 1970s failed to carry conviction. The Jews did not expect to obtain salvation on account of their own merits. Instead, they put their trust in divine mercy within the covenant. Their observance of the Law was indeed covenantal nomism. The great turning point in the history of research was all because of Sanders and his important contribution to the academic discussion through his monumental work *Paul and Palestinian Judaism*. Notwithstanding, he did not quite succeed in explaining why Paul still criticizes Judaism for vain self-righteousness and self-praise. At this point, H. Odeberg tentatively provided an opportunity to a much better understanding. He drew attention to the anthropological presuppositions (especially the question of free will) in a soteriological context. As a consequence, he thought that the Pauline criticism of Jewish self-righteousness and self-praise easily turns into a contradiction between Pauline pessimistic and Jewish optimistic anthropology. Until now, no one has dealt with such a perspective in academic research to the same extent as Odeberg. He showed the way ahead and set a path for future studies.

The chosen perspective increased in importance as it was made known that Sanders had not given enough attention to the anthropological presuppositions of Jewish and Pauline soteriology (chapter 3). In fact, the question of human ability was implicit in his new method, a necessary component of "a comparison of patterns of religion."

In the following section (chapter 4), the anthropological presuppositions of Jewish and Pauline soteriology were covered. A serious contrast showed up:

Judaism represents an optimistic anthropology with the affirmation of human free will, whereas Paul presents a pessimistic anthropology with the assertion of human depravity, a positition to which he consistently holds fast.

On the basis of the anthropological presuppositions, it turned out that the Jewish and the Pauline pattern of religion or respective soteriology do differ from each other (chapter 5). In the former case, final salvation takes place not only by divine grace. Human cooperation through the works of the Law is also needed. It is about synergism. In the latter case, salvation takes place really by divine grace. Human works of love rise out of Christ's action in the Christian and as a sign of living faith. It is about monergism.

Next, interest turned toward the categorical and clear-cut confrontation of Paul with contemporary Judaism (chapter 6). The exegetical analysis of the pertinent passages exposed that he rejects the Jewish soteriology particularly on the basis of his pessimistic anthropology and criticizes it for self-righteousness and self-praise.

Finally, the attention focused on the question if Paul thinks "backward" (from solution to plight) or not—in other words, if he has deduced his pessimistic anthropology from his soteriological conviction that only Christ saves (chapter 7). The goal of addressing the complicated issue of the direction and development of one's mindset disclosed that the right answer depends on a sharp difference between the autobiographical and theological perspective. In an autobiographical sense, Paul thought from solution to plight (he first encountered Christ as his Savior and then became aware of his own sinfulness), but in a theological sense he thought from plight to solution (the anthropological analysis of the human existence under sin points to the necessity of Christ's salvific death on the cross).

In conclusion, Paul has disregarded the Jewish soteriology both for Christological and for anthropological reasons.

EPILOGUE

A FAREWELL TO THE NEW PERSPECTIVE AND THE START OF A NEW QUEST FOR PAUL[1]

1. Introduction

In New Testament scholarship, Pauline research continues its triumph. The debate about the New Perspective on Paul broadens and gains depth, yet it also becomes more difficult and complicated. Interpretations diverge strongly, with most currently exhibiting diversity.[2]

The present debate was launched in 1977 with the publishing of E. P. Sanders's broad work *Paul and Palestinian Judaism: A Comparison of Patterns of Religion*. Since then, thousands of articles and essays, studies and investigations, volumes, monographs, and dissertations have taken up the topic. Among the large number of scholars especially two stand out: J. D. G. Dunn and N. T. Wright. They stand—so to speak—"taller than any of the people" (1 Sam. 9:2).[3] Additionally, in recent times J. M. G. Barclay has made his mark on the state

1 This epilogue is a modification of an article originally published in *The Doctrine on Which the Church Stands or Falls*, ed. M. Barrett (Crossway, 2019): 295–325. It is republished with permission. However, a short outline of the necessity of the new quest for Paul is added at the end (see below).

2 The New Perspective advocates are a large number of scholars who do not often find consensus in their interpretations. Still, they do have something in common; otherwise it would not make sense to speak of a fresh wave of research. For more on the research history, see S. Westerholm, "The 'New Perspective' at Twenty-Five," in *The Paradoxes of Paul*, vol. 2 of *Justification and Variegated Nomism*, ed. D. A. Carson et al. (Mohr Siebeck, 2004), 1–38.

3 Cf. D. J. Moo, "Israel and the Law in Romans 5–11: Interaction with the New Perspective," in *The Paradoxes of Paul*, vol. 2 of *Justification and Variegated Nomism*, ed. D. A. Carson et al. (Mohr Siebeck, 2004), 185.

of research and distinguished himself from his peers. He has presented fresh insights into some stagnating problems and imparted a welcome disturbance in a current debate.[4]

My task is to analyze critically the new direction in Pauline research that was taken by Dunn and Wright in the aftermath of Sanders. Last, but not least, the recent progress initiated by Barclay deserves to be observed. It goes without saying that not every detail in their overall views can be scrutinized. One must be selective while, at the same time, recognizing that all involved, the present author included, attempt to contribute through their own unique work. Therefore, certain crucial themes are picked up below and reflected upon in more depth. Clearly, they are distinct from case to case: these prominent scholars have their marked centers of gravity. To be sure, I hope that my selective use of their writings adequately embodies what they really want to say.

Since the academic debate with the prominent proponents of the New Perspective will end up in a kind of deadlock, a fresh approach is needed. Hence, there is a need for a new quest for Paul. The analysis of his theology finally substantiates his break with Judaism on the whole.

Interestingly, the New Perspective on Paul basically arises from the new perspective on Judaism. If the old perspective on Judaism as a religion of gaining merits and earning salvation is no longer valid, it is no more possible to stand up for the old perspective on Paul as preaching against the legalistic understanding of God's grace. As a result, we have to reconsider the reasons for his break with his former beliefs.

Sanders dubbed the common Jewish "pattern of religion" covenantal nomism. He helpfully summarizes the position as follows:

> God has (1) chosen Israel and (2) given the law, which implies both (3) God's promise to maintain the covenant and (4) the requirement of obedience. (5) God rewards obedience and punishes disobedience. (6) The law ordains means of expiation and (7) the expiation restores the broken covenant. (8) All who through obedience, expiation and God's grace remain in the covenant will be saved.[5]

In other words, one gets in the covenant through acceptance of the Law and remains in it through submission to the Law. Both the election (see point 1) and the salvation of Israel (see point 8) depend on God's grace, not on human merit. Succinctly, obedience as such earns neither election nor salvation. It effects the remaining within the covenant.[6]

4 See his major work: *Paul and the Gift* (Eerdmans, 2015).

5 E. P. Sanders, *Paul and Palestinian Judaism: A Comparison of Patterns of Religion* (Fortress Press, 1977), 422.

6 Sanders, *Paul and Palestinian Judaism*, 419–22.

Since Sanders insists that covenantal nomism is not at all based on self-righteousness, merit, and boasting, he concludes that Paul did not discard Jewish religion owing to its assumed legalistic soteriology. No, not in the slightest! The main reason was first and foremost Christological. Paul stands for a very exclusive Christology. He affirms that no other can save but Christ. He did not consent to Jewish soteriology simply (and somewhat simplified) because it was not Christianity.[7]

Over the years, the sketch of covenantal nomism as the common denominator of the Jewish religion has caused much debate. It has been defended. It has been rejected. It has been modified. It has been amplified.[8]

Still, Sanders absolutely has shown that Judaism should not be identified with a religion of complete self-salvation ("eine Religion völliger Selbsterlösung").[9] He rightly affirms God's grace as the basis of fulfilling the Law, in other words, covenant as the origin of nomism. Therefore, the concept of covenantal nomism as an interrelationship between given election and required obedience clarifies the main lines well enough.[10]

To say this is not to say that the concept of covenantal nomism does not lack precision and clarity. It leaves, indeed, a great deal to be desired. I have pointed out elsewhere that the idea of human free will amounts to *opinio communis* in Judaism. (One exception confirms the rule: the Qumran community seems to represent an absolute determinism.[11]) Consequently, in covenantal nomism the Jews are supposed to contribute to their attaining of eternal life by doing their very best. They can and should do it in their own strength, but not to the exclusion of any role by divine grace. The issue at stake is cooperation. Hence, covenantal nomism ends up as a synergistic soteriology.[12]

---

7 Sanders, *Paul and Palestinian Judaism*, 552: "In short, *this is what Paul finds wrong in Judaism: it is not Christianity*." Later, he clarifies his position as follows: "What is wrong with the law, and thus with Judaism, is that it does not provide for God's ultimate purpose, that of saving the entire world through faith in Christ, and without the privilege accorded to Jews through the promises, the covenants, and the law." See E. P. Sanders, *Paul, the Law and the Jewish People* (Fortress Press, 1983), 47.

8 Cf., e.g., the recent discussion in J. D. G. Dunn, "The New Perspective: Whence, What and Whither?" in *The New Perspective on Paul: Collected Essays* (Mohr Siebeck, 2005), 55–63. See above, chapter 3. My book is available in German as well. See T. Laato, *Paulus und das Judentum: Anthropologische Erwägungen* (Åbo Academy Press, 1991).

9 *Contra* P. Billerbeck, *Exkurse zu einzelnen Stellen des Neuen Testaments*, Kommentar zum Neuen Testament aus Talmud und Midrasch 4/1, ed. H. L. Strack and P. Billerbeck (C. H. Beck, 1928), 6. See above, chapter 2.

10 Dunn, "The New Perspective," 62.

11 See above 4.1.1. Later S. Westerholm, "Paul's Anthropological 'Pessimism' in Its Jewish Context," in *Divine and Human Agency in Paul and His Cultural Environment*, ed. J. M. G. Barclay and S. J. Gathercole (T&T Clark 2008), 71–98.

12 See above, chapter 5.

This much should be known about the ongoing debate before moving on in the critical evaluation of the main proponents of the New Perspective.

2. J. D. G. Dunn

A. The Question of Synergism

Initially, the New Perspective on Paul was so dubbed by J. D. G. Dunn. He also emphasizes that it in fact flows from the new perspective on Judaism (as has already been pointed out above).[13] Thus he principally shares the overall delineation of covenantal nomism.[14]

Yet Dunn argues that "it may well be the case, no doubt is the case, that some of Sanders' statements are imbalanced in that they overstate the covenant side of the inter-relationship."[15] Despite this, "there was an inter-relationship between given election and required obedience in the soteriology of Second Temple Judaism," an inner linkage "which prior to Sanders was not sufficiently recognized, and which can now be fairly and effectively characterized in the phrase 'covenantal nomism.' "[16] Accordingly, Dunn also here nicely consents to the outcome of the previous analysis (see above).

In addition, Dunn even acknowledges a clear-cut synergism in Judaism.[17] Therefore, he actually admits that Judaism does teach salvation by human cooperation, but based on God's amazing grace (covenant). Once again, his conclusion seems obvious (for the very reasons stated earlier).

Then Dunn goes one step further and suggests that Paul himself in his thinking allows for some synergistic tendencies which permeate his soteriology. He specifically refers to the thought of judgment according to works.[18] From this perspective, the reader wonders whether he has to face the past theological dispute relating to Pelagius and his heretical teachings. Were we not discussing the New Perspective on Paul? Frankly speaking, one must wonder at this point whether we are here involved in Pauline theology at all.

At long last, Dunn ends up fervently denying that "Paul's understanding of salvation was synergistic." Rather, his concern was "to question whether the charge of synergism should be laid so confidently at the door of Judaism when

---

13 Dunn, "The New Perspective," 15: the New Perspective on Paul "builds on Sanders' new perspective on Second Temple Judaism, and Sanders' reassertion of the basic graciousness expressed in Judaism's understanding and practice of covenantal nomism."

14 Dunn, "The New Perspective," 55–63.

15 Dunn, "The New Perspective," 56.

16 Dunn, "The New Perspective," 62.

17 Dunn, "The New Perspective," 54–80, especially 69–72 and 80.

18 Dunn, "The New Perspective," 72–79.

some of Paul's language seems vulnerable to the same charge" and "to take more seriously and with due seriousness the other Pauline teaching" (predominantly on judgment according to works).[19] By and large, Dunn's rhetoric back and forth seems to aim at downplaying the notion of human cooperation. He is not drawn in to prolonging the debate about that. Ultimately, he would be willing to drop the verdict against legalism of the Pauline soteriology, provided that the charge of synergism in Judaism is not taken at face value!

Dunn's overall thinking becomes even more bewildering on another occasion as he writes:

> In all these cases [that is Rom. 4:4–5; 10:2–4; Phil. 3:7–9], therefore, it is difficult to sustain the claim that Paul was polemicizing against "self-achieved righteousness." *Of course the texts just reviewed can be read that way.*[20]

In reality, Dunn admits here that his own reading of the Pauline texts is *not* the one and only. Indeed, it is possible to understand Paul polemicizing against self-achieved righteousness (which goes back to the synergistic trends in Judaism).[21] That is exactly what "the later Paul" (the one who wrote Ephesians)[22] does. Dunn suggests:

19 Dunn, "The New Perspective," 80.

20 J. D. G. Dunn, *The Theology of Paul the Apostle* (Eerdmans, 1998), 370 (italics mine). Cf. Dunn, "The New Perspective," 41: "Here again I do not question the fundamental statement of principle which Paul enunciates in these passages [Rom. 3:20; 4:4–5; 9:11–12]. But again I wonder if the conclusion that Paul is attacking a works-righteousness attitude, an attitude embraced by Jews of his time, is *quite so soundly* based as most think, and whether Paul's attack is again *somewhat broader*" (italics mine).

21 Cf. some remarkable passages in J. D. G. Dunn, *Romans 1–8* (Word Books, 1988): "What is attacked, therefore, is the self-confidence of the synagogue attender who faithfully hears the law being read Sabbath by Sabbath and who in consequence counts himself as one of the righteous, one of the chosen people (an equation encouraged not least once again by the Wisdom of Solomon and *Psalms of Solomon*), that is, one who is already assured of a favorable final verdict because as a member of the covenant people he has remained within the covenant, loyal to the covenant" (104–5). Or later: "In any case we must assume that Paul, in looking back on his life as a Pharisee, had long ago concluded that the law, far from binding individuals closer to God in truthful obedience, actually separated them from God and prevented them from accepting God's grace in its complete gratuitousness [. . .]" (352). Or later: "With insight born of his conversion Paul sees that attitude to have been motivated (subconsciously) in large part by fear—a fear of failing to match up to a standard of exact obedience, a fear in other words not so much of God as of what his fellow Pharisees might think or say of his failure to conform. Paul thus, in all probability, extrapolates his own experience to that of his readers, confident that his Jewish and God-worshipping audiences have found in Christianity the same liberation as he had himself (v 2)" (460).

22 Dunn, "The New Perspective," 51. The later Paul is the one who also wrote the Pastoral epistles (ibid., 53–54).

> That [the disapproval of self-achieved righteousness] may have happened already in Eph. 2:8–9, where the issue does seem to have moved from one of works of law to one of human effort.[23]

And later, in another context, he writes:

> Here [in Eph. 2:8–9] the thought seems to have broadened out to refer to human effort in general as inadequate to the demands of salvation; salvation could be accomplished only by grace alone through faith alone. At the very least that implies that the Reformation understanding of Paul's theology of justification was already shared by the first Christian commentator on that theology.[24]

All in all, Dunn seems to saw off the branch on which he is sitting. He acknowledges that

(1) Judaism was synergistic,
(2) some crucial Pauline texts can be read as polemicizing against self-achieved righteousness, and
(3) "the later Paul" does exactly that as he disapproves every kind of legalism.

So the question naturally arises: Why not interpret the theology of Paul and his break with Judaism along these lines? Is there any compelling or convincing need for the New Perspective? Truly, it looks as if there is none. Rather, one should simply say that the Judaism of what Sanders christened as covenantal nomism was synergistic. As a result, Paul has all reasons to criticize it exactly for that.

B. "Works of the Law" as Jewish Identity Markers

In his concise summary of the New Perspective on Paul, Dunn does not simply build on Sanders's new perspective on Second Temple Judaism (see above). He also observes and emphasizes "a social function" of the Law as an integral feature of covenantal nomism. To put it in a well-defined dictum: the Mosaic Law serves to mark off Israel from all the other nations.[25]

Accordingly, Dunn argues as follows:

> When Paul said in effect, "All are justified by faith and not by works," he meant *not* "Every individual must cease from his own efforts and simply trust in God's acceptance," however legitimate and important an interpretation of his words that is. What he meant was, "Justification is not confined to Jews as

23 Dunn, *The Theology of Paul*, 371.

24 Dunn, "The New Perspective," 52. That kind of reasoning continues also in the Pastoral epistles (ibid., 53–54).

25 Dunn, "The New Perspective," 15.

marked out by their distinctive works; it is open to all, to Gentile as well as Jew, through faith."[26]

Consequently, Dunn contends that "works of the Law" in the Pauline epistles serve as "Jewish identity markers." They especially indicate circumcision, food, and Sabbath laws, even if they should not be narrowed to boundary issues only. By focusing particularly on those regulations, the Judaizers in Galatia put to the test the willingness of the Gentiles to enter covenant membership, their readiness to remain faithful to the whole of Old Testament traditions and customs.[27]

The explicit emphasis on national separation or division by Dunn has caused much turbulence in the ongoing discussion. In the first place, M. Seifrid raises objections. He regards it as "highly questionable" that Jewish identity markers symbolize "*mere* national identity."[28] Rather, he contends that circumcision (for instance in Josephus's account of the circumcision of King Izates) symbolizes "not merely separation from other nations, but an ethically superior monotheism."[29]

On balance, Dunn seems not to have turned a deaf ear to a call for revision of his position. Later he writes as follows:

> I have no doubt that "works of the law" refer to what the law requires, the conduct prescribed by the Torah; whatever the law requires to be done can be described as "doing" the law, as a work of the law. [. . .] [T]he phrase "works of the law" is a way of describing the law observance required of all covenant members, and could be regarded as an appropriate way of filling out the second half of the Sanders' formula—"covenantal *nomism*."[30]

Taken at face value, the quotation shows undeniably that "works of the Law" point not simply to distinctive *ethnic* features but also to diverse *ethical* features. In that case, Paul renouncing "works of the Law" does not merely exclude Jewish national priority but human moral superiority as well. In full agreement with Seifrid: "All these observations give us reasons for thinking that in rejecting ἔργα νόμου as a guarantee of salvation, Paul rejects a moral superiority gained

---

26 J. D. G. Dunn, "The Justice of God: A Renewed Perspective on Justification by Faith," in *The New Perspective on Paul: Collected Essays* (Mohr Siebeck, 2005), 199.

27 Dunn, "The New Perspective," 22–26.

28 M. Seifrid, "Blind Alleys in the Controversy over the Paul of History," *TynBul* 45, no. 1 (1994): 77.

29 Seifrid, "Blind Alleys," 79. Later Seifrid adds: It is "impossible to sustain the claim that Jewish 'boundary markers' signalled exclusivism or national identity alone. I must confess considerable puzzlement that both Dunn and Wright, who recognise that some Jews could regard other Jews as outside the community of the elect on the basis of halakhah, regard distinctive practices as simply 'exclusivistic,' borders without interior meaning" (80–81).

30 Dunn, "The New Perspective," 22–23.

by obedience, notwithstanding that Jews who adopted such a stance would have attributed their progress to God's gracious covenant with Israel."[31]

Astoundingly, Dunn himself applauds these words in a footnote as "a basis for a richer synthesis,"[32] even though they actually overturn his New Perspective on Paul! Rejecting "a moral superiority gained by obedience," the apostle of the Gentiles at the same time abrogates every kind of synergism in the Jewish soteriology (see above). In the end, this is what he finds wrong with covenantal nomism.

C. The Request for Consistency

By and large, reading Dunn (and above all his copious commentary on Romans) puzzles me. He sends out a signal of having been rethinking his position. Surely, he has. However, one still gets the impression that he, despite his apparent reassessment, has not, to an adequate extent, read into his text any new meaning of the works of the Law. To quote his words: "I confess to being a little surprized by the difficulty apparently experienced by some respondents in recognizing how ἔργα νόμου can denote what the law requires, but with special reference to such crucial issues [as Jewish identity markers]."[33]

Without doubt, Dunn was obliged to reassess his previous position to avoid the morbid criticism that it caused. However, the extension of "works of the Law" as "what the Law requires" with special reference to Jewish identity markers is not the same as the notion of "works of the Law" as solely Jewish identity markers. All that the Law requires (notwithstanding the special reference to the Jewish identity markers) comprises not only *ethnic* but also *ethical* dimensions. This is completely at odds with what Dunn suggests. In that case, we are not just talking about Jewish national priority. At stake is moral human superiority (see point b above) combined with strong synergistic tendencies (see point a above).[34]

Elsewhere, I have emphasized that Dunn has modified his former stance considerably.[35] It is not surprising at all that he fervently denies such

---

31 Seifrid, "Blind Alleys," 85.

32 Dunn, "The New Perspective," 26 n. 107. In addition, Dunn affirms that Seifrid "is much more nuanced than the others."

33 See J. D. G. Dunn, "Yet Once More—'The Works of the Law': A Response," in *The New Perspective on Paul: Collected Essays* (Mohr Siebeck, 2005), 208.

34 For a recent discussion of the meaning of "works of the Law" especially in Galatians, see particularly N. Techow, *Sinners, Works of Law, and Transgression in Gal 2:14b–21: A Study in Paul's Line of Thought*, WUNT 602 (2. Reihe) (Mohr Siebeck, 2024), above all 245–370 (*et passim*).

35 See T. Laato, "Paul's Anthropological Considerations: Two Problems," in *The Paradoxes of Paul*, vol. 2 of *Justification and Variegated Nomism*, ed. D. A. Carson et al. (Mohr Siebeck, 2004), 356 n. 71.

a conclusion.[36] He maintains to have adjusted his "initial formulation" only.[37] However, the discussion above runs completely counter to any denial. The fact remains that Dunn has fundamentally altered the content of "works of the Law." Besides, he admits that Judaism is pervaded by human cooperation (synergism). As a result, what will be left of his New Perspective? On the whole, it seems to me that his overall interpretation has really collapsed under its own weight.

3. N. T. Wright

A. Preliminary Remarks

By and large, N. T. Wright (like Dunn) makes his case for the new perspective on Judaism. He wholeheartedly hails Sanders for bringing to light that "Judaism, so far from being a religion of works, is based on a clear understanding of grace, the grace that chose Israel in the first place to be a special people. Good works are simply gratitude, and demonstrate that one is faithful to the covenant [. . .]."[38] In addition, Wright also (like Dunn) understands especially circumcision "as a badge of national identity"[39] and acknowledges it as defining boundaries between Jews and Gentiles.[40] Therefore, I think, there is no need to prolong the discussion on those aspects beyond what has been confirmed so far.

Yet it might be added that even Wright (like Dunn) ultimately shows the necessity for an extension of "works of the Law" from "Jewish boundary markers" to embracing all that the Law requires. He maintains that Israel still lives in exile. Although she came back from Babylon, the divine promise of a glorious future remained unfulfilled. Thus, Wright asks, what should Israel be doing in the present to hasten the time when God would act on her behalf.[41] Accordingly, he indicates that she, "sheltered behind the religious boundary-markers," should do her very best to "keep the covenant" with all her might.[42] In that case, the Jews (as expected) are indeed to obey the *whole* Law, possibly concentrating on those aspects which isolate themselves from the Gentiles but not to the exclusion of other aspects in their Torah. For that reason, Jewish badges of covenant membership imply the wider reference to covenantal nomism, the entire body of Israel's sacred traditions (cf. above).

36 Dunn, "The New Perspective," 22 n. 94.

37 Dunn, "The New Perspective," 22.

38 N. T. Wright, "The Paul of History and the Apostle of Faith," *TynBul* 29 (1978): 80 and later *passim*.

39 Wright, "The Paul of History," 65.

40 N. T. Wright, *The Climax of the Covenant: Christ and the Law in Pauline Theology* (Fortress Press, 1993), 240–44. See also Dunn, "The New Perspective," 25 n. 106.

41 N. T. Wright, *The New Testament and the People of God* (Fortress Press, 1992), 268–69.

42 Wright, *The People of God*, 271–72.

Saying this is not tantamount to approving the thought of ongoing exile. Wright suggests that Israel (despite her strong emphasis on nomism in reliance on human freedom as a vital feature of covenant membership) is not guilty of any legalistic works-righteousness but, on the contrary, of what he calls "national righteousness." The Law functions "as a charter of national privilege."[43] The future return from exile would amount to the fulfillment of distinct *Jewish* longing. Then God will rescue his own people and do this by his grace. At that moment he brings the good old times (or even better times) back again. What is more, Gentiles were also supposed to be flocking into Zion to acknowledge him as their Lord. Their imminent coming occurs according to the Old Testament expectations.[44]

On the other hand, Wright suggests that on the road to Damascus Paul was brought to realize the astonishing accomplishment of his former national hopes. Surprisingly, the exile has already ended! Israel has truly been delivered from her oppression and oppressors. There is no need to yearn for her redemption anymore. The Messiah has come. He has exhausted the curse of sin and death.[45] Besides, the Gospel involves an extensive redefinition of Israel. She "is transformed from being an ethnic people into a worldwide family," including also Gentiles.[46] Hence, what counts is grace, not race.[47] To put it simply:

> *The one true God had done for Jesus of Nazareth in the middle of time, what Saul had thought he was going to do for Israel at the end of time.*[48]

Obviously, a short summary cannot do full justice to the overall picture of Wright's analysis. He has much more to say on Jewish and Pauline theology. Even so, his specific theory of Israel in exile is to be examined more closely next.

B. Israel Still in Exile?

(i) Old Testament

On the whole, Wright regards the so-called Deuteronomic view of history as "constitutive of the underlying narrative framework" in the Old Testament as well as in later writings.[49] He maintains that "a great many Second-Temple Jews interpreted *that part of the continuing narrative in which they were living* in terms of the so-called Deuteronomic scheme of sin—exile—restoration, with

43 Wright, "The Paul of History," 65, 71.

44 Wright, *The People of God*, 268–79.

45 Wright, *The Climax of the Covenant*, 141–55.

46 Wright, *The Climax of the Covenant*, 240.

47 Wright, *The Climax of the Covenant*, 168, 194, 238.

48 N. T. Wright, *What Saint Paul Really Said: Was Paul of Tarsus the Real Founder of Christianity?* (Eerdmans, 1997), 36.

49 N. T. Wright, *Paul and the Faithfulness of God* (SPCK, 2013), 162. See already 139–40, 142–43, 149–50.

themselves still somewhere in the middle stage, that of 'exile' [. . .]" (especially Deuteronomy 27–30).[50] A similar sequence of events culminating in a continuing exile and an ultimate return emerges in Leviticus 26.[51] Both Ezra (9:6–9) and Nehemiah (9:32–37), in their great prayers, speak of a constant calamity, which amounts to a hapless exile.[52] Also Daniel in chapter 9 "poured out his heart and soul in prayer, insisting that it must be time for the exile to end" (because Jeremiah predicted that it would last for seventy years).[53] But he was informed by the angel that "the exile will not last for seventy years, but for *seventy times seven*." He ought not run ahead of reality. There will be an extension of the time schedule. Until then the hoped-for restoration falls short.[54]

Despite some strong tendencies in the current academic debate, it has not been substantiated that Wright is right in his analysis of the biblical data.[55] Here, for obvious reasons, a full-scale evaluation of his arguments would go too far. Still, a number of germane aspects, not always taken at face value, are needed.

The most common word for "exile" in the OT is גולה or גלות. It stems from the verb גלה, which literally means "to uncover" and is used in various contexts. The phrase "to uncover the ear"—with either man or God as its subject—means "to show" or "to reveal." Although not a technical term for "divine revelation," it conveys that meaning too. In Leviticus 18 and 20, the verb גלה occurs in the expression "to uncover the shame," which denotes sexual intercourse in proscribed circumstances, usually incest. It occurs also in the prophetic complaint that Israel has "uncovered her nakedness," a metaphor implying that she has thrown off her loyalty to the Lord. As a rough punishment, her land will be "uncovered" as the people go into exile (e.g., Hos 2:12; Ezek. 16:36).[56] Here the idea of "uncovering" is associated with the conditions of a ruined land[57] and probably with the humiliation of the prisoners of war being led naked into

---

50 Wright, *Faithfulness*, 140.

51 Wright, *Faithfulness*, 149–50.

52 Wright, *Faithfulness*, 151.

53 Wright, *Faithfulness*, 142.

54 Wright, *Faithfulness*, 142. See also 140, 143–46, 151, 160–62.

55 Cf. Wright's own evaluation *Faithfulness*, 139 n. 263. He refers to Scott, who suggests that the notion of the ongoing exile is now widely recognized and speaks of a growing consensus. That is—Wright reasonably fears—"over-optimistic."

56 See especially Bruce K. Waltke, "גלה," in *Theological Wordbook of the Old Testament* (*TWOT*), ed. R. Laird Harris et al. (Moody Press, 1980), 160–61. He regards it as "an open question whether we are dealing with one or two roots" and discusses therefore the verb גלה under two main meanings: "to uncover," and "to depart, to go into exile." However, the two main meanings are connected as "the land is uncovered when people are removed." See Allen P. Ross, "Exile," in *New International Dictionary of Old Testament Theology and Exegesis*, ed. Willem A. VanGemeren, vol. 4 (Paternoster Press, 1996), 595.

57 Ross, "Exile," 595.

captivity.[58] During the time of Israel's "scattering" among the nations, her whole holy terrain will rest and "enjoy its Sabbaths," which it did not have as long as she lived in it (Lev. 26:33–34).

The Lord's judgment of leading (most) Israelites out of the land into captivity functions as an appropriate contrast to his fulfilling the promises to lead them into the land at the beginning of their history. Accordingly, his repeated warnings through the prophets to lead them out of the land correspond exactly to his recurring promises to the fathers to lead their descendants into the land.[59] Thus as God remembers his covenant with Abraham, Isaac, and Jacob, he certainly remembers also the land at the same time (see Lev. 26:42). Both aspects are very closely intertwined. Indeed, the thought of an ongoing exile would be awkward in Old Testament theology. Obviously, it does not make any more sense if the Lord brought back his people into the Promised Land but would then nevertheless leave them in a state of ongoing exile. He is a trustworthy God, not an arbitrary one.

Additionally, the notion of exile is both lexically and theologically linked with "nakedness" (see above). In other words, it is associated with heinous sins, such as idolatry (Israel uncovering her nakedness), forbidden sexual relationships (Israelites uncovering the shame of their relatives or neighbors), and constant violation of Sabbath rules. Those really loathsome connotations are included in the language of the Old Testament. Therefore, the theory of ongoing exile suggests that Israel still is involved in grievous transgressions in one way or another. I strongly suspect that it properly renders the common Jewish thinking after the rebuilding of the temple (see below).

To be precise, the Deuteronomic view of history does not amount to the scheme of sin—exile—restoration, but rather to the scheme of sin—punishments (of which the exile is the climax)—restoration. In Deuteronomy 28, the exile arises recurrently during the whole chapter as the harshest chastisement (e.g., vv. 21, 25, 32, 36–37, 41, 49–52, 63–68). The repetition aims to underline the seriousness and severity of the divine retribution. Transgressing the Law ushers in a catastrophe. In Leviticus 26, the whole long story ushers in the retribution of the exile (vv. 32–39). The line of thought is more linear, leading finally to the return and restoration of Israel (vv. 40–45).

The factual composition in Deuteronomy 28 and Leviticus 26 indicates that the exile will take place as the ultimate punishment invoked only when the other curses had failed to bring Israel out of her recurrent recalcitrance. The long list of punishments reaches the culmination there, with the last one

58 M. G. Klingbeil, "Exile," in *Dictionary of the Old Testament: Pentateuch*, ed. T. Desmond Alexander and David W. Baker (InterVarsity Press, 2003), 246.

59 Waltke, *TWOT*, 61, s.v. גלה.

being the absolute worst.[60] Cogently, if the exile is going on, at least most other chastisements (but not necessarily all and all the time) are likewise in force. In that case, Israel suffers as well from serious diseases; insanity; extreme drought and other environmental calamities; unceasing hunger and thirst; dire poverty; the burdens of huge debts; brutal robbery; constant oppression; the desire to be married to a woman but someone else ravishing her; building a house but not living in it; ploughing and sowing but not reaping the harvest; planting a vineyard but not enjoying its fruit; slaughtering an ox but not eating any beef; the curse of eating one's own children. To be sure, the Jews would not have been thinking to live in ongoing exile and on the whole to suffer from this kind of chaos and anarchy after having returned from Babylon to the Promised Land. Without doubt, life was hard in ancient times and circumstances but scarcely *so* tough, especially if you were released from your captivity among foreign nations (see also below).

The books of Ezra and Nehemiah shed more light on the crucial aspects included in the concept of exile. The rest of Israel has returned from Babylon to the Promised Land. As a result, they have started to rebuild the temple and soon after the tumbled walls of Jerusalem. In the meantime, it is important to learn from the mistakes of the past, repenting of them and definitely not repeating them once again. Otherwise the people run the risk of a new exile. They will be punished because of their inward stubbornness.

It is no coincidence that the books of Ezra and Nehemiah strictly forbid those sins which especially brought about the exile, in other words, offenses which are closely associated with "nakedness" (see above). Thus Israel is not to "uncover her nakedness," showing disloyalty to God and not completing the rebuilding of the temple or the fallen walls of Jerusalem (Ezra 4:1–6:22; Neh. 3:17–6:19). Neither is Israel to "uncover the shame of others" by marrying foreigners (Ezra 9–10; Neh. 13:1–6, 23–31). Neither should Israel reject the Sabbath and cause the land to become "naked" (or desolate) in order that it may enjoy its Sabbatical rest (Neh. 13:15–22).

Further, it should also be borne in mind that the punishment for the sins associated with "nakedness" is nothing less than exile. If Israel forsakes God, he, in turn, will forsake her, as well as the land where she lives (as already shown in Deuteronomy 28). Likewise, prohibited sexual relationships result in captivity.

60 Cf. S. M. Bryan, *Jesus and Israel's Traditions of Judgment and Restoration* (Cambridge University Press, 2002), 17. He examines the book of Jubilees and writes: "One obvious way of reading the curses of Deuteronomy 32 is to see exile as the ultimate punishment invoked only when the other curses had at last failed to bring Israel out of its recurrent recalcitrance. But in *Jubilees* 23 the significance of the exile has been reduced [. . .] captivity is simply one of a litany of curses [. . .]." In the Old Testament the significance of the exile has not been downgraded but upgraded as the worst curse. See my arguments below.

In fact, there are, strictly speaking, no offerings that bring reconciliation in that case. If Israel defiles the land, it will simply vomit her out (see Lev. 18:24, 28; cf. 20:22–24; 26:31). Similarly, if Israel does not keep the Sabbath laws, she will be driven out from her land, and the land will be laid waste. Then it will have the rest it needs (Lev. 26:34–35).

The seriousness of the situation makes it more understandable why both Ezra and Nehemiah are ready to use or threaten violence in order to avoid intermarriage or to prevent the recurring violation of Sabbath rules (Ezra 10:8; Neh. 13:15–22). Sins such as those have resulted in exile, a fact to which both explicitly refer (Ezra 9:10–15; Neh. 13:17–18). Thus there is definitely no room for laxity and vagueness. Restricted violence is better than the whole hell of savagery and bloodshed prompted by furious enemies who—if the worst comes—take Israel into captivity once again.

Also 4 Baruch (dated to the first half of the second century AD) shows much later the same line of thought. It announces the end of the exile. However, those who do not separate from their foreign wives have to return to Babylon. They go back but are not allowed to resettle there anymore. Therefore, they must come back and build a city (i.e., Samaria) for themselves (8:1–11). Here, a certain sin is closely connected with the punishment of exile, as in the Old Testament, to say nothing of the Gospels, where the Pharisees do their utmost to keep in particular the Sabbath rules and purity laws (not least those concerning sexuality). Without doubt, their devout practice maintains to a large extent substantial continuity with the national revival of Ezra and Nehemiah (cf. above).[61]

In addition, it is worth mentioning that the Deuteronomic scheme of sin—punishments (including the exile as the ultimate chastisement)—restoration is taken at face value in Haggai as well. Yet now the curses are made to function in reverse (or so to speak "backward"). They do not disappear all at once, but rather in the long run. To be sure, the exile is over. The rebuilding of the temple has begun without being finished. Therefore, the prophet urges his kinsmen to complete it. If God's own house remains a ruin, there are no abundant blessings. So far "the heavens above you have withheld the dew, and the earth has withheld its produce" (1:10). As soon as the work on the temple is making real progress and coming to the end, a fabulous change takes place. The Lord says, "From this day on I will bless you" (2:19). It denotes—as expected—the rich blessings of the heavens and the earth. To sum up: Not long ago Israel has returned from Babylon to the Promised Land. In a little while she will live in abundance in the land flowing with milk and honey.

The future will be even brighter. Notwithstanding the fact that the new temple seems "as nothing" in comparison with the old one (2:3), the Lord

61 For the Pharisees before AD 70, see particularly Jacob Neusner, *The Rabbinic Traditions about the Pharisees Before 70*, 3 vols. (Brill, 1971).

promises that he will fill it with glory (2:7). In the end, the glory of the new temple will be greater than the glory of the old one (2:9). The divine prophecy was fulfilled in at least two different ways. First, through the vast construction projects of Herod the Great as he enlarged the temple and made it one of the most astounding buildings in its own time. Second, through the entering of the Messiah (Jesus) into that temple.[62]

All this shows that the full restoration of Israel does not occur at once. It takes time. Much more time than it was thought originally. Yet it would be wrong to argue on that basis alone that the exile is still going on.

Neither does Daniel 9 infer something like the theory of the ongoing exile (both at present and in the remote future). On the contrary, it "explicitly and positively recalls Jeremiah's prediction of seventy years, suggesting that the author regarded Jeremiah's prophecy not as incorrect."[63] Then, by the same token, it assertively envisions the hope for the final atonement and everlasting righteousness (v. 24). In short: the exile will soon be over, but the full restoration will take time to be completed.

Largely, Wright's theory of Israel still in exile is not backed up by any noteworthy biblical data. For sure, the next issue concerns whether it could be traced to other Jewish texts.

(ii) Other Jewish Texts

On the whole, Wright has to deal with the fact that Jewish writings "in which exile language occurs are rare." Therefore, much of the evidence for his case is drawn from a more wide-ranging perspective.[64] Accordingly, Wright expands the textual basis for his theory of the ongoing exile. To support it, he quotes texts

(1) reflecting on the Diaspora,
(2) bemoaning the bondage of Israel (as already in Ezra 9:8–9 and Neh. 9:36–37), and
(3) underlying the non-restoration (or incomplete restoration) of Israel.[65]

Yet the equation of the Diaspora, the bondage, and the non-restoration of Israel to exile displays a serious methodological problem:

(1) Accurately, the Diaspora and exile are not synonymous. In the latter case, prisoners of war are not allowed to return from the

62 Strictly speaking, the temple that Herod the Great enlarged was still the second one (not the third one), since the sacrificial cult was not interrupted during the long construction work. Thus the prophecies in Haggai 2 (see above) were fulfilled in the long run.

63 Bryan, *Jesus and Israel's Traditions*, 18.

64 Bryan, *Jesus and Israel's Traditions*, 13, 19.

65 Wright, *Faithfulness*, 139–63.

land(s) of their captivity. In the former case, they have become accustomed to live outside their home country and by their own choice reside where they are. They could go back to their country of origin, but at present—for one reason or another—they won't.

(2) Similarly, living in bondage is not exactly tantamount to exile. In Old Testament times, occasionally Israel has been living in bondage in her own land without living in exile (which denotes the obligation to live in a foreign country).

(3) To be precise, the non-restoration of Israel does not absolutely suggest that exile still goes on. For certain, there was plenty of room for future revelations and end-time perfection also after the return of Israel from Babylon. The end of Babylonian captivity was not the end of all eschatology in the proclamation of the prophets.

Despite the indisputable fact that Jewish writings "in which exile language occurs are rare" (see above), Wright remarkably assumes that "we can no doubt go on *fine-tuning the details of what kind of exile* people thought they were living in."[66] There are at least geographical, political, cultural as well as theological adjustments to exile.[67] Yet "the sense of living within the middle term of the Deuteronomic scheme [of sin—exile—restoration]" is applied on all levels. It remains true:

(1) "Whether, for those concerned, 'exile' was still in fact a geographical reality, as it was for many in the Diaspora."

(2) "Whether they were aware of the continuing theological and cultural oppression of foreign nations as indicating that Daniel 9 had not yet been fulfilled."

(3) "Whether they believed that in some sense they themselves were the advance guard of the 'real return from exile,' indicating that it had been going on right up to their time and still was for everyone except themselves (as in Qumran)."[68]

Wright's efforts to fine-tune the details of what kind of exile it is run into grievous methodological shortcomings. He equates here again exile with the Diaspora (point 1) and with the non-restoration of Israel (point 2). To that extent, his conclusions are unwarranted—as already shown (see above). In addition, Wright argues from the sectarian viewpoint of Qumran that all other Israelites live in exile, as if the exclusive indoctrination of a religious minority correctly expressed the common Jewish desperation felt by the majority (point 3). Rather, one could understand the whole state of affairs very much to

66 Wright, *Faithfulness*, 140 (italics mine).

67 Wright, *Faithfulness*, 139–40.

68 Wright, *Faithfulness*, 140.

the contrary: although a rigorous sect such as that in Qumran is not ashamed of asserting that all the others of their kinsmen still live in exile, this suggests that the Israelites themselves in general did *not* think along those lines (see below).

Overall, Wright fails to convince. His methodological fallacies call into question his conclusions. The "fine-tuning" of the details in the notion of exile remains a flop. A meticulous exegetical analysis of data is missing. Wright has not shown that his way of reading varied Jewish texts is not only possible but even plausible. The proof of evidence lies on him.

Astonishingly, Wright himself admits that there are a number of remarkable exceptions to his theory of ongoing exile. As already stated, he considers the vast literature of the tiny sect in Qumran as one of them. Additionally, he mentions also the books of Sirach and Judith.[69] They all draw attention to the fact that Israel already has returned from her exile back to the Promised Land.

In the case of Tobit,[70] 1 Enoch,[71] and, as it seems, Jubilees,[72] Wright focuses on "a double return from exile." For sure, the first return has already taken place in the past. A number of Israelites have come back to the Promised Land. God has shown "mercy on them" (Tob. 14:5). Still, the second return will take place sometime in the future.

That said, Wright explains the double return from exile by downplaying the first one. He writes: "Yes, there had been a 'return from exile'—of sorts: but it had not been the real thing." Hence, Israelites have "experienced a kind of 'return,' but [are] still awaiting the *true* 'return.'"[73] On balance, the first return from exile does not override the second one. In fact, the exile has not ended but at the present goes on as ever.

Frankly, Wright's devaluation of the first return seems unwarranted. Leaving aside a large-scale discussion here, the most natural interpretation of the double return from exile denotes the gathering of *all* Jews: at the outset merely the *southern* tribes of Judah from Babylon, then also and especially the *northern* tribes of Israel (including all other Jews as well) from different countries. Since the northern tribes never came back, their future gathering was a matter of end-time dream. That vision will come true at long last—not before:

> God will again have mercy on them [= Israelites], and God will bring them back into the land of Israel; and they will rebuild the temple of God, but not like the first until the period when the times of fulfilment shall come. After

69 Wright, *Faithfulness*, 157–58.

70 Wright, *Faithfulness*, 154–55.

71 Wright, *Faithfulness*, 155.

72 Wright, *Faithfulness*, 156. After having acknowledged "a double return from exile" in Tobit and 1 Enoch, Wright continues: "So too with *Jubilees*."

73 Wright, *Faithfulness*, 155.

> this they *all* will return from their exile and will rebuild Jerusalem in splendour (Tob. 14:5).[74]

As a result, the whole of Israel (all her tribes) will be saved.

The fulfillment of the traditional hope as to the redemption and restoration of all Israel in the end is the content of the double return from exile. It does not indicate that the first return is not essentially a "true" one. Neither does it suggest that the Jews at year zero in general regarded themselves as being in exile and estranged from God. Wright is not right. He does not even discuss other alternatives but only his own previously established and closed position, taken for granted, that no critical remark should be thought through.

On the contrary, Wright is right that the view of an ongoing exile does occur in the book of Baruch. For sure, the alleged author is a pseudonym. He is portrayed as Jeremiah's secretary. Thus the book has a fictive setting in the Babylonian exile, though it is usually dated in the second century BC.[75] In Baruch, there are indeed passages which state that Israel will return from her exile in the future. Jerusalem is admonished to rejoice since her children are coming from everywhere (4:37). She should take off her garments of mourning and instead wear the marvelous clothes of divine glory at that moment (5:1).

Even so, the reader of Baruch is naturally supposed to understand that the "today of the exile" is simply a literary setting.[76] The long-promised foretelling as to the end of exile has already come true. Israel has returned from her captivity. What has been told Baruch is verified long ago. Accordingly, he has been confirmed as a trustworthy man, sent from God. To be sure, the book of Baruch was not written to show that it for the most part has completely failed (telling that Israel should return but in fact she did not)! In that case it is not to be used as evidence for the theory of ongoing exile.[77]

Neither of the books of the Maccabees indicate what Wright reads into them. Referring to "such exalted language about the results of Simon's rule,"[78] he—as expected—recognizes the difficulty "to imagine that in the heady days of Hasmonean success" the Jews generally "perceived themselves to be in exile."[79] However, he also now speaks of the "double return," asserting that God has already rescued Israel and will soon gather all Israelites from everywhere.[80] On

74 The quotation according to Wright, *Faithfulness*, 154.

75 Wright, *Faithfulness*, 151–52.

76 Seifrid, "Blind Alleys," 88.

77 *Pace* J. M. Scott, "Restoration of Israel," in *Dictionary of Paul and His Letters*, ed. G. F. Hawthorne and R. P. Martin (InterVarsity Press, 1993), 796–99 as well. He repetitively quotes the book of Baruch as evidence for an ongoing exile. A better understanding of the literary setting of the writing would have resulted in another conclusion.

78 Wright, *Faithfulness*, 159.

79 Wright, *Faithfulness*, 160, in reference to Bryan, *Jesus and Israel's Traditions*, 15.

80 Wright, *Faithfulness*, 159.

that basis he then suggests that "the promised time of full blessing" had not arrived. Accordingly, he concludes that the curse of being in exile prevails.[81]

Once again, Wright rushes into his vague methodological point of departure and simply overemphasizes the eschatological language of Israel's complete restoration. As pointed out, his line of reasoning falls short on account of

(1) the equation of incomplete restoration to exile and
(2) the devaluation of the first return while recurring to the idea of the double return from the exile.

Both former methodological fallacies cause Wright to misinterpret the obvious meaning and sense of the books of the Maccabees.

In the case of Josephus, Wright asserts that "the period of life under Rome was a time of *douleia*, 'slavery,' and it was all Israel's own fault."[82] So he therefore concludes that because of that enslavement Israel still lives in exile. But this is simply a blatant *non sequitur*! The equation of bondage (or slavery) to exile is another methodological fault which leads astray (as shown above).

What is more, Wright knows perfectly well that Josephus "regards the beginning of Jewish slavery as having occurred because of the Jewish civil strife leading to Pompey's entrance."[83] Thus: "Inasmuch as Josephus regards the enslavement that began under Pompey as the end of a preceding period of liberty, it is difficult to see how or why he would have connected this new situation of bondage with exile."[84] Astonishingly, the more detailed facts such as these are hidden in a footnote and hastily forgotten.[85] Why? Because, as a consequence, the view of an ongoing exile completely collapses. To put it bluntly: Wright distorts the plain meaning of the original text by his tendentious interpretation. He forces his sources to say what he likes.[86]

All in all, the theory of an ongoing exile lacks evidence. It does not do justice to the Jewish texts and their apparent message. On the contrary, a more comprehensive inquiry into the data shows that a number of Israelites have indeed returned back to the Promised Land. The end of exile was generally perceived and recognized. Not even the notion of a double return entails that the first return is not a "true" one.[87]

---

81 Wright, *Faithfulness*, 159–60.

82 Wright, *Faithfulness*, 159.

83 Bryan, *Jesus and Israel's Traditions*, 15.

84 Bryan, *Jesus and Israel's Traditions*, 15. Wright is acquainted with the arguments here (see *Faithfulness*, 160–62).

85 Wright, *Faithfulness*, 159 n. 332.

86 The texts like 4 Ezra (see Wright, *Faithfulness*, 156) are no more discussed here, since they are written after the devastation of the temple in AD 70. As a result, a new age of exile was launched.

87 Cf. Seifrid, "Blind Alleys," 87. He writes with more caution: "More precisely stated: the early Jewish tradition of an extended period of exile for Israel is more complicated than

(iii) Paul and His Pharisaic Past

All things considered, the theory of an ongoing exile is not to be assumed as Jewish background for the interpretation of the New Testament. As it happens, the Gospel of Matthew begins with a report of the genealogy of Jesus in which a clear distinction between the age before and after the exile to Babylon occurs (1:11–12 and 17), a kind of prelude that acts as a fitting introduction to the other canonical books as well. That is an important lesson to be learned!

For certain, Paul—once as a devout Pharisee—did not think of himself as living in exile because of his own fault or as a result of the guilt of the whole Israel. He returned from the Diaspora to Jerusalem in his youth. In addition, he regarded his former practice of the Law as "blameless" (Phil. 3:6). There is no hint of feeling culpable. Paul was one of the best and advanced in self-righteousness, beyond many others (Gal. 1:14). Further, his declaration of "the earthly Jerusalem being enslaved with her children" does not derive from the ongoing Roman occupation but as a consequence of the failure to believe the Gospel (Gal. 5:25). In Romans 9–11, it rather seems that a new exile has begun (or shortly will begin) in Israel's unbelief![88] It is well-known that the prediction was fulfilled in concrete history because of the fall of Jerusalem in AD 66–70 (cf. also the later revolt in AD 132–135).

There is no reason to dwell more on details in the Pauline letters. To state the obvious: the idea of Israel still living in exile fails to carry conviction. Accordingly, it is not to be taken for granted in the reading of the New Testament on the whole. A more comprehensive exegesis of certain features particularly in Galatians and Romans confirms that such is the case.

C. Concluding Remarks

As per usual among the proponents of the New Perspective, Wright rejects the notion of the "introspective conscience" in Pauline thinking. Paul did not struggle with an anguished mind and spirit before his conversion. Rather, he and the whole of Israel have lamented their corporate failures. This is what the theory of the ongoing exile implies (see above). Conversely, the proclaiming of the Gospel makes the difference: it insists that the end of the exile has already arrived in Jesus' cross and resurrection.[89]

---

recent advocates of this perspective often have taken into account. Dissatisfaction with the condition of Jerusalem and the Temple is not precisely the same as the theme of a continuing exile. And to view the exile as in some sense continuing is not the same as regarding 'all' of Israel as being in exile or estranged from God."

88 M. Seifrid, *Christ, Our Righteousness: Paul's Theology of Justification* (InterVarsity Press, 2000), 21–25.

89 Wright, *The People of God*, 268–79. See the well-known article by K. Stendahl, "The Apostle Paul and the Introspective Conscience of the West," *HTR* 56, no. 3 (1963): 199–215.

In truth, to shift from speaking of the burden of personal guilt to that of the nation is a mere variation on an older theme. It represents no real movement away from psychologism. "The Paul of the introspective conscience is ushered out the door," whereas "the Paul of the social conscience is welcomed in." Oddly, "an early twentieth-century existentialist Paul is replaced by a late twentieth-century Paul disturbed by the malaise of the world."[90]

Even worse: the compulsive need to explain the majority of the Jewish texts through the category of the ongoing exile characterizes that kind of interpretation to a great extent as artificial, as if practically the whole Jewish religion simply were an abject fiasco and in dire need of the reparation kit of the arising Christianity! Wright pushes through his theory whenever he thinks it feasible. When not, then he speaks of exceptions. Alternatively, he speaks of a double return from exile, underlining that the first one is not a true one. In addition, he confuses the idea of exile with that of the Diaspora, bondage, and the non-restoration of Israel (see above). Finally, he asserts that he has confirmed his main thesis as much as possible: Since Israel lives in exile she has failed.

Surprisingly, Wright's New Perspective is increasingly coming to resemble the outdated old perspective. The common denominator is the exaggerated proclivity to represent the Jewish religion as a failure which paves the way for the definite triumph of Christianity. Previously, the focus was laid on works-righteousness (with basically no sense for God's grace). This time, the emphasis is placed on the life in exile (with principally no sense for any relief). In both cases a flagrant distortion of the facts follows.[91]

It is no longer possible to discuss Wright's interpretation of the Pauline doctrine on justification. In part, it seems to be determined by his theory of Israel still being in exile. At least some anomalies in his overall thinking are easier to

---

90 Seifrid, "Blind Alleys," 90–91.

91 Wright refers frequently to O. H. Steck, *Israel und das gewaltsame Geschick der Propheten: Untersuchungen zur Überlieferung des deuteronomistischen Geschichtsbildes im Alten Testament, Spätjudentum und Urchristentum* (Neukirchener Verlag, 1967). He writes: "The fundamental study for this remains that of O. H. Steck, and I suspect from some of the reactions to further presentations of the theme that his work has remained unread" (*Faithfulness*, 139). But does Steck's notion of an ongoing exile in the end represent the *old* perspective on Judaism, something that Wright uncritically has adopted? The former writes in his book: "Die Gegenwart ist bestimmt von der Andauer des Gerichts, von der Andauer der Schuld des Volkes und von Umkehr und Gesetzesgehorsam als dem einzig möglichen Weg zu Jahwe" (203) and: "[. . .] muss es darum auch immer Verkündigung gegeben haben, die sich auf das vorfindliche Israel im ganzen richtete, es zur Umkehr aufrief, zum Gehorsam mahnte und darüber belehrte, was der Gebotswille Gottes ist. Entsprechend sind wir [. . .] immer wieder auf den Vorgang solcher Umkehrpredigt und Gesetzesbelehrung im Volk gestossen" (215–16). Similar passages are to be found also elsewhere. They outline the central thesis of the whole book (cf. 64–80). See also O. H. Steck, "Das Problem theologischer Strömungen in nachexilischer Zeit," *EvT* 28 (1968): 445–58.

get across on that basis. For instance, he affirms that justification first and foremost is a declaration of status ("you are already in"), but not ultimately a declaration of entrance ("welcome in"), as if the question is of living in the Promised Land or outside of it.[92] Likewise, Wright asserts that justification is twofold and presupposes also "the work of the Spirit," as if he is thinking of the new life in the Promised Land including the readiness to accomplish basic obligations in various conditions and circumstances therein.[93] Moreover, Wright speaks of the future justification and maintains that it is on account of the entire life, as if he is imagining a continued existence in the Promised Land.[94]

In any case, the cornerstone of Wright's theological position is his well-known theory of the ongoing exile. The foundering of his main thesis together with the critical remarks against his interpretation of "works of the Law" as "badges of identity" and his neglect of synergistic propensities in Judaism (see above)—all this calls into question the credibility of his overall view.

4. J. M. G. Barclay

A. Diverse Graces—Different Meanings

Recently, J. M. G. Barclay has made an important contribution to the present-day debate. He has studied the occurrence and meaning of the different words for "gift" in the sociopolitical context of the Greco-Roman and Jewish frames of reference. Within that wider perspective, he then situates the Pauline teaching on grace. His thorough exegetical analyses provide the basis for taxonomy of theologies of God's mercy.[95]

Barclay suggests that gift can be "perfected" (or drawn out into some essential or ultimate form) in a number of ways. He enumerates six perfections as follows:

(1) superabundance: the extravagance and the overwhelming scale of the gift;

(2) singularity: the attitude of the giver as marked solely and purely by benevolence and including no punishment for evil;

92 Wright, *What Saint Paul Really Said*, 139, 157.

93 Wright, *What Saint Paul Really Said*, 128–30, 159–79. See also his *Justification: God's Plan and God's Vision* (SPCK 2009), 122–24, 158–68.

94 Ibid. It is in this light I understand what Seifrid once wrote to me in an email: "I do think that there is a subtle connection between 'return from exile' and Wright's conception of justification—and his eschatology: it pictures redemption in terms of the transformation of the present world and opens the door to the minimizing of the final judgment that appears in Wright's thought."

95 See Barclay, *Paul and the Gift*.

(3) priority: the timing of the gift always before the recipient's initiative;
(4) incongruity: the bestowal of the gift without any regard to the worth of the recipient;
(5) efficacy: the impact of the gift on the nature or agency of the recipient; and
(6) non-circularity: no expected return for the gift, no cycle of reciprocity.[96]

As a result, "gift" is a polyvalent symbol. One does not necessarily have all six definitions in mind when using the word.[97] Definitely, there may be more perfections of gift. Still, no single one of them should be regarded as *conditio sine qua non*. Each has its own worth. Hence, it need not be completed by other meanings.[98] Nor is it the case that the more perfections various ancient texts have the better off they are.[99]

Further, Barclay claims that scholars often talk past each other by sharpening and perfecting gift or grace in one way but not making any allowance for another way of sharpening and perfecting gift or grace. He does his very best to avoid that kind of dichotomy which derails academic debate from the outset. Thus he provides a stable foundation for moving forward to an in-depth analysis of the ancient texts.[100]

In view of his methodology, Barclay is at the same time both strong and weak. As a specialist in New Testament theology and a professional scholar in the academic world, he is certainly a competent judge for his case. Yet he follows a similar procedure that has turned out to be problematic at least since the publication of G. Kittel's standard dictionary *Theologisches Wörterbuch zum Neuen Testament*. All entries there are written approaching—if possible—first the secular Greek literature, then the Old Testament as well as other Jewish sources, and after that finally relevant New Testament writings. This kind of reading runs the obvious risk of imposing an external model on the analysis of target texts (the canonical books). They should be interpreted related to their own defining characteristics.[101]

In the case of Barclay, he starts with some insights into cultural anthropology. Then he proceeds to the ancient Greco-Roman literature and analyzes most of it with discernment. Next, he surveys selected Jewish writings. In his inquiries, he principally concentrates on the concept of "gift" while examining

96 Barclay, *Paul and the Gift*, 70–75, 185–86 (for the concept of "perfection," see 67–68).
97 Barclay, *Paul and the Gift*, 75–76.
98 Barclay, *Paul and the Gift*, 68–70, 76–77.
99 Barclay, *Paul and the Gift*, 69–70.
100 Barclay, *Paul and the Gift*, 67–70.
101 See *TWNT* I–X/2, ed. G. Kittel (Kohlhammer, 1933–).

the Pauline teaching on grace. Barclay works as if he is making a long entry in Kittel's *Theologisches Wörterbuch*. He seems to paint with a broad brush and creates a wonderful canvas or an enchanting illustration in which the whole sequence from the distant past to the New Testament times and even across church history makes sense.[102] The question is whether the content is rendered everywhere as accurately as possible.

B. The Pauline Teaching on Grace

As to the Pauline teaching on grace, Barclay emphasizes particularly the idea of incongruity but also the subjects of superabundance, priority, and efficacy.[103] What he writes appears predominantly sound, so there is no need to go into the details. However, it seems that none of his six perfections of *gift* in truth depicts the Pauline notion of *grace*. Barclay himself properly delineates the exceptional understanding of God's mercy primarily in Romans and Galatians. His exegetical analysis is helpful in its basic outline. He affirms that "grace effects a new reality" that is "no ordinary existence, but the product of an impossibility, the resurrection of Christ." Hence, it is "a life whose source lies outside of themselves [Christians], the life of the risen Christ." In other words, it "is not some reformation of the self, or some newly discovered technique in self-mastery." On the contrary, it is rather an "eccentric" phenomenon or an "extrinsic" incident.[104] Further, it "is permanently at odds with the natural (post-Adamic) condition of the human being," no matter how much some Christians "may (and should) grow in holiness." Their inner "capacity depends on a transformation of the self or, better, a *new* self, derived from the risen Christ."[105] They do not achieve "a series of 'graces' won by increases in sanctification." Neither do they acquire a set of "competencies added to their previous capacities, nor an enhancement of their previous selves." To be brief: what is given to them "is a death and the emergence from that death of a new self."[106]

Overall and in most of its detail, the analysis of Barclay is straight to the point. However, it is so much the worse for his main thesis. How is that?

In view of the Pauline definition and interpretation of God's amazing grace, all other perfections of gifts outside the new reality, present in the risen Christ alone, fall short since they actually do not alter the human conditions and circumstances radically and completely but only improve them more or less. Then nothing has been changed ultimately, even though there are improvements of different kinds. No real transformation has taken place. The old life and the

102 Cf. Barclay's definition of his task in *Paul and the Gift*, 77–78.

103 Barclay, *Paul and the Gift*, 569.

104 Barclay, *Paul and the Gift*, 500–501.

105 Barclay, *Paul and the Gift*, 503.

106 Barclay, *Paul and the Gift*, 518.

old being are still the same in the midst of religious reformation agendas and programs. Thus a general divine benevolence, discovered in the many-faceted forms of gifts, does not make any difference. It does not precisely amount to the special divine grace as substantiated in Pauline theology. They are not strictly on a par with each other. The soteriological focus moves from the reparation of the old self in the former case to the rebirth of the new self in the latter case. For that reason, the gift in Greco-Roman culture can never replace in Pauline theology God's grace, which alone brings forth a totally new existence in contrast to the conventional old way of being and living.

The transformation of reality is centered on the "Christ-event" (his death and resurrection), not elsewhere, irrespective of how much talk there is about a general divine benevolence. Once again, in line with Barclay, it is apparently neither about "a narrative progression in human history" nor "an additional chapter in a developing human story." It is "no process of maturation" nor any series of "preceding epochs of human history," but more accurately "the *reversal* of previous human conditions." On the contrary, it "represents not continuity, but interruption," even "miracle"—indeed, "a new creation in the midst of the present evil age."[107] In brief: it is an "impossibility"[108] that surprisingly turns into a possibility and reality. Hence, it is "not a goal yet to be attained or a favor yet to be gained from God."[109] It already exists in the risen Lord.

On the whole, after having dusted down the fundamentals and distinctive understanding of grace in Pauline theology, Barclay astonishingly concludes as follows:

> It would be a mistake to regard the incongruity of grace as ubiquitous in Judaism, but equally wrong to consider this notion uniquely Pauline. Paul's is one Jewish voice in a chorus of divergent opinions, distinctive in certain respects, but not qualitatively or quantitatively *more distinct* than the voices of other Jews. Paul stands *among* fellow Jews in his discussion of divine grace, not *apart from* them in a unique or antithetical position.[110]

The quotation shows a blatant *non sequitur* compared with what Barclay in his exegetical analysis has brought forward. Here the nonbiblical taxonomy of *gifts* is imposed on the understanding of *grace* in Pauline theology, and the meaning of grace is reduced to one sense of gift, namely, to that of incongruity. The conclusion is neither justified nor substantiated in any way. Clearly, the evidence points in another direction. It results rather in the conclusion that none of the six perfections of gifts encompasses the Pauline definition of grace. This absolutely ruins the entire taxonomy used by Barclay in his investigation. But

107 Barclay, *Paul and the Gift*, 412–13.
108 Barclay, *Paul and the Gift*, 421.
109 Barclay, *Paul and the Gift*, 446.
110 Barclay, *Paul and the Gift*, 565.

he still remains stuck in his own categories without perceiving that they do not work in the soteriological matrix of Romans and Galatians. The methodological flaw, like that in Kittel's *Theologisches Wörterbuch* (see above), has caught up with him. To repeat: not even the incongruous perfection of the gift as recognized in the sociopolitical context of the Greco-Roman and Jewish frames of reference does justice to the Pauline concept of grace which assumes a totally new reality extrinsic to special human efforts and general divine benevolences (as more completely specified above).

By and large, the necessity of a totally new reality in the risen Christ makes all the definitions or perfections of gifts depending on human cooperation many-faceted divine benevolences. Therefore, the Pauline understanding of grace really makes the difference. It does not fit into a straitjacket of modern exegetical taxonomy taken from the sociopolitical context of the Greco-Roman and Jewish culture. Barclay affirms that the idea of the "pure gift" is a late interpretation. He does not find any traces of it in his ancient texts.[111] That may be right. (I have to leave it to the experts to resolve.) But at least the notion of "pure *grace*" does occur as an essential element in Pauline theology. It takes the form of a new creation, an extrinsic existence in the risen Christ. As such it is absolutely independent of any human efforts, even though a response certainly is expected or intended in return.

Oddly, it seems that Barclay's taxonomy of perfections of gifts does not have any sense for synergism in a soteriological setting. At the very least, he intentionally circumvents that kind of speech.[112] Instead, pretty much everything is labeled as a perfection of God's grace. The obvious methodological tendency of Barclay sticks out especially in the question of the Pelagian controversy. He asserts that both Augustine and Pelagius (and those in favor of his position) agree "in their emphasis on the priority of grace."[113] The latter "clearly believed in the *priority* and *superabundance* of grace."[114] However, the former insisted upon the *priority*, *incongruity*, and *efficacy* of grace.[115] Thus the controversy between them was in fact about different perfections of grace. The traditional question of synergism is conspicuous by its absence. Moreover, there is no clear-cut explanation for the shift in focus.[116] To be sure, old theological disputes are open to modern and fresh interpretations. That in itself is a good thing. But how can it be that Pelagius and his spiritual followers, who were declared heretics (by

---

111 Barclay, *Paul and the Gift*, 59–63, 66.

112 Quite strangely, it seems that Barclay only addresses the issue of synergism while criticizing me and others for making use of "the terminology of the Reformation tradition" (*Paul and the Gift*, 168–69).

113 Barclay, *Paul and the Gift*, 92.

114 Barclay, *Paul and the Gift*, 93.

115 Barclay, *Paul and the Gift*, 97.

116 Barclay, *Paul and the Gift*, 92–97.

the First Council of Ephesus in AD 431) because of their synergism, are unexpectedly the ones who have "perfected" God's grace in their own way? Why the need to condemn them at all then? It seems, at the least, Barclay owes a clarification to his readers. He does not pursue his investigation through to the end.

Even so, Barclay's clear statement of the impossibility of the "pure" gift is evidence for the synergistic thinking which permeates Greco-Roman and Jewish theology, something that he repeatedly shows in his analysis. In this respect, he fully agrees with the other main proponents of the New Perspective, particularly with Sanders, Dunn, and Wright (see above). Despite all differences in their overall position, they share at least one common denominator: they take for granted that Jewish soteriology without a doubt indicates a strong synergistic feature. On the other hand, the Pauline understanding of divine grace radically differs from that tendency. It is not based on human efforts or cooperation (as already recurrently recognized above). Salvation is found in the risen Lord, in a reality called into being through the Gospel, in an existence extrinsic to oneself. In brief: it is an impossible possibility, an exceptional life, where truly "it is no longer I who live, but Christ who lives in me" (Gal. 2:20). As a result, it necessarily ushers in a breakdown of Jewish soteriology.[117]

C. Beyond the New Perspective?

In his conclusions, Barclay regards his special contribution as going beyond the New Perspective, in other words as "a reconfiguration of 'the new perspective,' placing its best historical and exegetical insights within the frame of Paul's theology of grace."[118] His analysis of "works of the Law," a central issue in Pauline theology and absolutely decisive for the overall view of Dunn and Wright as already shown above, serves particularly well as a test case for his self-evaluation.

Right from the outset, Barclay emphasizes that works of the Law refer to the practice of the Jewish Law. The expression is, for certain, Pauline shorthand. It echoes the scriptural commands to "do" the Torah.[119] But even so, "what is significant is not the bare fact of practices (and thus not 'works' as such) but that they derive from, and are oriented to, the Torah." Palpably, the Gentile mission

117 To be sure, "Paul does not have to play the agency of the believer off against the agency of Christ/the Spirit" (Barclay, *Paul and the Gift*, 518). "God's grace does not exclude, deny, or displace believing agents; they are not reduced to passivity or pure receptivity" (ibid., 519). Cf. also 503 n. 17. Nevertheless, it is true that Paul lives only since Christ lives in him (Gal. 2:20), or he lives together with Christ only after having been put to death together with him (Rom. 6:4). In this sense, the real agent is indeed Christ (*pace* Barclay). See above 5.2.

118 Barclay, *Paul and the Gift*, 573. On the other hand, Barclay regards his special input "as a re-contextualization of the Augustinian-Lutheran tradition, returning the dynamic of the incongruity of grace to its original environment where it accompanied the formation of new communities" (ibid.).

119 Barclay, *Paul and the Gift*, 373–74.

threw some works into special relief (e.g., circumcision and dietary regulations). Yet "there is no reason to restrict the referent of ἔργα νόμου" principally to "those rules that created boundaries between Jews and Gentiles (*pace* Dunn)." Rather, "the issue is the validity of the Torah" in defining and establishing righteousness. Then "it becomes clear" that the real question is about "the practice of the Torah as though it were the authoritative cultural frame of the good news."[120]

Despite his stout criticism of works as mere "identity markers," Barclay still shares Dunn's conviction that the major shift in the interpretation of ἔργα νόμου "may be traced in the deutero-Pauline letters, where works are refocused as moral achievements" (Eph. 2:8–10; 2 Tim. 1:9; Titus 3:5).[121] Neither does boasting indicate "the cultural confidence of the Jew in the Torah (or of the Greek in wisdom), but pride in achievement" (Eph. 2:9).[122] Concisely, the previous apostolic missionary theology is now "turned inwards."[123]

Principally, Barclay's critique of the practice of the Torah as "the authoritative cultural frame of the good news" derives from his downplaying of synergism in Jewish soteriology. Therefore, he has to find other reasons for the apostolic disapproval of works of the Law. Despite the fact that he explains his reading of the Pauline texts at length, the exact meaning of his interpretation remains vague. It leaves the impression of unnecessary hairsplitting. In the end, how precisely does Barclay come to his conclusion that works of the Law express "the authoritative cultural frame of the good news" and should be discarded for that very reason? Elsewhere, I have argued that Paul in Galatians not only raises the requirement of a quantitatively but even of a qualitatively impeccable Law observance.[124] Thus he "maintains that those who rely on works of the law fail to do the works of the law!"[125] The question is simply about works as such. Accordingly, the severe denunciation is leveled against synergism in the so-called covenantal nomism.[126]

Evidently there is no alteration of the interpretation in the allegedly deutero-Pauline letters. The line of thought is similar everywhere in *corpus Paulinum*. For instance, Eph. 2:8–10 summarizes the theological substance in Romans and

---

120 Barclay, *Paul and the Gift*, 374, see also 444 and 567–68.

121 Barclay, *Paul and the Gift*, 571. Formerly, Barclay makes the following clarification: "What changes is not that a specific Pauline rule ('works of the Law') becomes generalized as 'works,' but that Paul's critique of the *criteria* of worth being applied in the formation of the community becomes a critique of the *achievement* of worth whose criteria, in an established Christian tradition, are themselves unproblematic" (see ibid., 546 n. 57).

122 Barclay, *Paul and the Gift*, 571.

123 Ibid.

124 Laato, "Paul's Anthropological Considerations," 353–59.

125 Laato, "Paul's Anthropological Considerations," 357.

126 Laato, "Paul's Anthropological Considerations," 359.

Galatians. It remains unmistakable that works of the Law stand for every kind of human striving and yearning in a soteriological context.

It follows that Barclay's analysis here fails to carry conviction.

5. Summary

All in all, considering soteriological issues, the most popular advocates of the New Perspective to a large extent ignore the principal importance of anthropology in that context. To be sure, they do agree and admit that Judaism is synergistic. Yet they try to downplay their observation one way or another. This is true in the cases of E. P. Sanders, J. D. G. Dunn, N. T. Wright, and J. M. G. Barclay.

It seems that strong synergistic facets in Judaism are regarded as problematic because they easily explain why Paul disregarded his former Pharisaic past. As a result, many alternative ways of expounding his conversion, advocated by the representatives of the New Perspective, fail to carry conviction or fall short as an overall account of it. Dunn especially raises the question of synergistic inclinations in Pauline theology but wisely rejects them in the end. Those outdated and old-fashioned (in the deepest sense heretical) accusations hardly fit the image of the New Perspective.

It follows that an anthropological approach is surpassed neither by a Christocentric nor an ethnocentric reading of Pauline theology—important as they are in themselves. Works of the Law are not eradicated simply for the reason that they are not based on Christ (*pace* Sanders) or that they are based on ethnic privileges (*pace* in the first place Dunn and Wright). On the contrary, they are abandoned because they are human efforts (for certain, not to the exclusion of divine grace) to guarantee one's own salvation. Therefore, different anthropological presuppositions lead to different soteriological conclusions. A correlation exists between them both. Paul emphasizes the necessity of becoming an entirely new creature. He promotes a life outside of oneself, attained in the risen Christ alone. In view of that, all various definitions of gifts in the sociopolitical context of the Greco-Roman and Jewish culture and all divine benevolences perfected in them do not prevail. They do not actually do justice to the meaning in Pauline theology of pure grace, which stands out as a unique masterpiece in the midst of the ancient religious world (*pace* Barclay).

Besides, the theory of Israel's ongoing exile as the black background of the New Testament proclamation of salvation in the risen Lord is to be rejected (*contra* Wright).

When all is said and done, the fact still remains that the Jewish soteriology was synergistic despite divine benevolences and compassion in the covenantal context. For sure, also the most acknowledged advocates of the New Perspective admit it, although not showing a lot of enthusiasm for the result. It seems that it is time for a new opening in research.

6. The New Quest for Paul

A. Initial Observations

For many decades, the so-called New Perspective on Paul has dominated the academic research. Sometimes the impression is given that there are no longer any alternatives: "They have spoken; the matter is settled." I doubt that. The New Perspective has run its course. It has failed to explain Paul's break with Judaism. It is far from the final word on the issue. The confrontation with the prominent proponents of the New Perspective has shown the deplorable state of affairs. The discussion has to be continued on a wider scale. Apparently, there is a need for a wholly new quest for Paul.

As shown above, Barclay has outlined a feasible sketch of Pauline soteriology as an "impossible possibility" that turns into a reality in the risen Lord. However, he has not drawn the urgent conclusions from his own presentation. His overall understanding of the textual evidence does not do full justice to the data. His exegetical analyses actually usher in another kind of result.

B. The Basics in the Overall Pauline Understanding of the "Christ-Event"

The necessity of becoming a new creature and obtaining a true life outside of oneself in the risen Christ alone has an impact on Paul's understanding of his own Pharisaic past or any other form of Jewish religiosity. In other words, his emphasis lies on "writing the law on the heart" of believers (Jer. 31:33) and "putting God's Spirit" (Ezek. 36:27) in them. He draws attention to the many Old Testament visions of re-creation, regeneration, resuscitation, resurrection, and revitalization.[127] They are the characteristics of the messianic era. Hence, they are a reality in the presence of the Messiah. Since it is all about a new mode of existence, there is no room for the old manner of living as Jews truthfully try to do what is written in the Torah. All the same, they still do it "in flesh" and in reliance on their innate moral power.

Accordingly, the dominion of sin is not broken by the Mosaic Law but eschatologically through Christ's salvific death and resurrection in the majestic power of the Spirit. Strictly, the opposite of wrongdoing is not right doing. We all know

127 See T. Laato, *The New Quest for Paul and His Reading of the Old Testament: The Contrast Between the "Letter" and the "Spirit" in 2 Corinthians 3:1–18* (1517 Publishing, 2023), 44–68.

too well that vices cannot simply be replaced by virtues. It never functions like that in practice. Astonishingly, to be "under sin" and to be "under law" are ultimately synonymous (Rom. 6:14). More to the point, the opposite of transgression is the union with Christ and, in him, the defeat of all evil's supremacy because of the subsequent empowering of the Spirit in the new life of Christians. They have died to the Law in order to fulfill it in love and charity. Paradoxically, their one step back is their one step forward. Quite clearly, the baptismal parenesis of chapter 6 lies behind the exhortatory composition in 12:1–2. As Christians are advised to offer themselves—respectively, their members—to God as weapons of righteousness (6:13, 19), so they are admonished to offer their bodies to God as living sacrifices (12:1). In both texts, the verb is the same (παριστάνω and/or παρίστημι). The object of the verb is similar: in the former case, the persons themselves or their members; in the latter case, their bodies. In other words, the reign of sin in one's life has not been annulled ever since the promulgation of the Mosaic Law but on account of the change of rule, commenced in Baptism. From then on, Christ exerts total control of Christians and bestows his Spirit on them. Therefore, they are truly transformed.[128]

As a result, Paul concludes that unbelieving Jews absolutely do not comply with the Law. He maintains that they transgress it. He denounces them as great sinners like everyone else. In consequence, they are without exception bound to fail. It is indeed about a total failure. To say this is not to say that old-fashioned and outdated distortions (or conscious falsifications) of the Jewish religion in exegetical research in the end prove right. Absolutely not; they should never come back to the agenda of modern scholarship.[129] Still, Paul puts himself at odds with any kind of Judaism. On purpose, he moves into a frontal collision with it in his reading of the Old Testament. He speaks for a new mode of existence. That is why his break with Judaism remains an invincible obstacle.

C. The Contrast Between the "Letter" and the "Spirit"

In addition, the contrast between the "letter" and the "Spirit" (see especially 2 Cor. 3:6) sheds light on Paul's break with Judaism as a whole. It substantiates his totally different way of thinking "outside the box." Elsewhere, I have analyzed the difference more in-depth.[130] Here, some highlights will suffice.

The "letter" simply denotes the Mosaic Law, especially as a compilation of various legal records that should be read and observed very strictly in punctilious

128 See especially T. Laato, "Crucified with Christ and the New Life of Christians: Romans 6:1–14 (and 15–23) Revisited," in *Fri och bunden: En bok om teologisk antropologi*, ed. J. Hellberg, R. Imberg, T. Johansson, Församlingsfakultetens skriftserie 13 (Församlingsförlaget, 2013), 103, 123–24.

129 See above, chapter 2.

130 See Laato, *The New Quest for Paul.*

accordance with their literal meaning. It does not call for the pouring out of the Spirit or the divine writing of the Torah on human hearts that will take (or has already taken) place in the new covenant, as written in Jer. 31:31–34 and Ezek. 36:26–27. Jews follow the letter of the Torah. They try to do whatever is prescribed in the Pentateuch. Their religious zeal focuses on the literal meaning of the written texts and pushes for unconditional devotion. Therefore, they do not (necessarily) leave out of account inner motives for their good works. They really try to do their very best to do what they should. Nevertheless, their moral efforts largely remain from a position of their own ability and activity. The characteristics of the new covenant, namely, "writing the law on their hearts" (Jer. 31:33) and "putting God's Spirit in them" (Ezek. 36:27), are missing. Hence, the Jewish religiosity refers back to human capacity and leads to boasting. As a Pharisee, Saul did not "boast in Christ Jesus" but rather about himself. He put his "confidence in the flesh" and did not trust in his Lord (Phil. 3:3–9). In the churches of Galatia, Judaizers likewise boasted about themselves and tried to convince Christians to rely upon their own flesh in terms of circumcision (Gal. 3:1–5; 5:1–6; 6:12–15). Further, Jews boast about their superiority in comparison with Gentiles and yearn for praise from God. In their vanity, they heavily lean on their obedience to the Law even though they transgress his will (Rom. 2:17–29). For sure, Saul before his conversion, Judaizers, and Jews in general provide here the warning examples of those who do not fulfill the Law.[131]

In contrast, the Christian existence does not depend on attempts to work for one's own devout religiosity in severe adherence to the Mosaic Law. Instead, it harks back to God's stunning and sovereign re-creation out of nothing (*ex nihilo*). He makes his light shine on repentant sinners "in the face of Jesus Christ" (2 Cor. 4:6). He shows his mercy upon them without any merits from their side. Jer. 31:31–34 and Ezek. 36:26–27 are fulfilled in them as they believe the Gospel. Just at that moment, they become alive. Immediately, they also start to live their life and follow the Law, not according to the "letter" but explicitly in Spirit.[132]

Accordingly, Paul does mean that Christians fulfill the whole Law. But he does not expect that they fulfill the whole Law rigorously or categorically according to the Jewish norms or standards. Rather, they have circumcised their mind and self, not only a small part of their flesh (Rom. 2:26–29; Phil. 3:3). They are circumcised in their hearts or in their entire being. Similarly, they offer their bodies, instead of sheep or goats, as living sacrifices to God (Rom. 12:1–2). Paul even speaks of his own violent death as a drink offering (Phil. 2:17), the

131 For the Pauline passages, see above, chapter 6. The Jewish boasting amounts not only to a national pride. It is more about a moral superiority. Further, see Laato, *The New Quest for Paul*, 119–20.

132 Laato, *The New Quest for Paul*, 119–25 *et passim*.

pouring out of his blood at the end of his sacrificial service as an apostle. To top it off, Christians fulfill the whole Law in love as they live their life in the Spirit (Rom. 13:8–10; Gal. 5:14).[133]

Remarkably, Paul nowhere affirms that the several Mosaic commandments are reduced to one single commandment of love. He does not simply ignore or disregard them as redundant. Rather, he transposes them all into practice with immediate effect: he maintains that the whole Law is truly fulfilled in genuine love of neighbor (Rom. 13:8–10; Gal. 5:14). Neither does Paul affirm anywhere that the cultic aspects have become passé whereas the moral precepts remain valid. Instead, he insists that Christians are circumcised, and they offer themselves as living sacrifices and undertake the temple service, though they do not carry out any of it exactly to the letter but in Spirit.[134]

As a consequence, a fresh insight into the contrast between the "letter" and the "Spirit" opens up. The modern distinction between the literal (or verbatim) and nonliteral (or metaphorical) meaning has not a lot to offer here. The differentiation between the conservative and liberal interpretation has even less to bring to the table. No doubt, Paul thinks in an innovative way. He does believe in the Scriptures. Nowhere does he suggest that they could be annulled (cf. Rom. 3:4; 9:6). Quite the opposite, he maintains that "*whatever* was written in former days was written for our instruction" (Rom. 15:4). That concerns truly everything, for instance, the decree on circumcision, the rules for temple service, and the tiny principle of "not muzzling the ox as it threshes the grain (1 Cor. 9:9). However, nothing of that should be fulfilled "in flesh" or according to the "letter," but "in Spirit" or through faith that shows itself in love. The two alternatives, the Jewish and the Pauline, exclude each other. Paradoxically, they both represent a word-for-word reading. We might speak of the "literal-letteral" and "literal-spiritual" study of the Old Testament Scripture. Even if they function on totally different levels, they both are pragmatic and realistic. The former exemplifies knowledge that is based on human understanding, while the latter epitomizes knowledge that is based on divine understanding. In other words, the former Jewish alternative relates to life "in flesh," while the latter Pauline alternative pertains to life "in Spirit." Ultimately, the pivotal issue turns on the question whether to read the Old Testament according to the "literal-letteral" or "literal-spiritual" sense. In both options, firm trust and strong confidence in Scripture prevails.[135]

In keeping with his conviction, Paul seems to work on the assumption that since the Law is written on the *hearts* in the course of the new covenant, it is indeed no longer observed in the "*flesh*," and since the *Spirit* is poured out in the

133 Laato, *The New Quest for Paul*, 108–19.

134 Laato, *The New Quest for Paul*, 118–19.

135 Laato, *The New Quest for Paul*, 122.

hearts of Christians, their obedience is no more bound to the "*letter*" of the Law. As a consequence, it turns out that he succeeds in "Christianizing" his preceding Pharisaic ideal to extend the purity rules of the clergy to pertain to an ordinary person's daily life. His theological persuasion already introduced a sort of universal priesthood in the church.[136]

Without doubt, the current discussion could be extended still more, though it would scarcely add much to the ensuing outcomes. Suffice it to say that some parts of the Mosaic Law exclusively relate to Christ and the Christological creed of the early church. He alone is the offering for the sins of the world (for instance, see Rom. 8:3; 2 Cor. 5:21). He alone is the bloody sacrifice on the Day of Atonement that is sprinkled on the atonement cover (or "mercy seat") in the Most Holy Place (Rom. 3:25). He alone is the Passover Lamb who has been slaughtered on the cross (1 Cor. 5:7) even if Christians are exhorted to get rid of the "old leaven" and become "a new lump" and keep the Jewish ritual and feast, "not with the old leaven, the leaven of malice and evil, but with the unleavened bread of sincerity and truth" (1 Cor. 5:7–8). Adding this and that—it would not alter or change the undeniable fact that the new covenant does not abolish "the Law or the Prophets" but fulfills them. Truly, nothing will "pass from the Law" until "all is accomplished" (cf. Matt. 5:17–18). In Pauline theology, the goal is not reached in the sphere of the flesh according to the "literal-letteral" meaning of the Law. Instead, it will come to reality only through Christ in the sphere of the Spirit according to the "literal-spiritual" meaning of the Law. The Christians really fulfill the Law because they no longer stand under it. Since they once died from it, they always live in harmony with it. Paradoxically, continuity takes full effect as a result of discontinuity. The contrast between the "letter" and the "Spirit" gains importance just here.[137]

D. Conclusions

Often, the ambiguous approach to the Old Testament legislation in the context of the apostolic argumentation has been pressed into the separation between the moral and cultic law. Allegedly, the former remains valid, but the latter has become obsolete. The opposite poles of ethics and ritual ceremonies make the difference in understanding the contents as having permanent or impermanent value. Something of the kind proves to be prominent and provides much for the traditional differentiation between the two categories in the Christian Church. Without doubt, the distinction between the moral and cultic law accounts well for the practical consequences that pertain to the extension of certain definite parts of the Mosaic legislation into the New Testament period. However, Paul never says that explicitly. Neither does he suggest it. In contrast,

136 Laato, *The New Quest for Paul*, 123.
137 Laato, *The New Quest for Paul*, 138–39.

he overtly maintains that the prescription of circumcision and the precepts of sacrifices or temple service in general are fulfilled by Christians although they do not carry them out exactly to the letter.

The fresh insights into the antithesis between the "letter" and the "Spirit" as well as its various important implications to Pauline theology throw light on the parting of the ways between Christianity and Judaism. The process of separation of the two religions looks much more complicated than generally assumed. For certain, a brief exegetical study such as this does not track and trace the entire historical development. Nevertheless, the pulling apart of Paul from his Pharisaic past did not grow out of the naive and very simplistic notion that his previous beliefs were not his present faith. Allegedly, he rejected Judaism precisely because it was not Christianity.[138] Neither did he depreciate "the works of the Law" supposedly as "Jewish identity markers" (circumcision, Sabbath, kosher food or food regulations in general).[139] Nor did he pretend that the main failure of Israel amounts to an imaginary state of their ongoing exile.[140] All those speculative made-up interpretations (including some others) of the New Perspective fail to explain the core of the religious conflict or the bone of scriptural contention between Paul and Judaism. They are not radical enough. In a sense, they err on the side of caution. Evidently, the New Perspective has run its course. It should be laid to rest and rather leave the space for the New Quest that comprises the outcomes of the research at hand. Paul definitively breaks with Judaism and pulls down "the works of the Law" because he rejects the illusion of observing the Torah "in flesh" and according to the "literal-letteral" meaning of the text. He considers that kind of religious interest and pursuit as the worst form of human self-righteousness and self-praise (notwithstanding the efforts to true piety and absolute dedication). In terms of innate capacity and capability, there is no way out of the quandary and dilemma. The shortage of remedies promising any solution depends on the fact that the actuality and reality of the new covenant, namely, the writing of the Torah on hearts (Jer. 31:31–34) and the pouring out of the Spirit (Ezek. 36:26–27), are missing. Thus every hope for something better including even the last, desperate chance for change is doomed. It is all gone.

Hence, Paul's rejection of the works of the Law does not aim at a limitation of the works as Jewish identity markers or signs of national priority. He does not say anything about that kind of definition. It has been disastrously (mis)read into his writings. In his theology, the works of the Law *are* simply the works of the Law, namely, whatever is done out of obedience to the Torah. In a Christian context, they are excluded. For sure, Christians do fulfill the whole Mosaic Law.

138 *Pace* Sanders, *Paul and Palestinian Judaism*, 552.

139 *Pace* Dunn, "The New Perspective," 22–26.

140 *Pace* Wright, *Faithfulness*, 139–62.

Yet they fulfill it "in Spirit" and not "in flesh," in other words, according to the "literal-spiritual" and not "literal-letteral" meaning of Scripture. For that reason, they do not boost or bolster their self-righteousness and self-praise. Their good works show that they live a new life that has taken place in their inner being through the apostolic proclamation of the Gospel. They live in a new covenant where the Torah has been written in their hearts (Jer. 31:31–34) and the Spirit poured out in their souls (Ezek. 36:26–27). It makes all the difference. Christians have undergone a transformation in terms of re-creation, regeneration, resuscitation, resurrection, revitalization. The Spirit gives them life. He remains and reigns in them.

All in all, Paul shows a radical and innovative shift in his thinking. It carries weight and makes his break with Judaism unreconcilable. He really thinks "outside the box." Because the New Perspective has failed to explain the actual difference in the apostle's line of reasoning, the utter necessity for the New Quest for Paul becomes apparent.

ABBREVIATIONS AND WORKS CITED

The following abbreviations are used in this bibliography as taken from *The SBL Handbook of Style* and *Theologische Realenzyklopädie*.

AnBib	Analecta biblica
ANRW	*Aufstieg und Niedergang der römischen Welt: Geschichte und Kultur Roms im Spiegel der neueren Forschung*. Edited by H. Temporini and W. Haase. De Druyter, 1972–
ATANT	Abhandlungen zur Theologie des Alten und Neuen Testaments
BECNT	Baker Exegetical Commentary on the New Testament
BEvT	Beiträge zur evangelischen Theologie
BHT	Beiträge zur historischen Theologie
Bib	*Biblica*
BJS	Brown Judaic Studies
BNTC	Black's New Testament Commentaries
BTB	*Biblical Theology Bulletin*
BWANT	Beiträge zur Wissenschaft vom Alten und Neuen Testament
CBQ	*Catholic Biblical Quarterly*
CTQ	*Concordia Theological Quarterly*
EKKNT	*Evangelisch-katholischer Kommentar zum Neuen Testament*
EvT	*Evangelische Theologie*
EWNT	Exegetisches Wörterbuch zum Neuen Testament
FRLANT	Forschungen zur Religion und Literatur des Alten und Neuen Testaments
GTA	Göttinger theologischer Arbeiten
GUS	Göttinger Universitätsschriften
HNT	Handbuch zum Neuen Testament
HTKNT	Herders theologischer Kommentar zum Neuen Testament
HTR	*Harvard Theological Review*
ICC	International Critical Commentary
JBL	*Journal of Biblical Literature*
JQR	*Jewish Quarterly Review*
JSNT	*Journal for the Study of the New Testament*
JSNTSup	*Journal for the Study of the New Testament: Supplement Series*
JSHRZ	Jüdische Schriften aus hellenistisch-römischer Zeit
JTS	*Journal of Theological Studies*
Jud	*Judica*
KD	*Kerygma und Dogma*
KEK	Kritische-exegetischer Kommentar über das Neue Testament (Meyer-Kommentar)
KNT	Kommentar zum Neuen Testament

LCL	Loeb Classical Library
MTZ	*Münchener theologische Zeitschrift*
NICNT	New International Commentary on the New Testament
NIGTC	The New International Greek Testament Commentary
NKB	Nobels Kulturbibliothek
NovT	*Novum Testamentum*
NovTSup	Supplements to Novum Testamentum
NTAbh	Neutestamentliche Abhandlungen
NTD	Neue Testament Deutsch
NTS	*New Testament Studies*
RGG	*Religion in Geschichte und Gegenwart*. 3rd ed. Edited by K. Galling. 7 vols. J. C. B. Mohr, 1957–65
RelSRev	*Religious Studies Review*
SBLDS	Society of Biblical Literature Dissertation Series
SEÅ	*Svensk exegetisk årsbok*
SIESÅA	Skrifter utgivna av Institutet för ekumenik och socialetik vid Åbo Akademi
SJT	*Scottish Journal of Theology*
SNTSMS	Society for New Testament Studies Monograph Series
SNTSU	*Studien zum Neuen Testament und seiner Umwelt*
ST	*Studia theologica*
STK	*Svensk teologisk kvartalskrift*
TAik	*Teologinen Aikakauskirja*
TBei	*Theologische Beiträge*
THKNT	Theologischer Handkommentar zum Neuen Testament
ThSt	Theologische Studien
TLZ	*Theologische Literaturzeitung*
TNT	Tolkning av Nya Testamentet
TQ	*Theologische Quartalschrift*
TRE	*Theologische Realenzyklopädie*. Edited by G. Krause and G. Müller. De Gruyter, 1977–
TWNT	*Theologische Wörterbuch zum Neuen Testament*. Edited by G. Kittel and G. Friedrich. Kohlhammer, 1932–79
TZ	*Theologische Zeitschrift*
TynBul	*Tyndale Bulletin*
UTB	Uni-Taschenbücher
WBC	Word Biblical Commentary
WMANT	Wissenschaftliche Monographien zum Alten und Neuen Testament
WUNT	Wissenschaftliche Untersuchungen zum Neuen Testament
ZBK	Zürcher Bibelkommentare
ZNW	*Zeitschrift für die neutestamentliche Wissenschaft*
ZTK	*Zeitschrift für Theologie und Kirche*

Publications by the same author are arranged chronologically with those published in the same year indicated by distinguishing lowercase letters.

Aids, Text Editions, and Translations

The Apocrypha and Pseudepigrapha of the Old Testament in English: With Introductions and Critical and Explanatory Notes to the Several Books. Edited by R. H. Charles. 2 vols. Clarendon Press, 1963–64 (= 1913).

Biblia Hebraica Stuttgartensia editio funditus renovata. Edited by K. Elliger and W. Rudolph. Deutsche Bibelstiftung, 1977.

Die Lehren des Judentums nach den Quellen. Edited by W. Homolka. Vol. 1. Wissenschaftliche Buchgesellschaft, 1999.

Josephus. With an English translation by H. St. J. Thackeray, R. Marcus, A. Wikgren, and L. H. Feldman. 9 vols. LCL. Heinemann, 1956–69.

Konkordanz zum Novum Testamentum Graece von Nestle-Aland, 26. Auflage und zum Greek New Testament, 3rd edition. Edited by Institut für neutestamentliche Textforschung and the Rechenzentrum der Universität Münster with special assistance from H. Bachmann and W. A. Slaby. De Gruyter, 1987.

Mekhilta according to Rabbi Ishmael: An Analytical Translation. Translated by J. Neusner. 2 vols. Scholars Press, 1988.

Mekilta de-Rabbi Ishmael. A critical edition on the basis of the manuscripts and early editions with an English translation, introduction, and notes by J. Z. Lauterbach. 3 vols. Jewish Publication Society, 1976 (= 1933–35).

Mishna S. *Talmud*.

The Talmudic Anthology: Tales and Teachings of the Rabbis, a Collection of Parables, Folktales, Fables, Aphorisms, Epigrams, Sayings, Anecdotes, Proverbs, and Exegetical Interpretations. Edited by L. J. Newman and S. Spitz. Behrman House, 1947.

Novum Testamentum Graece. 26th ed. Post Eb. Nestle et E. Nestle communicter ediderunt K. Aland, M. Black, C. M. Martini, B. M. Metzger, A. Wikgren. Deutsche Bibelgesellschaft, 1979.

Philo. With an English translation by F. H. Colson and G. H. Whitaker. 10 vols and 2 supplementary vols. LCL. Heinemann, 1929–63.

Septuaginta: Id est Vetus Testamentum Graece iuxta LXX interpretes. Edited by A. Rahlfs. 2 vols. Deutsche Bibelgesellschaft, 1979.

Siddur. The Hirsch Siddur: The Order of Prayers for the Whole Year. Translation and commentary by S. R. Hirsch. New (2nd) ed. Feldheim, 1978.

Sifra. Halachischer Midrasch zu Leviticus. Translated by J. Winter. Münz, 1938.

Siphre [Sifre] ad Deuteronomium. H. S. Horovitzii schedis usus cum variis lectionibus et adnotationibus. 2nd ed. Edited by L. Finkelstein. New York, 1969 (= 1939).

Sifre to Deuteronomy: An Analytical Translation. Translated by J. Neusner. 2 vols. Scholars Press, 1987.

Sifré to Numbers: An American Translation and Explanation. Translated by J. Neusner. 2 vols. Scholars Press, 1986.

Siphre d'Be Rab: Fasciculus primus: Siphre ad Numeros adjecto Siphre zutta. Cum variis lectionibus et adnotationibus. Edited by H. S. Horovitz. Wahrmann Books, 1966 (= 1917).

Talmud. *Der babylonische Talmud I–IX. Mit Einschluss der vollstaendigen Mišnah; hrsg. nach der ersten, zensurfreien bombergschen Ausgabe (Venedig 1520–23), nebst Varianten der spaeteren, von S. Lorja, J. Berlin, J. Sirhes u.aa. rev. Ausgaben und der muenchener Talmudhandschrift, moeglichst sinn- und wortgetreu uebersetzt und mit kurzen Erklaerungen versehen von L. Goldschmidt.* Nijhoff, 1933–35.

Der Jerusalemische Talmud in seinen haggadischen Bestandtheilen. Translated into German for the first time by A. Wünsche. Olms, 1967 (= Zürich, 1880).

The Talmud of Babylonia: An American Translation.

I: Tractate Berakhot. Translated by J. Neusner. Scholars Press, 1984.

XXIX: Tractate Menahot I–III. Translated by J. Neusner. Scholars Press, 1991.

XXXVI: Tractate Niddah I–III. Translated by J. Neusner. Scholars Press, 1990.

The Tosefta: Translated from the Hebrew I–VI. Translated by J. Neusner. KTAV, 1977–86.

Secondary Literature

Aageson, J. W. 1987. "Typology, Correspondence, and the Application of Scripture in Romans 9–11." *JSNT* 10 (31): 51–72.

Aejmelaeus, L. 1992. Review of Paulus und das Judentum: Anthropologische Erwägungen, by Timo Laato. SJS 13: 168–70.

Alexander, Ph. S. 1983. "Rabbinic Judaism and the New Testament." *ZNW* 74: 237–46.

Althaus, P. 1951. "'. . . Daß ihr nicht tut, was ihr wollt': Zur Auslegung von Gal. 5,17." *TLZ* 76: 15–18.

Althaus, P. 1951a. *Paulus und Luther über den Menschen, ein Vergleich.* 2nd ed. Studien der Luther-Akademie 14. Bertelsmann.

Althaus, P. 1952. "Zur Auslegung von Röm. 7,14ff.: Antwort an Anders Nygren." *TLZ* 77: 475–80.

Althaus, P. 1966. *Der Brief an die Römer.* 10th ed. NTD 6. Vandenhoeck & Ruprecht.

Amir, Y. 1983. *Die hellenistische Gestalt des Judentums bei Philon von Alexandrien.* Neukirchener.

Andrews, M. E. 1935. "Paul and Repentance." *JBL* 54: 125.

Bacher, W. 1903. *Von Hillel bis Akiba: Von 30 vor bis 135 nach der gew. Zeitrechnung.* 2nd ed. Vol. 1 of *Die Agada der Tannaiten.* Trübner.

Bader, G. 1981. "Römer 7 als Skopus einer theologischen Handlungstheorie." *ZTK* 78: 31–56.

Bailey, L. R. 1981. *Biblical Perspectives on Death.* 2nd ed. Fortress Press.

Barclay, J. M. G. 2015. *Paul and the Gift.* Eerdmans.

Barrett, C. K. 1967. *A Commentary on the Epistle to the Romans.* BNTC. A. & C. Black (= 1957).

Barrett, C. K. 1968. *A Commentary on the First Epistle to the Corinthians.* BNTC. A. & C. Black.

Barrett, C. K. 1973. *A Commentary on the Second Epistle to the Corinthians*. BNTC. A. & C. Black.

Barrosse, T. 1953. "Death and Sin in Saint Paul's Epistle to the Romans." *CBQ* 15: 438–59.

Barth, G. 1979. *Der Brief an die Philipper*. ZBK 9. Theologischer Verlag.

Barth, K. 1928. *Erklärung des Philipperbriefes*. Chr. Kaiser.

Bassler, J. M. 1982. *Divine Impartiality: Paul and a Theological Axiom*. SBLDS 59. Scholars Press.

Bassler, J. M. 1984. "Divine Impartiality in Paul's Letter to the Romans." *NovT* 26: 43–58.

Bauer, K-A. 1971. *Leiblichkeit das Ende aller Werke Gottes: Die Bedeutung der Leiblichkeit des Menschen bei Paulus*. Studien zum Neuen Testament 4. Gütersloher.

Bauer, W. 1988. *Griechisch-deutsches Wörterbuch zu den Schriften des Neuen Testaments und der frühchristlichen Literatur*. 6th ed. Edited by K. and B. Aland. De Gruyter.

Baumgärtel, Fr. 1966. "σάρξ B-3a." *TWNT* 7:105–8.

Becker, J. 1976. *Der Brief an die Galater*. 14th ed. NTD 8:1–85. Vandenhoeck & Ruprecht.

Becker, J. 1981. "Buße IV." *TRE* 7:446–51.

Becker, J. 1989. *Paulus: Der Apostel der Völker*. Mohr.

Behm, J. 1942. "μετανοέω/μετάνοια D–E." *TWNT* 4:991–1001.

Beker, J. C. 1978. Review of *Paul and Palestinian Judaism* by E. P. Sanders. *Theology Today* 35: 108–11.

Beker, J. C. 1980. *Paul the Apostle: The Triumph of God in Life and Thought*. T&T Clark.

Belkin, S. 1940. *Philo and the Oral Law: The Philonic Interpretation of Biblical Law in Relation to the Palestinian Halakah*. Harvard Semitic Studies 11. Harvard University Press.

Berger, K. 1966. "Abraham in den paulinischen Hauptbriefen." *MTZ* 17: 47–89.

Bergmeier, R. 1985. "Röm 7,7–25a (8,2): Der Mensch—das Gesetz—Gott—Paulus—die Exegese im Widerspruch?" *KD* 31: 162–72.

Best, Th. F. 1982. "The Apostle Paul and E. P. Sanders: The Significance of Paul and Palestinian Judaism." *Restoration Quarterly* 25: 65–74.

Betz, H. D. 1974. "Geist, Freiheit und Gesetz: Die Botschaft des Paulus an die Gemeinden in Galatien." *ZTK* 71: 78–93.

Betz, H. D. 1988. *Der Galaterbrief: Ein Kommentar zum Brief des Apostels Paulus an die Gemeinden in Galatien*. Aus dem amerikanischen übersetzt und für die deutsche Ausgabe redaktionell bearbeitet von S. Ann. C. Kaiser.

Betz, O. 1978. "Die heilsgeschichtliche Rolle Israels bei Paulus." *TBei* 9: 1–21.

Beyer, H. W. 1972. *Der Brief an die Galater*. Neu bearbeitet von P. Althaus. In *Die kleineren Briefe des Apostels Paulus*, 1–55. NTD 8. Vandenhoeck & Ruprecht.

Bialoblocki, S. 1930. *Die Beziehungen des Judentums zu Proselyten und Proselytentum*. NKB 1. Berlin.

Bietenhard, H. 1986. Rezension E. P. Sanders: *Paulus und das palästinische Judentum: Ein Vergleich zweier Religionsstrukturen*. *KBRS* 142: 279.

Billerbeck, P. 1922. *Das Evangelium nach Matthäus: Erläutert aus Talmud und Midrasch*. Vol. 1 of *Kommentar zum Neuen Testament aus Talmud und Midrasch*. Edited by H. L. Strack and P. Billerbeck. Beck.

Billerbeck, P. 1924. *Das Evangelium nach Markus, Lukas und Johannes und die Apostelgeschichte. Erläutert aus Talmud und Midrasch.* Vol. 2 of *Kommentar zum Neuen Testament aus Talmud und Midrasch.* Edited by H. L. Strack and P. Billerbeck. Beck.

Billerbeck, P. 1926. *Die Briefe des Neuen Testaments und die Offenbarung Johannes erläutert aus Talmud und Midrasch.* Vol. 3 of *Kommentar zum Neuen Testament aus Talmud und Midrasch.* Edited by H. L. Strack and P. Billerbeck. Beck.

Billerbeck, P. 1928. *Exkurse zu einzelnen Stellen des Neuen Testaments: Abhandlungen zur neutestamentlichen Theologie und Archäologie.* Vol. 4/1 of *Kommentar zum Neuen Testament aus Talmud und Midrasch.* Edited by H. L. Strack and P. Billerbeck. Beck.

Binder, H. 1968. *Der Glaube bei Paulus.* Evangelische Verlagsanstalt.

Blank, J. 1969. "Der gespaltene Mensch: Zur Exegese von Röm 7,7–25." In *Schriftauslegung in Theorie und Praxis*, 158–73. Biblische Handbibliothek 5. Kösel Verlag.

Blocher, H. 2004. "Justification of the Ungodly (Sola Fide): Theological Reflections." In *The Paradoxes of Paul*, 465–500. Vol. 2 of *Justification and Variegated Nomism.* Edited by D. A. Carson, P. T. O'Brien, and M. A. Seifrid. WUNT 2/181. Mohr Siebeck.

Borgen, P. 1964. Rezension Hugo von Odeberg, *Pharisaism and Christianity. JBL* 83: 445–46.

Borgen, P. 1980. "Observations on the Theme 'Paul and Philo': Paul's Preaching of Circumcision in Galatia (Gal. 5:11) and Debates on Circumcision in Philo." In *Die Paulinische Literatur und Theologie*, 85–102. Edited by S. Pedersen. Forlaget Aros.

Borgen, P. 1982. "Paul Preaches Circumcision and Pleases Men." In *Paul and Paulinism: Essays in Honour of C. K. Barrett*, 37–46. Edited by M. D. Hooker and S. G. Wilson. SPCK.

Borgen, P. 1987. "Debates on Circumcision in Paul and Philo." In *Philo, John, and Paul: New Perspectives on Judaism and Early Christianity*, 233–54. BJS 131. Scholars Press.

Bormann, P. 1965. *Die Heilswirksamkeit der Verkündigung nach dem Apostel Paulus: Ein Beitrag zur Theologie der Verkündigung.* Konfessionskundliche und kontroverstheologische Studien 14. Bonifacius-Druckerei.

Bornemann, E., and E. Risch. 1978. *Griechische Grammatik.* 2nd ed. Diesterweg.

Bornkamm, G. 1966. "Paulinische Anakoluthe." In *Das Ende des Gesetzes: Paulusstudien*, 76–92. 5th ed. Vol. 1 of *Gesammelte Aufsätze.* BEvT 16. C. Kaiser.

Bornkamm, G. 1966a. "Sünde, Gesetz und Tod: Exegetische Studie zu Röm 7." In *Das Ende des Gesetzes: Paulusstudien*, 51–69. 5th ed. Vol. 1 of *Gesammelte Aufsätze.* BEvT 16. C. Kaiser.

Bornkamm, G. 1970. "Gesetz und Natur, Röm. 2:14–16." In *Studien zu Antike und Urchristentum*, 93–118. 3rd ed. Vol. 2 of *Gesammelte Aufsätze.* BEvT 28. Chr. Kaiser.

Bornkamm, G. 1987. *Paulus.* 6th ed. Kohlhammer Urban-Taschenbücher 119. Kohlhammer.

Bosch, J. S. 1970. *"Gloriarse" segun San Pablo: Sentido y teología de καυχάομαι.* AnBib 40. Biblical Institute Press.

Bousset, W. 1966. *Die Religion des Judentums im späthellenistischen Zeitalter.* 4th ed. In dritter, verbesserter Auflage. Edited by H. Gressmann. HNT 21. Mohr.

Bousset, W. 1967. *Kyrios Christos: Geschichte des Christusglaubens von den Anfängen des Christentums bis Irenaeus*. 6th ed. Vandenhoeck & Ruprecht (= 1913).

Brandenburger, E. 1962. *Adam und Christus: Exegetisch-religionsgeschichtliche Untersuchung zu Röm. 5,12–21 (1. Kor. 15)*. WMANT 7. Neukirchener.

Braun, H. 1953. "'Umkehr' in spätjüdisch-häretischer und in frühchristlicher Sicht." *ZTK* 50: 243–58.

Braun, H. 1959. "Römer 7,7–25 und das Selbstverständnis des Qumran-Frommen." *ZTK* 56: 1–18.

Brockelmann, C. 1956. *Hebräische Syntax*. K. Moers.

Brooke, G. 1979. Review of E. P. Sanders, *Paul and Palestinian Judaism: A Comparison of Patterns of Religion*. *Journal of Jewish Studies* 30: 247–50.

Bruce, F. F. 1963. *The Epistle of Paul to the Romans*. Tyndale New Testament Commentaries. Eerdmans.

Bruce, F. F. 1982. "The Curse of the Law." In *Paul and Paulinism: Essays in Honour of C. K. Barrett*, 27–36. Edited by M. D. Hooker and S. G. Wilson. SPCK.

Bruce, F. F. 1982a. *The Epistle of Paul to the Galatians: A Commentary on the Greek Text*. NIGTC 2. Paternoster.

Bruce, F. F. 1982b. *1 and 2 Thessalonians*. WBC 45. Word Books.

Bruckner, J. K. 1995. "The Creational Context of Law before Sinai: Law and Liberty in Pre-Sinai Narratives and Romans 7." *Ex auditu* 11: 91–110.

Bryan, S. M. 2002. *Jesus and Israel's Traditions of Judgment and Restoration*. Cambridge University Press.

Bultmann, R. 1930. "Paulus." *RGG* 4:1019–45.

Bultmann, R. 1932. "Römer 7 und die Anthropologie des Paulus." In *Imago Dei: Beiträge zur theologischen Anthropologie. Gustav Krüger zum siebsigsten Geburtstage dargebracht*. Edited by H. Bornkamm. Töpelmann.

Bultmann, R. 1938. "καυχάομαι κτλ." *TWNT* 3:646–54.

Bultmann, R. 1940. "Christus des Gesetzes Ende." In R. Bultmann and H. Schlier, *Christus des Gesetzes Ende*, 3–27. BEvT 1. A. Lempp.

Bultmann, R. 1947. "Glossen im Römerbrief." *TLZ* 72: 197–202.

Bultmann, R. 1954. *Das Urchristentum im Rahmen der antiken Religionen*. 2nd ed., 59–75. Artemis-Verlag.

Bultmann, R. 1959. "Adam und Christus nach Rm 5." *ZNW* 50: 145–65.

Bultmann, R. 1976. *Der zweite Brief an die Korinther*. KEK Sonderband. Vandenhoeck & Ruprecht.

Bultmann, R. 1984. *Theologie des Neuen Testaments*. 9th ed. Durchgesehen und ergänzt von O. Merk. UTB 630. Mohr.

Bultmann, R. 1988. *Neues Testament und Mythologie: Das Problem der Entmythologisierung der neutestamentlichen Verkündigung*. 3rd ed. BEvT 96. C. Kaiser (= 1941).

Burgland, L. A. 1997. "Eschatological Tension and Existential *Angst*: 'Now' and 'Not Yet' in Romans 7:14–25 and 1QS 11 (Community Rule, Manual of Discipline)." *CTQ* 61: 163–76.

Busch, A. 2004. "The Figure of Eve in Romans 7:5–25." *Biblical Interpretation* 12: 1–36.

Byrne, Br. 1979. *Sons of God—Seed of Abraham: A Study of the Idea of the Sonship of God of All Christians in Paul against the Jewish Background*. Biblical Institute.

Byskov, M. 1976. "Simul Iustus et Peccator: A Note on Romans vii. 25b." *ST* 30: 75–87.

Caird, G. B. 1978. Review of *Paul and Palestinian Judaism: A Comparison of Patterns of Religion* by E. P. Sanders. *JTS* 29: 538–43.

Campbell, D. H. 1980. "The Identity of ἐγώ in Romans 7:7–25." In *Studia Biblica 1978. III. Papers on Paul and Other New Testament Authors. Sixth International Congress on Biblical Studies*, 57–64. Edited by E. A. Livingstone. JSNTSup 3. JSOT Press.

Campbell, W. S. 1981. "The Freedom and Faithfulness of God in Relation to Israel." *JSNT* 4 (13): 27–45.

Carson, D. A. 2001. "Summaries and Conclusions." In *The Complexities of Second Temple Judaism*. Vol. 1 of *Justification and Variegated Nomism*, 505–48. Edited by D. A. Carson, P. T. O'Brien, and M. A. Seifrid. WUNT 2/140. Mohr Siebeck.

Chancey, M. A. 2017. Foreword to *Paul and Palestinian Judaism: A Comparison of Patterns of Religion*. 40th anniversary ed., xi–xxvi. Fortress Press.

Charles, R. H. 1963. See *The Apocrypha and Pseudepigrapha*.

Charles, R. H. 1964. See *The Apocrypha and Pseudepigrapha*.

Childs, Br. S. 1974. *Exodus: A Commentary*. Old Testament Library. SCM Press.

Clarke, E. G. 1973. *The Wisdom of Solomon*. Cambridge Bible Commentary. Cambridge University Press.

Conzelmann, H. 1981. *Der erste Brief an die Korinther*. 2nd ed. KEK 5. Vandenhoeck & Ruprecht.

Conzelmann, H. 1987. *Grundriß der Theologie des Neuen Testaments*. 4th ed. Edited by A. Lindemann. UTB 1446. J. C. B. Mohr (P. Siebeck).

Cooper, K. T. 1982. "Paul and Rabbinic Soteriology: A Review Article." *Westminster Theological Journal* 44: 123–39.

Cranfield, C. E. B. 1981. *Commentary on Romans 9–16 and Essays*. Vol. 2 of *A Critical and Exegetical Commentary on the Epistle to the Romans*. ICC. T&T Clark (= 1979).

Cranfield, C. E. B. 1982. *Introduction and Commentary on Romans 1–8*. Vol. 1 of *A Critical and Exegetical Commentary on the Epistle to the Romans*. ICC. T&T Clark (= 1975).

Dahl, N. A. 1944. Recension H. Odeberg: *Fariséism och kristendom*. *STK* 20: 133–36.

Dahl, N. A. 1952. "Two Notes on Romans 5." *ST* 5: 37–48.

Dahl, N. A. 1977. "The One God of Jews and Gentiles (Romans 3:29–30)." In *Studies in Paul: Theology for the Early Christian Mission*, 178–91. Augsburg.

Dahl, N. A. 1978. Review of *Paul and Palestinian Judaism: A Comparison of Patterns of Religion* by E. P. Sanders. *RelSRev* 4: 153–58.

Danker, F. W. 1968. "Romans V. 12. Sin under Law." *NTS* 14: 424–39.

Das, A. A. 2007. *Solving the Romans Debate*. Fortress Press.

Davies, W. D. 1980. *Paul and Rabbinic Judaism: Some Rabbinic Elements in Pauline Theology*. SPCK.

Deidun, T. 1986. "E. P. Sanders: An Assessment of Two Recent Works. 1. 'Having His Cake and Eating It,' Paul on the Law." *Heythrop Journal* 27: 43–52.

Deissmann, A. 1925. *Paulus: Eine kultur- und religionsgeschichtliche Skizze*. 2nd ed. J. C. B. Mohr (P. Siebeck).

Demke, C. 1976. "'Ein Gott und viele Herren': Die Verkündigung des einen Gottes in den Briefen des Paulus." *EvT* 36: 473–84.

Deuser, H. 1979. "Glaubenserfahrung und Anthropologie: Röm 7,14–25 und Luthers These: totum genus humanum carnem esse." *EvT* 39: 409–31.

Dietrich, E. K. 1936. *Die Umkehr: (Bekehrung und Busse) im Alten Testament und im Judentum bei besonderer Berücksichtigung der neutestamentlichen Zeit*. Kohlhammer.

Dihle, A. 1973. "ψυχή κτλ. C I 1–5." *TWNT* 9:630–33.

Dobbeler, A. von. 1987. *Glaube als Teilhabe: Historische und semantische Grundlagen der paulinischen Theologie und Ekklesiologie des Glaubens*. WUNT 2/22. Mohr.

Dochhorn, J. 2009. "Röm 7,7 und das zehnte Gebot: Ein Beitrag zur Schriftauslegung und zur jüdischen Vorgeschichte des Paulus." *ZNW* 100: 59–77.

Dodd, C. H. 1947. *The Epistle of Paul to the Romans*. Moffat New Testament Commentary 6. Hodder & Stoughton.

Donfried, K. P. 1976. "Justification and Last Judgment in Paul." *ZNW* 67: 90–110.

Drury, J. 1978. Review of *Paul and Palestinian Judaism* by E. P. Sanders. *Theologica* 81: 235–36.

Dunn, J. D. G. 1975. "Rom.7,14–25 in the Theology of Paul." *TZ* 31: 257–73.

Dunn, J. D. G. 1983. "The New Perspective on Paul." *Bulletin of the John Rylands University Library of Manchester* 65: 95–122.

Dunn, J. D. G. 1988. *Romans 1–8*. WBC 38A. Word Books.

Dunn, J. D. G. 1998. *The Theology of Paul the Apostle*. Eerdmans.

Dunn, J. D. G. 2005. "The Justice of God: A Renewed Perspective on Justification by Faith." In *The New Perspective on Paul: Collected Essays*, 187–205. WUNT 185. Mohr Siebeck.

Dunn, J. D. G. 2005a. "The New Perspective: Whence, What and Whither?" In *The New Perspective on Paul: Collected Essays*, 1–88. WUNT 185. Mohr Siebeck.

Dunn, J. D. G. 2005b. "Yet Once More—'The Works of the Law': A Response." In *The New Perspective on Paul: Collected Essays*, 207–20. WUNT 185. Mohr Siebeck.

Eising, H. 1959. "Der Weisheitslehrer und die Götterbilder." *Bib* 40: 393–408.

Ellwein, E. 1955. "Das Rätsel von Röm VII." *KD* 1: 247–68.

Enslin, M. S. 1982. "Paul and Repentance: A Conspicuous Silence." *Eretz-Israel* 16: 37–42.

Epstein, I. 1960. *The Faith of Judaism: An Interpretation for Our Times*. 3rd ed. Soncino Press.

Eriksson, L. 1982. *Filipperbrevet*. Kommentar till Nya Testamentet 11. EFS-Förlaget.

Espy, J. M. 1985. "Paul's 'Robust Conscience' Re-examined." *NTS* 31: 161–88.

Fascher, E. 1975. *Der erste Brief des Paulus an die Korinther*. Erster Teil: *Einführung und Auslegung der Kapitel 1–7*. THKNT 7/1. Evangelische Verlagsanstalt.

Feine, P. 1899. *Das gesetzesfreie Evangelium des Paulus nach seinem Werdegang dargestellt*. Leipzig.

Feldmann, F. 1926. *Das Buch der Weisheit*. Vol. 6/4 of *Die Heilige Schrift des Alten Testaments*. Hanstein.

Fichtner, J. 1938. *Weisheit Salomos*. Handbuch zum Alten Testament 6. J. C. B. Mohr.

Flückiger, F. 1952. "Die Werke des Gesetzes bei den Heiden (nach Röm. 2,14 ff.)." *TZ* 8: 17–42.

Flückiger, F. 1954. "Zur Unterscheidung von Heiden und Juden in Röm. 1,18–2,3." *TZ* 10: 154–58.

Foerster, W. 1962. "Der Heilige Geist im Spätjudentum." *NTS* 8: 117–34.

Freundorfer, J. 1927. *Erbsünde und Erbtod beim Apostel Paulus: Eine religionsgeschichtliche und exegetische Untersuchung über Römerbrief 5,12–21*. NTAbh 13/1–2. Aschendorff.

Friedländer, M. 1905. *Die religiösen Bewegungen innerhalb des Judentums im Zeitalter Jesu*. Berlin.

Friedrich, G. 1952. "Ἁμαρτία οὐκ ἐλλογεῖται Röm. 5,13." *TLZ* 77: 523–28.

Friedrich, G. 1954. "Das Gesetz des Glaubens Röm. 3,27." *TZ* 10: 401–17.

Friedrich, G. 1957. "Bekehrung III." *RGG* 1:979–80.

Friedrich, G. 1976. *Der Brief an die Philipper*. 14th ed. NTD 8:125–75. Vandenhoeck & Ruprecht.

Friedrich, G. 1982. "Glaube und Verkündigung bei Paulus." In *Glaube im Neuen Testament: Studien zu Ehren von H. Binder anläßlich seines 70. Geburtstags*, 93–113. Edited by F. Hahn and H. Klein. Biblisch-theologische Studien 7. Neukirchener.

Fuchs, E. 1949. *Die Freiheit des Glaubens: Römer 5–8 ausgelegt*. BEvT 14. Kaiser.

Fuchs, E. 1962. "Existentiale Interpretation von Römer 7,7–12 und 21–23." *ZTK* 59: 285–314.

Furnish, V. P. 1968. *Theology and Ethics in Paul*. Abingdon.

Gager, J. G. 1983. *The Origins of Anti-Semitism: Attitudes Toward Judaism in Pagan and Christian Antiquity*. Oxford University Press.

Garlington, D. B. 1990. "Romans 7:14–25 and the Creation Theology of Paul." *Trinity Journal* n.s. 11: 197–235.

Garnet, P. 1980. "Qumran Light on Pauline Soteriology." In *Pauline Studies: Essays Presented to Professor F. F. Bruce on His 70th Birthday*, 19–32. Edited by D. A. Hagner and M. J. Harris. Eerdmans.

Gaston. L. 1987. *Paul and the Torah*. University of British Columbia Press.

Gaventa, B. R. 1980. "Comparing Paul and Judaism: Rethinking Our Methods." *BTB* 10: 37–44.

George, T. 2004. "Modernizing Luther, Domesticating Paul: Another Perspective." In *The Paradoxes of Paul*, 437–63. Vol. 2 of *Justification and Variegated Nomism*. Edited by D. A. Carson, P. T. O'Brien, and M. A. Seifrid. WUNT 2/181. Mohr Siebeck.

Georgi, D. 1980. *Weisheit Salomos. JSHRZ* 3/4. Gütersloher.

Giblin, C. H. 1975. "Three Monotheistic Texts in Paul." *CBQ* 37: 527–47.

Gieschen, C. A. 2004. "Paul and the Law: Was Luther right?" In *The Law in Holy Scripture: Essays from the Concordia Theological Seminary Symposium on Exegetical Theology*, 113–47. Edited by C. A. Gieschen. Concordia Publishing House.

Glombitza, O. 1959. "Mit Furcht und Zittern: Zum Verständnis von Philip. II 12." *NovT* 3: 100–106.

Gnilka, J. 1976. *Der Philipperbrief*. HTKNT 10/3. Herder.

Goldhahn-Müller, I. 1989. *Die Grenze der Gemeinde: Studien zum Problem der Zweiten Buße im Neuen Testament unter Berücksichtigung der Entwicklung im 2. Jh. bis Tertullian*. GTA 39. Vandenhoeck & Ruprecht.

Goodenough, E. R. 1935. *By Light, Light: The Mystic Gospel of Hellenistic Judaism*. Oxford University Press.

Goppelt, L. 1954. *Christentum und Judentum im ersten und zweiten Jahrhundert: Ein Aufriß der Urgeschichte der Kirche*. Bertelsmann.

Goppelt, L. 1980. *Theologie des Neuen Testaments*. 3rd ed. Edited by J. Roloff. Teil 1: *Jesu Wirken in seiner theologischen Bedeutung*. Teil 2: *Vielfalt und Einheit des apostolischen Christuszeugnisses*. Vandenhoeck & Ruprecht.

Gräßer, E. 1981. "'Ein einziger ist Gott' (Röm 3,30): Zum christologischen Gottesverständnis bei Paulus." In *"Ich will euer Gott werden": Beispiele biblischen Redens von Gott*, 177–205. Stuttgarter Bibelstudien 100. Katholisches Bibelwerk.

Gräßer, E. 1981a. "Zwei Heilswege? Zum theologischen Verhältnis von Israel und Kirche." In *Kontinuität und Einheit: Für F. Mußner*, 411–29. Edited by P-G. Müller and W. Stenger. Herder.

Grosheide, F. W. 1980. *Commentary of the First Epistle to the Corinthians*. NICNT 7. Eerdmans (= 1953).

Grundmann, W. 1960. "Paulus, aus dem Volke Israel, Apostel der Völker." *NovT* 4: 267–91.

Gundry, R. H. 1980. "The Moral Frustration of Paul Before His Conversion: Sexual Lust in Romans 7:7–25." In *Pauline Studies: Essays Presented to Professor F. F. Bruce on His 70th Birthday*, 228–45. Edited by D. A. Hagner and M. J. Harris. Eerdmans.

Gundry, R. H. 1985. "Grace, Works, and Staying Saved in Paul." *Bib* 66: 1–38.

Haacker, K. 1975. "Die Berufung des Verfolgers und die Rechtfertigung des Gottlosen. Erwägungen zum Zusammenhang zwischen Biographie und Theologie des Apostels Paulus." *TBei* 6: 1–19.

Haacker, K. 1982. "Das Evangelium Gottes und die Erwählung Israels: Zum Beitrag des Römerbriefs zur Erneuerung des Verhältnisses zwischen Christen und Juden." *TBei* 13: 59–72.

Hafemann, S. 1981. "Entering and Remaining: E. P. Sanders' View of Palestinian Judaism." *Studia Biblica et Theologica* 11: 139–49.

Hagner, D. A. 1979. "Salvation, Faith, Works." *Reformed Journal* 29: 25–27.

Hagner, D. A. 1993. "Paul and Judaism: The Jewish Matrix of Early Christianity: Issues in the Current Debate." Bulletin for Biblical Researcg 3: 111–30

Hahn, F. 1976. "Das Gesetzesverständnis im Römer- und Galaterbrief." *ZNW* 67: 29–63.

Hahn, W. T. 1937. *Das Mitsterben und Mitauferstehen mit Christus bei Paulus: Ein Beitrag zum Problem der Gleichzeitigkeit des Christen mit Christus*. Bertelsmann.

Hall, D. R. 1983. "Romans 3.1–8 Reconsidered." *NTS* 29: 183–97.

Hansen, G. W. 2009. *The Letter to the Philippians*. Pillar New Testament Commentary. Eerdmans.

Harnack, A. 1900. *Das Wesen des Christentums: Sechzehn Vorlesungen vor Studierenden aller Facultäten im Wintersemester 1899/1900 an der Universität Berlin gehalten*. Leipzig.

Harris, M. J. 2005. *The Second Epistle to the Corinthians: A Commentary on the Greek Text*. NIGTC. Eerdmans.

Harrison, J. R. 2003. *Paul's Language of Grace in Its Graeco-Roman Context*. WUNT 2/172 Mohr Siebeck.

Hartman, L. 1980. "Bundesideologie in und hinter einigen paulinischen Texten." In *Die Paulinische Literatur und Theologie*, 103–18. Edited by S. Pedersen. Forlaget Aros.

Hay, D. M. 1979. "Philo's References to Other Allegorists." *Studia Philonica* 6: 41–75.

Hayman, A. P. 1984. "The Fall, Freewill and Human Responsibility in Rabbinic Judaism." *SJT* 37: 13–22.

Hedegård, D. 1951. *Seder R.Amram Gaon*. Part I. *Hebrew Text with Critical Apparatus, Translation with Notes and Introduction*. Lindstedts Universitets-Bokhandel.

Heil, J. P. 1987. *Romans—Paul's Letter of Hope*. AnBib 112. Biblical Institute.

Heiligenthal, R. 1983. *Werke als Zeichen: Untersuchungen zur Bedeutung der menschlichen Taten im Frühjudentum, Neuen Testament und Frühchristentum*. WUNT 2/9. Mohr.

Heiligenthal, R. 1985. Rezension E. P. Sanders: *Paulus und das palästinische Judentum: Ein Vergleich zweier Religionsstrukturen. Deutsche Pfarrerinnen- und Pfarrerblatt* 85: 546–47.

Heinemann, I. 1932. *Philons griechische und jüdische Bildung: Kulturvergleichende Untersuchungen zu Philons Darstellung der jüdischen Gesetze*. M. & H. Marcus.

Hengel, M. 1961. *Die Zeloten: Untersuchungen zur jüdischen Freiheitsbewegung in der Zeit von Herodes I. bis 70 n. Chr.* Arbeiten zur Geschichte des Spätjudentums und Urchristentums 1. Brill.

Hengel, M. 1969. *Judentum und Hellenismus: Studien zu ihrer Begegnung unter besonderer Berücksichtigung Palästinas bis zur Mitte des 2. Jh. v. Chr.* WUNT 10. J. C. B. Mohr.

Hill, D. 1967. *Greek Words and Hebrew Meanings: Studies in the Semantics of Soteriological Terms*. SNTSMS 5. Cambridge University Press.

Hoffmann, P. 1963. "Umkehr." *Handbuch Theologischer Grundbegriffe* 2:719–24.

Hofius, O. 2002. "Der Mensch im Schatten Adams." In *Paulusstudien II*, 104–54. WUNT 143. Mohr.

Hoheisel, K. 1978. *Das antike Judentum in christlicher Sicht: Ein Beitrag zur neueren Forschungsgeschichte*. Studies in Oriental Religions 2. Harrassowitz.

Holm-Nielsen, S. 1977. *Die Psalmen Salomos. JSHRZ* 4/2. Gütersloher.

Hommel, H. 1961. "Das 7. Kapitel des Römerbriefes im Licht antiker Überlieferung." *Theologia viatorum* 8: 90–116.

Hooker, M. D. 1982. "Paul and 'Covenantal Nomism.'" In *Paul and Paulinism: Essays in Honour of C. K. Barrett*, 47–56. Edited by M. D. Hooker and S. G. Wilson. SPCK.

Horbury, W. 1979. "Paul and Judaism." *Expository Times* 90: 116–18.

Horn, F. W. 1991. "1 Korinther 15,56—ein exegetischer Stachel." *ZNW* 82: 88–105.

Howard, G. 1979. *Paul: Crisis in Galatia: A Study in Early Christian Theology*. SNTSMS 35. Cambridge University Press.

Hruby, K. 1965. "Begriff und Funktion des Gottesvolkes in der rabbinischen Tradition." *Jud* 21: 230–56.

Hruby, K. 1966. "Begriff und Funktion des Gottesvolkes in der rabbinischen Tradition." *Jud* 22: 167–91.

Hruby, K. 1967. "Begriff und Funktion des Gottesvolkes in der rabbinischen Tradition (Fortsetzung)." *Jud* 23: 30–48.

Hruby, K. 1968. "Begriff und Funktion des Gottesvolkes in der rabbinischen Tradition (Fortsetzung)." *Jud* 24: 224–45.

Hruby, K. 1969. "Gesetz und Gnade in der rabbinischen Überlieferung." *Jud* 25: 30–63.

Hübner, H. 1975. "Das ganze und das eine Gesetz: Zum Problemkreis Paulus und die Stoa." *KD* 21: 239–56.

Hübner, H. 1980. "Pauli Theologiae Proprium." *NTS* 26: 445–73.

Hübner, H. 1981. "ἐπιθυμία κτλ." EWNT 2:68–71.

Hübner, H. 1982. *Das Gesetz bei Paulus: Ein Beitrag zum Werden der paulinischen Theologie.* 3rd ed. FRLANT 119. Vandenhoeck & Ruprecht.

Hübner, H. 1982a. Rezension W. Schmithals: *Die theologische Anthropologie des Paulus: Auslegung von Röm 7,17–8,39. TLZ* 107: 817–19.

Hübner, H. 1984. *Gottes Ich und Israel: Zum Schriftgebrauch des Paulus in Römer 9–11.* FRLANT 136. Vandenhoeck & Ruprecht.

Hübner, H. 1985. Rezension H. Räisänen: *Paul and the Law. TLZ* 110: 894–96.

Hübner, H. 1986. Rezension E. P. Sanders: *Paulus und das palästinische Judentum: Ein Vergleich zweier Religionsstrukturen*; *Paul, the Law, and the Jewish People*; *Jesus and Judaism. SNTSU* 11: 238–45.

Hübner, H. 1987. "Paulusforschung seit 1945: Ein kritischer Literaturbericht." In *ANRW* 2.25/4:2649–840. De Gruyter.

Huggins, R. V. 1992. "Alleged Classical Parallels to Paul's 'What I Want to Do I Do not Do, But What I Hate, That I Do' (Rom 7:15)." *Westminster Theological Journal* 54: 153–61.

Hughes, P. E. 1980. *Paul's Second Epistle to the Corinthians.* NICNT 8. Eerdmans.

Jacques, X. 1979. Review of E. P. Sanders. *Paul and Palestinian Judaism: A Comparison of Patterns of Religion. La nouvelle revue théologique* 101: 896–98.

Jervell, J. 1960. *Imago Dei: Gen.1,26f. im Spätjudentum, in der Gnosis und in den paulinischen Briefen.* FRLANT 76. Vandenhoeck & Ruprecht.

Jervis, L. A. 2004. "'The Commandment Which Is for Life' (Romans 7.10): Sin's Use of the Obedience of Faith." *JSNT* 27: 193–216.

Joest, W. 1951. *Gesetz und Freiheit: Das Problem des Tertius usus legis bei Luther und die neutestamentliche Parainese.* Vandenhoeck & Ruprecht.

Joest, W. 1955. "Paulus und das Luthersche These Simul Iustus et Peccator." *KD* 1: 269–320.

Jones, F. St. 1987. *"Freiheit" in den Briefen des Apostels Paulus: Eine historische, exegetische und religionsgeschichtliche Studie.* GTA 34. Vandenhoeck & Ruprecht.

Jüngel, E. 1963. "Das Gesetz zwischen Adam und Christus: Eine theologische Studie zu Röm 5,12–21." *ZTK* 60: 42–74.

Käsemann, E. 1961. "Gottesgerechtigkeit bei Paulus." *ZTK* 58: 367–78.

Käsemann, E. 1969. "Der Glaube Abrahams in Röm. 4." In *Paulinische Perspektiven*, 140–77. Mohr.

Käsemann, E. 1980. *An die Römer*. 4th ed. HNT 8a. Mohr.

Kaye, B. N. 1979. *The Thought Structure of Romans: With Special Reference to Chapter 6*. Schola Press.

Kertelge, K. 1967. *"Rechtfertigung" bei Paulus: Studien zur Struktur und zum Bedeutungsgehalt des paulinischen Rechtfertigungsbegriffs*. NTAbh 3. Aschendorff.

Kertelge, K. 1971. "Exegetische Überlegungen zum Verständnis der paulinischen Anthropologie nach Römer 7." *ZNW* 62: 105–14.

Keuck, W. 1961. "Dienst des Geistes und des Fleisches: Zur Auslegungsgeschichte und Auslegung von Röm 7,25b." *TQ* 141: 257–80.

Kietzig, O. 1957. "Bekehrung zum Glauben an Jesus Christus. Zur Problematik religiöser Bekehrung." *TLZ* 82: 891–902.

Kim, S. 1981. *The Origin of Paul's Gospel*. WUNT 2/4. J. C. B. Mohr.

King, N. 1980. Review E. P. Sanders: *Paul and Palestinian Judaism: A Comparison of Patterns of Religion*. *Bib* 61: 141–44.

Kirby, J. T. 1987. "The Syntax of Romans 5.12: A Rhetorical Approach." *NTS* 33: 283–86.

Kjær, T. 2010. *"Jeg'et" i Romerbrevet 7,7–13 og 14–25*. Copenhagen.

Klauck, H-J. 1984. *1. Korintherbrief*. Die neue Echter Bibel: Kommentar zum Neuen Testament 7. Echter.

Klauck, H-J. 1986. *2. Korintherbrief*. Die neue Echter Bibel: Kommentar zum Neuen Testament 8. Echter.

Klauck, H-J. 1986a. Rezension E. P. Sanders, *Paulus und das palästinische Judentum: Ein Vergleich zweier Religionsstrukturen*. *Wissenschaft und Weisheit* 49: 77–79.

Klein, G. 1963. "Römer 4 und die Idee der Heilsgeschichte." *EvT* 23: 424–47.

Klein, G. 1964. "Exegetische Probleme in Römer 3,21–4,25: Antwort an U. Wilckens." *EvT* 24: 676–83.

Klein, G. 1966. "Heil und Geschichte nach Römer IV." *NTS* 13: 43–47.

Klein, G. 1988. "Ein Sturmzentrum der Paulusforschung." *Verkündigung und Forschung* 33 (1): 40–56.

Klijn, A. F. J. 1976. *Die syrische Baruch-Apokalypse*. *JSHRZ* 5/2:103–91. Gütersloher.

Klingbeil, M. G. 2003. "Exile." In *Dictionary of the Old Testament: Pentateuch*. Edited by T. Desmond Alexander and David W. Baker. InterVarsity Press.

Knox, J. 1950. *Chapters in a Life of Paul*. Abingdon-Cokesbury.

König, A. 1976. "Gentiles or Gentile Christians? On the Meaning of Romans 2:12–16." *Journal of Theology for Southern Africa* 15: 53–60.

Kraus, H-J. 1979. *Theologie der Psalmen*. Biblischer Kommentar Altes Testament 15/3. Neukirchener.

Krauter, S. 2010. "Röm 7: Adam oder Eva?" *ZNW* 101: 145–47.

Krauter, S. 2011. "'Wenn das Gesetz nicht gesagt hätte . . .': Röm 7,7b und antike Äusserungen zu paradoxen Wirkungen von Gesetzen." *ZTK* 108: 1–15.

Kreß, H. 2022. "'[S]o viel Verständnis für [. . .] unser nationalsozialistisches Denken': Gerhard Kittel und Hugo Odeberg." In *Auf dem Weg zu einer Biographie Gerhard Kittels (1888–1948)*. Edited by L. Bormann and A. W. Zwiep. Mohr Siebeck.

Kruyf, Th. de. 1978. "The Perspective of Romans VII." In *Miscellanea Neotestamentica II*, 127–41. Edenda curaverunt T. Baarda, A. F. J. Klijn, and W. C. van Unnik. NovTSup 48. Brill.

Kuhr, Fr. 1964. "Römer 2,14f. und die Verheißung bei Jeremia 31,31ff." *ZNW* 55: 243–61.

Kümmel, W. G. 1974. *Römer 7 und das Bild des Menschen im Neuen Testament: Zwei Studien*. Theologische Bücherei: Neues Testament 53. C. Kaiser.

Kürzinger, J. 1963. "Der Schlüssel zum Verständnis von Röm 7." *Biblische Zeitschrift* 7: 270–74.

Kuß, O. 1954. "Die Heiden und die Werke des Gesetzes (nach Röm 2,14–16)." *MTZ* 5: 77–98.

Kuß, O. 1963. "Der Glaube nach den paulinischen Hauptbriefen." In *Aufsätze zur Exegese des Neuen Testamentes*. Vol. 1 of *Auslegung und Verkündigung*. Pustetet.

Kuula, K. 1999. *Paul's Polemical Treatment of the Law in Galatians*. Vol. 1 of *The Law, the Covenant and God's Plan*. Publications of the Finnish Exegetical Society 72. Vandenhoeck & Ruprecht.

Laato, T. 1995. "Room 7,7–25: Lain apologiaa vai kristityn omakuva?" In *Paavali ja laki*, 17–28. Iustitia 6. Suomen teologinin instituutti.

Laato, T. 2004. "Paul's Anthropological Considerations: Two Problems." In *The Paradoxes of Paul*, 343–59. Vol. 2 of *Justification and Variegated Nomism*. Edited by D. A. Carson, P. T. O'Brien, and M. A. Seifrid. WUNT 2/181. Mohr Siebeck.

Laato, T. 2007. "Att göra rättvisa åt ett geni: Om Hugo Odebergs bok 'Fariseism och kristendom.'" *STK* 83: 169–74.

Laato, T. 2008. "'God's Righteousness'—Once Again." In *The Nordic Paul: Finnish Approaches to Pauline Theology*, 40–73. Edited by L. Aejmelaeus and A. Mustakallio. Library of New Testament Studies 374. ESCO 374. T&T Clark.

Laato, T. 2010. "Die paulinische Denkweise: Von der Lösung aus auf den Ausgangspunkt hin?" *Lutherische Beiträge* 15: 88–98.

Laato, T. 2013. "Crucified with Christ and the New Life of Christians: Romans 6:1–14 (and 15–23) Revisited." In *Fri och bunden: En bok om teologisk antropologi*, 95–127. Edited by J. Hellberg, R. Imberg, and T. Johansson. Församlingsfakultetens skriftserie 13. Församlingsförlaget. Published simultaneously in the electronic journal *SEE-J* 4 (2013): 68–88.

Laato, T. 2018. "Salvation by God's Grace, Judgment According to Our Works: Taking a Look at Matthew and Paul." *CTQ* 82: 163–78.

Laato, T. 2018a. "*Simul Iustus et Peccator* through the Lenses of Paul." *Journal of the Evangelical Theological Society* 61: 735–66.

Laato, T. 2019. "The New Quest for Paul: A Critique of the New Perspective on Paul." In *The Doctrine on Which the Church Stands or Falls: Justification in Biblical, Theological, Historical, and Pastoral Perspective*, 291–321. Edited by M. Barrett. Crossway.

Laato, T. 2021. *Hermeneutics in Romans: Paul's Approach to Reading the Bible*. Translated by B. Erickson, W. Odom, and K. Odom. 1517 Publishing.

Laato, T. 2023. *The New Quest for Paul and His Reading of the Old Testament: The Contrast Between the "Letter" and the "Spirit" in 2 Corinthians 3:1–18*. 1517 Publishing.

Langerbeck, H. 1967. *Aufsätze zur Gnosis: Aus dem Nachlaß*. Edited by H. Dörries. Vandenhoeck & Ruprecht.

Leeste, T. 1979. *ΕΓΩ I Rom. 7:14–25: En undersökning av tolkningshistoriens huvudlinjer*. SIESÅA 8. Åbo.

Léon-Dufour, X. 1973. "Arbeitspapier zu Röm 7." In *Exegese in Methodenkonflikt: Zwischen Geschichte und Struktur*. Edited by X. Léon-Dufour. Translated (into German) by G. Haeffner and H. Schöndorf. Kösel-Verlag.

Lichtenberger, H. 1985. *Studien zur paulinischen Anthropologie in Römer 7*. 2 vols. Tübingen.

Lichtenberger, H. 2004. *Das Ich Adams und das Ich der Menschheit: Studien zum Menschenbild in Römer 7*. WUNT 164. Mohr Siebeck.

Liebers, R. 1989. *Das Gesetz als Evangelium: Untersuchungen zur Gesetzeskritik des Paulus*. ATANT 75. Theologischer Verlag.

Liechtenhan, R. 1946. "Paulus als Judenmissionar." *Jud* 2: 56–70.

Lietzmann, H. 1969. *An die Korinther I/II*. 5th ed. Ergänzt von W. G. Kümmel. HNT 9. Mohr (Siebeck).

Lietzmann, H. 1971. *An die Galater*. 4th ed. HNT 10. Mohr (Siebeck).

Lietzmann, H. 1971a. *An die Römer*. 5th ed. HNT 8:19–134. Mohr.

Limbeck, M. 1971. *Die Ordnung des Heils: Untersuchungen zum Gesetzesverständnis des Frühjudentums*. Kommentare und Beiträge zum Alten und Neuen Testament. Patmos-Verlag.

Limbeck, M. 1972. *Von der Ohnmacht des Rechts: Untersuchungen zur Gesetzeskritik des Neuen Testaments*. Theologische Pespektiven. Patmos-Verlag.

Lindeskog, G. 1938. *Die Jesusfrage im neuzeitlichen Judentum: Ein Beitrag zur Geschichte der Leben-Jesu-Forschung*. Almquist & Wiksells.

Ljungman, H. 1964. *Pistis: A Study of Its Presuppositions and Its Meaning in Pauline Use*. Gleerup.

Loewe, R. 1966. *The Position of Women in Judaism*. SPCK.

Lohmeyer, E. 1928. *Der Brief an die Philipper*. 11th ed. KEK 9. Vandenhoeck & Ruprecht.

Lohmeyer, E. 1929. *Grundlagen paulinischer Theologie*. BHT 1. J. C. B. Mohr.

Lohmeyer, E. [1954]. *Probleme Paulinischer Theologie*. Kohlhammer.

Lohse, E. 1966. Foreword in W. Bousset: *Die Religion des Judentums im späthellenistischen Zeitalter*, v–x. Mohr.

Lohse, E. 1973. "ὁ νόμος τοῦ πνεύματος τῆς ζωῆς: Exegetische Anmerkungen zu Röm.8,2." In *Neues Testament und christliche Existenz: Festschrift für Herbert Braun*, 279–87. Edited by H. D. Betz and L. Schottroff. J. C. B. Mohr (Paul Siebeck).

Lohse, E. 1977. "Emuna und Pistis: Jüdisches und urchristliches Verständnis des Glaubens." *ZNW* 68: 147–63.

Lohse, E. 1978. "Glauben im Neuen Testament." In H-J. Hermisson and E. Lohse, *Glauben*, 102–17. Kohlhammer-Taschenbücher: Biblische Konfrontationen 1005. Kohlhammer.

Lübking, H.-M. 1986. *Paulus und Israel im Römerbrief: Eine Untersuchung zu Römer 9–11*. Europäische Hochschulschriften 260. Lang.

Lüdemann, G. 1983. *Paulus und das Judentum*. Theologische Existenz heute 215. Kaiser.

Lüdemann, G. 1987. "Die Religionsgeschichtliche Schule." In *Theologie in Göttingen: Eine Vorlesungsreihe*, 325–61. Edited by B. Moeller. Göttinger Universitätsschriften 1. Vandenhoeck & Ruprecht.

Lührmann, D. 1965. *Das Offenbarungsverständnis bei Paulus und in paulinischen Gemeinden*. WMANT 16. Neukirchener.

Lührmann, D. 1978. *Der Brief an die Galater*. ZBK 7. Theologischer Verlag.

Luz, U. 1968. *Das Geschichtsverständnis des Paulus*. BEvT 49. C. Kaiser.

Luz, U. 1981. "'Das Gesetz im Frühjudentum' und 'Das differenzierte Nein zum Gesetz: Paulus.'" In R. Smend and U. Luz, *Gesetz*, 45–57, 89–112. Kohlhammer-Taschenbücher: Biblische Konfrontationen 1015. Kohlhammer.

Lyonnet, S. 1962. "'Tu ne convoiteras pas' (Rom. vii 7)." In *Neotestamentica et Patristica: Eine Freundesgabe, Herrn Professor Dr. O. Cullmann zu seinem 60. Geburtstag überreicht*, 157–65. Brill.

Maier, G. 1971. *Mensch und freier Wille: Nach den jüdischen Religionsparteien zwischen Ben Sira und Paulus*. WUNT 12. J. C. B. Mohr (Paul Siebeck).

Malina, Br. J. 1978. Review of E. P. Sanders, *Paul and Palestinian Judaism: A Comparison of Patterns in [of] Religion*. *BTB* 8: 190–91.

Marcus, J. 1989. "The Circumcision and the Uncircumcision in Rome." *NTS* 35: 67–81.

Marquardt, F.-K. 1971. *Die Juden im Römerbrief*. ThSt (B) 107. Theologischer Verlag.

Martin, B. L. 1981. "Some Reflections on the Identity of ἐγώ in Rom. 7:14–25." *SJT* 34: 39–47.

Martin, B. L. 1989. *Christ and the Law in Paul*. NovTSup 62. Brill.

Martin, R. P. 1986. *2 Corinthians*. WBC 40. Word Books.

Mattern, L. 1966. *Das Verständnis des Gerichtes bei Paulus*. ATANT 47. Zwingli Verlag.

Mauerhofer, E. 1981. *Der Kampf zwischen Fleisch und Geist bei Paulus: Ein Beitrag zur Klärung der Frage nach der Stellung des Gläubigen zur Sünde im paulinischen Heiligungs- und Vollkommenheitsverständnis*. 2nd ed. TELOS-Skript 1702. Trachsel Verlag.

McEleney, N. J. 1974. "Conversion, Circumcision and the Law." *NTS* 20: 319–41.

McKnight, S., and B. J. Oropeza. 2020. *Perspectives on Paul: Five Views*, ix–x. Edited by S. McKnight and B. J. Oropeza. Baker Academic.

McNamara, M. 1979. Review of E. P. Sanders, *Paul and Palestinian Judaism: A Comparison of Patterns of Religion*. *JSNT* 5: 67–73.

Meeks, W. A. 1980. "Toward a Social Description of Pauline Christianity." In vol. 2 of *Approaches to Ancient Judaism*, 27–41. Edited by W. S. Green. BJS 9. Scholars Press.

Mengel, B. 1982. *Studien zum Philipperbrief: Untersuchungen zum situativen Kontext unter besonderer Berücksichtigung der Frage nach der Ganzheitlichkeit oder Einheitlichkeit eines paulinischen Briefes*. WUNT 2/8. Mohr.

Merk, O. 1969. "Der Beginn der Paränese im Galaterbrief." *ZNW* 60: 83–104.

Merklein, H. 1981. "μετάνοια/μετανοέω." *EWNT* 2:1022–31.

Meyer, R. 1937. *Hellenistisches in der rabbinischen Anthropologie: Rabbinische Vorstellungen vom Werden des Menschen*. BWANT 74. Kohlhammer.

Michaelis, W. 1927. "Rechtfertigung aus Glauben bei Paulus." In *Festgabe für A. Deissmann zum 60. Geburtstag*, 116–38. J. C. B. Mohr (Paul Siebeck).

Michel, O. 1978. *Der Brief an die Römer*. 5th ed. KEK 4. Vandenhoeck & Ruprecht.

Middendorf, M. P. 1997. *The "I" in the Storm: A Study of Romans 7*. Concordia.

Miguens, M. 1971. Review of J. S. Bosch: *"Gloriarse" según San Pablo: Sentido y teología de χαυχάομαι*. *CBQ* 33: 603–5.

Modalsli, O. 1965. "Gal. 2,19–21; 5,16–18 und Röm. 7,7–25." *TZ* 21: 22–37.

Möller, H. 1939. "Röm. 7 ist und bleibt das Bild des Christen I–II." *Deutsche Theologie* 6: 5–27, 68–79.

Montefiore, C. G. 1901. "Rabbinic Judaism and the Epistles of St. Paul." *JQR* 13: 161–217, 552.

Montefiore, C. G. 1904. "Rabbinic Conceptions of Repentance." *JQR* 16: 209–57.

Montefiore, C. G. 1914. *Judaism and St. Paul: Two Essays*. Max Goschen.

Moo, D. J. 2004. "Israel and the Law in Romans 5–11: Interaction with the New Perspective." In *The Paradoxes of Paul*, 185–216. Vol. 2 of *Justification and Variegated Nomism*. Edited by D. A. Carson, P. T. O'Brien, and M. A. Seifrid. WUNT 2/181. Mohr Siebeck.

Moo, D. J. 2013. *Galatians*. BECNT. Baker Academic.

Moo, D. J. 2018. *The Letter to the Romans*. 2nd ed. NICNT. Eerdmans.

Moore, G. F. 1921. "Christian Writers on Judaism." *HTR* 14: 197–254.

Moore, G. F. 1948–50. *Judaism in the First Centuries of the Christian Era: The Age of the Tannaim*. 3 vols. Harvard University Press (= 1927–30).

Moule, C. F. D. 1967. "Obligation in the Ethic of Paul." In *Christian History and Interpretation: Studies Presented to J. Knox*, 389–406. Edited by W. R. Farmer, C. F. D. Moule, and R. R. Niebuhr. Cambridge University Press.

Müller, F. 1941. "Zwei Marginalien im Brief des Paulus an die Römer." *ZNW* 40: 249–54.

Müller, H. 1967. "Der rabbinische Qal-Wachomer-Schluß in paulinischer Typologie: Zur Adam-Christus-Typologie in Rm 5." *ZNW* 58: 73–92.

Müller, J. J. 1976. *The Epistles of Paul to the Philippians and to Philemon*. NICNT 11. Eerdmans (= 1955).

Müller, K. 1983. *Das Judentum in der religionsgeschichtlichen Arbeit am Neuen Testament: Eine kritische Rückschau auf die Entwicklung einer Methodik bis zu den Qumranfunden*. Judentum und Umwelt 6. Peter Lang.

Müller, K. 1989. "Zur Datierung rabbinischer Aussagen." In *Neues Testament und Ethik: Für S. Schnackenburg*, 551–87. Edited by H. Merklein. Herder.

Mundle, W. 1932. *Der Glaubensbegriff des Paulus: Eine Untersuchung zur Dogmengeschichte des ältesten Christentums*. M. Heinsius.

Mundle, W. 1934. "Zur Auslegung von Röm 2,13ff." *Theologische Blätter* 13: 249–56.

Murphy-O'Connor, J. 1978. Revue *Paul and Palestinian Judaism: A Comparison of Patterns of Religion* par E. P. Sanders. *Revue Biblique* 85: 122–26.

Murray, J. 1982. *The Epistle to the Romans*. Vol. 1: *Chapters 1 to 8*. Vol. 2: *Chapters 9 to 16*. NICNT 5. Eerdmans (= 1968).

Mußner, F. 1974. *Der Galaterbrief*. 2nd ed. HTKNT 9. Herder.

Mußner, F. 1977. "'Christus (ist) des Gesetzes Ende zur Gerechtigkeit für jeden, der glaubt' (Röm. 10,4)." In *Paulus, Apostat oder Apostel? Jüdische und christliche Antworten*, 31–44. Pustet.

Mußner, F. 1979. *Traktat über die Juden*. Kösel.

Mußner, F. 1986. "Das Toraleben im jüdischen Verständnis." In *Das Gesetz im Neuen Testament*, 28–45. Edited by K. Kertelge. Quaestiones disputatae 108. Herder.

Napier, D. 2002. "Paul's Analysis of Sin and Torah in Romans 7:7–25." *Restoration Quarterly* 44: 15–32.

Neusner, J. 1971. *The Rabbinic Traditions about the Pharisees Before 70*. Vol. 1: *The Masters*. Vol. 2: *The Houses*. Vol. 3: *Conclusions*. Brill.

Neusner, J. 1978. "Comparing Judaisms." *History of Religions* 18: 177–91.

Neusner, J. 1980. "The Use of Later Rabbinic Evidence for the Study of Paul." In vol. 2 of *Approaches to Ancient Judaism*, 43–63. Edited by W. S. Green. BJS 9. Scholars Press.

Neusner, J. 1984. *Ancient Judaism: Debates and Disputes*. BJS 64. Chico.

Neusner, J. [1984a]. *Pirke Avot: A New American Translation and Explanation*. Rossel.

Neusner, J. 1986. *Reading and Believing: Ancient Judaism and Contemporary Gullibility*. BJS 113. Scholars Press.

Neusner, J. 1986a. *Understanding Seeking Faith: Essays on the Case of Judaism*. Vol. 1: *Debates on Method, Reports of Results*. BJS 116. Scholars Press.

Neusner, J. 1988. *Judaism: The Evidence of the Mishnah*. 2nd ed. BJS 129. Scholars Press.

Neusner, J. 1988a. *A Religion of Pots and Pans? Modes of Philosophical and Theological Discourse in Ancient Judaism: Essays and a Program*. BJS 156. Scholars Press.

Nickelsburg, G. W. E. 1979. Review of E. P. Sanders, *Paul and Palestinian Judaism: A Comparison of Patterns of Religion*. *CBQ* 41: 171–75.

Nikolainen, A. 1943. *Ihmisen ongelma: Raamatun myöhäisjuutalaisessa ja hellenistisessä ympäristössä*. Helsinki.

Nikolainen, A. 1975. *Roomalaiskirje*. Suomalainen Uuden Testamentin Selitys 6. Hämeenlinna.

Nikolainen, A. 1978. "Samalla kertaa uusi ja vanha: Eräs näkökulma apostoli Paavalin eskatologiaan." *TAik* 83: 313–24.

Nissen, A. 1974. *Gott und der Nächste im antiken Judentum: Untersuchungen zum Doppelgebot der Liebe*. WUNT 15. J. C. B. Mohr (Paul Siebeck).

Nolland, J. 1981. "Uncircumcised Proselytes?" *Journal for the Study of Judaism in the Persian, Hellenistic, and Roman Periods* 12: 173–94.

Nygren, A. 1979. *Pauli brev till romarna*. TNT 6. Verbum.

Oberforcher, R. 1987. Rezension von E. P. Sanders, *Paulus und das palästinische Judentum: Ein Vergleich zweier Religionsstrukturen*. *Zeitschrift für katholische Theologie* 109: 213–14.

O'Brien, P. T. 2004. "Was Paul a Covenantal Nomist?" In *The Paradoxes of Paul*, 249–96. Vol. 2 of *Justification and Variegated Nomism*. Edited by D. A. Carson, P. T. O'Brien, and M. A. Seifrid. WUNT 2/181. Mohr Siebeck.

Odeberg, H. 1944. *Pauli brev till korintierna*. TNT 7. Lund.

Odeberg, H. 1964. *Pharisaism and Christianity*. Translated by J. M. Moe. Concordia.

Odeberg, H. 1968. *The Fourth Gospel*. 2nd ed. B. R. Grüner.

Odeberg, H. 1980. *Fariseism och kristendom*. Pro veritate (= 1943).

Oepke, A. 1979. *Der Brief des Paulus an die Galater*. 4th ed. Edited by J. Rohde. THKNT 9. Evangelische Verlagsanstalt.

Osborne, G. R. 2011. "The Flesh Without the Spirit: Romans 7 and Christian Experience." In *Perspectives on Our Struggle with Sin: Three Views of Romans 7*, 6–47. Edited by T. L. Wilder. B & H Academic.

Osten-Sacken, P. von der. 1975. *Römer 8 als Beispiel paulinischer Soteriologie*. FRLANT 112. Vandenhoeck & Ruprecht.

Osten-Sacken, P. von der. 1989. *Die Heiligkeit der Tora: Studien zum Gesetz bei Paulus*. Chr. Kaiser.

Packer, J. I. 1964. "The 'Wretched Man' in Romans 7." In *Studia Evangelica*, vol. 2: *Papers Presented to the Second International Congress on New Testament Studies*; part 1: *The New Testament Scriptures*, 621–27. Edited by F. L. Cross. Texte und Untersuchungen 87. Akademie-Verlag.

Packer, J. I. 1999. "The 'Wretched Man' Revisited: Another Look at Romans 7:14–25." In *Romans and the People of God: Essays in Honor of G. D. Fee on the Occasion of His 65th Birthday*, 70–81. Edited by S. K. Soderlund and N. T. Wright. Eerdmans.

Patte, D. 1983. *Paul's Faith and the Power of the Gospel: A Structural Introduction to the Pauline Letters*. Fortress Press.

Paulsen, H. 1974. *Überlieferung und Auslegung in Römer 8*. WMANT 43. Neukirchener.

Paulsen, H. 1980. "Einheit und Freiheit der Söhne Gottes: Gal 3,26–29." *ZNW* 71: 74–95.

Pedersen, S. 1978. "'Mit Furcht und Zittern' (Phil. 2,12–13)." *ST* 32: 1–31.

Perles, F. 1903. *Bousset's Religion des Judentums im neutestamentlichen Zeitalter: Kritisch untersucht*. W. Peiser.

Poschmann, B. 1940. *Paenitentia secunda: Die kirchliche Buße im ältesten Christentum bis Cyprian und Origenes: Eine dogmengeschichtliche Untersuchung*, 20–38. Peter Hanstein.

Räisänen, H. 1976. "'Myyty synnin alaisuuteen': Kuvaako Rm 7:14–25 kristittyä?" *TAik* 81, 426–38.

Räisänen, H. 1979. "Zum Gebrauch von ΕΠΙΘΥΜΙΑ und ΕΠΙΘΥΜΕΙΝ bei Paulus." *ST* 33: 85–99.

Räisänen, H. 1980. "Das 'Gesetz des Glaubens' (Röm. 3:27) und das 'Gesetz des Geistes' (Röm. 8:2)." *NTS* 26: 101–17.

Räisänen, H. 1980a. "Legalism and Salvation by the Law. Paul's Portrayal of the Jewish Religion as a Historical and Theological Problem." In *Die Paulinische Literatur und Theologie*, 63–83. Edited by S. Pedersen. Forlaget Aros.

Räisänen, H. 1980b. "Paul's Theological Difficulties with the Law." In *Studia Biblica 1978. III. Papers on Paul and Other New Testament Authors. Sixth International Congress on Biblical Studies*, 301–20. Edited by E. A. Livingstone. JSNTSup 3. JSOT Press.

Räisänen, H. 1983. *Paul and the Law*. WUNT 29. J. C. B. Mohr (Paul Siebeck).

Räisänen, H. 1986. "Paul's Call Experience and His Later View of the Law." In *The Torah and Christ: Essays in German and English on the Problem of the Law in Early Christianity*, 55–92. Finnish Exegetical Society.

Räisänen, H. 1987. Preface to the second edition, *Paul and the Law*, xi–xxxi. WUNT 29. J. C. B. Mohr (Paul Siebeck).

Räisänen, H. 1987a. "Römer 9–11: Analyse eines geistigen Ringens." *ANRW* 2.25/4:2891–939. De Gruyter.

Reese, J. M. 1983. *The Book of Wisdom: Song of Songs*. Old Testament Message 20:1–202. M. Glazier.

Reichrath, H. 1967. "Römer 9–11: Ein Stiefkind christlicher Theologie und Verkündigung." *Jud* 23: 160–81.

Rese, M. 1975. "Die Vorzüge Israels in Röm. 9,4f. und Eph. 2,12: Exegetische Anmerkungen zum Thema Kirche und Israel." *TZ* 31: 211–22.

Rese, M. 1988. "Israel und Kirche in Römer 9." *NTS* 34: 208–17.

Rhyne, C. T. 1981. *Faith Establishes the Law*. SBLDS 55. Scholars Press.

Ridderbos, H. 1981. *The Epistle of Paul to the Churches of Galatia*. NICNT 9. Eerdmans (= 1953).

Ridderbos, H. 1987. *Paul: An Outline of His Theology*. 2nd ed. Translated by J. R. de Witt. Eerdmans (= 1975).

Riedl, J. 1965. *Das Heil der Heiden nach R 2,14–16.26.27*. St. Gabrieler Studien 20. St. Gabriel-Verlag.

Rissi, M. 1969. *Studien zum zweiten Korintherbrief: Der alte Bund, Der Prediger, Der Tod*. ATANT 56. Zwingli Verlag.

Robinson, J. T. A. 1966. *The Body: A Study in Pauline Theology*. Studies in Biblical Theology 5. SCM (= 1952).

Rohde, J. 1989. *Der Brief des Paulus an die Galater*. THKNT 9. Evangelische Verlagsanstalt.

Röhser, G. 1987. *Metaphorik und Personifikation der Sünde: Antike Sündenvorstellungen und paulinische Hamartia*. WUNT 2/25. J. C. B. Mohr (Paul Siebeck).

Ross, Allen P. 1996. "Exile." In vol. 4 of *New International Dictionary of Old Testament Theology and Exegesis*. Edited by Willem A. VanGemeren. Paternoster Press.

Routila, L. 1969. *Die aristotelische Idee der ersten Philosophie: Untersuchungen zur onto-theologischen Verfassung der Metaphysik des Aristoteles*. Helsinki.

Saldarini, A. J. 1979. Review of *Paul and Palestinian Judaism: A Comparison of Patterns of Religion*, by E. P. Sanders. *JBL* 98: 299–303.

Sand, A. 1984. "Der Mensch als 'Fleisch': Zur anthropologischen Dimensionen der Sünde bei Paulus." *Katechetische Blätter* 109: 608–12.

Sanday, W., and A. Headlam. 1920. *A Critical and Exegetical Commentary on the Epistle to the Romans*. 5th ed. ICC 6. T&T Clark (= 1902).

Sanders, E. P. 1973. "Patterns of Religion in Paul and Rabbinic Judaism: A Holistic Method of Comparison." *HTR* 66: 455–78.

Sanders, E. P. 1976. "The Covenant as a Soteriological Category and the Nature of Salvation in Palestinian and Hellenistic Judaism." In *Jews, Greeks and Christians: Religious Cultures in Late Antiquity. Essays in Honor of W. D. Davies*, 11–44. Edited by R. Hamerton-Kelly and S. Scroggs. Studies in Judaism in Late Antiquity 21. Brill.

Sanders, E. P. 1977. *Paul and Palestinian Judaism: A Comparison of Patterns of Religion*. SCM.

Sanders, E. P. 1978. "On the Question of Fulfilling the Law in Paul and Rabbinic Judaism." In *Donum Gentilicium: New Testament Studies in Honour of D. Daube*, 103–26. Clarendon Press.

Sanders, E. P. 1980. "Puzzling Out Rabbinic Judaism." In vol. 2 of *Approaches to Ancient Judaism*, 65–79. Edited by W. S. Green. BJS 9. Scholars Press.

Sanders, E. P. 1982. "Jesus, Paul and Judaism." In *ANRW* 25/1:390–450. De Gruyter.

Sanders, E. P. 1983. *Paul, the Law, and the Jewish People*. Fortress Press.

Sanders, E. P. 1985. *Paulus und das palästinische Judentum: Ein Vergleich zweier Religionsstrukturen*. Translated (into German) by J. Wehnert. Studien zur Umwelt des Neuen Testaments 17. Vandenhoeck & Ruprecht.

Sanders, E. P. 1990. *Jewish Law from Jesus to the Mishnah: Five Studies*. SCM.

Sanders, E. P. 2009. "Covenantal Nomism Revisited." *Jewish Studies Quarterly* 16: 23–55.

Sanders, E. P. 2016. *Comparing Judaism and Christianity: Common Judaism, Paul, and the Inner and the Outer in Ancient Religion*. Augsburg Fortress.

Sanders, E. P. 2017. Preface to the 40th anniversary edition of *Paul and Palestinian Judaism: A Comparison of Patterns of Religion*, xxvii–xxviii. Fortress Press.

Sandmel, S. 1978. Review of *Paul and Palestinian Judaism: A Comparison of Patterns of Religion* by E. P. Sanders. *Religious Studies Review* 4: 158–60.

Sandmel, S. 1979. *Philo of Alexandria: An Introduction*. Oxford University Press.

Sauer, G. 1981. *Jesus Sirach (Ben Sira)*. *JSHRZ* 3/5. Gütersloher Gerd Mohn.

Schechter, S. 1975. *Aspects of Rabbinic Theology*. 5th ed. New York (= 1909).

Schelkle, K. H. 1986. Rezension E. P. Sanders, *Paulus und das palästinensische Judentum: Ein Vergleich zweier Religionsstrukturen*. *TQ* 166: 64–65.

Schlier, H. 1938. "Von den Heiden: Römer 1,18–32." *EvT* 5: 113–24.

Schlier, H. 1938a. "Von den Juden in Römer 2,1–29." *EvT* 5: 263–75.

Schlier, H. 1971. *Der Brief an die Galater*. 5th ed. KEK 7. Vandenhoeck & Ruprecht.

Schlier, H. 1977. *Der Römerbrief*. HTKNT 6. Herder.

Schmidt, H. W. 1962. *Der Brief des Paulus an die Römer*. THKNT 6. Evangelische Verlagsanstalt.

Schmithals, W. 1980. *Die theologische Anthropologie des Paulus: Auslegung von Röm 7,17–8,39*. Kohlhammer.

Schmitt, R. 1984. *Gottesgerechtigkeit—Heilsgeschichte—Israel in der Theologie des Paulus*. Europäische Hochschulschriften 240. Lang.

Schnabel, E. J. 1985. *Law and Wisdom from Ben Sira to Paul: A Tradition Historical Enquiry into the Relation of Law, Wisdom, and Ethics*. WUNT 2/16. J. C. B. Mohr (Paul Siebeck).

Schnackenburg, R. 1975. "Römer 7 im Zusammenhang des Römerbriefes." In *Jesus und Paulus: Festschrift für W. G. Kümmel zum 70. Geburtstag*, 283–300. Edited by E. E. Ellis and E. Gräßer. Vandenhoeck & Ruprecht.

Schoeps, H.-J. 1944. Recension *Fariseism och kristendom. Särtryck ur Judisk Tidskrift*.

Schoeps, H.-J. 1950. *Aus frühchristlicher Zeit: Religionsgeschichtliche Untersuchungen*. Mohr.

Schoeps, H.-J. 1959. *Paulus: Die Theologie des Apostels im Lichte der jüdischen Religionsgeschichte*. Mohr.

Schottroff, L. 1979. "Die Schreckensherrschaft der Sünde und die Befreiung durch Christus nach dem Römerbrief des Paulus." *EvT* 39: 497–510.

Schreiner, J. 1981. *Das 4. Buch Esra*. *JSHRZ* 5/4. Gütersloher Gerd Mohn.

Schreiner, T. R. 1991. "'Works of Law' in Paul." *NovT* 33: 217–44.

Schreiner, T. R. 1998. *Romans*. BECNT 6. Baker Academic.

Schubert, P. 1967. "Paul and the New Testament Ethic in the Thought of John Knox." In *Christian History and Interpretation: Studies Presented to J. Knox*, 363–88. Edited by W. R. Farmer, C. F. D. Moule, and R. R. Niebuhr. Cambridge University Press.

Schulz, S. 1958. "Die Anklage in Röm.1,18–32." *TZ* 14: 161–73.

Schunack, G. 1967. *Das hermeneutische Problem des Todes: Im Horizont von Römer 5 untersucht*. Hermeneutische Untersuchungen zur Theologie 7. J. C. B. Mohr.

Schweizer, E. 1966. "σάρξ E II." *TWNT* 7:124–36.

Scott, J. M. 1993. "Restoration of Israel." In *Dictionary of Paul and His Letters*, 796–99. Edited by G. F. Hawthorne and R. P. Martin. InterVarsity Press.

Segal, A. F. 1985. "Covenant in Rabbinic Writings." *Studies in Religion* 14: 53–62.

Segal, A. F. 1987. *The Other Judaisms of Late Antiquity*. BJS 127. Scholars Press.

Seifrid, M. 1992. *Justification by Faith: The Origin and Development of a Central Pauline Theme*. NovTSup 68. Brill.

Seifrid, M. 1992a. "The Subject of Rom 7:14–25." *NovT* 34: 313–33.

Seifrid, M. 1994. "Blind Alleys in the Controversy over the Paul of History." *TynBul* 45 (1): 73–95.

Seifrid, M. 2000. *Christ, Our Righteousness: Paul's Theology of Justification*. New Studies in Biblical Theology 9. InterVarsity Press.

Seifrid, M. 2004. "Unrighteous by Faith: Apostolic Proclamation in Romans 1:18–3:20." In *The Paradoxes of Paul*, 105–45. Vol. 2 of *Justification and Variegated Nomism*. Edited by D. A. Carson, P. T. O'Brien, and M. A. Seifrid. WUNT 2/181. Mohr Siebeck.

Seifrid, M. 2011. "Romans 7: The Voice of the Law, the Cry of Lament, and the Shout of Thanksgiving." In *Perspectives on Our Struggle with Sin: Three Views of Romans 7*, 111–65. Edited by T. L. Wilder. B & H Academic.

Siegert, F. 1985. *Argumentation bei Paulus gezeigt an Röm 9–11*. WUNT 34. J. C. B. Mohr.

Sjöberg, E. 1939. *Gott und die Sünder im palästinischen Judentum nach dem Zeugnis der Tannaiten und der apokryphisch-pseudepigraphischen Literatur*. BWANT 27 (4. Folge). Kohlhammer.

Sjöberg, E. 1944. Recension H. Odeberg: *Fariseism och kristendom*. *SEÅ* 9: 109–12.

Sjöberg, E. 1959. "πνεῦμα/ πνευματικός III 4." *TWNT* 6:374–79.

Sloan, R. B. 1991. "Paul and the Law: Why the Law Cannot Save." *NovT* 33: 35–60.

Smith, E. W. 1971. "The Form and Religious Background of Romans VII 24–25a." *NovT* 13: 127–35.

Smith, M. 1968. "On the Shape of God and the Humanity of Gentiles." In *Religions in Antiquity: Essays in Memory of E. R. Goodenough*, 315–26. Edited by J. Neusner. Studies in the History of Religions 14. Brill.

Snodgrass, K. R. 1986. "Justification by Grace—to the Doers: An Analysis of the Place of Romans 2 in the Theology of Paul." *NTS* 32: 72–93.

Souček, J. B. 1956. "Zur Exegese von Röm.2,14ff." In *Antwort: Karl Barth zum siebzigsten Geburtstag*, 99–113. Evangelischer Verlag.

Sprinkle, P. M. 2013. *Paul and Judaism Revisited: A Study of Divine and Human Agency in Salvation*. IVP Academic Press.

Stalder, K. 1962. *Das Werk des Geistes in der Heiligung bei Paulus*. EVZ-Verlag.

Stauffer, E. 1947. *Die Theologie des Neuen Testaments*. 3rd ed. Kohlhammer.

Steck, O. H. 1967. *Israel und das gewaltsame Geschick der Propheten: Untersuchungen zur Überlieferung des deuteronomistischen Geschichtsbildes im Alten Testament, Spätjudentum und Urchristentum*. Neukirchener Verlag.

Steck, O. H. 1968. "Das Problem theologischer Strömungen in nachexilischer Zeit." *EvT* 28: 445–58.

Stein, J. B. 1977. *Claude Goldsmid Montefiore on the Ancient Rabbis: The Second Generation of Reform Judaism in Britain*. BJS 4. Scholars Press.

Stendahl, K. 1963. "The Apostle Paul and the Introspective Conscience of the West." *HTR* 56: 199–215.

Stendahl, K. 1976. *Paul among Jews and Gentiles and Other Essays*. Fortress Press.

Stiegman, E. 1979. "Rabbinic Anthropology." In *ANRW* 2.19/2:487–579.

Stowers, S. K. 1994. "Romans 7.7–25 as a Speech-in-Character (Προσωποποιία)." In *Paul in His Hellenistic Context*, 180–202. Edited by T. Engberg-Pedersen. T&T Clark/ Fortress Press.

Strack, H., and P. Billerbeck. *See* Billerbeck, P.

Strobel, A. 1989. *Der erste Brief an die Korinther*. ZBK 6/1. Theologischer Verlag.

Stuhlmacher, P. 1966. *Gerechtigkeit Gottes bei Paulus*. 2nd ed. FRLANT 87. Vandenhoeck & Ruprecht.

Stuhlmacher, P. 1966a. "Glauben und Verstehen bei Paulus." *EvT* 26: 337–48.

Stuhlmacher, P. 1985. "Paul's Understanding of the Law in the Letter to the Romans." *SEÅ* 50: 87–104.

Stuhlmacher, P. 2002. *Biblische Theologie und Evangelium: Gesammelte Aufsätze*. WUNT 146. Mohr Siebeck.

Sutherland, D. D. 1982. *Genesis 15:6: A Study in Ancient Jewish and Christian Interpretation*. Louisville, KY.

Svartvik, J. 2006. *Bibeltolkningens bakgator: Synen på judar, slavar och homosexuella i historia och nutid*. Verbum.

Svartvik, J. 2007. "Att göra rättvisa åt inte enbart genier: Fem synpunkter på Timo Laatos artikel 'Att göra rättvisa åt ett geni: Om Hugo Odebergs bok "Fariseism och kristendom." ' " *STK* 2007: 175–80.

Synofzik, E. 1977. *Die Gerichts- und Vergeltungsaussagen bei Paulus: Eine traditionsgeschichtliche Untersuchung*. GTA 8. Vandenhoeck & Ruprecht.

Techow, N. 2024. *Sinners, Works of Law, and Transgression in Gal 2:14b–21: A Study in Paul's Line of Thought*. WUNT 2/602. Mohr Siebeck.

Theißen, G. 1983. *Psychologische Aspekte paulinischer Theologie*. FRLANT 131. Vandenhoeck & Ruprecht.

Theobald, M. 1981–82. "Das Gottesbild des Paulus nach Röm 3,21–31." *SNTSU* 6/7: 131–68.

Thielman, F. 1989. *From Plight to Solution: A Jewish Framework for Understanding Paul's View of the Law in Galatians and Romans*. NovTSup 61. Brill.

Thompson, R. W. 1986. "Paul's Double Critique of Jewish Boasting: A Study of Rom 3,27 in Its Context." *Bib* 67: 520–31.

Thurén, J. 1977. *Israelin usko*. Helsinki.

Thurén, J. 1986. "Paulus och torah: Reflexioner kring Heikki Räisänens arbete Paul and the Law, 1983." In vol. 1 of *Judendom och kristendom under de första århundradena*, 165–92. Stavanger.

Thurén, J. 1994. *Roomalaiskirje*. Hämeenlinna.

Thurén, L. 2000. *Derhetorizing Paul: A Dynamic Perspective on Pauline Theology and the Law*. WUNT 124. Mohr Siebeck.

Thurén, L. 2002. "Romans 7 Derhetorized." In *Rhetorical Criticism and the Bible*, 420–40. Edited by St. E. Porter and D. L. Stamps. JSNT 195. Sheffield Academic Press.

Tyson, J. B. 1968. "Paul's Opponents in Galatia." *NovT* 10: 241–54.

Ulonska, H. 1966. "Die Doxa des Mose: Zum Problem des Alten Testaments in 2. Kor. 3,1–16." *EvT* 26: 378–88.

Uotila, T. 1986. Resensio E. P. Sanders, *Paulus und das palästinische Judentum: Ein Vergleich zweier Religionsstrukturen*. *TAik* 91: 512–13.

Urbach, E. E. 1979. *The Sages: Their Concepts and Beliefs*. 2nd ed. Translated from the Hebrew by I. Abrahams. Magnes Press.

Van den Beld, A. 1985. "Romans 7:14–25 and the Problem of *Akrasia*." *Religious Studies* 21: 495–515.

Van der Minde, H.-J. 1976. *Schrift und Tradition bei Paulus: Ihre Bedeutung und Funktion im Römerbrief*. Paderborner theologische Studien 3. Wien.

Van Dülmen, A. 1968. *Die Theologie des Gesetzes bei Paulus*. Stuttgarter biblische Monographien 5. Katholisches Bibelwerk.

Varo, F. 1984. "La lucha del hombre contra el pecado: Exégesis de Rom 7,14–25." *Scripta Theologica* 16: 9–53.

Vergote, A. 1973. "Der Beitrag der Psychoanalyse zur Exegese: Leben, Gesetz und Ich-Spaltung im 7.Kapitel des Römerbriefs." In *Exegese im Methodenkonflikt: Zwischen Geschichte und Struktur*. Edited by X. Léon-Dufour. Translated (into German) by G. Haeffner and H. Schöndorf. Kösel-Verlag.

Vermes, G. 1961. *Scripture and Tradition in Judaism*. Studia post-biblica 4. Brill.

Vicent, R. 1986. Recension E. P. Sanders, *Paulus und das palästinische Judentum: Ein Vergleich zweier Religionsstrukturen*. *Salvationist* 48: 428.

Vischer, W. 1950. "Das Geheimnis Israels: Eine Erklärung der Kapitel 9–11 des Römerbriefs." *Jud* 6: 81–132.

Volf, J. M. G. 1990. *Paul and Perseverance: Staying In and Falling Away*. WUNT 2/37. J. C. B. Mohr.

Vollenweider, S. 1989. *Freiheit als neue Schöpfung: Eine Untersuchung zur Eleutheria bei Paulus und in seiner Umwelt*. FRLANT 147. Vandehoeck & Ruprecht.

Walker, R. 1960. "Die Heiden und das Gericht: Zur Auslegung von Römer 2, 12–16." *EvT* 20: 302–14.

Waltke, Bruce K. 1980. "הלך." In *Theological Wordbook of the Old Testament*. Edited by R. Laird Harris et al. Moody Press.

Wasserman, E. 2007. "The Death of the Soul in Romans 7: Revisiting Paul's Anthropology in Light of Hellenistic Moral Psychology." *JBL* 126: 793–816.

Wasserman, E. 2008. *The Death of the Soul in Romans 7: Sin, Death, and the Law in Light of Hellenistic Moral Psychology*. WUNT 2/256. Mohr Siebeck.

Watson, F. 1986. *Paul, Judaism and the Gentiles: A Sociological Approach*. SNTSMS 56. Cambridge University Press.

Watson, N. M. 1983. "Justified by Faith; Judged by Works—An Antinomy?" *NTS* 29: 209–21.

Weber, F. 1897. *Jüdische Theologie auf Grund des Talmud und verwandter Schriften*. 2nd ed. Nach des Verfassers Tode edited by F. Delitzsch and G. Schnedermann. Leipzig.

Weder, H. 1981. *Das Kreuz Jesu bei Paulus: Ein Versuch, über den Geschichtsbezug des christlichen Glaubens nachzudenken*. FRLANT 125. Vandehoeck & Ruprecht.

Weiß, J. 1910. *Der erste Korintherbrief*. KEK 5. Vandenhoeck & Ruprecht.

Wendland, H.-D. 1980. *Die Briefe an die Korinther*. 15th ed. NTD 7. Vandenhoeck & Ruprecht.

Wengert T. J. 2013. "The 'New' Perspectives on Paul at the 2012 Luther Congress in Helsinki." *Lutheran Quarterly* 27: 89–91.

Wenham, D. 1980. "The Christian Life: A Life of Tension? A Consideration of the Nature of Christian Experience in Paul." In *Pauline Studies: Essays Presented to Professor F. F. Bruce on His 70th Birthday*, 80–94. Edited by D. A. Hagner and M. J. Harris. Eerdmans.

Werblowsky, R. J. Z. 1973. "Tora als Gnade." *Kairos* 15: 156–63.

Westerholm, S. 1979. Recension E. P. Sanders, *Paul and Palestinian Judaism: A Comparison of Patterns of Religion*. *STK* 55: 131–33.

Westerholm, S. 1984. "'Letter' and 'Spirit': The Foundation of Pauline Ethics." *NTS* 30: 229–48.

Westerholm, S. 1986–87. "On Fulfilling the Whole Law (Gal. 5:14)." *SEÅ* 51/52: 229–37.

Westerholm, S. 1988. *Israel's Law and the Church's Faith: Paul and His Recent Interpreters*. Eerdmans.

Westerholm, S. 2004. "The 'New Perspective' at Twenty-Five." In *The Paradoxes of Paul*, 1–38. Vol. 2 of *Justification and Variegated Nomism*. Edited by D. A. Carson, P. T. O'Brien, and M. A. Seifrid. WUNT 2/181. Mohr Siebeck.

Westerholm, S. 2006 (2008). "Paul's Anthropological 'Pessimism' in Its Jewish Context." In *Divine and Human Agency in Paul and His Cultural Environment*, 71–98. Edited by J. M. G. Barclay and S. J. Gathercole. Library of New Testament Studies 335. T&T Clark.

Wieser, F. E. 1987. *Die Abrahamvorstellungen im Neuen Testament*. Europäische Hochschulschriften 317. P. Lang.

Wilckens, U. 1961. "Die Rechtfertigung Abrahams nach Römer 4." In *Studien zur Theologie der alttestamentlichen Überlieferungen*, 111–27. Edited by R. Rendtorff and K. Koch. Neukirchener.

Wilckens, U. 1964. "Zu Römer 3,21–4,25: Antwort an G. Klein." *EvT* 24: 586–610.

Wilckens, U. 1978. *Der Brief an die Römer*. 1. Teilband. *Röm.1–5*. EKKNT 6. Cologne.

Wilckens, U. 1980. *Der Brief an die Römer*. 2. Teilband. *Röm.6–11*. EKKNT 6. Cologne.

Willi, Th. 1972. "Das Erlöschen des Geistes." *Jud* 28: 110–16.

Windisch, H. 1970. *Der zweite Korintherbrief*. 9th ed. KEK 6. Vandenhoeck & Ruprecht.

Winston, D. 1979. *The Wisdom of Solomon: A New Translation with Introduction and Commentary*. Anchor Bible 43. Doubleday.

Wißmann, E. 1926. *Das Verhältnis von ΠΙΣΤΙΣ und Christusfrömmigkeit bei Paulus*. FRLANT 40. Vandenhoeck & Ruprecht.

Witherington, B. 1981. "Rite and Rights for Women—Galatians 3.28." *NTS* 27: 593–604.

Wolff, C. 1982. *Der erste Brief des Paulus an die Korinther*. Zweiter Teil: *Auslegung der Kapitel 8–16*. THKNT 7/2. Evangelische Verlagsanstalt.

Wolff, C. 1986. Rezension E. P. Sanders, *Paulus und das palästinische Judentum: Ein Vergleich zweier Religionsstrukturen*. *TLZ* 111: 421–25.

Wolff, C. 1989. *Der zweite Brief des Paulus an die Korinther*. THKNT 8. Evangelische Verlagsanstalt.

Wolff, H. W. 1984. *Anthropologie des Alten Testaments*. 4th ed. Chr. Kaiser.

Wolfson, H. A. 1948. *Philo: Foundations of Religious Philosophy in Judaism, Christianity, and Islam*. 2nd ed. 2 vols. Structure and Growth of Philosophy Systems 11. Harvard University Press.

Wright, N. T. 1978. "The Paul of History and the Apostle of Faith." *TynBul* 29: 61–88.

Wright, N. T. 1992. *The New Testament and the People of God*. Fortress Press.

Wright, N. T. 1993. *The Climax of the Covenant: Christ and the Law in Pauline Theology*. Fortress Press.

Wright, N. T. 1997. *What Saint Paul Really Said: Was Paul of Tarsus the Real Founder of Christianity?* Eerdmans.

Wright, N. T. 2009. *Justification: God's Plan and God's Vision*. SPCK.

Wright, N. T. 2013. *Paul and the Faithfulness of God*. SPCK.

Zahn, Th. 1922. *Der Brief des Paulus an die Galater*. 3rd ed. Durchgesehen von F. Hauck. KNT 9. Deichert.

Zahn, Th. 1925. *Der Brief des Paulus an die Römer*. 3rd ed. Durchgesehen von F. Hauck. KNT 6. Deichert.

Zeller, D. 1973. *Juden und Heiden in der Mission des Paulus: Studien zum Römerbrief*. Forschung zur Bibel 1. Katholische Bibelwerk.

Ziener, G. 1970. *Das Buch der Weisheit*. Welt der Bibel 12. Patmos.

Ziesler, J. A. 1988. "The Role of the Tenth Commandment in Romans 7." *JSNT* 10 (33): 41–56.